# The Conservatives
# and British Society, 1880–1990

# The Conservatives and British Society, 1880–1990

edited by

MARTIN FRANCIS

and

INA ZWEINIGER-BARGIELOWSKA

UNIVERSITY OF WALES PRESS
CARDIFF
1996

British Cataloguing-in-Publication Data.
A catalogue record for this book is available from
the British Library.

ISBN 0-7083-1363-9

Jacket design by John Garland, Pentan Partnership, Cardiff
Typeset at University of Wales Press
Printed in Great Britain by Dinefwr Press, Llandybïe

# Contents

# Foreword

It is a great personal pleasure to be invited to write the foreword to this most interesting volume on the Conservatives and British society over the past hundred years. It originates from a conference at the University of Wales's residential hall at Gregynog, Powys, held in September 1995 in the last few weeks of my time as Vice-Chancellor of the University of Wales, Aberystwyth, and I had the pleasure of attending part of it myself. The result is an important and impressive contribution to the understanding of the history and social evolution of modern Britain which will be welcomed by all students in the field at whatever level.

The Conservative Party has, until recently, fared rather less well at the hands of historians than have British parties of the centre-left. This may have been for technical, archival reasons. It may, alternatively, have reflected the ideological outlook of many university historians, still influenced perhaps by the words at the base of Gladstone's bust in the National Liberal Club that 'Toryism is distrust of the people qualified by fear'. Much of the historical writing that there has been tended to focus rather narrowly on institutional or organizational aspects of British Conservatism. This present volume breaks new ground in emphasizing the social dynamics, ethnic and other identities, and gender relationships of the Conservative Party, as well as policy formulation and the development of ideology. The view that the Tories were a movement indifferent to ideology, prior to the dramatic emergence and later downfall, of Thatcherism, is shown to be a myth. So, too, is the notion that British political empiricism made them more inclined to a value-free 'muddling through' than to exploring purposively (and for good or ill) the subtler relationships between the state and society.

The contributors to this volume are, with the distinguished exception of Lord Gilmour, mainly younger scholars from universities in England, Scotland and Canada as well as from the national University of Wales. All of them are pushing hard at the frontiers of new knowledge and fresh understanding of key themes and concepts central to modern British history. There are many new discoveries here. We even have a serious study of Welsh Conservatism, long the academic equivalent of Banquo's ghost at the feast of us Welsh historians. It may be hoped that, in a subsequent colloquium, the authors will explore other relatively unexplored features of the recent Conservative tradition. A treatment of Tory views and divisions on foreign and imperial issues (which, after all, led to major splits over empire and tariff reform in 1903, the overthrow of the Lloyd George coalition in 1922, appeasement of Germany in 1938, and relations with Europe more or less continuously from the later 1980s to the present) would be no less fascinating. So, too, would be a comparative history of British Conservatism taken in parallel to the distinct experiences of, say, continental Christian Democracy or the American radical right. The importance of this volume as a contribution to political, social and intellectual history is such that it leads on to further questions such as these. On behalf of my former colleagues in the University of Wales and as a historian myself, I am delighted and honoured to welcome this book.

KENNETH O. MORGAN
Oxford, May Day 1996

# Acknowledgements

This collection brings together many of the papers presented at a conference on the Conservative Party since the late nineteenth century held at the University of Wales conference centre at Gregynog on 12–14 September 1995, which was organized by the editors. First of all we wish to express our gratitude to Siân Nicholas who helped in the organization of the conference. This conference was made possible through the generosity of the University of Wales and the Department of History and Welsh History at Aberystwyth.

Duncan Tanner, Terry Jenkins, L. J. Williams, Jose Harris, Harriet Jones and Aled Jones acted as discussants for the sessions at the conference. We are grateful to these colleagues, as well as to Stephen Brooke, Ewen Green, Brian Harrison and David Jarvis, for comments and advice at various stages of the project. We wish to thank Kenneth O. Morgan for his address to the conference, and for his foreword to this volume. Finally we are grateful to Ned Thomas of University of Wales Press for his interest in the project from its earliest stages and his supportive editorship throughout.

Martin Francis
Ina Zweiniger-Bargielowska
Aberystwyth, July 1996

# The Contributors

**Felix Aubel** is Associate Lecturer in History at the University of Wales, Lampeter.

**Stephen Brooke** is Professor of History at Dalhousie University, Halifax, Nova Scotia, Canada.

**Martin Daunton** is Professor of British History at University College, London.

**Richard Finlay** is Lecturer in History at the University of Strathclyde.

**Martin Francis** is Fulbright-Robertson Visiting Professor of British History at Westminster College, Fulton, Missouri, USA.

**Mark Garnett** is Lecturer in Politics at the University of Bristol.

**Lord Gilmour of Craigmillar** was a Cabinet Minister in the Heath and Thatcher governments and is author of *Dancing with Dogma*.

**E H. H. Green** is Fellow and Tutor in Modern History at Magdalen College, Oxford.

**David Jarvis** is British Academy Postdoctoral Fellow at Lady Margaret Hall, Oxford.

**Harriet Jones** is Senior Lecturer in History at the University of Luton.

**Rodney Lowe** is Professor of Contemporary History at the University of Bristol.

**Siân Nicholas** is Lecturer in History at the University of Wales, Aberystwyth.

**Ian Packer** is Lecturer in History at the University of Teesside.

**Jeremy Smith** is Lecturer in History at the University of Wales, Lampeter.

**Jim Tomlinson** is Reader in Government at Brunel University.

**Ina Zweiniger-Bargielowska** is Lecturer in Social and Economic History at the University of Wales, Aberystwyth.

# Introduction

MARTIN FRANCIS and INA ZWEINIGER-BARGIELOWSKA

This collection analyses the relationship between the Conservative Party and British society since 1880 from a perspective which is informed by recent developments in cultural theory and historical methodology. We seek a fuller understanding of the party's extraordinary electoral success in the period by focusing on the four key themes of ideology, national identity, gender and policy.

It is a commonplace that while volumes have been lavished on the history of the Liberal and Labour Parties, the study of the Conservative Party since 1880 was for a long time relatively neglected. In the words of one recent commentator, 'Considering that we are talking about the world's most successful political party the published material doesn't add up to much.'[1] Indeed most of the standard textbooks on British Conservatism date from the mid-1970s.[2] The Ford Lectures, on which Lord Blake's long-serving account was based, were originally delivered over a quarter of a century ago.[3] It was not until 1978 that Ramsden's engaging and authoritative *Age of Balfour and Baldwin* provided the first overview of the party in the first half of the twentieth century to be based on extensive primary research.[4] At around the same time a number of monographs appeared which offered insight into various aspects of late Victorian and Edwardian Conservatism.[5] Before the mid-1980s the post-1918 (and particularly the post-1945) Conservative Party was largely unexplored by historians.[6] It was left to political scientists, notably Gamble, Harris, and Norton and Aughey, to provide some of the more interesting studies of Conservative thought and policy.[7]

Over the last decade, both the quantity and quality of the historiography of British Conservatism have improved dramatically. Pugh's pioneering studies of popular Conservatism rejected ahistorical sociological explanations of working-class Toryism, stressing instead the changing patterns of the party's responses to a mass electorate, and in particular the incorporation of women into the Conservative constituency.[8] An awareness of the dynamism of Conservative responses to the post-1884 mass electorate has informed recent studies of Edwardian Conservatism, most notably Green's *Crisis of Conservatism*, and Lawrence's study of the construction of political alliances in the West Midlands.[9] By contrast, the historiography of inter-war Conservatism remains patchy. Ball and Williamson have analysed the period up to 1932, particularly the deceptively straightforward personality and politics of Baldwin, but there has been no sustained investigation of the National Government after that date.[10] Two stimulating contributions are McKibbin's and Jarvis's explanations of the ideological underpinning to Conservative electoral hegemony in the 1920s and 1930s.[11]

The most dramatic growth in the literature has been on post-1945 Conservatism, as a direct result of the recent release of previously closed official records. Ramsden's *Age of Churchill and Eden* elaborates on his address to the Royal Historical Society in 1986, which proposes a rigorous critique of old myths about a revolutionary shift in Conservative policy and strategy after 1945.[12] This subject has also been addressed by a number of revisionist historians who explicitly reject the traditional 'consensus' model of post-war Conservative policy-making.[13] There is already a growing secondary literature on several aspects of the 1951–64 Conservative governments.[14] While works on the decade between 1965 and 1975 are thinner on the ground, Campbell's biography of Heath has initiated a revaluation of the 1970–4 government which will be extended in forthcoming publications.[15] Not surprisingly, the change in the Conservative leadership in 1990 has prompted an outpouring of works on the significance of the Thatcher years,[16] which supplement an already voluminous body of contemporary commentary provided during the 1980s.[17] This debate on the nature of Thatcherism has included the participation of many of the leading Conservative figures of the 1975–90 period, principally through the vehicle of autobiography, including of course, the former premier herself.[18] The desire to provide a *historical* interpretation of Thatcherism, placing it in the context of earlier varieties of Conservative politics, was one of the themes of the special issue of *Twentieth Century British History* devoted exclusively to the Conservative Party in 1994.[19]

Therefore this collection is part of a growing body of literature which reflects an increased interest among historians in modern British Conservatism. The writing which has appeared in the last decade, while more sophisticated than previously, none the less remains fragmented and incomplete. Most of it is in the form of specialized monographs and articles. With the exception of Seldon and Ball's *Conservative Century* there are no wider studies which cover the entire period since the late nineteenth century.[20] Regardless of its pioneering aspect, *Conservative Century* has severe limitations since it is essentially a study of the Conservative Party as an institution rather than an appraisal of the party's wider significance in British political culture.

By contrast, the idea behind this collection is to analyse the dynamic and complex relationship between the Conservative Party and British society since 1880. This is not to deny the obvious success of the party during the period. Between 1880 and 1990 the party won sixteen of the twenty-eight general elections held and their share of the vote rarely fell below 40 per cent. As a result of this electoral success, the party was in power for seventy of the 109 years which separate the death of Disraeli and the fall of Thatcher. Even defeat frequently meant only a tenuous hold on power by the opposition parties. The only exceptions were the parliaments of 1906–10, 1945–50 and 1966–70 when the Liberals and later Labour could command an overwhelming majority. Despite such evidence, it is too simplistic to see the Conservatives as the natural party of government. We hold that Conservative success was both problematic and historically contingent.

Our aim is to explore this Conservative domination of British politics during the last one hundred years from a perspective which does not take class as a starting point. This collection is informed by the challenge to established historiography posed by recent intellectual developments and particularly post-modernism and post-structuralism, the so-called linguistic turn. We appreciate the importance of class-based analyses to illuminating the history of the Conservative Party,[21] and the contributors to this volume show how both ideology and policy are partly dictated by the social bases of the party's support such as landowners before 1914 or middle-class pressure groups in the 1950s. However, we explicitly reject the conventional perspective of class as the overarching framework. This approach, emanating from electoral sociology and political science in which British politics is conceptualized in terms of a class-based two-party system, has always had difficulty in explaining how a party led by the landed aristocracy and bourgeoisie has sustained a dominant position in an emerging parliamentary democracy in which the majority of the electorate were working class. Indeed, it was the party's exceptional ability to construct a broad base of support which was central to its success and made the Conservatives the principal beneficiary of the arrival of the mass electorate after both 1884 and 1918.

The explanatory capacity of the class-based approach to British electoral behaviour has always been severely limited due to its inability to explain Conservative electoral success, and attempts to conceptualize working-class Tories as deferential are unsatisfactory.[22] Indeed, confidence in the explanatory power of class as a central organizing category is now questioned from the perspective of political science[23] as well as by historians.[24] In view of this growing awareness of the problematic nature of class as a concept and of the relationship between class and political parties, this collection examines the Conservative Party from a perspective directed away from the paradigm of class. Our starting point is not the question: how could the party of the rich survive and indeed thrive in a parliamentary democracy in which the majority of the electorate are working class? Rather, we aim to understand the party's unrivalled success in constructing and reconstructing electoral majorities from a perspective which highlights the importance of ideology, national and ethnic identity as well as gender.

This approach is informed by the emergence of post-modernist and post-structuralist theory. Traditional British political history of the later nineteenth and twentieth century is primarily empiricist and frequently grounded in an essentially Marxian materialism. Social relations are founded on an objective material reality – the base – from which the political and cultural superstructure arises in a deterministic form. Post-modernism questions this faith in the primacy of class which has provided the dominant 'grand narrative'. Thus concepts such as class, the social or politics themselves become historicized or, as Joyce puts it, 'far from being anti-historical . . . [the] relativism and scepticism' of post-modernist thought 'are deeply historical'.[25] Post-structuralist and feminist theory has raised awareness of the complexities of identity which is no longer perceived to be ahistorical. To quote Joyce again, 'identity is composed through the relations of systems of difference . . . it is marked by conflict . . . plural, diverse and volatile.' It is not one-dimensional but rather 'many "identities" press in and react with one another'.[26] Class is only one aspect of identity competing with gender, ethnicity and many other facets. According to Lawrence 'political constituencies are not pre-established social blocs awaiting representation, but painstakingly constructed (and often socially heterogeneous) alliances.' Political parties have a 'conscious and creative role . . . moulding . . . a political constituency out of the diverse subjective identities and interests of voters'.[27] This is a process of continual adaptation and re-creation of electoral alliances in which class plays a role but need not take centre stage alongside other identities such as ethnicity or gender. Ideology provides a means of communication between parties and their constituencies.

Michael Freeden, bemoaning the persistence of residual myths about the unideological nature of British politics, observed that in the writing of British political history, ideology long remained 'the stranger at the feast'.[28] Indeed the history of modern British politics has traditionally concentrated on policies and their consequences, rather than on the ideological assumptions which underpinned them. However, since the late 1960s several scholars have succesfully blended the previously separate concerns of political history and political theory.[29] Moreover the 1990s have seen a new emphasis among historians of late nineteenth- and twentieth-century Britain on the significance of ideas in politics, largely (although not exclusively) as a result of assertions by cultural historians about the significance of language in the creation of identities and the shaping of political behaviour.[30] Most of this recent scholarship has focused on the left rather than the right of the political spectrum.[31] This bias is explicable in the light of Conservative insistence on the dangers of pursuing a purely intellectual approach to politics.[32] However, by stating their preference for empiricism and 'common sense', Conservatives are actually making a profoundly ideological assertion. Conservatives may prefer to think of themselves as non-doctrinal and undogmatic (although in the light of the Thatcher years even this notion is seriously open to question), but this does not mean that they are unideological.[33] Our emphasis, in contrast to those who practise the 'history of ideas', is not on a few 'great thinkers', but rather on the interrelationship between ideology and public policy. This reflects the fact that 'the evidence for political thinking is unobservable and hence its reflection must be sought in acts – of expression, of writing, of doing'.[34] In other words we are less interested in the abstract nature of political ideas than in the relationship of those ideas to political action.

The study of national and ethnic identity has become increasingly fashionable among historians since the 1980s. Influenced by developments in sociological and cultural theory,[35] advocates of the 'new British history' (a generic term which embraces a wide variety of methodologies and themes) have shown that national identity in modern Britain has been continually constructed and reshaped by its interaction with others.[36] In the words of a leading expert in ethnic relations, 'You know who you are, only by knowing who you are not.'[37] It is often assumed that the Conservatives' self-identification as the 'patriotic' party *par excellence* has been a straightforward electoral asset.[38] However, if the shape of British identity is essentially fluid, it necessarily follows that the relationship between Conservatives and the nation state is more complex than might be immediately thought.[39] The first frontier of identity is within the British Isles itself, the association between the Scots, Welsh and Irish on the one hand and the English on the other. At times – the 1880s or the 1980s for instance – Conservatives appeared to be the party of English nationalism, defending the interests of England against what were portrayed as the unrepresentative and erratic fads of the Celtic fringe. However, at the same time, Conservatives have been staunch defenders of the notion of a United Kingdom, fearful of the 'Balkanization' of Britain, and even willing to change their name in 1886 to defend the Union with Ireland. Moreover as recent deconstructions of the national heritage have suggested, the notion of 'Englishness' is problematic, even within England itself.[40] Mass immigration from Britain's former colonies made it impossible by the 1960s to exclude 'the other' by a simple territorialization of national identity. Conservatives were obliged to recode their patriotism in order to create a specifically racial and post-colonial variety of nationalist discourse.[41] The use of the term *British* society in the title of this book is therefore considered and deliberate, and we insist on the placing of Conservative thought and action in the context of a multinational, multi-ethnic and multiracial society.

In the last fifteen to twenty years women's history, informed by the feminist movement and feminist theory, has become a rapidly growing branch of historical research challenging conventional orthodoxies in many areas. This focus on women has raised awareness of gender differences in life cycle, attitudes and political behaviour. Gender, which Joan Scott defines as the 'social organisation of sexual difference . . . is not absolute or true, but always relative'.[42] It can no longer be relegated to the status of a minor background variable. The recognition that all basic categories are shot through with gendered meanings has also drawn attention to masculinity which is not an ahistorical norm from which women deviate but constructed in relation to femininity.[43] It is thus impossible to generalize about men and women since gender identities are historically specific and continually changing.

It should already be clear that we believe questions of ideology and identity do more than provide the context in which Conservative economic and social policies are made: they decisively and profoundly affect the shape these policies take. The decision to place five of our contributions in a separate section on 'policy' is a simple organizational expedient, not an intellectual or methodological premise, and the four sections of the book are of course not hermetically sealed. Conservative policy-making is invested with its full complexity and dynamism, and old stereotypes about the opportunist or defensive nature of Conservative policies are eschewed. Judging from the ideological cleavages of the Edwardian era or the speed of recovery after 1945 and 1966, Conservatives clearly prefer to be in office rather than out of it. But to see Conservative policy as a pragmatic exercise in the pursuit (or retention) of power is a crude reductionism not borne out by the historical record.

Obviously a collection of this type cannot be either

comprehensive or definitive. Among the important subjects which
receive limited treatment here are the role of religion, education
policy and Conservative responses to pre-1945 immigration into
Britain. Our intention has not been to provide an even textbook-
style coverage, but to illuminate a number of key themes and
incidents in the history of the Conservative Party since 1880.
However, in raising questions through the application of recent
developments in historical methodology, we seek to stimulate
further research rather than to provide a definitive study. While
Parts One to Three encompass a fairly even chronological spread,
Part Four is heavily weighted towards the period 1945–70. This is
a natural consequence of the release of public records for this
period in the last decade.

Part One of the volume addresses Conservative ideology. All
contributors reject the persistent myth that the Conservative Party
is not an ideological party. However they suggest that
Conservative ideology was fluid and unstable and that this helps
to explain the complexity of Conservative policy during the last
one hundred years. Smith traces the ideological flux which
characterized Conservative representations of the Union with
Ireland between 1885 and 1914. He argues that by 1910 the
traditional 'defence of the Union' was ideologically exhausted. The
party leadership was faced with a series of competing definitions
of what the Union and Unionism now stood for, ranging from a
fully federated United Kingdom to the simple exclusion of Ulster
from Irish Home Rule. The difficulty of reconciling these
alternative representations explains the extraordinary and extreme
stance taken by Bonar Law during the crises of 1911–14. This
sense of ideological fragmentation in Edwardian Conservatism is
also evident in Packer's reconstruction of Conservative responses
to the 'land question' in the years 1910–14. He contends that the
Conservatives found it increasingly difficult to protect the power
and status of the landowning élites without sacrificing the party's
wider interests. The alternative strategies proposed to counter
Lloyd George's 1912–14 Land Campaign demonstrate that the
Tory leadership lacked a definite ideology of social reform, and
were deeply divided on the role of the state. The tensions and
ambiguities created by the dichotomy between individualist and
collectivist aspirations are explored in Francis's study of
Conservative attitudes to the state in the middle decades of the

twentieth century. He insists that an examination of Conservative attitudes to the regulation of moral and sexual behaviour reveals the ongoing debate between libertarianism and paternalism. Conservative attitudes to the state ranged from the defence of personal freedom against an intrusive state to the use of state coercion by Tory Home Secretaries in the 1920s and 1950s to reform public morals. The contribution by Garnett and Gilmour appraises the nature of 'Thatcherism'. Placing Thatcherism in a long-term historical perspective, they argue that the period since 1975 has seen a radical break in the history of Conservatism, with the party's traditional emphasis on pragmatism being abandoned in favour of an ideological crusade. They conclude that the inspiration for Thatcherism came not from British Conservatism but from nineteenth-century British liberalism and contemporary theory and practice in the United States.

Part Two analyses Conservative discourse and policy on the multinational and culturally diverse character of the United Kingdom. Aubel provides the first substantial treatment of the Conservative Party in Wales between 1880 and 1935. The party's performance in the Principality has undeniably been one of consistent electoral failure, but Aubel shows that failure can prove to be just as illuminating as success in terms of clarifying the nature of Conservatism. Conservative hostility to Church disestablishment is not a sufficient explanation for Conservative weakness, and attention has to be given to the narrow socio-economic composition of the party hierarchy in Wales. Finlay surveys the changing relationship between Conservatism and Unionism in Scotland since 1918. He suggests that the Conservatives endeavoured to maintain a distinctive Scottish identity in the period after 1945, by the use of the British state apparatus to regenerate the Scottish economy and alleviate social deprivation. This was to restore the appeal of Unionism, which had become increasingly moribund in the 1920s and 1930s. However, Thatcher's attack on both corporatism and the welfare state after 1979 robbed the Scots of an acceptable vision of Britain, and led to the dramatic decline of Scottish Conservatism in the last decade. While Conservatism in Scotland and Wales clearly suffered at various times from its identification as 'English' and alien, this does not mean that questions of national identity were unproblematic in England itself. Nicholas insists that

Baldwin's image as the essential Englishman was not simply a conventional publicity device, but an integral part of his political identity. However, she also shows that this identity was carefully and deliberately constructed through radio and film. The new mass media (unlike the press) shared Baldwin's preference for consensus and class harmony as opposed to confrontation, a preference which was presented as reflecting the essential 'Englishness' of inter-war Conservatism. In the post-war era the most serious challenge to traditional Conservative conceptions of national identity has arisen over the issue of immigration from Britain's former colonies. Brooke argues for the essential complexity of Conservative reactions to immigration, as was suggested by the dialogue between Heath and Powell in 1968. Brooke asserts that the advent of non-white immigration after 1945 enveloped the question of national identity with more explicit concerns about race and colour, and led to the abandonment of the promotion of the multiracial Commonwealth in favour of the defence of the traditional nation.

Part Three focuses on gender. The contributions by Jarvis and Zweiniger-Bargielowska examine the gendered nature of popular politics and the Conservative response within the context of the equal franchise in the twentieth century. Jarvis discusses Conservative concerns over shifting and unstable gender identities between 1900 and 1939. He juxtaposes the Conservatives' success among women with male ambivalence and resentment about female intrusion into a previously masculine domain. The party believed it had to strike a balance between the conflicting demands of a softer and more home-centred discourse to appeal to the new women voters and the need to prevent a new generation of 'virile' and 'energetic' young men from turning to extremes of both left and right. Zweiniger-Bargielowska focuses on the gender gap in voting behaviour between 1945 and 1970. Gallup Poll data shows a gap of up to seventeen points and a strong female preference for the Conservative Party. Conventional structural explanations of female Conservatism are based on simplistic notions of female domesticity. Zweiniger-Bargielowska rejects these assumptions since the gender gap was not static and a small majority of women voted Labour in 1945 and 1966. She emphasizes historical factors, namely the Conservatives' distinctive appeal to women as consumers and citizens, including the introduction of equal pay in the public sector, during the 1950s when the gender gap was most significant.

The final part examines Conservative approaches to practical policy. All contributions discuss how Conservative perceptions of the relationship between the state and society are translated into specific aspects of social and economic policy. Green, Jones and Lowe analyse the recurring debate within the Conservative Party about social policy during a period of major changes in the relationship between the state and the individual as a result of the emergence of the welfare state. Green examines the Conservatives' complex and fragmented response to 'the social question' of the late Victorian and Edwardian period. The discussion of Conservative thought on this issue incorporates both libertarian and collectivist approaches and shows that the party was engaged in prolonged discussion about the role of agencies of state in civil society dealing with social issues. Specific social policy initiatives are examined through the work of the Unionist Social Reform Committee which, through the idea of an organic state, seemed to have the potential to reconcile party conflicts. Jones focuses on the difficult period of adjustment facing Conservative social policy-makers after 1945. The party had to balance the conflicting claims of ideological beliefs on the proper relationship between the individual and the state and financial constraints as well as political assessments over the best way to regain and maintain power against the backcloth of the Cold War. High growth and full employment allowed the Conservatives to shelve painful policy decisions temporarily and to indulge in delivering presents in the form of high public expenditure combined with a consumer boom – the 'Santa Claus syndrome'. Lowe follows on directly from Jones and examines how the Conservative Party replanned the welfare state and came to accept high public expenditure between 1957 and 1964. Lowe sees Thorneycroft's resignation in 1958 and the refusal to cut public expenditure in 1962 as an indication of the Conservatives' growing commitment to the welfare state. Over and above the electoral advantage to be gained, welfare policy was seen as a means to promote both social justice and economic efficiency. This was so among the party leadership as well as a younger generation of Conservatives such as Macleod or Heath who were sympathetic to modernization through state action. Tomlinson and Daunton examine the ideological and political

implications of economic and taxation policy during the 1950s
and 1960s. Tomlinson's analysis of Conservative economic policy
between 1951 and 1964 highlights the party's distinctive
ideological approach through the twin themes of liberty and order.
Going beyond a focus on macro-economic policy and the
conventional epithet of 'wasted years', Tomlinson argues that the
Conservative governments both knew about and tried to respond
to mounting evidence of relatively slow economic growth.
However, a combination of ideological constraints and political
calculations about feasible policy options inhibited any kind of
adequate response. Finally, Daunton focuses on Conservative
attempts to reform the tax system after 1960. While they stressed
the importance of both the legitimacy and buoyancy of the fiscal
system, the problem facing the Conservatives in the 1960s was
that this fiscal constitution showed signs of strain due to rising
welfare costs. The party discussed a range of tax reforms intended
to create an 'opportunity state' which was based on economic
growth but would not entail harm to others. However, the
integrated tax package proposed by 1970 was never implemented
in the face of political resistance and economic downturn. The
alternative electoral strategy developed after the mid-1970s, based
on home ownership and share ownership, was a blatant appeal to
self-interest with scant regard either for the creation of efficiency
or the well-being of the poor.

Our contributors often draw very different conclusions, for
example on the commitment of Conservatives to social reform in
both the Edwardian period and the 1950s and 1960s, or on the
status of Thatcherism in the Conservative tradition. However, they
share a common concern to recast the historiography of modern
Conservatism, and to provide a novel approach to the relationship
between politics and people in twentieth-century Britain.

*Notes*
[1] A. J. Davies, *We, The Nation: The Conservative Party and the Pursuit of
Power* (London, 1995), 414.
[2] D. Southgate (ed.), *The Conservative Leadership, 1832–1932* (London,
1974); T. F. Lindsay and M. Harrington, *The Conservative Party,
1918–1979* (London, 1979); Lord Butler (ed.), *The Conservatives: A
History from their Origins to 1965* (London, 1977).

[3] R. Blake, *The Conservative Party from Peel to Churchill* (London, 1970).

[4] J. Ramsden, *The Age of Balfour and Baldwin, 1902–1940* (London, 1978).

[5] For example, P. Marsh, *The Discipline of Popular Government: Lord Salisbury's Domestic Statecraft, 1881–1902* (Hassocks, 1978); A. Sykes, *Tariff Reform in British Politics, 1903–13* (Oxford, 1979); G. D. Phillips, *The Diehards: Aristocratic Society and Politics in Edwardian England* (Cambridge, Mass., 1979).

[6] Among the exceptions are J. Ramsden, *The Making of Conservative Party Policy: The Conservative Research Department since 1929* (London, 1980) and A. Seldon, *Churchill's Indian Summer: The Conservative Government, 1951–55* (London, 1981).

[7] A. Gamble, *The Conservative Nation* (London, 1974); N. Harris, *Competition and the Corporate Society: British Conservatives, the State and Industry, 1945–1964* (London, 1972); P. Norton and A. Aughey, *Conservatives and Conservatism* (London, 1981).

[8] M. Pugh, 'Popular Conservatism in Britain: Continuity and Change, 1880–1987', *Journal of British Studies* 27 (1988); *idem, The Tories and the People, 1880–1935* (Oxford, 1985).

[9] E. H. H. Green, *The Crisis of Conservatism: The Politics, Economics and Ideology of the British Conservative Party, 1880–1914* (London, 1995); J. Lawrence, 'Class and Gender in the Making of Urban Toryism, 1880–1914', *English Historical Review* 108 (1993). Other recent studies of Edwardian Conservatism are F. Coetzee, *For Party or Country? Nationalism and the Dilemmas of Popular Conservatism in Edwardian England* (Oxford, 1990); D. Dutton, *'His Majesty's Loyal Opposition': The Unionist Party in Opposition, 1905–15* (Liverpool, 1992); M. Fforde, *Conservatism and Collectivism, 1886–1914* (Edinburgh, 1990).

[10] S. Ball, *Baldwin and the Conservative Party: The Crisis of 1929–31* (New Haven, Conn., 1988); P. Williamson, *National Crisis and National Government: British Politics, the Economy and Empire, 1926–32* (Cambridge, 1992); *idem,* 'The Doctrinal Politics of Stanley Baldwin', in M. Bentley (ed.), *Public and Private Doctrine* (Cambridge, 1993).

[11] R. McKibbin, 'Class and Conventional Wisdom: The Conservative Party and the 'Public' in Inter-War Britain', in his *The Ideologies of Class* (Oxford, 1990); D. Jarvis, 'The Shaping of Conservative Electoral Hegemony, 1918–39', in J. Lawrence and M. Taylor (eds.), *Party, State and Society: Electoral Behaviour in Modern Britain* (Aldershot, 1996).

[12] J. Ramsden, *The Age of Churchill and Eden, 1940-1957* (London, 1995); *idem,* '"A Party for Owners or a Party for Earners": How Far did the British Conservative Party Really Change after 1945?', *Transactions of the Royal Historical Society*, 5th ser, 37 (1987). The remaining volumes in the Longman History of the Conservative Party dealing with the post-1880 period are *idem, Age of Balfour and Baldwin; idem, The Winds*

*of Change: Macmillan to Heath, 1957–1975* (London, 1996); and R. Shannon, *The Age of Salisbury, 1881–1902* (London, 1996).

[13] H. Jones, 'The Conservative Party and Social Policy, 1942–1955', unpublished Ph.D. thesis, University of London, 1992; *idem*, 'New Tricks for an Old Dog? The Conservatives and Social Policy, 1951–1955', in A. Gorst et al. (eds.), *Contemporary British History, 1931–1961* (London, 1991); I. Zweiniger-Bargielowska, 'Rationing, Austerity and the Conservative Party Recovery after 1945', *Historical Journal* 37 (1994); N. Rollings, 'Poor Mr Butskell: A Short Life, Wrecked by Schizophrenia?', *Twentieth Century British History* 5 (1994); M. Kandiah, 'Lord Woolton's Chairmanship of the Conservative Party, 1945–1951', unpublished Ph.D. thesis, University of Exeter, 1992. A similar emphasis on the distinctiveness of Conservative policies for the years immediately *before* 1945 is made in K. Jefferys, *The Churchill Coalition and Wartime Politics, 1940–1945* (Manchester, 1991).

[14] For example, J. Barnes and A. Seldon, '1951–64: Thirteen Wasted Years?', *Contemporary Record* 1 (1987); K. Burk, *The First Privatisation: The Politicians, the City and the Denationalisation of Steel* (London, 1988); R. Lamb, *The Failure of the Eden Government* (London, 1987); *idem, The Macmillan Years, 1957–63: The Emerging Truth* (London, 1995).

[15] J. Campbell, *Edward Heath: A Biography* (London, 1993); S. Ball and A. Seldon, *The Heath Government: A Reappraisal* (London, 1996). One exception to the general neglect of 1964–70 is L. Johnman, 'The Conservative Party in Opposition, 1964–70', in R. Coopey et al. (eds.), *The Wilson Governments, 1964–1970* (London, 1993).

[16] For example, P. Clarke, 'Margaret Thatcher's Leadership in Historical Perspective', *Parliamentary Affairs* 45 (1992); A. Adonis and T. Hames (eds.), *A Conservative Revolution? The Thatcher-Reagan Decade in Perspective* (Manchester, 1994).

[17] For example, A. Gamble, *The Free Economy and the Strong State: The Politics of Thatcherism* (Basingstoke, 1988); K. Minogue and M. Biddiss (eds.), *Thatcherism: Personality and Politics* (Basingstoke, 1987); R. Skidelsky (ed.), *Thatcherism* (London, 1988); H. Young, *One of Us: A Biography of Margaret Thatcher* (London, 1989); S. R. Letwin, *The Anatomy of Thatcherism* (London, 1992).

[18] M. Thatcher, *The Downing Street Years* (London, 1993); N. Lawson, *The View from No. 11: Memoirs of a Tory Radical* (London, 1992); N. Tebbit, *Upwardly Mobile* (London, 1988); I. Gilmour, *Dancing with Dogma* (London, 1992). G. Howe, *Conflict of Loyalty* (London, 1994).

[19] *Twentieth Century British History* 5, 2 (1994).

[20] A. Seldon and S. Ball, *Conservative Century: The Conservative Party since 1900* (Oxford, 1994).

[21] McKibbin, 'Class and Conventional Wisdom'; J. Cornford, 'The

Transformation of Conservatism in the Late Nineteenth Century',
*Victorian Studies* 7 (1963).
22 E. Nordlinger, *The Working Class Tories* (London, 1967); R. McKenzie
and A. Silver, *Angels in Marble: Working Class Conservatives in Urban
England* (London, 1968); H. Newby, *The Deferential Worker: A Study of
Farm Workers in East Anglia* (London, 1977).
23 A. Heath et al., *Understanding Political Change: The British Voter
1964–1987* (Oxford, 1991), 62–84; J. Curtice, 'Political Sociology
1945–92', in J. Obelkevich and P. Catterall (eds.), *Understanding Post-
War British Society* (London, 1994), 31–44.
24 E. F. Biagini and A. J. Reid (eds.), *Currents of Radicalism: Popular
Radicalism, Organised Labour and Party Politics in Britain, 1850–1914*
(Cambridge, 1991); Lawrence and Taylor (eds.), *Party, State and
Society: Electoral Behaviour in Modern Britain*; P. Joyce (ed.), *Class*
(Oxford, 1995).
25 P. Joyce, 'The End of Social History?', *Social History* 20 (1995), 74. For
this debate see D. Mayfield and S. Thorne, 'Social History and its
Discontents: Gareth Stedman Jones and the Politics of Language',
*Social History* 17 (1992); J. Lawrence and M. Taylor, 'The Poverty of
Protest: Gareth Stedman Jones and the Politics of Language - A Reply',
*Social History* 18 (1993); comments by Joyce and Mayfield and Thorne
in ibid.; J. Vernon, 'Who's Afraid of the "Linguistic Turn"? The Politics
of Social History and its Discontents', *Social History* 19 (1994).
26 Joyce, 'The End of Social History?', 82.
27 Lawrence, 'Class and Gender in the Making of Urban Toryism', 631.
28 M. Freeden, 'The Stranger at the Feast: Ideology and Public Policy in
Twentieth-Century Britain', *Twentieth Century British History* 1 (1990),
34.
29 M. Freeden, *The New Liberalism* (Oxford, 1978); and *idem, Liberalism
Divided* (Oxford, 1986); P. F. Clarke, *Liberals and Social Democrats*
(Cambridge, 1978).
30 Here modern historians clearly lag behind their early modern
counterparts, most notably J. G. A. Pocock and Q. Skinner, who have
long appreciated the importance of political language. See A. Padgen
(ed.), *The Languages of Political Theory in Early-Modern Europe*
(Cambridge, 1987).
31 For example, E. F. Biagini, *Liberals, Retrenchment and Reform*
(Cambridge, 1992); D. Tanner, 'Ideological Debate in Edwardian
Labour Politics', in E. F. Biagini and A. J. Reid (eds.), *Currents of
Radicalism,* (Cambridge, 1991); S. J. Brooke, 'Problems of "Socialist
Planning": Evan Durbin and the Labour Government of 1945',
*Historical Journal* 34 (1991); M. Francis, 'Economics and Ethics: The
Nature of Labour's Socialism, 1945-1951', *Twentieth Century British
History* 6 (1995). The major exceptions to this weighting towards

Liberals and Labour are Green, *Crisis of Conservatism;* M. Bentley, 'Liberal Toryism in the Twentieth Century', *Transactions of the Royal Historical Society,* 6th ser, 4 (1994); J. Barnes, 'Ideology and Factions', in Seldon and Ball, *Conservative Century.*

[32] W. Elliot, *Toryism and the Twentieth Century* (London, 1927), 4; Q. Hogg, *The Case for Conservatism* (London, 1947), 13; R. Scruton, *The Meaning of Conservatism* (London, 1980), 11.

[33] See E. H. H. Green, 'The Strange Death of Tory England', *Twentieth Century British History* 2 (1991), 70–1.

[34] Freeden, 'Stranger', 11.

[35] For example, E. Said, *Culture and Imperialism* (London, 1994); H. Bhabba (ed.), *Nation and Narration* (London, 1990).

[36] For example, A. Grant and K. Stringer (eds.), *Uniting the Kingdom? The Making of British History* (London, 1995). Studies specifically on the post-1880 period include R. Samuel (ed.), *Patriotism,* 3 vols. (London, 1989); R. Colls and P. Dodd (eds.), *Englishness: Politics and Culture, 1880–1920* (London, 1986). A useful commentary on some of this literature is provided by M. Taylor, 'Patriotism, History and the Left in Twentieth-Century Britain', *Historical Journal* 33 (1990).

[37] R. Cohen, *Frontiers of Identity: The British and the Others* (London, 1994), 1.

[38] Blake, *Peel to Churchill,* 274.

[39] H. Cunningham, 'The Conservative Party and Patriotism', in Colls and Dodd, *Englishness;* J. Turner, 'Letting Go: The Conservative Party and the End of the Union with Ireland', in Grant and Stringer (eds.), *Uniting the Kingdom?*

[40] Colls and Dodd, *Englishness;* R. Porter (ed.), *Myths of the English* (Oxford, 1992).

[41] A. M. Smith, *New Right Discourse on Race and Sexuality: Britain, 1968–1990* (Cambridge, 1994), 23–4.

[42] J. W. Scott, *Gender and the Politics of History* (New York, 1988), 2; D. Riley, *'Am I that Name?' Feminism and the Category of 'Women' in History* (Basingstoke, 1988).

[43] K. McClelland, 'Some Thoughts on Masculinity and the "Representative Artisan" in Britain, 1850–1880', *Gender and History* 1 (1989); S. O. Rose, *Limited Livelihoods: Gender and Class in Nineteenth Century England* (London, 1992).

# Part One

# Ideology

# Conservative Ideology and Representations of the Union with Ireland, 1885–1914

## JEREMY SMITH

## I

For many years the Conservative Party struggled to promote itself as unideological, disclaiming any systematic ideological tendencies in favour of understanding their creed as more of 'a habit of mind, a mode of feeling, a way of living'.[1] This originated in a mis-understanding (and mistrust) of ideology, as something rather narrow, un-English and alien, the refuge of revolutionaries and radicals who chased rainbows and utopias, and thus not the stuff of serious politicians. By contrast, Conservatives imagined they had no fixed destination and only the loosest of guiding principles, usually culled from the writings and speeches of previous leaders. They saw themselves operating, therefore, according to the world around them and not motivated by ideas or projects; thus one of the more scholarly accounts of Conservative principles could still claim that 'Conservatism is not so much a philosophy as an attitude, a constant force'.[2] Their craft was premised upon the application of a rugged common-sense and practical turn of mind, rather than the pursuit of an unrealizable and idealized society. Government, for them, was a limited, administrative task, a 'technocratic Conservatism',[3] designed solely to recalibrate the institutions of state to changing social and cultural circumstances, and not the implementation of a programme, agenda or plan. It was a self-representation that was reinforced by notions, popular during the 1950s and 1960s, of an 'end of ideology' and the triumph of empirical social science, and from a tendency for Conservative aspirations and values to express themselves not in constitutions, manifestos, philosophical treatises or Yellow Books, but in less systematic and ideological forms, such as speeches, biographies and memoirs, or the deeds of past leaders.

By the 1970s the assertion that Conservatism was simply 'grounded in practice',[4] appeared less sustainable. This resulted from cracks within the political consensus and broadening definitions of ideology towards more 'inclusive' meanings,[5] according to which all politics, even the least self-conscious, were in some sense ideological. Political scientists and historians now began to investigate the existence of a Conservative doctrine, although, interestingly, these questions had already received attention within American academic circles from the late 1950s.[6] What emerged, in place of a Conservative 'spirit' or 'atmosphere', was a more distinct and intelligible Conservative value and belief system or dogma, of which perhaps the most thorough account has been Roger Scruton's formulation of a systematic structure to Conservative assumptions.[7] Most researches stressed an assortment of 'common aims, arguments and assumptions',[8] a canon of ideals sometimes referred to as the Conservative tradition. This includes a pessimism about human nature, a belief in an organically based and hierarchically structured society, the paramountcy of property-ownership and a firm maintenance of the established social order and established basis of authority. Several studies traced these assumptions back to the nineteenth century, revealing a fairly consistent doctrinal bedrock, despite dramatic shifts in policy and rhetoric.[9] Others, such as Eccleshall and Cowling, rather than assembling a coherent dogma, have struggled to locate a core impulse to Conservatism, which lay, for both of them, in its 'vindication of inequality'.[10]

Conservative dogma therefore not only existed but had, as it were, always done so, although it tended to disclose its quintessence most clearly when under attack. At such moments it was forced into greater transparency and a 'firmer sense of identity'[11] by the necessity of defining and legitimating the resistance of an established social order to a threat to its economic and political power. The period of the French Revolution is frequently cited as the location of the origins of modern Conservatism, when Edmund Burke, 'the prophet of

Conservatism',[12] laid out the 'fundamental philosophical, political, social and religious details' of a self-conscious Conservatism.[13] Similarly, the 1880s, with changes in the electoral system, the rise of an independent working-class politics and the rising threat of socialism, generated a much sharper Conservative definition, as can be gleaned from the speeches and works of W. H. Mallock, Disraeli, Sir Henry Maine and Lord Salisbury.[14] And the so-called New Right upsurge from the late 1960s drew nourishment from a series of threats in the form of an emergent New Left, the Cold War, increased trade union power, a radicalized Labour Party and spiralling demands on welfare.[15]

Yet dogma is not the same thing as ideology, for ideology is something animated, that embraces the interplay of those various Conservative assumptions and traditions within political activity. It is a discourse, as Martin Seliger argues, between the fundamental and operative[16] or, for Scruton, between dogma and policy,[17] whilst Greenleaf similarly asserts that dogma is 'intended primarily to justify action', with ideology representing a 'confluence of ideas and policies'.[18] Only, then, when dogma is applied or grounded in political action, does it become ideological and assume numerous dynamic roles. These include the mobilization of networks of electoral support, often from dissimilar regions, communities, religions, classes and ethnic groups, as well as converting new recruits to the party, the manufacture and strengthening of loyalty towards the political leadership, the recommendation and legitimation of policy and political response, and at a wider, cultural level, the creation of a Conservative thought-world or 'universe of meaning',[19] that would define and guide political, social and moral activities for the wider party.

Ideology must therefore operate within a political context that is determined by various dynamic forces, such as tactical options, perceptions of public opinion and audience reaction, electoral calculation, personal advancement, influence from interests and groups, prevailing economic conditions or foreign affairs. To win or secure power in such a setting, an ideology must maintain its effective appeal and relevance, which necessitates a process of continued reinterpretation, a constant modification in the representation and expression of Conservatism, or aspects of it, and alteration in the selection, emphasis and prioritizing of its assorted aims and beliefs. Those Conservative beliefs might themselves grow, modify or perhaps depreciate, in line with wider changes in social, political and cultural circumstances. As with all ideologies Conservatism is unstable and pliant, subject to redefinition and repackaging: what a recent study has referred to as 'porous and open to a wide variety of influences and interpretations: consequently it can never have a complete or comprehensive or essential statement philosophically, dogmatically or practically.'[20] Two brief observations should be added to this.

Firstly, not all would decipher these considerations in the same way; thus points of tension and division were built into the process and rival conservatisms would exist at the same time. This, in turn, reinforces the second point, that ideological conflict was indigenous to Conservatism rather than foreign to it. Such conflict could operate at different levels and strengths and with differing amounts of enthusiasm, leaders, for example, being more constrained in their ideological proclivities by the immediate needs of circumstance and context than supporters or lesser political actors, who enjoyed more freedom to indulge their opinions. It could focus upon one aspect of policy or embrace a broader refashioning of Conservative dogma, as some imagined with Chamberlain's tariff reform crusade. At these moments conflict could be bitter and deep-rooted, with different representations struggling for ascendancy, as occurred within the party between 1903 and 1914 and again between 1975 and 1983. On other occasions a degree of stability was achieved by a dominant ideological representation being imposed, thus temporarily marginalizing any alternatives, as occurred with Salisburian Conservatism after 1886–7 and Baldwin's representation of Conservatism after 1923.

At a general level, this chapter will attempt to display some of these inner workings of Conservative ideology and the processes by which an aspect of it was constructed and reconstructed, by exploring Conservative reactions towards Liberal attempts to grant Home Rule for Ireland, between 1885 and 1914. Ireland was, after all, a central issue during this period of intense political struggle, when Home Rule, according to Conservatives, threatened the very basis of the United Kingdom. Ireland and the Union also triggered (or were made to trigger) a variety of deep

Conservative assumptions and is therefore an effective spotlight with which to examine those ideas. More specifically, the chapter will argue that the activities of the Conservative Party during the Ulster crisis of 1911–14, and more precisely the extreme and unparliamentary campaign of resistance to the Liberal Home Rule bill, launched by the Tory leadership, was a consequence of acute ideological conflict and confusion. In particular, how the late nineteenth-century Conservative ideological characterization of Ireland and Union seemed to lose much of its relevance by the early twentieth century, as its founding representations were gradually weakened or sullied. This resulted in ideological uncertainty, encouraging, on the one hand, those surviving elements, and especially the cause of Ulster, to strengthen their pull and significance, and on the other, to elevate alternative ideological approaches, or ones previously dormant or suppressed. Together, these developments nurtured an environment of acute ideological conflict, which underlay and indeed provoked the drift towards extreme political methods.

## II

Several different ideological representations of Ireland competed for dominance within Conservative politics during the complex and fluid political situation from 1884 onwards.[21] One, sponsored by Randolph Churchill, Lord Carnarvon and Michael Hicks Beach, and which drew support from Dublin Tories – the 'Howth set', such as Plunkett and Gibson – was constructed around a moderate and mildly progressive stance, where the Union with Ireland was represented as a partnership and an alliance of mutual benefit.[22] In policy terms it advocated the appeasement of Irish unrest and undercutting the appeal of Home Rule by conciliatory measures, which included a refusal to introduce a Crimes bill, a scheme of educational reform and the state purchase of land which was then sold back to tenants at low rates of interest. They also recommended, though more hesitantly, the grant of specific devolved governmental powers to a local Irish assembly, and even, with Carnarvon, to the point of Irish Home Rule. This stance was legitimated by appeals to a number of Conservative assumptions and traditions. It evoked Burkean notions of 'change in order to conserve' and could echo Peelite methods of removing sources of friction to buy off Irish discontent, as in 1829 and again in 1845–6. It reflected a practical, Palmerstonian approach to Empire, whilst facilitating the exercise of power at a local level overlapped with Conservative small-state leanings. Land-purchase measures, as shown by Ashbourne's Act of 1885, reinforced property-ownership for single owner-occupiers, by negating Liberal dual-ownership principles, as enshrined in the 1881 Land Act, even if they were Irish tenant farmers rather than landed élites. It could also draw legitimacy from previous co-operation between the Conservatives and Isaac Butt's Home Rulers, and from their common attitudes towards education and Fair Trade.

During 1885, this ideological representation gained in appeal as a result of its tactical relevance, with a moderate, reformist approach helping to sustain an alliance with the Irish Nationalists from July 1885. Also, in a period of enormous electoral change and uncertainty, many Conservatives believed a sensible and practical response to Irish problems would be preferred by the electorate to more radical Gladstonian initiatives or hard-line Tory methods. It was these considerations that led Salisbury, against his previously stated attitude and to the disgruntlement of many of his right-wing friends, temporarily to endorse such views, agreeing to Carnarvon's secret meeting with Parnell and postponing a new Crimes bill.[23] On the other hand, for Churchill, it enhanced his position and importance, in a political atmosphere thick with speculation about the creation of a centrist coalition.[24]

Conflicting with this approach was a less consensual ideological representation of Ireland, closely associated with sentiments on the Tory right. According to this vision, Ireland was a hotbed of disloyalty, and a land ridden with priests and rebels, plotting against the established Protestant order, and a potential ally for Britain's enemies. The Irish were criminalized, feminized and imagined as racially inferior. As such, 'In Ireland', Lord Salisbury believed, 'it is essential that you govern',[25] rather than partner, a conviction that firmly denied the legitimacy of Irish political grievances. What grievances existed were the product of economic hardship, moral laxity and exploitation by ambitious Nationalist politicians, rather than arising from genuine iniquity.[26] By this interpretation any grant of Irish self-rule was foolhardy, although it left room for limited economic reforms and financial investment, once law and order was established. Such images were used to highlight many Conservative assumptions and traditions. Some of these overlapped with other representations, such as the safeguarding of property ownership. However, others were represented differently or were prioritized in a way Churchill's more consensual line had not. In particular, it foregrounded a firm commitment to upholding the law and the existing social order, through the effective deployment of a Crimes bill. Tough measures to preserve the sanctity of the law would also advertise the dominance of the imperial Parliament at Westminster to the rest of the Empire.[27]

This latter representation of Ireland and Irish grievances was initially of a limited appeal for Conservatives. Not until the end of 1885 and early 1886 did the situation alter with Gladstone's conversion to Home Rule. This proved a tremendous bounty to Salisbury,[28] recommending to him the viability of his hard-line representation of Ireland and the Union. Salisbury was now able to polarize politics between Gladstonian Home Rule and his own rigid defence of the Union, a breach that led the Liberal Unionists, under Hartington and Chamberlain, to cross the floor of the Commons and into a Unionist alliance with Tories. The realignment also helped Salisbury consolidate his position as leader, by collapsing the prospects for a centrist coalition, so forcing his main rival Churchill, who had previously sailed close to Home Rule, to distance himself from a stance associated with Gladstone. Churchill warmed to the new task, throwing off his consensual line and repositioning himself behind Salisbury, in a dramatic speech at Ulster Hall in February 1886, where he declared, 'Ulster will fight and Ulster will be right.'[29]

More significantly, Gladstone's promotion of Home Rule allowed Salisbury to construct a highly influential political representation of the Union. It drew upon, and aligned with, a populist, nationalistic, anti-Catholic and anti-Irish tradition, that was long established in many working-class communities, particularly Lancashire and parts of the north-east. These prejudices connected the party to sections of working-class support, in an 'English, British Nationalist and Protestant patriotic alliance',[30] and was of vital importance at a moment when the electoral system was undergoing rapid expansion. Salisbury's representation also drew sanction from a Pittite legacy, a legacy of national defence and struggle during a period of acute danger to the United Kingdom, not least as a consequence of revolt in Ireland. Peace and social order had eventually been restored by Pitt's Act of Union, a political settlement that secured British interests, and laid the basis for a century of rapid commercial and economic progress. 'Was there any doubt', Salisbury asked his audience at St James's Hall, 'as to the policy of Mr Pitt and Lord Castlereagh, and Mr Canning and Sir Robert Peel and Lord Beaconsfield. The maintenance of the Act of Union was the unbroken tradition of the Tory party.'[31] This was a powerful invocation, and perhaps symbolized most explicitly by the disparity in wealth between 'loyal' northern Ireland and the 'disloyal' south, with loyalists after 1886 increasingly organizing their parliamentary representatives behind the Tory party.[32] Union was, by these representations, inextricably linked with national prosperity and imperial security, and therefore a vital structural prop for the British state and British interests. Attempts to alter or reform it were quickly caricatured as attacks on the British state itself. Hence the Liberal Party, in taking up Home Rule, was portrayed by Tories as a force for subversion at the heart of the British political system, especially once the 'loyal' minority had fled from their ranks.

Yet the Conservative values raised around the defence of the Union resonated with similar anxieties within the domestic political environment of the 1880s. This was a period of rising trade union militancy, growing republican and socialist activity, disturbance in several parts of the Empire, constitutional innovation, and attacks upon the existing structure of landowner-ship from progressive radicals such as Henry George, and which found an echo in government legislation. Defence of the Union was therefore embellished and manufactured into a more general defence of existing British society against various disintegrative forces. Union with Ireland became a totem to bind together all those interests, bodies and groups fearful or injured by recent trends in society. It was used to represent the protection of property and freedom of contract, the vigorous defence of law and order, the preservation of established authority, a bulwark against socialism and radical agitators, an insurance against religious intolerance, an upholding of existing constitutional arrangements and resistance to full democracy and the maintenance of imperial unity and national defence. In electoral terms this evolved into an effective appeal that operated in the classic Conservative style above class, region and ethnicity, and which, at the 1886 general election, helped gain 394 seats for the Unionist alliance, a majority of 118 over all other parties. Victory cemented Salisbury's ideological representation onto the party and established a paradigm through which Conservatives would imagine and interpret Ireland and the Union. It proved, however, to be a severe obstacle, for it consolidated a representation from which the party would find it difficult to escape, even after changing circumstances had rendered it unsustainable; a 'mould which could not, apparently, be broken'.[33] It would also be a particular millstone to the party in government when faced with the problem of actually administering Ireland. The political maelstrom of 1885–6 was, as Gailey has observed, a baptism by fire which left deep birthmarks.[34]

These restraints became evident in new circumstances, from the autumn of 1886. With the party's return to office came responsibility for administering Ireland, and the necessity of co-operation with Liberal Unionists. Liberal Unionists looked for something more than the rigid protection of the Union.[35] In this they could count on some Conservative support, and particularly on that of Churchill, who, buoyed up by the active co-operation of Chamberlain, continued to look to a centrist realignment.[36] These designs were bolstered by the fading threat of Home Rule, with the Liberal Party divided and shrunk to just 191 MPs and the Nationalists no longer numerically dominant. Similarly, public concern with Ireland now also fell away (if it had ever existed in the first place). These political considerations persuaded Salisbury, working through his nephews Arthur and Gerald Balfour, successive Conservative Chief Secretaries for Ireland from 1887 through until 1900, and then George Wyndham between 1900 and 1904, to repackage the Union with a more progressive hue, and yet at the same time maintain, at least publicly, its founding, defensive representation. It blended a hardline Unionist ideology with more conciliatory methods and reforms on the ground in Ireland.[37]

This proved a difficult balance; asserting the Union as the rigid bulwark of property, law, established authority and imperial unity (a line that appealed to many sections of the party, particularly

Irish and Ulster Unionists and Conservative grassroots) whilst at the same time characterizing Union as a source of practical reform, economic improvement and a constructive imperial connection (for Liberal Unionist opinion and a wider, British public sentiment). Much of this practical reform was able to keep within the margins of the founding Conservative representation of Union, with, for example, extensions to land purchase, in 1891, 1896 and 1903, and the creation of a Congested Districts Board to co-ordinate economic revitalization, such as the dredging of harbours and construction of light railways. Other measures, however, clearly stepped beyond those margins and encountered intense resistance. The Land Act of 1887, which extended Gladstone's controversial legislation of 1881 and further interfered with property relations, provoked a great deal of animosity from Irish Unionists as well as Conservatives.[38] Gerald Balfour's Irish Local Government bill of 1898, which devolved extensive powers to local county councils, similarly encountered resistance. And perhaps most vociferously, Arthur Balfour's attempts to establish a Catholic university, in 1889 and again in 1897–8, were swept aside by a surge of Protestant resentment, from Liberal Unionists as much as English Tories.[39] It was, however, the plan to devolve power to some form of Dublin government, supported by Sir Antony MacDonnell, Under-Secretary at the Irish Office, and more hesitantly, by George Wyndham, the Chief Secretary, that provoked the bitterest reaction from Conservatives and especially from Irish Unionists.[40]

Such opposition revealed the strength and pull which the founding representation could still effect, even though, by the early twentieth century, many of its ideological appeals now appeared exhausted and at odds with the realities of Irish society and the domestic British political environment. For example, land purchase and the creation of a local government structure, which redistributed power to Nationalist agitators, diluted perceptions of the Conservatives' commitment to upholding traditional ruling élites and established authority. Union, as the resolute guardian of property, appeared less sustainable after the 1887 Land Act and the sale of land under what was perceived as radical Nationalist pressure. Similarly, representation of the Union as the bulwark against socialism and Nationalist radicalism seemed less appropriate. A perception grew of the Nationalists as a rather conservative movement, symbolized by their mild-mannered and portly leader, John Redmond. This was fuelled by the emergence of various radical forces, which included the foundation of James Connolly's Irish Socialist Republican Party in 1896, Cummann na nGaedheal under Griffith in 1900, and the growing radical activity of James Larkin, leader of the Irish TGWU, who was especially singled out by Redmond for attack.[41] In such a changing environment and with ties to the Catholic Church, Nationalists could now be depicted as a force for stability and traditionalism within Irish society. Indeed, if anywhere was a threat to law and order and political stability, it was Belfast and the north. Thus, whereas Conservatives in the mid-1880s had been able to define and identify themselves and the Union against a radical, disloyal Nationalist, Home Rule, Celtic 'other', this representation was far less distinct and potent by the 1900s.

In addition, representation of the Union as the linchpin of imperial unity no longer held the same rigour. Government-directed investment in Ireland, and the Conservative promotion of tariff reform after 1903, suggested that the economic foundations to imperial connections were perhaps more significant than constitutional ones; an impression reinforced by the Nationalist enthusiasm for tariff reform. Constitution-making elsewhere in the Empire, early in the new century, made justification for a negative approach to Ireland even more difficult. The successful federation of Australia in 1900 and, more dramatically, South Africa by 1910, indicated that colonies, even previously unruly and warlike ones, could be trusted with political responsibility. In any case, after 1905 imperial concerns were less dominant within British politics than they had been in the mid-1880s. The Boer war redirected public attention to social and welfare issues, and worked to undermine the Conservative self-portrait of itself as the party of Empire. Therefore, attempts to cloak the Union with images and representations derived from the mid-1880s were much more problematic by the 1900s. Its founding, Salisburian characterization had, so it appeared, lost much of its ideological purchase and pull, a perception ruthlessly brought home to Conservatives at the 1906 election, where traditional appeals to secure the Union could not prevent a massive collapse in their parliamentary standing.

This ideological exhaustion continued once in opposition. The

1906 defeat emptied the party of a whole generation of Tory MPs raised on a diet of negative, Salisburian defence of the Union. In their place came new members reared on tariff reform, national efficiency sentiment and radical Unionism.[42] This development signified the growing importance of Chamberlainite ideas, and more generally collectivist sympathies, which embodied a reformulation and repackaging of Conservative values and assumptions along more constructive, pro-active and reformist lines. It was a shift in the general direction of Conservatism that further undermined the utility of more traditional, negative appeals, which Union had been used to represent. By 1910 this slippage had progressed so far that one leader of the party could claim that the struggle over the Union was 'a dead quarrel for which neither the country nor the party cares a damn'.[43]

The period of acute constitutional struggle of 1910–11 proved, however, to be something of a climacteric. The January 1910 election, in providing no party with an outright majority, returned the Irish Nationalists to a position of strategic influence, comparable to that of the 1885–6 and 1892 parliaments. Unfortunately, for Tories, the renewed threat of Home Rule was accompanied by (and indeed helped to motivate) the removal of the House of Lords' power of veto and the resignation of Balfour as party leader, both in 1911 – and both champions of a traditional approach to defence of the Union. In addition, the party suffered two election defeats, in which those same traditional, if now rather hollow, appeals to the firm defence of the Union failed to unseat the Liberal–Labour–Nationalist alliance. These electoral rebuffs helped to consolidate the impression, for some in the party, that representation of the Union as a defensive bastion for property, established élites, law and order, religious toleration and imperial unity, as constructed by Salisbury in 1885–6, was of limited appeal and relevance in the political context of 1910–11.

This combination of pressures encouraged alternative representations of the Union to be constructed or clarified that reinterpreted or prioritized selected Conservative values and drew upon different legacies. One such alternative was a federal or devolutionary representation, which grew steadily in popularity from 1910.[44] This could vary from support for full-blown federalization of the UK, associated with Milner's Kindergarten and the Round Table Movement,[45] through to milder forms of devolved local government adopted by some forward-thinking southern Unionists, such as Lord Dunraven. Yet they all shared a sympathy for the liberal, progressive approach of Churchill in the mid-1880s, where timely, pre-emptive concessions and partnership were methods for securing law and order, property rights and religious toleration. Federal/devolutionary plans, therefore, imagined Union less as a defensive rampart and more as an integral, self-governing component of a larger interlocking imperial framework, assumptions that appeared more appropriate to political circumstances after 1910, where constructive sentiments were so strong, and with questions of constitutional relations central to most political issues after 1909.

However, another representation to unpick itself from Salisbury's founding portrayal was the cause of the Protestant communities of Ulster. Defending these interests had, since 1885–6, been a central element of the traditional Conservative characterization of Union. As this representation crumbled and the influence of southern Unionism declined, from land purchase and Nationalist domination of local government, so the cause of Ulster grew in importance as the most significant surviving element.[46] For many Conservatives, Ulster now became almost synonymous with Union itself; certainly it proved a more workable representation of the defence of property, law and order, religious toleration, loyalism and patriotism, against a confiscating and Catholic Dublin parliament, than an all-Ireland definition. In other words, Ulster became a microcosm for all those Conservative assumptions once projected onto Union with all Ireland. In addition, the prominence of Ulster as a leading representation of Conservative values resulted from its rising profile, by the early 1900s, as a consequence of internal reorganization within the province, with the formation of the Ulster Unionist Council in 1905, and then full-scale mobilization after 1910. It also resulted from the influence certain well-positioned friends of Ulster, such as Carson and Walter Long, were able to wield in Tory leadership circles.

And yet, other Conservatives clung obstinately to older representations, derived from the 1880s, that denied the integrity of federal experiments or the narrowing of Union with Ireland onto an Ulster remnant. Union, for them, was still a pact with all Ireland that was non-negotiable and based upon the clear, unequivocal dominance of the imperial Parliament at Westminster.[47] For these sections, which included much of the Tory right, die-hards and southern Unionists, the traditional representation of Union was, if anything, even more apposite in a political context shaped by rising trade union activity, suffragette militancy, revolutionary constitutional changes and Lloyd Georgian finance and land tax initiatives. Union as the symbol for defence and consolidation still had pertinence for the Edwardian period. The more extreme elements from these sections, such as Willoughby de Broke, Lord Winterton and Page Croft, already anxious at the prospects for their class and the disintegrative movements within society, extended Union to represent a sort of last stand or rearguard action, in defence of an idealized image of British society which they believed was slipping away.[48]

From these dissimilar representations of Union different tactical priorities and policy concerns arose, fuelling serious internal division. For example, representing Union as Ulster implied that Ireland might be partitioned, with Home Rule acceptable for the rest of Ireland, a view opposed by federal and more traditional, all-Ireland representations of Union. Alternatively, Union as a self-governing part of a wider interlocking Empire found little favour with those who asserted the dominance of the Westminster Parliament or regarded Union as corresponding to Ulster, since it created a Dublin legislature with powers over northern Protestants, and suggested colony status for Ulster rather than an integral part of the United Kingdom. And traditional all-Ireland representations of the Union were, for both federalists and supporters of Ulster, impractical and of little electoral value after 1910–11. Division also occurred within each representative strain, with a variety of different shades of opinion nestling uneasily together. Those who imagined Union as part of an interlocking Empire divided between mild devolutionists, such as Lord Lansdowne, to full-blown federalists, such as Earl Grey, Lords Selborne and Hythe, and Leo Amery. Traditional exponents of Union split between those more constitutionally restrained, like A. V. Dicey, and those who saw defence of all-Irish Union a matter of life and death. Even supporters of Ulster divided between liberal and more hard-line defenders, and over whether, in the last instance, Ulster was to be defined as either a nine-, six- or even a four-county unit.[49]

By 1910–11 the party was, therefore, in a state of ideological confusion, upon how to imagine and represent Union with

Ireland, and what conservative values and assumptions Union now symbolized and embodied.[50] This confusion, in turn, generated tactical and policy disagreement as, for example, on 22 and 23 January 1912, during a speaking tour of the north-west, the party leadership all supported slightly different things. Walter Long and Lord Midleton concentrated on opposing Home Rule for all Ireland, whereas Austen Chamberlain appeared to favour a devolutionary scheme, and Sir Edward Carson and F. E. Smith fastened their arguments onto the position of Ulster.[51] It presented the new Tory leader, Andrew Bonar Law, with a very difficult situation, facing the imminent prospect of another Home Rule bill yet with the party squabbling over conflicting representations of what Union was and how best to secure it.

Unable to impose one representation of Union onto the party, as Salisbury had in 1886, he sought instead to construct a basis of agreement or consensus. This emerged during the hiatus period, between the Lords crisis of August 1911 and introduction of Home Rule in April 1912, and developed from arguments raised in opposition to the Parliament Act, and from his campaign during November and December against government corruption. It took the form of steering party attention away from questions about what Union represented, and thus what Home Rule challenged, and onto a more neutral stance that the Home Rule bill was itself unconstitutional. It was a shift from criticizing the substance of Home Rule, so avoiding the need for a clear conception of Union, towards an attack on the method and means by which the government were trying to introduce it. According to this, Home Rule was unconstitutional because it had not figured in ministerial addresses during the December 1910 election, and followed directly on from the Parliament Act, despite the constitution still being in suspension and before reconstruction, as promised in the preamble to the Parliament bill. Only some form of appeal to the people, with an election or referendum, would re-inject constitutionality into the bill's progress, which now became the central demand for most Conservatives.[52] The struggle over Home Rule was, therefore, absorbed into the wider struggle over the Constitution running between the parties since 1909. Nothing indicates the ideological exhaustion of Union better than Bonar Law's concentration upon the Home Rule bill's technical flaws.

Yet such a neutral, if not negative, line brought significant political advantages. Pre-eminent among these was that it enabled Bonar Law to establish a basis of agreement between the different representations of Union. It provided the political width for Tories to emphasize the predicament of Ulster as the most obvious victim of Liberal constitutional illegality, and even support its rebellion against Home Rule as 'a righteous one',[53] if no election was held to restore a degree of constitutional convention. It was a line that won the support of Ulstermen and their sympathizers within the Tory die-hards. Yet concentrating upon constitutional questions also endeared the approach to federalists, devolutionists and southern Unionists, with its implication of constitutional reconstruction and, by prioritizing an election, avoided any approval for partitionist ideas. It was a stance that also won him the backing of traditional sponsors of all-Ireland Union. The combination of Bonar Law's strong language, itself vaguely reminiscent of Salisbury, and the clear populist undertones and focus upon an election, won support from a wide cross-section of Conservative groups. And at the very least, these qualities helped disguise the conflict of ideas and representations over Union.

It was also an approach that could draw upon alternative Tory assumptions, such as a regard for a balanced constitution and apprehension of an overpowerful executive. This last consideration had been particularly important to Conservatives since the late nineteenth century, and a major worry for Lord Salisbury, observing the executive grow steadily in power and independence from changes in parliamentary procedure.[54] These arguments now clearly resonated, for many, within the political context after 1909, shaped by Liberal constitutional experiments. Making the cry 'Constitution in danger', responded, then, to long-established anxieties within Tory circles and, more immediately, to the deep sense of frustration within the Conservative Party. In addition, employing the language of democracy, by demanding an election and appealing to the people as the ultimate sovereign power, reactivated a strong populist strand within Toryism. This aligned the constitutional crusade of 1911–14 with earlier populist appeals, against Catholic Emancipation in the 1820s, Disraeli on Empire and social reform and Randolph Churchill with Tory Democracy.

Unfortunately, shifting the focus onto a constitutional footing was an approach riddled with dangers. Although it balanced out the competing representations of Union, this could only ever be a short-term consensus. Once political pressure built up, and particularly if no election materialized and the government remained steadfast to their legislative programme, so the various alternatives would unravel themselves from Bonar Law's constitutional line, to pursue their own, more limited campaigns. More dramatically, parliamentary debate was now injected with the images, language and arguments of other great constitutional struggles, particularly those of the 1640s and 1680s. This altered the whole tone and basis of discussion, with focus shifting from consideration of the details of the bill onto wider questions of constitutionality and the need for an election to legitimate it. It was a discourse that increasingly radicalized sections of the party, helping to loosen those attachments to custom and form that sustained loyalty and regard for the parliamentary system. It also rendered bargaining over the particulars of the bill of little importance – indeed the government's use of the fast-track Parliament Act and willingness to speed up the legislative process with guillotining simply added more substance to Tory arguments – and made any movement towards a compromise far more difficult. Even more seriously, imagining the Home Rule bill as illegal justified a whole range of extreme and precariously open-ended options and possibilities, which the leadership might undertake if constitutional precedent was not restored with an election. The options included the disruption of parliamentary business, enticing the king to use his prerogative powers, plans to amend the Army Annual Act,[55] right through to disobeying the elected government by supporting the Ulster Unionist Council in resisting the implementation of Home Rule.

The foundations for the extreme and extraordinary political methods undertaken by the leadership after 1911 are, then, to be located in the Conservative leadership's shift towards a constitutional basis for resisting the third Liberal Home Rule bill. This was the product of important changes both in Irish and British domestic political circumstances, during the late Victorian and Edwardian periods. Changes that weakened the ideological components of the founding representation of Union, as set in place by the convulsive events of 1885–6, and encouraged the gradual rise of alternative, competing definitions of Union with Ireland, to fill the vacuum. These developments forced Bonar Law, as the new leader of a rapidly disintegrating party, to fashion a workable, if negative, basis of agreement between them, one that held certain political advantages but also opened up a whole vista of potentially disastrous consequences. At a broader, historiographical level these developments suggest that notions about a crisis of Conservatism, and particularly notions of an ideological crisis within the party,[56] also had a clear Irish and indeed constitutional, dimension to them. These areas are either missing or badly underrated, playing a poor second fiddle in many accounts to interpretations that orientate their arguments almost solely towards tariff reform.[57]

## Notes

I would like to thank Mr Alan Beattie for all his help and encouragement well beyond a supervisor's call of duty.

1 R. J. White, *The Conservative Tradition* (London, 1950), 1.

2 Q. Hogg, *The Case for Conservatism* (London, 1947), 13.

3 B. Girvin, *The Transformation of Contemporary Conservatism* (London, 1988), 2.

4 R. Scruton, *The Meaning of Conservatism* (London, 1980), 11.

5 N. O'Sullivan, 'The Politics of Ideology', in N. O'Sullivan (ed.), *The Structure of Modern Ideology* (London, 1989), 188.

6 S. Huntington, 'Conservatism as an Ideology', *American Review of Political Science* 6 (1957); H. Glickman, 'The Toryness of English Conservatism', *Journal of British Studies* 1 (1961); S. Beer, *Modern British Politics* (London, 1965).

7 Scruton, *The Meaning*.

8 W. Greenleaf, *The British Political Tradition: The Ideological Heritage* (London, 1983), 8.

9 F. O'Gorman, *British Conservatism from Burke to Thatcher* (London, 1986): R. Eccleshall, *English Conservatism since the Reformation: An Introduction and Anthology* (London, 1990).

10 R. Eccleshall, 'Conservatism', in R. Eccleshall et al. (eds.), *Political Ideologies* (London, 1984), 73; M. Cowling, 'Introduction', in M. Cowling (ed.), *Conservative Essays* (London, 1978), 1–24.

11 J. D. Fair and J. A. Hutcheson, 'British Conservatism in the Twentieth Century: An Emerging Ideological Tradition', *Albion* 19 (1987), 550.

12 R. Nisbet, *Conservatism: Dream and Reality* (Milton Keynes, 1986), x.

13 O'Gorman, *British Conservatism*, 12.

14 Fair and Hutcheson, 'British Conservatism in the Twentieth Century', 549–78.

15 Girvin (ed.), *The Transformation*, 1–12.

16 M. Seliger, *Ideology and Politics* (London, 1976).

17 Scruton, *The Meaning*, 11–12.

18 Greenleaf, *The British Political Tradition*, 7.

19 Z. Bauman, 'Sociology and Postmodernity', in P. Joyce (ed.), *Class* (Oxford, 1995), 75.

20 A. Aughey, G. Jones and W. Riches, *The Conservative Political Tradition in Britain and the United States* (London, 1992), 21.

21 A. B. Cooke and J. Vincent, *The Governing Passion: Cabinet Government and Party Politics in Britain, 1885–6* (Brighton, 1974). A very different account of events during the 1885–6 period is W. C. Lubenow, *Parliamentary Politics and the Home Rule Crisis: The British House of Commons in 1886* (Oxford, 1988).

22 P. Marsh, *The Discipline of Popular Government: Lord Salisbury's Domestic Statecraft, 1881–1902* (London, 1978), 73–6; R. Foster, 'To the Northern Counties Station: Lord Randolph Churchill and the prelude to the Orange Card', in F. L. S. Lyons and R. A. Hawkins (eds.), *Ireland under the Union: Varieties of Tension* (Oxford, 1980); R. E. Quinault, 'Lord Randolph Churchill and Home Rule', in *Reactions to Irish Nationalism, 1865–1914* (London, 1987), 319–45.

23 Ibid., 71–3.

24 R. Foster, *Lord Randolph Churchill: A Political Life* (Oxford, 1981), 214–44.

25 A. L. Kennedy, *Salisbury 1830–1903: Portrait of a Statesman* (London, 1953), 176.

26 For a tightly reasoned account of such opinions, see Lord Salisbury, 'Disintegration', in P. Smith (ed.), *Lord Salisbury on Politics* (Cambridge, 1972), 361–76. Also, 'Swashbuckle Salisbury on the Stump', *The Nation*, 27 April 1889, in A. Mitchell and P. O'Snodaigh (eds.), *Irish Political Documents, 1869–1916* (Dublin, 1989), 76. For a useful overview of Salisbury's views on Ireland see Kennedy, *Salisbury*, 172–5.

27 A. V. Dicey, *England's Case against Home Rule* (London, 1886). Dicey passionately believed Home Rule to be destructive to the authority of Parliament, the constitution and the unity of the Empire. See also R. A. Cosgrove, 'The Relevance of Irish History: The Gladstone–Dicey debate about Home Rule, 1886–7', *Eire-Ireland* 13 (1978).

28 Marsh, *The Discipline*, 68.

29 A. Jackson, *The Ulster Party: Irish Unionists in the House of Commons, 1884–1911* (Oxford, 1989), 117–18.

30 D. G. Boyce, *The Irish Question and British Politics, 1868–1986* (London, 1988), 32.

31 *The Times*, 17 May 1886, Lord Salisbury's speech to NUCA at St James's Hall in London. See also Marsh, *The Discipline*, 71; and Kennedy, *Salisbury*, 174–5.

32 Jackson, *The Ulster Party*, chapter 2.

33 Boyce, *The Irish Question*, 32.

34 A. Gailey, *Ireland and the Death of Kindness: The Experience of Constructive Unionism, 1890–1905* (Cork, 1987).

35 P. Davies, 'The Liberal Unionist Party and the Irish Policy of Lord Salisbury's Government, 1886–1892', *Historical Journal* 18 (1975), 85–104.

36 G. R. Searle, *Country before Party: Coalition and the Idea of National Government in Modern Britain, 1885–1987* (London, 1995), 34–7.

37 L. P. Curtis, *Coercion and Conciliation in Ireland, 1880–1892: A Study of Conservative Unionism* (Princeton, 1963).

38 Jackson, *The Ulster Party*, 133–7.

39 Ibid., 178–9.

40 F. S. L. Lyons, 'The Irish Unionist Party and the Devolution Crisis of 1904–5', *Irish Historical Studies* 6 (1948), 1–22: Gailey, *Ireland and the Death*, part 2; Jackson, *The Ulster Party*, chapter 6.

41 P. Bew, *Ideology and the Irish Question: Ulster Unionism and Irish Nationalism, 1912–1916* (Oxford, 1994), 79.

42 J. Ramsden, *A History of the Conservative Party: The Age of Balfour and Baldwin, 1902–1940* (London, 1978), 20: D. Dutton, *'His Majesty's Loyal Opposition': The Unionist Party in Opposition, 1905–1915* (Liverpool, 1992), 18–20.

43 F. E. Smith to A. Chamberlain, 20 October 1910, in the Second Earl of Birkenhead, *The Life of F. E. Smith, First Earl of Birkenhead* (London, 1959), 156.

44 J. Kendle, *Ireland and the Federal Solution: The Debate over the United Kingdom Constitution, 1870–1921* (Montreal, 1989): P. Jalland, 'United Kingdom Devolution 1910–1914: Political Panacea or Tactical Diversion', *English Historical Review* 94 (1979), 757–85.

45 D. G. Boyce and J. Stubbs, 'F. S. Oliver, Lord Selborne and Federalism', *Journal of Imperial and Commonwealth History* 5, 1 (1976), 53–81; J. Kendle, 'The Round Table Movement and "Home Rule all Round"', *Historical Journal* 11 (1968), 332–53.

46 A. T. Q. Stewart, *The Ulster Crisis: Resistance to Home Rule, 1912–1914* (London, 1967); R. McNeill, *Ulster's Stand for Union* (London, 1922); W. S. Rodner, 'Leaguers, Covenanters, Moderates: British Support for Ulster, 1913–1914', *Eire-Ireland* 17 (1982), 68–85.

47 A. V. Dicey, *A Fool's Paradise: Being a Constitutionalist's Criticism on the Home Rule Bill of 1912* (London, 1913); *The Times*, 27 March 1913, manifesto on behalf of the British League for the Support of Ulster and the Union.

48 D. Cannadine, *The Decline and Fall of the British Aristocracy* (New Haven, 1990), 526–30.

49 For some of the different ideas and strains within Ulster Unionism see Bew, *Ideology and the Irish Question*, chapter 2.

[50] A. Sykes, 'The Radical Right and the Crisis of Conservatism before the First World War', *Historical Journal* 26 (1983), 661–76. Sykes points to a deep, if more general, ideological cleavage within the party, between traditionalists, social imperialists and a radical right, a division not dissimilar to what emerges over the Union.

[51] *The Morning Post*, 23 and 24 January 1912.

[52] J. Smith, 'Bluff, Bluster and Brinkmanship: Andrew Bonar Law and the Third Home Rule Bill', *Historical Journal* 36 (1993), 161–78.

[53] *Hansard* 5th ser XXXVII, col. 89, 15 April 1912 (Hugh Cecil).

[54] G. H. L. Le May, *The Victorian Constitution: Conventions, Usages and Contingencies* (London, 1979), chapter 6; C. Weston, 'Salisbury and the Lords 1868–1895', *Historical Journal* 25 (1982), 105–29; J. Ridley, 'The Unionist Opposition and the House of Lords', *Parliamentary History* 11 (1992), 235–53.

[55] J. Smith, 'Paralysing the Arm: Unionists and the Army Annual Act, 1911–1914', *Parliamentary History* 15 (1996), 191–207.

[56] E. H. H. Green, *The Crisis of Conservatism: The Politics, Economics and Ideology of the British Conservative Party, 1880–1914* (London, 1995).

[57] Ibid.; in an excellent work with 330 pages of text, Green devotes just seven to Conservatives and the Irish crisis between 1910 and 1914.

# The Conservatives and the Ideology of Landownership, 1910–1914

IAN PACKER

British Conservatives have usually been described as reluctant to philosophize about their ideas, or even to define them. As W. H. Mallock, one of the Tories' most tireless writers and propagandists in the late nineteenth and early twentieth centuries, lamented, Conservatism was no more than a 'vague sentiment' to most of its supporters and the whole movement exhibited a profound 'intellectual apathy'.[1] This approach is rather misleading, though, when considering Edwardian Conservatism. It produced a flood of books, pamphlets and newspaper articles on party policy and a number of works by well-known Tories like Hugh Cecil, F. E. Smith and Willoughby de Broke on the nature of Conservatism.[2] However, these sources do not provide a clear picture for the historian who wishes to uncover the central core of Conservative thought and belief in the Edwardian era. The flood of writing and rhetoric produced by the Tories emphasized how divided the party was, especially about tariff reform, rather than the principles that Conservatives held in common. Certainly, none of the attempts in this period to define the party's creed were accepted as authoritative, and most took the form of intra-party polemics. One way to circumvent this problem, though, is to examine the party's actions and priorities, in government and opposition, and to use these to build up a picture of the assumptions that bound Conservatives together.

All Tories, for instance, believed that there were elements in the nation's life that had to be protected at virtually any cost from the

malice and theoretical constructs of Liberalism. Probably the most
important of these features for Edwardian Conservatives were
grouped around their thinking about the nation – its position in
the world, its Empire and its national integrity. Conservatives
insisted that Britain should retain a leading role in world affairs,
supported by a sufficient military and naval force – a principle that
mainly took the form when they were in opposition in 1905–14 of
a demand for increased naval construction.[3] Tories also
increasingly identified themselves with the maintenance of the
Empire and, where necessary, as in South Africa, its expansion.
Indeed, one of the many attractions of tariff reform for
Conservatives was that it hoped to bind the Empire more tightly
together by creating a great imperial trading bloc.[4] Most
fundamentally of all, the Conservatives were the party that wished
to preserve the Union with Ireland – it was, after all, officially
styled the Unionist Party after 1912. On this issue its leaders were
willing to countenance civil war and insurrection in Ireland and
even disobedience to orders in the armed forces.[5]

Second only to this group of issues for most Conservatives was
their devotion to the country's constitution. This included the
maintenance of the established Churches in England, Wales and
Scotland and their role in society. The Edwardian party fought
Welsh Church disestablishment almost as vigorously as Home
Rule and managed successfully to sabotage attempts to increase
local authority control of Church schools after a long and bitter
battle in 1906–8.[6] The constitution also, of course, had a secular
aspect, though many Tories accorded the monarch a semi-
religious status as the embodiment of the nation. They certainly
saw themselves as the most fervently pro-royal party and the only
one that was prepared to accord the sovereign an active role in
moments of national crisis – as in 1913–14 when many senior
Conservatives, including Law, Lansdowne and Balfour, urged the
monarch to intervene to 'settle' the Home Rule imbroglio.[7] The
party also vigorously defended the right of the House of Lords to
play an active role in legislation, especially in blocking unwelcome
proposals from the Liberal government of 1905–14.[8] Even after
the Lords' veto was removed in 1911, Tories insisted on its right to
delay legislation like Home Rule. In effect, while Conservatives
accepted a qualified form of adult male democracy for elections to
the Commons, they did not see elections or Commons majorities

as the sole source of authority, let alone wisdom. Church, King and Lords still had a role to play in the constitution.

Most Conservatives had little trouble agreeing on the need to preserve the nation's might and its constitution. But the party was also committed to preserving the existing social order and distribution of property. This was a much more wide-ranging and less concrete concept than the party's devotion to subjects like the Empire or the monarchy. It also lacked the glamour and resonance of these simple appeals and had an obvious ability to divide a party with widespread support. For all these reasons, it was less obviously and straightforwardly promoted on Tory platforms. However, it did have some important implications that informed Conservative behaviour. Firstly, the party was very suspicious of attempts to 'confiscate' property – whether through Church disendowment, cancelling liquor licences or taxation like the 1909 budget that 'penalized' wealth or property.[9] Secondly, Conservatives actively supported the social and political leadership of men of wealth and power – an ideal institutionalized in the Primrose League, whose grades and ranks were fine-tuned to provide 'appropriate' roles for the different classes, with working men mainly a silent and appreciative audience.[10] This did not mean, of course, that Tories believed property was in all cases inviolate, nor that men could not rise out of their social class. But this merely reflects the complex nature of issues of property and class when transformed into political practice.

However, all these central themes in Conservative ideology involved the party in a close and intricate relationship with landowners, even if, by the Edwardian era anyway, the party accorded no specific role to landownership in its thought. Landowners were, for instance, intimately associated with Conservative ideas about the nation's role in the world. They were still a class that saw itself in the role of a 'warrior élite' and they provided well over a third of army officers (many more in the prestigious regiments), leading naval figures like Lord Charles Beresford and much of the leadership of the reserve forces.[11] Aristocrats were also increasingly associated with the glories of the Empire, where they presided over the most important colonies and dominions.[12] In addition, landowners provided the backbone of the Unionist cause throughout Ireland outside of Ulster.[13] Thus it was scarcely possible to think in a Conservative way about the

nation's greatness and integrity without recognizing the crucial
contribution the landed classes made to sustaining these ideas.

Landowners were even more closely enmeshed in the
Conservative view of the constitution. The Church of England was
slowly throwing off its reputation as a haven for younger sons of
the aristocracy, but landowners still held the right of presentation
to about half of all livings, and patrician bishops like Hon.
Augustus Legge, Edward Talbot and Charles Gore were not hard
to find in Edwardian Britain.[14] The monarch led the life of a
country landowner, with George V particularly addicted to the
slaughter of wild animals on his estates at Sandringham and
Balmoral, and the Court was staffed almost entirely by
landowners and their relatives.[15] But perhaps most significantly of
all, the House of Lords remained very much a house of landlords.
Despite the gradual intrusion of non-landed peers from the mid-
1880s, the vast majority of the Lords inherited their titles and even
in 1914 over 80 per cent were substantial landowners.[16] Finally,
landowners still retained much of their position at the apex of the
social order in Edwardian Britain, even if 'Society' had been
diluted by the admission of a motley group of plutocrats. The vast
extent of their landed estates had also not been seriously
undermined by sales before 1914.[17] Landowners could obviously
look to the Conservatives as the party of property and the social
order to defend their property and position.

Given the links between Conservative ideology and landownership, it was scarcely surprising that, after 1886, the overwhelming
majority of landowners were Conservatives. Indeed, they remained
one of the party's central pillars of support. Financial
contributions from landowners were crucial to the party's success,
and landowners continued to play a central role in many
constituency associations.[18] Even in 1914 at least a quarter of Tory
MPs were landed, and men like Lansdowne, Long, Derby,
Curzon, Salisbury and Steel-Maitland played a crucial role in the
party leadership.[19] But this should not obscure the central point
that the Edwardian Tory party was not just a landed party. If it had
been, it could never have held such a dominant position in late
nineteenth-century British politics. The secret of its success, as
James Cornford pointed out, was its ability to recruit all forms of
wealth and property to its side, as well as maintaing a large
working-class electoral base.[20] In 1914 most Conservative MPs

were from a professional or business background and the party
was led by Bonar Law – a former businessman who knew nothing
of London Society.[21] In the country the party was sustained, not
only by landed influence, but by the freely given votes of
Conservatives from the lower middle and working classes. The
Tory party was just as much the party of Liverpool or Birmingham
as it was the political expression of the English counties.[22]

A party with such a broad base of support could only function if,
ultimately, its devotion to subjects like the Empire and the Union
could transcend, however painfully, any narrow identification with
landed interests. Usually, there was no conflict between the party's
wider ideological concerns and the defence of landownership, as
the two were so closely entwined. But the policies of the Salisbury
and Balfour governments in Ireland, where they were prepared to
end landed domination of local government and encourage massive
land sales, were a sign that the party could, in some situations, put
issues like the preservation of the Union before the defence of
landownership.[23] The 'conciliation' of the Irish tenantry caused
much anguish to Irish landowners, but the real difficulties of
separating out landownership from Tory principles were not
apparent until the crisis over the Lords in 1909–11. Although the
Conservatives fully supported the peers' rejection of the budget in
1909, the leadership's analysis of the January 1910 election led
them to the conclusion that their Lordships had been a serious
electoral handicap in much of urban Britain.[24] As a result, the party
undertook a long-drawn-out and ultimately fruitless series of
attempts to modify its defence of the landed position. It refused to
make any commitment to repeal the land taxes in the 1909 budget,
and throughout 1910–11 it gradually brought forward a succession
of distinctly half-hearted proposals to change the composition of
the Lords and to adapt its powers.[25] Even Lansdowne accepted the
need to dilute the hereditary character of the Lords and he was
prepared to contemplate a referendum to settle contentious issues
between the two Houses of Parliament. However, these manœuvres
were only undertaken with some distaste, and it was clear that both
Lansdowne and Balfour regarded the existing House of Lords as
more or less incapable of improvement from a Conservative
viewpoint. Moreover, they refused to end the Lords' association
with the peerage altogether, or even to change its name. Many
Tories were, though, deeply unhappy with the proposals, as they

seemed to violate the very constitution the party was pledged to defend. It was perhaps as well for Conservative unity that the party was never in a position to enact any of its proposals. However, the result of the December 1910 election, which was again largely fought on the Lords' powers and actions, made it clear that none of the party's contortions had allowed it to escape the electorate's unfavourable verdict on their Lordships. Nor did they prevent the emasculation of the Lords' powers in 1911 and damaging Conservative divisions over how to resist the Parliament bill.[26] The party was torn between the idea that it was the Tories' role to defend the landowners' position in the constitution as an integral part of that edifice and the need to distance itself from an unpopular position for the sake of wider considerations like the Union, which would be threatened by Liberal victory. The result was confusion, inertia and defeat.

Thus, by 1911 the intricate relationship between Conservatism and landownership was already showing signs of acute strain. In 1912–14 the strain became even greater as the party struggled to formulate a response to the Liberal Land Campaign.[27] This ingenious initiative was the brainchild of the Liberal Chancellor of the Exchequer, David Lloyd George. It sought to build on the successful formula he devised for his 'People's Budget' of 1909, of combining an assault on landownership with substantial measures of social reform. This strategy was widely credited with reviving the government's fortunes in 1909 and the Chancellor hoped to perform a similar feat in time for the next election, due in 1915. However, unlike some of his initiatives, Lloyd George prefaced his campaign with a lengthy investigation, designed to accumulate facts and figures and round out his initial ideas. He appointed a Land Inquiry, whose most prominent figure was Seebohm Rowntree, in June 1912 to consider the whole 'land question' and develop suitable policies. It produced a lengthy Rural Report in October 1913 and an Urban Report in April 1914. The proposals of the former were largely accepted by the cabinet in October 1913 and formed the basis of the Land Campaign conducted by the Liberal Party up to the outbreak of the First World War. The urban proposals were produced too late to have much impact before domestic politics were suspended in August 1914, and the Conservatives were faced by a largely rural campaign in the months leading up to the war.

Nevertheless, its proposals filled the Tory party with alarm and some horror. The Liberals offered agricultural labourers a minimum wage enforced by local wages boards and a scheme of state encouragement for rural house-building. Farmers were enticed with promises of security of tenure and fixed rents.[28] These plans threatened both to erode English landowners' profits and control of their agricultural estates and to wipe out the Tory hold on the English counties, especially by offering the labourers an attractive new programme of benefits. The Conservatives' immediate response to the launching of the Land Campaign in October 1913 was one of lofty disdain. The chief whip and the chairman of Central Office issued instructions to 'treat Lloyd George's land policy with ridicule or contempt' and to focus attention on the Home Rule crisis.[29] However, as the Unionist whip and rural MP Robert Sanders found, this was 'not very practicable in county divisions'.[30] What worried Tories most was the appeal of the minimum wage proposal to agricultural labourers, and F. B. Mildmay's agent in Totnes declared it was 'absolutely necessary' to produce a response to the wages board policy.[31] If no such response was forthcoming from the party, the agent for the West Country warned, 'this is going to lose us a lot of votes among the agricultural classes and some seats.'[32] This was a matter of serious concern to the leadership. Despite public pronouncements to the contrary, they were not at all sanguine that a forthcoming general election would produce an overwhelming Tory victory, especially as the Liberals seemed to have passed their trough of unpopularity at by-elections in 1912.[33] Serious losses in English agricultural seats, together with Liberal plans to abolish plural voting by 1915, might turn a close election against the Conservatives.

However, formulating the required response to the Liberal initiative proved agonizingly difficult for the party. At one level this was surprising, for the party seemed to have a ready-made policy to hand. Previous attempts by Liberals to win over the agricultural labourers had focused on the promise to provide them with plots of land for smallholdings and allotments – the famous 'three acres and a cow' – a promise most effectively embodied in the 1907 Smallholdings Act. The intention was to give labourers the opportunity of economic independence from the squire and farmer. But Conservatives had been willing to match these promises and had produced Allotments Acts in 1887 and 1890 and a Smallholdings Act in 1892. Balfour had also made a number of rather vague endorsements of the value of promoting owner occupancy in 1909–10.[34] The thinking behind this approach was fairly explicit. While the Liberals offered labourers the tenancy of land acquired by local councils, Conservatives offered labourers the chance to take up state loans and become property-owners and hence, it was hoped, bulwarks of the social order. As Lord Onslow put it, 'I think you would go far before you would find a small owner who was a Radical.'[35] This policy could obviously be extended to providing loans to tenant farmers to buy their land, as in Ireland, and in 1912 and 1913, the party's commitment to small ownerships was reiterated and extended to cover loans to farmers where landowners were willing to sell to sitting tenants, especially when a whole estate changed hands.[36]

The Tories continued to promote these policies down to 1914, with the most committed tariff reformers as their staunchest advocates. They hoped that making the labourers into direct agricultural producers would overcome their objections to tariffs on food.[37] But, as their response to the launch of the Land Campaign in October 1913 showed, this did not necessarily mean that the leadership had a great deal of faith in owner occupancy. They placed most confidence in the idea of providing loans for farmers. There was some evidence from agricultural areas that the small wave of estate sales in 1910–14 to take advantage of rising land prices had produced a sense of insecurity among tenant farmers, as a change of ownership in an estate necessarily entailed notice to quit for all tenants.[38] Loans were a useful antidote to the Liberal promise of security of tenure. But, unfortunately for the Conservatives, they were far less worried about the farmers' vote in 1912–14 than they were about the labourers' intentions. In fact, most Tories were fairly confident that Liberal policies like the 1909 land taxes had already distanced the government from the farmers and that the minimum wage proposal in the Land Campaign would complete the process, however unhappy some farmers might be about the decision to drop food taxes from the Conservative programme.[39]

The Conservatives' real problem lay with the labourers and it was precisely the application of the 'loans for land' policy to them that caused most difficulties in the Tory camp. Their 1892

Smallholdings Act had been so cumbersome as to be virtually inoperative and as Steel-Maitland, the party chairman, wrote in March 1912, even before the Land Campaign was devised, 'we have absolutely no data to show that a system of small cultivators based on ownership rather than tenancy is possible and desirable.'[40] To remedy this situation, no fewer than three Conservative committees examined land policy in 1912–14 – itself a sign of the difficulties the party encountered. The first committee consisted of three MPs – Bathurst, Peto and Mills.[41] All were ardent tariff reformers and they produced a report focusing on the need for a guaranteed price for wheat, bounties on agricultural produce and imperial preference. They also suggested that labourers' wages might be linked to food prices. The party was unlikely to accept recommendations so unpalatable to the urban consumer. But an interesting portent in the report was its scepticism about smallholdings. It declared that this policy was not 'a panacea for a decaying agriculture or is of itself sufficient' as a rural programme. Smallholdings could only be successful in a few areas of the country and only then if colonies with co-operative facilities were planned. Otherwise, 'we do not believe that even ownership will secure success in the case of many smallholdings.'

These doubts were an important indicator of the reaction that greeted the second Conservative land report, drawn up by Milner and circulated by Steel-Maitland for comment in March 1913.[42] Milner was a firm believer in the need to promote smallholdings, 'if the present Social Order is to endure'. He advocated a programme that centred on the creation of colonies of small-holders, the 'reconstruction' of villages to ensure the distribution of common rights, and loans to farmers to purchase their land. Milner was a figure of some weight in the Tory party and his views had to be taken seriously. However, he did not control Conservative policy on the land issue – Bonar Law effectively delegated that responsibility to the Tory leader in the Lords, Lord Lansdowne. He was a substantial landowner in both Ireland and England who could be expected to judge what policies would be acceptable to his class and whose pronouncements would carry weight with them. Moreover, Lansdowne ensured that the devising of the Tories' official response to the Land Campaign was kept firmly in the hands of fellow landowners. Much of the routine organization, for instance, fell on Steel-Maitland, the chairman of

Central Office but also a large landowner in Scotland. Again, it was not coincidental that when Steel-Maitland circulated Milner's report for comment, all the recipients whose remarks survive – Lord Clinton, George Wyndham, R. E. Prothero and of course Steel-Maitland and Lansdowne themselves – were large landowners (or ex-land agents in Prothero's case).[43]

There was a certain similarity in all their comments. They were all horrified at the cost of Milner's plans. Steel-Maitland, for instance, believed that Milner's recommended rate of interest on loans was far too low. The unspoken fear was of higher taxes or rates to pay for the scheme. This problem had not stopped Lansdowne accepting state loans for farmers, but that was seen as a limited scheme, rather than an open-ended commitment to restructure rural life. Loans for labourers also presented two extra difficulties that did not apply to loans for farmers. Firstly, Clinton, Prothero, Steel-Maitland and Wyndham all balked at the idea of the state compulsorily purchasing land for smallholders. They suggested that this would alienate farmers who would fear losing their land, but obviously landowners would be in a similar position. Secondly, all used their experience of agriculture (something Milner, pointedly, did not have) to pour cold water on the idea that smallholdings would be a popular or viable alternative to the system of great estates and large farms. Steel-Maitland was filled with doubt by the whole owner-occupancy strategy and called for further investigation. Wyndham emphasized the need for 'tentative' experiments and predicted that as few as 5 per cent of labourers would become smallholders, with 'only a small percentage' even of them succeeding. Lansdowne's report was a masterpiece of damning Milner's work with faint praise. He concluded, 'I fear that it may not be possible to construct out of the above materials a rural policy likely to inspire great enthusiasm.'

The policy of owner-occupied smallholdings was not officially dropped. To do so would have annoyed its advocates, especially amongst enthusiastic tariff reformers. It was the natural counterpart of land purchase for farmers and it might bring dividends with some labourers. But it was not promoted with any great enthusiasm either, and those who controlled rural policy had little faith in it. To them, it was not a policy that could be called Conservative. It threatened property rights through increased taxation and compulsory purchase. Moreover, it implicitly criticized the existing system of great estates on which land-owners' wealth, prestige and power were based, and sought to transform the social order and distribution of property in the English countryside. This episode revealed the extreme difficulty the party had in coming to terms with the Land Campaign. It desperately needed to combat the Campaign's appeal and the party was sufficiently broader than a mere landed clique to be unwilling to offer just a negative defence of the status quo. But it still contained a very significant landed element which continued to identify Conservatism with the defence of landownership. The result was inertia and confusion, as the party could neither unite around a policy of owner occupancy nor just defend the landowners' position.

The more immediate outcome was the appointment of yet another committee to look into land policy in July 1913, headed by Lord Salisbury.[44] It went over the same ground again, and was similarly dubious about large-scale land purchase. On smallholdings, the committee reported it did 'not anticipate that the number of these is likely to be very large nor will they probably be suitable for all parts of the country'. The Tories would have to find another policy to combat the minimum wage. But the committee could only suggest that 'further study' was needed to produce such a policy. The Salisbury committee was reconvened in January 1914 to consider the matter again. Their main topic of debate was a memorandum from Lord Salisbury in which he proposed the establishment of wages boards in known low-wage areas.[45] However, these boards would have no power to compel farmers to raise wages. Instead, they would rely on 'public opinion' to enforce their recommendations. The committee had difficulty accepting this plan, and Lansdowne and Steel-Maitland were dubious, but continued fears about the Land Campaign finally convinced them. On 21 April 1914 Salisbury and Lansdowne floated the idea of 'voluntary' wages boards in the House of Lords.[46] This was the leadership's final response to the Land Campaign before the intervention of the First World War. It was scarcely a rallying cry to the faithful, because it was never made clear exactly what status Salisbury and Lansdowne's remarks possessed. Bonar Law, for instance, never referred to the matter in public and Lansdowne himself did not subsequently give his new line much publicity – he even omitted it from an article on land policy he wrote for the party's monthly journal, *Our Flag*, in June 1914.[47]

Nevertheless, as the party's final word on the Land Campaign, it is a revealing statement. Firstly, it says much about the continued significance of landownership in the Tory approach to the Land Campaign. The voluntary wages board policy was an attempt to neutralize the appeal of the Liberals in the countryside while providing maximum protection for the landowners' position. Unlike the owner-occupancy strategy it did not threaten that position either through envisaging rate or tax rises or compulsory purchase. Nor did it foresee the end of the great estates. Rather, it suggested that the state should try to sponsor agreement between landowners, farmers and labourers on local rates of pay. Landowners would have an important role on the wages boards and through the county councils that would organize the scheme. As wage rises would have to be in line with local 'public opinion' to be enforced, landowners could hope to have a good deal of influence in forming that opinion as the leaders of local society. Landowners were not unwilling to look at local wage rates – the Central Landowners Association asked its members to do just that in December 1913. The key was that landowners would not accept any form of compulsion.[48]

This approach by the leadership can be put into a wider pattern of Tory attitudes to the state's role in society in the late nineteenth and early twentieth centuries. As over wages boards, the party was willing to accord the state a significant role in social policy. When in office the Conservatives had important measures of social reform like the Workmen's Compensation Act of 1897 and the Unemployed Workmen's Act of 1905 to their names.[49] The key was how state intervention was managed. In both these cases the state's role was confined to that of supplementing and bringing together various forms of voluntary effort to increase social cohesion. Walter Long's Act of 1905, for instance, was primarily concerned with co-ordinating charitable and local authority work to relieve unemployment. State compulsion was confined to the tentative promotion of experiments like labour exchanges in London, financed by a $1d.$ rate. The wages board proposal clearly fitted into this pattern of state action.

The problem for the Conservatives, though, was that while this approach might have been implicit in some of the party's measures in government it had no agreed or explicit way of approaching issues like social reform and state intervention. This sort of activity was only just beginning to emerge as central to the way in which Conservatives defined their identity in the Edwardian era. Most of the party's energies remained focused on the need to fight traditional enemies like Home Rule, abolition of the House of Lords' veto, temperance reform and Welsh Church disestablishment. It was these issues that united and enthused the party. As a result, it contained a variety of opinions about what the 'truly' Conservative approach to social reform might be. This had not mattered very much in the 1880s and 1890s when such matters were not usually of central political concern at the national level. However, when, after 1908, the Liberal government began to espouse major initiatives in social policy, these divisions became much clearer and started to prove a major handicap for the party. On issues like old age pensions and National Insurance, Conservative opinion ranged from forthright opposition to warm endorsement and even calls to outbid the Liberals.[50]

These difficulties were repeated and magnified in the Conservative response to the Land Campaign. Under the intense pressure of a new, popular Liberal initiative that threatened interests close to the party's heart and endangered its electoral success, it proved impossible for the leadership to suppress differing opinions within the party. On the one hand, some Tories were deeply angered by the leadership's attempts once again to distance themselves from the public defence of landlordism and to admit the state's right to interfere with the conduct of landed estates. The most vocal spokesman for this point of view was the Tory MP for Chelmsford, future minister (and substantial landowner), E. G. Pretyman.[51] He headed a body grandly entitled the Land Union, which had been set up in 1910 to campaign against the land taxes in the 1909 budget. Its activities then had been embarrassing enough for the leadership, but in 1913–14 it was, if anything, even more active and extreme in rebutting the need to make concessions to combat the Land Campaign. Pretyman persisted in stating that the existing agricultural system was a magnificent institution and that rural conditions should not be criticized because worse problems could be found in urban slums. His associate, Trustram Eve, declared that the evidence that Edwardian farm labourers could afford coats was conclusive evidence of their prosperity. On 17 February 1914, two of Pretyman's allies launched an amendment to the address which played straight into Lloyd George's hands by defending every aspect of the land system and blaming any problems on the chancellor's speeches and past actions.[52] Furthermore, the Land Union representatives on Salisbury's committee vigorously opposed his plan for voluntary wages boards, and Pretyman refused to be silenced throughout 1914. The very existence of the Land Union was proof that the Conservatives were not just a landlord party. But Pretyman's activities could still give the impression that it was, thus undoing all the leadership's good work in establishing the party's distance from a negative defence of the landed position. Moreover, the Land Union's approach commanded considerable support amongst Tory peers and in the party at large and this was probably one reason why the voluntary wages board policy was presented in such a half-hearted fashion in 1914.[53]

Pretyman's views were so popular with Tories at least partly because he could describe his position as more rigorously Conservative than that of the leadership. Landowners were still closely bound up with Conservative definitions of their party's goals, and the Land Union was merely suggesting that they should not be forced to compromise their role in society once again. But, just as importantly, Pretyman denounced any sort of state intervention in the conduct of landed estates as bureaucratic and economically disastrous. He claimed that the state had no business undertaking this sort of task. Not all Tories agreed with Pretyman, but it was difficult to refute the claim that this was one possible Conservative response to the Land Campaign. The party was hostile to interference with property rights and it had a long tradition of presenting state interference with institutions like Church endowments and schools and liquor licences as 'robbery', motivated by spite, sectional concerns or impractical theories. This approach could easily be transferred to attacks on landowners. Moreover, Pretyman was able to gain plenty of support from sympathetic professionals engaged in land management for his claim that the labourers themselves would be harmed by state intervention, which would ruin agricultural prosperity and create unemployment.[54] Classical economics thus boosted elements in traditional Tory attitudes to consolidate Pretyman's case.

On the other wing of the party, the Unionist Social Reform Committee (USRC), founded by about thirty-five MPs in 1911 under the patronage of F. E. Smith, argued the case for more extensive state intervention.[55] In 1913 and 1914 they introduced bills providing for wages boards with compulsory powers and, like the Land Union, they refused to unite behind the leadership's initiatives.[56] This disagreement was partly a matter of tactics. USRC members like Leslie Scott saw Lloyd George's scheme as so popular that the only way to neutralize it was to make it a cross-party issue.[57] Behind this opinion lay the assumption that Conservatism's association with landownership was no longer beneficial. Landlords had become an electoral liability, and threats like Home Rule could only be defeated by showing the Conservatives were in earnest about social reform.[58] But the USRC also contained members like Charles Bathurst and Christopher Turnor, who wished to revitalize the landowners' role in agriculture and society by making them the leaders of rural reform.[59] What held the two positions together was a belief that compulsory wages boards were an authentic Conservative response to the Land Campaign. USRC members shared a common devotion to fleshing out and modernizing the tradition of 'Tory Democracy' derived from Disraeli and Lord Randolph Churchill. This tradition may have been something of a myth, but it allowed the USRC to legitimize policies like compulsory wages boards by providing a long-standing Conservative pedigree of social reform. Also, the party did have the capacity to promote social reform with some vigour at the local level. Many USRC figures, like Griffith-Boscawen in the field of housing, were merely transferring their experience on local authorities to national politics.[60] Support for state initiatives could also be gleaned from enthusiasts for 'national efficiency' like Milner and his followers, who were always ready to combat any 'Cobdenite' leanings in the party. Milner was an enthusiast for smallholdings, but he and friends like Fabian Ware had also played an important role in supporting previous minimum-wage legislation like the 1909 Trade Boards Act.[61] The USRC view on wages boards was very much a minority opinion in the party, but it was one that would not be silenced and its distance from the Land Union's position is eloquent testimony to the ideological fractures in Edwardian Conservatism.

Thus, by the time war broke out in August 1914, the Conservatives were no closer to producing an effective response to the Land Campaign. It presented them with a dual ideological dilemma: how to separate out the party's involvement with landlordism from its wider concerns; and how to respond to a popular programme of social reform. In focusing on these issues, Lloyd George once again showed his unerring eye for his opponents' weak spots, for neither element could easily be resolved. Conservatism's emergence from the landed embrace was still in its most painful stage and the party had no agreed approach to social issues. If these problems are put in the context of the intense difficulties the party faced over tariff reform and how to combat Home Rule it is easy to see why some contemporaries and historians have seen the Edwardian era as a time of crisis for Conservatism rather than Liberalism.

## Notes

1 W. H. Mallock, *Memoirs of Life and Literature*, 2nd edn. (London, 1920), 156–7.

2 Lord H. Cecil, *Conservatism* (London, 1912); F. E. Smith, *Unionist Policy and Other Essays* (London, 1913); Lord Willoughby de Broke, 'The Tory Tradition', *National Review* 58 (1911), 201–13.

3 A. J. A. Morris, *The Scaremongers: The Advocacy of War and Rearmament, 1896–1914* (London, 1984), 164–84, 203–23.

4 F. Coetzee, *For Party or Country? Nationalism and the Dilemmas of Popular Conservatism in Edwardian England* (Oxford, 1990), 55–61.

5 D. Dutton, *'His Majesty's Loyal Opposition': The Unionist Party in Opposition, 1905–15* (Liverpool, 1992), 203–50.

6 G. I. T. Machin, *Politics and the Churches in Great Britain, 1869–1921* (Oxford, 1987), 284–92, 305–10.

7 H. Nicolson, *King George the Fifth: His Life and Reign* (London, 1952), 221–43.

8 R. Jenkins, *Mr Balfour's Poodle* (London, 1954), 20–38.

9 M. Fforde, *Conservatism and Collectivism, 1886–1914* (Edinburgh, 1990), 25–6 for a very strong statement of the anti-collectivist side of Tory thinking.

10 M. Pugh, *The Making of Modern British Politics, 1867–1939* (Oxford, 1982), 51

11 D. Cannadine, *The Decline and Fall of the British Aristocracy* (London, 1990), 264–80.

12 A. Adonis, *Making Aristocracy Work: The Peerage and the Political System in Britain, 1884–1914* (Oxford, 1993), 210–39.

13 P. Buckland, *Irish Unionism*, I: *The Anglo-Irish and the New Ireland, 1885–1922* (Dublin, 1972), 1–28.

14 Cannadine, *Decline and Fall*, 255–64.

15 Nicolson, *King George the Fifth*, 142; Cannadine, *Decline and Fall*, 245–50.

16 F. M. L. Thompson, *English Landed Society in the Nineteenth Century* (London, 1963), 297.

17 Ibid., 299–303, 322–6.

18 Adonis, *Making Aristocracy Work*, 181–6.

19 J. Ramsden, *The Age of Balfour and Baldwin* (London, 1978), 94–5, 97–8.

20 J. Cornford, 'The Transformation of Conservatism in the Late Nineteenth Century', *Victorian Studies* 7 (1963), 35–66.

21 Ramsden, *Age of Balfour and Baldwin*, 90–2, 98–9.

22 H. Pelling, *Social Geography of British Elections, 1885–1910* (London, 1967), 414–20.

23 C. Shannon, *Arthur J. Balfour and Ireland, 1874–1922* (Washington DC, 1988), 99–106, 112–29.

24 Bodleian Library, Oxford, Selborne MSS 6, ff. 33–9, Lord Salisbury to Lord Selborne, 11 January 1910; BL, Add. MSS 49736 (Balfour MSS), ff. 63–5, A. Chamberlain to Balfour, 29 January 1910.

25 Jenkins, *Mr Balfour's Poodle*, 92–109, 134–45.

26 Dutton, *'His Majesty's Loyal Opposition'*, 97–104.

27 H. V. Emy, 'The Land Campaign: Lloyd George as a Social Reformer, 1909–14', in A. J. P. Taylor (ed.), *Lloyd George: Twelve Essays* (London, 1971), 35–70.

28 Report of the Land Enquiry Committee, *The Land*, I (London, 1913), 65–7, 133–5, 321–3, 382–3.

29 Scottish Record Office [SRO], GD 193/119/99 (Steel-Maitland MSS), Lord Lansdowne to Steel-Maitland, 31 October 1913.

30 J. Ramsden (ed.), *Real Old Tory Politics: The Political Diaries of Robert Sanders, Lord Bayford, 1910–35* (London, 1984), 67 (13 November 1913).

31 Hatfield House, 4th Marquess of Salisbury MSS, 74/78, F. Mildmay to Lord Salisbury, 11 February 1914.

32 SRO, GD 193/119/5/60, E. Hely to J. Boraston, 12 January 1914.

33 E. H. H. Green, *The Crisis of Conservatism: The Politics, Economics and Ideology of the British Conservative Party, 1880–1914* (London, 1995), 268.

34 R. Douglas, *Land, People and Politics: A History of the Land Question in the United Kingdom, 1878–1952* (London, 1976), 103–6, 138–9; Fforde, *Conservatism and Collectivism*, 117–19.

35 Birmingham University Library, A. Chamberlain MSS, 8/1/12, Lord Onslow to A. Chamberlain, 30 January 1910.

[36] Speeches by Lansdowne, *The Times*, 25 July 1912 and 23 June 1913.

[37] Green, *Crisis of Conservatism*, 215–16.

[38] Board of Agriculture, *Report of Departmental Committee on Tenant Farmers and Sales of Estates*, Cd 6030 (London, 1912), 5–6

[39] P. Williamson (ed.), *The Modernization of Conservative Politics: The Diaries and Letters of William Bridgeman, 1904–35* (London, 1988), 68–9 (13 February 1913).

[40] SRO, GD 193/274/244–51, Memorandum by Steel-Maitland, 4 March 1912.

[41] House of Lords Record Office, Bonar Law MSS, 27/1/17, W. Long to Bonar Law, 5 August 1912, enclosing Report of 1 August 1912.

[42] Bodleian, Milner MSS 159, ff. 9–51.

[43] Bodleian, Milner MSS 159, ff. 75–82, 'Land Scheme: Mr Steel-Maitland's Criticisms'; Milner MSS 159, ff. 67–74, 'Lord Clinton's Notes on Lord Milner's Memorandum'; Milner MSS 39, ff. 74–8, Prothero to Steel-Maitland, 4 February 1913; Milner MSS 39, ff. 144–54, G. Wyndham, 'Notes on Lord Milner's Memorandum on Land Policy', 30 April 1913; SRO, GD 193/119/5/163–94, Lord Lansdowne, 'Observations on Lord Milner's Memorandum', 8 April 1913.

[44] Bodleian, Milner MSS 40, ff. 61–2, Lord E. Talbot to Milner, 15 July 1913; Milner MSS 40, ff. 91–4, 'Report of the Committee appointed to consider the Land Policy of the Unionist Party', 12 August 1913.

[45] SRO, GD 193/119/5/34–46, Lord Salisbury, 'Memorandum on the Agricultural Labourers' Wages Question', 20 January 1914.

[46] *Hansard* 5th ser, 1914, XV, 942–55, 976–89.

[47] *Our Flag* (June 1914), 85.

[48] University of Reading, Institute of Agricultural History, CLA MSS, AII/3, executive committee minutes, 10 December 1913.

[49] Even Fforde, *Conservatism and Collectivism*, 78–80, cannot deny this.

[50] Dutton, *'His Majesty's Loyal Opposition'*, 257–8, 264–5; Green, *Crisis of Conservatism*, 288–9.

[51] A. Offer, *Property and Politics, 1870-1914* (Cambridge, 1981), 366–7.

[52] *The Times*, 14 February 1914; Hatfield, Salisbury MSS (4) 74/170–3, T. Eve to Lord Salisbury, n.d. [January 1914]; *Hansard* 5th ser, 1914, LVIII, 800–916.

[53] Bodleian, MSS Film 1107 (Lincolnshire MSS), Lord Carrington's Diary, 21 April 1914; Hatfield, Salisbury MSS (4) 74/167, Steel-Maitland to Lord Salisbury, 25 April 1914.

[54] Land Agents Society, *Facts about the Land* (London, 1916), 61–6.

[55] J. Ridley, 'The Unionist Social Reform Committee: Wets before the Deluge', *Historical Journal* 30 (1987), 391–413.

[56] *Hansard* 5th ser, 1913, LII, 2070; *Hansard* 5th ser, 1914, LXI, 776.

[57] Scott's letter to *The Times*, 12 May 1913.

[58] Joynson-Hicks's letter to *Pall Mall Gazette*, 28 October 1913.

[59] C. Turnor, *Land Problems and National Welfare* (London, 1911), 1–51.

[60] A. Griffith-Boscawen, *Memories* (London, 1925), 134–43, 154–6.

[61] J. Rickard, 'The Anti-Sweating Movement in Britain and Victoria: The Politics of Empire and Social Reform', *Historical Studies* 18 (1978–9), 582–97.

# 'Set The People Free'? Conservatives and the State, 1920–1960

## MARTIN FRANCIS

The ideology of the Conservative Party has long been a blend of paternalist and libertarian traditions. As Anthony Eden reminded the 1947 party conference, 'We are not a party of unbridled, brutal capitalism, and never have been. Although we believe in personal responsibility and personal initiative in business, we are not the political children of the laissez faire school. We opposed them decade after decade.'[1] However this implicit reference to the myth, if not the reality, of Disraelian paternalism was elsewhere tempered by ominous warnings about the dangers of collectivism. A year previously Eden had conceded that 'complete individualism is an impossibility'. 'Yet', he continued, 'complete State domination is utterly repugnant to our democratic traditions and to the whole political instinct of our people. The function of the State is to give the fullest possible scope to the free development of the individual . . . We must therefore choose our course avoiding both extremes'.[2]

However while Conservative policies have usually blended individualist and collectivist aspirations, the balance between these elements has frequently appeared uneven. For a long time the conventional narrative of changing Conservative responses to the role of the state went something like the following. In the late nineteenth century the influx of middle-class businessmen into the Tory Party led to a partial, but nevertheless distinct, shift away from Tory paternalism towards the defence of the free market. This anti-collectivist sentiment was further reinforced by the traumas created by the reforms of the 1906–14 Liberal governments, by the 1917 Russian revolution, and by unprecedented state intervention during the First World War. Tariff reform was quickly shorn of its potential for social reform and functioned throughout this period as an alternative to, rather than as an instrument of, collectivism. In the inter-war years Conservative ideology and policy were dominated by those 'hard-faced men' who had entered Parliament in 1918 with an explicit commitment to rolling back the state and upholding the principle of sound finance, and who seemed to exhibit a callous indifference to the social cost of mass unemployment. This effectively *laissez-faire* approach to economic and social questions proved little handicap to the party's electoral fortunes in the 1920s and 1930s, but it left the party high and dry in the wake of the collectivist tide which rushed through British politics during the Second World War. It was only then, faced with the electoral catastrophe of 1945, that the Conservatives once again embraced the notion of the active state by reconciling themselves to a post-war settlement built around the mixed economy and the welfare state. The Conservatives finally came to abandon this refurbished Disraelian paternalism in the late 1970s, when Margaret Thatcher's ascendancy saw the adoption of a radically ambitious and uncompromising libertarianism, which held sway in the party throughout the 1980s.[3]

This chronology still has much to recommend it, but it is ultimately too simplistic, underplaying as it does the consistent ambiguities which existed in Conservative attitudes to the state. This chapter intends to highlight these ideological tensions by examining Conservative policies between the 1920s and the 1950s, in particular the period 1945–55, usually seen as the formative years of the post-war 'New Conservatism'. Close attention to party rhetoric shows that in many respects the Conservatives were actually much less collectivist in the late 1940s than they had been in the 1930s, as is obvious from Churchill's war cry of 'set the people free'. The ambiguous and fluid nature of Conservative responses to the state becomes even more apparent when the focus is widened to include not just questions of economic and social policy, but other areas which have received much less attention from historians, for example the regulation of sexual and moral behaviour and the related issue of public order.

Here the full range of Conservative attitudes to the state is on display, ranging from a libertarian desire to defend personal freedom against an intrusive state to the full-blooded use of state coercion by Joynson-Hicks in the 1920s and Maxwell Fyfe in the 1950s to reform public morals and ensure social control. Certainly Tories often took a very different attitude to the question of state intervention in the field of social purity from that which they were simultaneously adopting towards the state's role in industry or in the provision of welfare.

For too long the inter-war years were viewed through the distorting prism created by Labour's post-war hegemony. The British public quickly came to accept Labour's image of Conservative governments in the 1920s and 1930s as ruthlessly applying the principles of *laissez-faire*, refusing to countenance the use of state action to alleviate the poverty and unemployment produced by the unrestricted forces of market capitalism. Some Conservatives did attempt to counter this new orthodoxy,[4] but they received little encouragement from Churchill, who not surprisingly had little compelling desire to laud the party's former leadership which had kept him excluded from office throughout the 1930s. The self-conscious use of the label 'New Conservatism' to describe the policies formulated after 1945 reflected a promise to break with a past which was now seen as an electoral handicap.[5] Historians now generally accept that the image of the 1930s which was dominant in political culture in the immediate post-war era was little more than a stereotype.[6] It was true that having endured over a decade of collectivism from both the 1906 Liberal government and the wartime coalition, Conservatives after 1918 were committed to a return to an economic liberalism and a minimal state, as was evident from the financial retrenchment of the 'Geddes axe' in 1920–2. However Tory anti-collectivism had already become more even-tempered by the end of the decade, when Chamberlain's tenure of the ministry of health marked a dramatic increase in public responsibility for the provision of welfare.[7] In the 1930s the National Government was remarkably interventionist in the economic sphere, pursuing cheap money policies to encourage investment, creating public corporations and marketing boards to aid industrial efficiency. Some have gone so far as to talk of an (albeit non-Keynesian) 'managed economy' in the decade before the war.[8] When it came to issues of law and order in the 1930s, the Conservatives certainly did not favour a minimal state, implementing Public Order Acts intended to deal with the perceived threat of political extremism from both left and right. Such legislation substantially increased the coercive power of the state and posed in many people's eyes a serious threat to civil liberties.[9]

However the epilogue to the old stereotypes of the 1930s has remained much more resilient.[10] In this part of the narrative the Conservatives were allegedly forced, largely by the electoral defeat of 1945, to abandon their previous commitment to economic liberalism, and instead embraced a new collectivism, reconciling themselves to a managed economy, a substantial public sector in industry and an extensive welfare state paid for out of taxation.[11] In fact it seems fair to claim that in many senses the Conservatives were much less collectivist in the late 1940s than they had been in the 1930s. Certainly the degree to which the party felt comfortable with the notion of an active state after 1945 has been exaggerated, and the libertarian rhetoric which was prominent in policy statements and speeches has been seriously downplayed. Recent research has highlighted how the Conservatives hoped to draw electoral dividends in 1950 and 1951 from their pledge to abandon controls over foodstuffs and other consumer goods.[12] However, the Conservative desire, in Churchill's words, to 'set the people free' was not confined to questions of consumption. When the party's Central Office plundered the press for stories of petty and unnecessary restrictions for use by their canvassers,[13] their motives were not just the securing of ammunition in the propaganda war with their political opponents. Tories under the Attlee government were genuinely alarmed by a whole series of developments which appeared cumulatively to be eroding the long-cherished liberties of the free-born Englishman and woman. The cutting of the House of Lords' veto under the 1949 Parliament Act seemed to imply that the government was committed to removing constitutional safeguards against doctrinaire and unrepresentative policies being imposed by the Labour-dominated Commons. The government's insistence on retaining wartime controls and regulations seemed the thin end of the wedge of totalitarianism, and the imagery of Churchill's infamous 'Gestapo' speech was not as unrepresentative of Tory rhetoric in 1945–51 as is usually presented. In 1951, for instance,

Butler described Labour's preference for physical planning as the 'Reichstag method of government'.[14] Bernard Braine calculated in 1947 that seventeen separate ministries had the power to authorize the entry of no less than 11,000 enforcement officers into private houses and premises: 'Today it is an official coming in to search your larder; tomorrow it may well be an official coming in to inspect your books and private papers. Today it is direction of labour; tomorrow it may well be a fascist state in which no man can call his soul his own.'[15] Tories also detected ominous signs in the government's frequent complaints about press bias and its decision, during the economic crises of 1947, to cut the availability of newsprint. As Macmillan insisted, it was both symbolic and sinister that the Magna Carta had been allowed to go out of print.[16] There were motions expressing concern about the erosion of the 'liberties of the subject' at most Conservative Party conferences in the Attlee years, and while Tories had little sympathy for a written constitution, some did go so far as to demand that the party produce a 'charter of liberties'.[17]

The Conservatives argued that the growing omnipotence of the state not merely threatened the rights and opportunities of the individual. It was also undermining the sanctity of family life. The party's Committee on Women's Questions, reporting in 1949, argued that socialist doctrine, by teaching 'that the State will provide for all', had undermined the family and promoted a 'general lowering of the moral standard in this country at the present time'. The committee demanded that social services provided by the state should be used to 'strengthen family life instead of being used as a substitute for it'.[18] Such sentiments were repeated by leading Conservative figures. Eden stressed that Conservatives did not regard 'the social centre, valuable as it can be, as a substitute for the family', while Butler declared, 'no state, however wise and paternal, can take the place of the family home.' Socialism had used the state to impose a uniformity alien to the 'many-sidedness of human life and activity' which was inherent in both Conservative philosophy and the British way of life.[19]

However, at the same time Conservatives were reluctant to give themselves up entirely to libertarianism. This was even true in economic policy, as is evident from the party's unwillingness to co-operate openly with anti-collectivist pressure groups such as Aims of Industry and Ernest Benn's Society for Individual

Freedom, and their emollient attitude towards industrial relations.[20] Moreover the outbreak of the Korean war in 1950 made the removal of controls much more difficult. In June 1950 the Conservative Research Department conceded that the party's previously uncompromisingly hostile attitude to the Supply and Services Acts might have to be modified in the light of the deteriorating international situation and the possible move 'towards a war economy'.[21] With regard to social policy, the party was keen to dispel the reactionary label foisted on it by their opponents and was therefore obliged to promise to maintain the welfare state constructed by Labour after 1945. True, the Conservatives sought to replace Labour's universalism by the targeting of benefits, but this still left the state with a huge ongoing commitment to the social services. Not surprisingly therefore, the Tories' return to office in 1951 was not the prelude to a new era of economic liberalism. Conservative ministers did boast of their success in rolling back the state. In 1954 Butler told an audience in Gloucester, 'in the past three years we have burned our identity cards, torn up our ration books, halved the number of snoopers, decimated the number of forms and said good riddance to nearly two-thirds of the remaining wartime regulations. This is the march of freedom on which we are bound. And the pace must quicken as we go forward.'[22] In fact the pace was still insufficient in the eyes of many grassroots Tories who vented their frustrations on the party leadership at party conferences throughout the 1950s, or by campaigning through organizations such as the People's League for the Defence of Freedom and the Middle Class Alliance. Complaints were frequently made that levels of public expenditure, and consequently of taxation, remained too high.[23] Concerns about the liberties of the subject did not, as might be expected, vanish with Labour's departure from office in 1951. The government's powers over the requisition of private property were still felt to be unnecessarily extensive, a claim which seemed to have been borne out in 1954 when criticisms of the methods used by the government in the compulsory acquisition of land at Crichel Down in Dorset forced the resignation of the Minister of Agriculture, Sir Thomas Dugdale. At the 1955 party conference there were no less than fourteen motions put forward relating to the 'rights of individuals in relation to the state', and the government was forced to appoint the Franks committee to investigate the contentious issue of administrative tribunals.[24] Some of the committee's recommendations were incorporated into the Tribunals and Inquiries Act, 1958.

But the leadership argued that it would be both unwise and impractical fully to embrace libertarianism in economic and social policy. At the 1957 party conference, Enoch Powell, Financial Secretary to the Treasury, reminded the government's critics that in the previous six Conservative budgets, the fraction of national income collected in taxes had already been reduced by 20 per cent, and that ministers were determined to make further reductions in public expenditure. However (ironically in the light of his later passion for the minimal state), Powell concluded that as long as the Cold War necessitated high levels of defence spending and the party was making electorally popular pledges in areas such as housing, reducing the burden of taxation was 'not easy'.[25] Contrary to the expectations raised by the bald rhetoric of 'set the people free' which had been so loudly proclaimed in 1950 and 1951, Conservative governments in the 1950s looked more to Disraeli than to Hayek as the inspiration for their programme of 'New Conservatism' in action. The conflict between libertarian and paternalist traditions within the leadership had largely been decided in favour of the latter by the mid-1950s. However the libertarian impulse of the late 1940s was not entirely banished, as the ideological debates surrounding 'robot' in 1952 and Thorneycroft's resignation in 1957 clearly showed.[26] Moreover, the perennial confrontations between platform and floor at party conferences in the late 1950s and 1960s on the issues of taxation and expenditure revealed that the ongoing tension between Tory collectivism and economic liberalism remained a critical motif in the discourse of the party as a whole.

This ambiguous response to the role of the state can be highlighted even more effectively if our focus is widened to include not just questions of economic and social policy, but also Conservative attitudes to the regulation of sexual and moral behaviour, and to the related issue of law and order. These are areas which have largely been ignored in the existing historiography of mid-twentieth-century Britain. The political dimension to issues such as gambling, prostitution and homosexuality in the twentieth century has been traditionally confined to legal historians, and they have tended to concentrate their attention on the 'permissive moment' of the 1960s, rather than what went before.[27] In contrast to the centuries before 1900, the history of sexuality in twentieth-century Britain remains surprisingly unexplored and undeveloped. Even Jeffrey Weeks's excellent survey *Sex, Politics and Society* effectively confines its analysis of the middle decades of this century to changing sexual behaviour, rather than to its political implications.[28] In fact, surveying changing reactions to these issues can help further our understanding of the tension between libertarian and paternalist traditions in Conservatism, and demonstrate how problematic the notion of 'freedom' has been for Tories in this century.

As Jon Lawrence has argued, in late Victorian and Edwardian Britain the Conservatives had presented themselves as the defenders of the Englishman's right to his private pleasures, in particular the public house, free from interference from the regulatory moral reformers of the Liberal Party.[29] However this libertarian impulse sat rather uneasily with Tory desire for social control, and increasingly as the century went on, with a desire to promote 'respectable' bourgeois domesticity among the working class. After 1918 this contradiction became even more acute as the enfranchisement of women over thirty in 1918 caused notions of 'decency' to rise in the political agenda, and the 'proletarian distemper' of the 1920s increased anxieties about law and order. While Tory economic policy in the 1920s saw an initial rolling back of the wartime state, at the Home Office William Joynson-Hicks, the infamous 'Jix', sought to use the power of the state to reform public morals and contain the 'red menace'. In 1929 the Home Secretary insisted that 'the Government has a general responsibility for the moral welfare of the community'.[30] This end was pursued by using the Home Office's residual powers of censorship to ensure that people were not sexually contaminated by what they saw or read. The most notorious outcome of this monitoring of literature and film was the prosecution for obscenity of Radclyffe Hall's lesbian novel *The Well of Loneliness* in 1928, but other works (including Richard Aldington's *Death of a Hero* and Shane Leslie's *The Cantab*) were also subjected to Jix's crusade against filth.[31] The Home Secretary's desire to clean up vice also extended into a campaign against unlicensed night clubs, which in the 1920s enjoyed a boom period among the young and fashionable, culminating in the frequent and farcical prosecutions

of the club proprietor Kate Meyrick.[32] Joynson-Hicks was also
agitated by 'degrading' activities behind the bushes in Hyde Park
and 'undesirable conduct among the audience' in badly lit
cinemas, but here the Home Office's intrusive monitoring proved
impractical and ineffective.[33]

Of course it could be argued that Joynson-Hicks's desire to act
as a guardian of public morals came less from any tradition of
Conservatism, and more from his own highly personal puritanism.
Indeed contemporary critics were keen to present him as both
absurd and unrepresentative of his party. When the Home
Secretary observed that 'the old days of the right of every man to
do as he likes are a relic of the eighteenth and nineteenth centuries
and will not work in the twentieth', his official biographer noted
that such sentiments were seen by many as 'wholly repugnant to
the Conservative creed'.[34] A. G. Gardiner argued that Joynson-
Hicks's Conservatism exhibited a certain 'streakiness'. As a
teetotaller, anti-gambler and 'a foe even of King Alcohol's sinister
consort, my Lady Nicotine', the Home Secretary looked a little
out of place in a party where 'puritanism is not a strongly marked
characteristic'. For, 'drink, after all, is the Gibraltar of Toryism,
and even night clubs have their friends in the inner shrine of the
party.'[35] Others attributed Joynson-Hicks's reforming zeal in moral
matters to his innate Victorianism, rather than to his Conservatism. The Home Secretary continually reminded others that
he was born in the year of Palmerston's death, leading one
infamous lampoon to assert:

> In 1865
> When little Jix was born, or came alive
> The Great Queen ruled and everyone was good
> And England stood where Mr Gladstone stood.
> Since then the times have changed, the clock has clicked;
> Jix does not think so, Jix was brought up strict.[36]

But it was no accident that Joynson-Hicks remained at the
Home Office throughout Baldwin's 1924–9 administration.
Joynson-Hicks's evangelism was not just a personal faith. It stood
in the wider tradition of Disraelian anti-ritualism and also
reflected the anti-Catholicism of Lancashire Toryism, that
critically influential model of popular Conservatism and the
environment in which (as MP for North West Manchester) he had

first come to political prominence. Moreover, his belief that there had been a deterioration in moral standards since 1914 (and that this development was intrinsically linked with the rise of communism) was widely shared in the party. The Solicitor-General, Thomas Inskip, also actively supported the movement for moral purity in the 1920s,[37] while the Rothermere press and Tory backbenchers raged against the apparent androgyny and 'unnatural' behaviour of the female 'flappers', whose high public profile attested to a decline in morals, a blurring of traditional gender hierarchies and the growing degeneracy of the British racial stock.[38] Joynson-Hicks certainly regarded himself, in the words of one of his officials at the Home Office, as 'a man with a mission'. But that mission, to 'smash the Communist menace in Britain' by means of both moral reform and the suppression of Soviet subversion, was one which was central to Conservative ideology and policy in the 1920s.[39] If this task demanded a more active state than the anti-collectivist rhetoric of 1918 seemed prepared for, the traumas of the first Labour government and the General Strike suggested that it was a price worth paying.

A similar desire to use the powers of the state to check an apparent collapse in moral standards at the very time that the party was preaching the merits of libertarianism in the economic sphere was also evident in the decade after the Second World War. Conventional histories[40] have downplayed or indeed completely ignored the fact that the political debates of 1945–60 took place against the backcloth of what at times can only be termed a 'moral panic' in Britain. The most immediate reflection of this phenomenon was concern about the increase in recorded crime since the war: the number of indictable offences in England and Wales had risen from 283,000 in 1938 to 545,000 in 1957.[41] This rise may have reflected changes in the methods of police reporting, but for many contemporaries they were a symptom of moral decline. Under the Labour government, Conservatives argued that a substantial part of the increase in recorded crime was due to unnecessary state controls and regulations which had created a 'spiv's paradise', and which had also caused (in Churchill's words) ordinary people engaging in a 'a whole series of actions hitherto free and unchallenged' to become lawbreakers. But it also reflected in their eyes the erosion of traditional moral values as a result of the war and the corrosive effects of socialism.[42] The abolition of corporal punishment in 1948 and the (unsuccessful) attempt in that same year to suspend the death penalty added to Tory anxieties about crime. A particular concern was the increase in juvenile delinquency, exaggerated in the public mind through the sensationalist press coverage of the Heath, de Antiquis and Haigh murder cases in 1946–9, and through the cinema releases in 1948 of *No Orchids for Miss Blandish* and *Good Time Girl*, which both dealt with the seedier aspects of the criminal underworld.[43] Significantly, while the chief film censor criticized film makers for the growing prevalence on screen of 'brutal and sadistic incidents', he accepted that this trend reflected the reality of a post-war world in which violence had become a 'familiar accompaniment of daily life'.[44] In the 1950s the attention of concerned Tories, particularly the hanging and flogging battalions, focused on a new arrival. As early as May 1954 Thomas Moore was expressing alarm in Parliament about 'Edwardian gangs', and throughout the 1950s Conservative Home Secretaries were bombarded with requests from Moore and Gerald Nabarro to deal with Teddy boys, to take steps (in the latter's words) to 'whack the thugs'.[45] In fact corporal punishment was not to be restored, much to the disgust of the party's rank and file, whose anger spilled over in the bad-tempered debate on law and order at the 1958 party conference. Interestingly that same conference saw the first post-war conference debate on immigration, and by the early 1960s fear of crime had become increasingly linked by many Tories with the issue of race.[46]

If the post-war 'crime wave' was perceived as one indicator of a decline in moral standards, the dramatic increase in the divorce rate in the late 1940s was seen as equally symptomatic, as was an apparent increase in promiscuity among young single women.[47] However the real anxieties about sexual freedom were focused on two other issues. First was the increasing visibility of prostitutes on the streets of Britain's cities, which seemed to be providing overseas visitors to both the 1951 Festival of Britain and the 1953 Coronation with a deplorable impression of the country's morality, and had led to London being labelled the 'vice capital of the world'.[48] Second was the increase in the number of prosecutions for homosexual acts. In December 1953 Home Secretary David Maxwell Fyfe claimed that while in 1938 the number of 'unnatural offences' in England and Wales was 134, the number of 'attempts to commit unnatural offences'was 822 and the number of 'offences of gross indecency' was 320, the corresponding figures for 1952 were 670, 3,087 and 1,686 respectively. While the figures were still relatively low, this did not alleviate official and public anxiety. Moreover the homosexual issue was brought to increased public attention by the high-profile trial of Lord Montagu of Beaulieu, Peter Wildeblood and Michael Pitt-Rivers in 1953–4.[49] In the words of one commentator, parts of what had previously been a 'largely submerged iceberg' were starting to appear above the surface of British public life.[50] Therefore amidst the more general concern among Tories about the increase in crime was a more specific concern: what to do about the post-war increase in forms of what were then termed 'sexual deviancy'? When was the state entitled to intervene to restrict the pursuit of private pleasure?

The libertarian tradition in Conservatism was undoubtedly much less pronounced in regard to moral questions in the 1940s and 1950s than it was in the sphere of economic and social policy. But it was not entirely absent. Iain Macleod, one of the most prominent policy-makers in the 1950s, took a consistently liberal view on issues such as gambling and sexual behaviour.[51] And it remained true that generally Conservatives adopted a more indulgent approach towards drinking and betting than their opponents on the left, where residual fears that such pursuits diverted workers' attention from the class struggle (or, in the late 1940s, from the productivity drive which would lay the foundations for socialism) still persisted. Indeed, faced with the puritanical and austere regime of the Attlee government, the Tories were unable to resist the temptation to refurbish some of the classic appeals of late Victorian Toryism. In 1948 they exploited popular fears that under the new Licensing Act both the playing of darts and drinking while standing at the bar would be officially discouraged in the state-owned pubs built in the New Towns.[52] In the Crippsian climate of the time, Labour's response that such claims were merely mischief-making lacked conviction.[53] Gaming and betting also had plentiful friends in the party, resulting from a happy coincidence of a desire to court the working man and the tendency of many (especially landed) Tories to own racehorses themselves. There was general agreement as early as the 1920s that the nineteenth-century laws on gambling were anachronistic and class-biased, and in 1925 Churchill, ultimately without success, had attempted to introduce a betting duty.[54] However, when in 1951 the Royal Commission on Betting, Lotteries and Gambling recommended legalizing off-course betting, the Conservatives were surprisingly coy in their reaction. The Conservative Research Department recommended parliamentary candidates to be noncommittal when replying to questions as to whether the party supported the Royal Commission's findings, and pointed out that both the Anglican and Nonconformist hierarchies were unsympathetic to any change in the law.[55] At the 1954 and 1955 party conferences there were rank-and-file protests about the government's failure to act on the Commission's report, which seemed to indicate an unwillingness by the government to throw off some of the 'nanny state' inclinations of its Labour predecessor.[56] Indeed a belief that the existing law was excessively restrictive was shared by Sir Hugh Lucas-Tooth, a prominent figure on the party's Betting and Gambling subcommittee.[57] However Butler at the Home Office, despite his desire to remove 'what might be described as the "Victoriana" [*sic*] attitude in legislation relating to our social habits', remained cautious, keen not to arouse opposition from the churches.[58] It was not until 1960 that Macmillan's Betting and Gaming Act finally legalized off-course bookmakers. And even this act should not necessarily be seen as a triumph for the libertarian strain in Conservatism. Rather it reflected pressure from the police, who found the pursuit of illegal betting an unnecessary drain on their manpower, and the Treasury's growing interest in tapping the growth in expenditure on commercialized gambling.[59] In the moral, as in the economic and social, sphere, the notion of 'set the people free' was rarely straightforward. Eden had declared that Conservatism, unlike socialism, stood for 'liberty of the individual, his right to . . . respect for his own distinctive personality'.[60] But Tories were not going to tolerate individualism and diversity if these led to deviance and a challenge to traditional moral authority.

Despite their rhetoric of 'freedom', Conservatives could never wholeheartedly give themselves up to libertarianism, which is evident in relation to the reform of laws relating to prostitution and homosexuality. In the decade after 1945 there was heightened emphasis on the importance of family life, which underlined the exclusion of those 'deviants' who sought sexual gratification outside marriage, or with a partner of the same sex. There was a wider acceptance than previously of the importance of mutual sexual pleasure, but this was applicable only to those engaged in 'normal', i.e. monogamous and heterosexual, relationships. However it increasingly became evident that the state would have to respond to forms of sexual behaviour which lay outside this norm and which had become more manifest since 1945. A political response to this issue was necessitated by the appointment of the Wolfenden committee to investigate the existing laws relating to prostitution and homosexuality.[61] In 1959 the Macmillan government, keen to dispel the moral panic produced by the increased visibility of prostitution, implemented many of the key recommendations of the Wolfenden report of 1957. The Street Offences bill of that year increased the maximum penalties for soliciting and eliminated the previous requirement of proving 'annoyance'.

This apparently straightforward response masked a dialogue within the party about how best to control prostitution, as is illustrated by the very different agenda adopted on this issue by Tory women. Beatrix Campbell has caricatured Tory women as the leading advocates in the party of notions of 'purity' and 'decency', and as key figures in the 'moral backlash' against permissiveness in this period.[62] Certainly women's conferences often echoed to the sound of full-blooded cries for the retention of capital punishment and the restoration of corporal punishment, the latter singled out as the only way to deal with sex pests and child molesters.[63] But there are other strains in the ideology of Conservative women which should not be underestimated, most notably a genuine interest in reducing inequalities between the sexes (at least in terms of rights of citizenship). Thus the Conservatives' 'charter for women', A True Balance: In the Home, in Employment, as Citizens, published in 1949, outlined a number of proposals to secure this end, in particular equal pay.[64] The egalitarian motif also found its way into a section of the pamphlet on 'The Moral Standard'.

> We in no way wish to encourage legislation which would make prostitution either more common or less abhorrent to the public mind, but the present attitude of the law on the subject (and in particular with regard to solicitation) presses sometimes unfairly upon women to the exclusion of male co-offenders. Existing legislation survives from

the days when women had much less voice in public affairs than they have now and in our opinion it results in pushing the whole distasteful subject underground, making it appear a nuisance committed by women of a certain class, rather than a social evil for which both sexes are equally to blame. The attitudes of the law to such a question should take some account of the male co-offender.[65]

This passage impressed the Association for Moral and Social Hygiene, who decided that the Conservatives, rather than Labour, provided the best opportunity for modifying the prostitution laws in a humane way.[66] A meeting between Association members and Evelyn Emmet, chair of the Central Women's Advisory Committee proved productive. A male Association representative argued, 'When a woman is no longer selected as the only punishable partner it would [be] an enormous step forward.' When he concluded his contribution with the rhetorical question, 'Why treat men dffferently?', Emmet rather pointedly interjected that it was 'perhaps because the law was made by men in the first place'. Emmet concluded the meeting by telling the Association that Central Office 'was very interested in all that you have said'.[67] However, Michael Fraser in the Conservative Research Department was more sceptical, and in January 1952 recommended that Tory MPs should not be allowed to sponsor a bill devised by the Association.[68] Despite a reference in his speech introducing the Street Offences bill to his ancestor Josephine Butler, R. A. Butler failed to enact the more radical changes Tory women had demanded, and instead accepted Wolfenden's priority: 'to help clear the streets'. Emmet's feminist cry in the debate on the Wolfenden report that 'if we can prosecute a woman for offering wares we should be able to prosecute a man for accepting them' reflected a discourse among Tory women which failed to become integrated into the legislative priorities of the party leadership.[69]

At least the government was willing to act on Wolfenden's recommendations on prostitution. By contrast the Conservatives were extremely reluctant to countenance Wolfenden's other proposal, that homosexual conduct in private between consenting adults should be decriminalized. There were libertarians, most notably the maverick Bob Boothby, who supported this demand.[70] But more representative of backbench opinion were the visceral pronouncements of Norman Cole, MP for Bedfordshire South, who argued that homosexuality was 'a sin' and should remain illegal.[71] Indeed only a few years before Wolfenden reported, Sir David Maxwell Fyfe at the Home Office was carrying out a relentless purge of homosexuals. The intensity of this campaign owed much to neuroses about the supposed link between sexual deviation and communist subversion, especially in the light of the Burgess and Maclean affair.[72] But it also reflected the exigencies of the post-war 'moral panic' and the fact that Maxwell Fyfe (like Joynson-Hicks) had spent his political apprenticeship amidst the evangelical prerogatives of Lancashire Toryism.[73] Conservative promises of 'freedom' made in 1951 were certainly not intended to relate to Britain's gay community, who found themselves the victims of police raids (often carried out at night) of dubious legality.[74] Under Butler, there was a degree of liberalization at the Home Office, but he rejected Wolfenden, arguing that he was unconvinced that homosexual conduct between consenting adults would not prove to be a source of harm to others, for 'a homosexual group may tend to draw in and corrupt those who are bisexual by nature and capable of living normal lives, but are led by curiosity, weakness, or . . . purely mercenary motives, into homosexual society.'[75] Butler was also privately concerned that public opinion was not ready for a change in the law.[76]

Conservatives therefore never desired to be complete libertarians. Their pursuit of freedom in the 1940s and 1950s (and the 1920s) was always tempered by a concern to preserve conventional morality, even if this required authoritarian policing by the state to banish 'deviancy'. In the late 1970s Margaret Thatcher revived the libertarian rhetoric of the late 1940s, arguing that the Tories had a duty to combat the socialist challenge to individual liberty, or otherwise Britain would be turned into an 'iron curtain tyranny'. Peregrine Worsthorne, articulating the views of the Salisbury Group, poured scorn on this notion, arguing that most Tories were not worried about a 'lack of freedom', rather by 'its excessive abundance': the freedom to commit crime, to undertake wildcat strikes, to distribute pornography and to take drugs. The real threat was not the Big Brother state of *Nineteen Eighty-Four* but the violent anarchy of *A Clockwork Orange*.[77] Worsthorne was worrying needlessly here. Thatcher, despite her self-proclaimed radicalism, was still the heir to earlier variants of twentieth-century Conservatism, and appreciated the importance of balancing market individualism with social discipline. Her preference for 'a free economy and a strong state', to borrow Andrew Gamble's neat summary of her ideology, had a definite precedent in the ambiguous and complex Conservative discourse which dominated the party in the middle decades of this century.[78]

*Notes*

I have benefited greatly in the writing of this chapter from discussions with Stephen Brooke, Brian Harrison, Ian Packer and Ina Zweiniger-Bargielowska, and I thank them for their help.

[1] Conservative Party, *Annual Conference Report* (hereafter *CPCR*) (1947), 42.

[2] A. Eden, *Freedom and Order: Selected Speeches, 1939–1946* (London, 1947), 395.

[3] R. Blake, *The Conservative Party from Peel to Thatcher* (London, 1985), 202–70; T. F. Lindsay and M. Harrington, *The Conservative Party, 1918–1979* (Basingstoke, 1979).

[4] For example, M. Maybury, *The Truth About the Interwar Years* (London, 1949).

[5] For example, Conservative and Unionist Central Office (hereafter CUCO), *The New Conservatism: An Anthology of Post-War Thought* (London, 1955).

[6] P. Williamson, *National Crisis and National Government: British Politics, the Economy and the Empire, 1926–1932* (Cambridge, 1992), 528–30.

[7] D. Dilks, *Neville Chamberlain, I: Pioneering and Reform, 1869–1929* (Cambridge, 1984), 405–587.

[8] A. Booth, 'Britain in the 1930s: A Managed Economy?', *Economic History Review* 2nd ser, 40 (1987), 499–522.

[9] G. D. Anderson, *Fascists, Communists and the National Government: Civil Liberties in Britain, 1931–1937* (Columbia, 1983).

[10] This is despite the rigorous challenge to old myths of post-war reorientation offered by J. Ramsden, ' "A Party for Owners or a Party for Earners?": How Far did the British Conservative Party Really Change after 1945?', *Transactions of the Royal Historical Society* 5th ser, 37 (1987), 49–63.

[11] A. Seldon, 'Conservative Century', in A. Seldon and S. Ball (eds.), *Conservative Century: The Conservative Party since 1900* (Oxford, 1994), 41–6.

[12] I. Zweiniger-Bargielowska, 'Rationing, Austerity and the Conservative Party Recovery after 1945', *Historical Journal* 37 (1994), 173–97.

[13] CPA, CCO 4/4/59, 'Ridiculous Controls', 1950.

14 Quoted in CUCO, *The Campaign Guide 1951* (London, 1951), 101–2.

15 *CPCR* (1947), 59.

16 Ibid, 114.

17 For example, *CPCR* (1947), 58–60; ibid. (1948),132–5; (1950), 21.

18 CUCO, *A True Balance: In the Home, in Employment, as Citizens* (London, 1949), 7.

19 *CPCR* (1947), 42 (Eden); CUCO, *New Conservatism*, 23 (Butler).

20 Conservative Party Archive, Bodleian Library, Oxford (hereafter CPA), CCO 3/l/85, Correspondence with Outside Organisations: Society for Individual Freedom; CCO 3/2/56 and CCO 3/343, ibid., Aims of Industry. For industrial relations, CUCO, *The Right Road for Britain* (London, 1949), 23–5.

21 CPA, CRD 2/52/12, Advisory Committee on Control of Executive Power, 1950.

22 Quoted in CUCO, *The Campaign Guide 1955* (London, 1955), 68.

23 A. Gamble, *The Conservative Nation* (London, 1974), 78–81. See also, CPA, CCO 120/3/1–6, Committee to examine the People's League for the Defence of Freedom and the Middle Class Alliance, 1956.

24 *CPCR* (1954), 66–8; ibid. (1955), 50–3.

25 Ibid. (1957), 44.

26 N. Rollings, 'Poor Mr Butskell: A Short Life, Wrecked by Schizophrenia?', *Twentieth Century British History* 5 (1994), 196–7.

27 For example, T. Newburn, *Permission and Regulation: Law and Morals in Post-War Britain* (London, 1992).

28 J. Weeks, *Sex, Politics and Society: The Regulation of Sexuality since 1800*, 2nd edn. (London, 1989). This statement could be applied with equal justification to two more recent studies, C. Haste, *Rules of Desire: Sex in Britain, World War One to the Present* (London, 1992), and P. Ferris, *Sex and the British: A Twentieth Century History* (London, 1993).

29 J. Lawrence, 'Class and Gender in the Making of Urban Toryism, 1880–1914', *English Historical Review* 108 (1993), 629–52.

30 Viscount Brentford, *Do We Need a Censor?* (London, 1929), 10.

31 R. Hall, *The Well of Loneliness* (London, 1928); R. Aldington, *Death of a Hero* (London, 1929); J. R. S. Leslie, *The Cantab* (London, 1926).

32 H. A. Taylor, *'Jix': Viscount Brentford* (London, 1933), 242–51.

33 A. Kuhn, *Cinema, Censorship and Sexuality, 1909–1925* (London, 1988), 120.

34 Taylor, *'Jix'*, 279.

35 A. G. Gardiner, *Certain People of Importance* (London, 1929 edn.), 224–5.

36 P. R. Stephensen, *Policeman of the Lord: A Political Satire* (London, 1929).

37 E. J. Bristow, *Vice and Vigilance: Purity Movements in Britain since 1700* (Dublin, 1977), 223–4.

[38] B. Melman, *Women and the Popular Imagination in the Twenties: Nymphs and Flappers* (London, 1988), 18–36.

[39] Sir H. Scott, *Your Obedient Servant* (London, 1959), 52–3.

[40] See, for example, K. O. Morgan, *The People's Peace: British History, 1945–1989* (Oxford, 1990), part 1.

[41] Figures cited in CUCO, *The Campaign Guide 1959* (London, 1959), 345–6.

[42] *CPCR* (1947), 32; HC Deb vol.460 (3 February 1949), c.1862.

[43] R. Murphy, *Realism and Tinsel: Cinema and Society in Britain, 1939–49* (London, 1989), 90–3, 187–90.

[44] J. C. Robertson, *The British Board of Film Censors: Film Censorship in Britain, 1896–1950* (London, 1985), 174–6.

[45] HC Deb vol.527 (6 May 1954) c.557; ibid. vol.612 (5 November 1959), c.1181.

[46] *CPCR* (1958), 95–102,149–51. See Brooke, 'Conservative Party, Immigration and National Identity' in this volume.

[47] Weeks, *Sex, Politics and Society*, 232–9; J. Costello, *Love, Sex and War: Changing Values, 1939–1945* (London, 1986 edn.), 356–61.

[48] Weeks, *Sex, Politics and Society*, 239–40.

[49] J. Weeks, *Coming Out: Homosexual Politics in Britain from the Nineteenth Century to the Present* (London, 1977), 161–4.

[50] H. Montgomery Hyde, *The Other Love: An Historical and Contemporary Survey of Homosexuality in Britain* (London, 1970), 197.

[51] R. Shepherd, *Iain Macleod* (London, 1994), 549.

[52] HC Deb vol.459 (14 December 1948), cc.1049–50.

[53] Labour Party, *The People and the Pubs* (1948).

[54] D. Dixon, *From Prohibition to Regulation: Bookmaking, Anti-gambling and the Law* (Oxford, 1991), 269–97.

[55] CPA, CRD 2/44/15, Memorandum on Gambling, 18 October 1951.

[56] *CPCR* (1954), 95–7; ibid. (1955), 104–6.

[57] CPA, CRD 2/44/15, H. Lucas-Tooth, 'Off-Course Betting', n.d. [1956].

[58] Ibid, CRD 2144/1, minutes of Parliamentary Home Office Affairs Committee, 15 July 1957 and 11 November 1959.

[59] Dixon, op. cit., 329–40.

[60] *CPCR* (1947), 42.

[61] Weeks, *Coming Out*, 156–8.

[62] B. Campbell, *The Iron Ladies: Why Do Women Vote Tory?* (London, 1987), 93–100.

[63] For example, Central Women's National Advisory Committee, resolutions for the Women's Conference agendas, 12 June 1956, 24 June 1959.

[64] See Zweiniger-Bargielowska, 'Explaining the Gender Gap' in this volume.

[65] CUCO, *A True Balance*, 19–20.

[66] CPA, CCO 3/3/46, meeting between C. Collison and F. R. Fletcher, n.d.

[67] Ibid., meeting between Association members and E. Emmet, 22 October 1951.

[68] Ibid., M. Fraser to Miss Fletcher, 10 January 1952.

[69] HC Deb vol.596 (22 November 1958), c.372, 451; ibid. vol.598 (29 January 1959), c.1271.

[70] Ibid. vol.521 (3 December 1953), c.1297.

[71] Ibid. vol.596 (22 November 1958), c.482.

[72] Weeks, *Coming Out*, 161–2.

[73] Lord Kilmuir, *Political Adventure* (London, 1964), 25–34.

[74] Montgomery Hyde, op. cit., 216–22.

[75] HC Deb vol.496 (26 November 1958) c.369.

[76] CPA, CRD 2/44/1, Minutes of meeting of Parliamentary Home Affairs Committee, 25 November 1957.

[77] P. Worsthorne, 'Too Much Freedom', in M. Cowling (ed.), *Conservative Essays* (London, 1978), 145–9.

[78] A. Gamble, *The Free Economy and the Strong State: The Politics of Thatcherism* (Basingstoke, 1988). Thatcher's puritanical background was significant here. See, for example, her comments that while she broadly welcomed the relaxation of restrictions on the free market after 1951, she did not pretend 'to have liked, or even understood, all the expressions of this new popular freedom', since rock and roll 'never eclipsed *The Desert Song* in my affections' (M. Thatcher, *The Path to Power* (London, 1995), 77).

# Thatcherism and the Conservative Tradition

### MARK GARNETT and LORD GILMOUR

The Conservative Party's electoral record during the twentieth century is unrivalled. Only in the disastrous year of 1906 has its representation in the Commons dipped below 200; its lowest share of the vote since 1900 was around 36 per cent in October 1974. As a result, the Conservatives have either ruled alone or dominated coalitions for seventy of the last hundred years.[1]. This impressive performance, in a century which has witnessed many changes, suggests a party which successfully adapts to new circumstances and enjoys much more than a sectional appeal.

Until 1979, this explanation of the Conservative Party's election victories was broadly accurate. In the general election of that year the Conservatives confronted a Labour Party which had clung to office for five years without ever holding a secure majority. Even this hand-to-mouth administration might have won re-election if the right moment had been chosen, but a succession of crippling strikes in the winter of 1978–9 brought an ironic end to a government which had told the electorate that it was uniquely capable of managing the trade unions. This 'Winter of Discontent' ensured that the poor performance of the Wilson and Callaghan governments was the dominant issue of the 1979 election campaign. Labour's fall from office was followed by years of internal party conflict, and the rise of the SDP split the opposition in the 1983 and 1987 contests. For most of the decade, the Conservatives enjoyed a rare opportunity to govern without effective challengers or the need to placate coalition partners.

The existence of an electable opposition is an invaluable buttress against divisive policies. If the traditional approach of the Conservative Party had been followed after 1979, the weakness of the opposition would have had less effect. Regrettably, this was not the case. Both critics and admirers of Margaret Thatcher have generally agreed that she was a different kind of politician from her post-war predecessors; what remains to be considered is the nature of this difference, and how far it affected the policies of her governments.

# I

A statement of Conservative principles published in 1950 declared that the party 'rejects all doctrines and all actions which seek to divide the nation against itself'.[2] To a Conservative, this principle represents nothing more than common sense; after all, a nation is far easier to govern when its people feel united. Even so, there have been occasions when the party has rebelled against its sensible ethos. After three defeats between 1906 and 1910, for example, the Conservatives pursued extremist and divisive policies, using the House of Lords to veto Liberal legislation and coming near to countenancing civil war in Ireland. Significantly, this uncharacteristic lapse occurred during a period of opposition, and it was brought to an end by renewed experience of power during the First World War. Between the wars the Conservatives 'were still the rich man's party', but the leadership of Stanley Baldwin – an enlightened industrialist – prevented the 'hard-faced' men of the party from pursuing a course which might have led the country towards all-out class war.[3] Although the virtues of Keynesian demand management were not fully appreciated by Conservatives as a remedy for the economic problems of the 1930s, this was a shortcoming which was widely shared; within the confines of prevailing economic orthodoxy, Neville Chamberlain was an interventionist Chancellor of the Exchequer.[4] Apart from programmes of public works and assistance to special areas, the inter-war Conservative Party was also willing to extend state ownership, nationalizing electricity generation (1926) and airlines (1939), while mergers were promoted in other key industries. Despite the unsettling developments of those years, the

Conservative Party never wedded itself to an ideology, as Conservatives themselves understand the word. Ideological politics, for Conservatives, is based on 'abstract principles, and arbitrary and general doctrines'.[5] Whether it results in socialism, *laissez-faire* or any other rigid government programme, ideology in this sense is clearly opposed to Conservatism. Faced with an increasingly complex world, Conservatives accept that government demands continual adaptation under the guidance of events. The patience required for this task is unsuited to the disposition of the ideologue, who prefers to think that the problems of government can be overcome by simply following a pre-designed formula. This approach can only result in damage to society. The experience of power has sometimes taught ideologues to change before too much harm has been done, but for others the challenge of reality has only spurred on their crusade to make the world conform to their beliefs.

In the twentieth century, the main battleground of ideas has concerned the role of the state. Between the wars, Conservatives like Baldwin and Chamberlain steered a middle course between the competing ideologies of socialism and *laissez-faire* liberalism. As Anthony Eden later put it, Conservatives were determined 'not to be tempted by the doctrinaire approach of our Socialist opponents to fall ourselves into the pit of doctrinaire anti-Socialism'.[6] Unlike socialists, Conservatives are too aware of human frailties to regard the state as an ideal instrument. Even so, they differ from *laissez-faire* liberals because they seek to uphold necessary authority, not to minimize its scope in the pursuit of an illusory model of freedom (especially in the economic sphere, where 'freedom' is impossible even to define).[7] Any abstract attempt to demarcate the proper limit of government activity invites disaster in an unpredictable world. At its best, government can act as an essential bond of national unity, and actively promote the social harmony which Conservatives desire; however, concentrations of power can lead to abuses, and the Conservative tradition has always promoted local government as a barrier against over-centralization.

During the post-war period the general lines of policy marked out by Keynes, Beveridge and others have been welcomed by most Conservatives as a satisfactory response to the problems of society. Although there is room for disagreement over the details of these 'consensual' measures, they represent the most likely means of securing the Conservative priority of social harmony, and fulfil Churchill's promise to 'promote all measures to improve the health and social conditions of the people'.[8] The welfare state is wholly compatible with a Conservative outlook; since there will always be people who cannot support themselves through no fault of their own, natural justice and the well-being of the public demand that there is a more reliable safety-net for them than private charity. While Conservatives are unconvinced that any society can reflect true 'merit', they do acknowledge that state support must be available to make sure that every citizen has a reasonable chance of overcoming the disadvantages of birth into a deprived environment. While the dangers of overdependency on the state cannot be ignored, the alternatives are far worse, and for most people 'dependency' of some kind is unavoidable. Conservatives were wary of the Attlee government's national-ization programme, but they had no objection to the principle of state ownership in itself.[9] Hence the Churchill government kept denationalization 'to a bare minimum' when Labour lost office in 1951.[10] Over the next thirteen years of Conservative rule the emphasis of policy fluctuated in response to circumstances, but the post-war priorities of full employment, sustained economic growth and an adequately funded welfare state were never seriously endangered.[11]

When the Conservative Party defeated Harold Wilson's Labour at the general election of 1970, inflation, uncompetitiveness and trade union power were the main problems facing Britain. Prior to the election, Edward Heath had been accused of wishing to break the post-war consensus by implementing a right-wing *laissez-faire* programme. Wilson attempted to emphasize the anachronistic nature of this approach by coining the phrase 'Selsdon Man' (after the Selsdon Park Hotel where the shadow cabinet held its manifesto deliberations). A small minority of Conservatives might have wished this caricature to be true, but Heath never intended to live down to it. He certainly felt that the Wilson governments had mismanaged the economy, but this was the fault of particular individuals, and not the general approach to government which had been prevalent since 1945. Like his Conservative pre-decessors, Heath sought a balance between the priorities of high and stable growth, low inflation, and minimal unemployment.

When he took office, growth and inflation were the most urgent priorities, but unemployment would undoubtedly have been tackled first had that presented his government with the most pressing immediate difficulties.

Unfortunately for the subsequent fortunes of both Heath and the Conservative Party, the media misinterpreted the change of direction after 1971 as a complete 'U-turn' – implying that the government had reversed its policy direction, abandoning free-market priorities in the face of difficulties. Subsequently this version of events has proved useful for Thatcherites wishing to discredit Heath, even though some of their most prominent champions sat in the cabinets which committed this treason.[12] In their hands, the record of these years has been transformed into myth. As we have seen, Conservatives are always ready to change in response to new challenges; the Heath government can be accused of originally underestimating the potential threat from unemployment, but the Prime Minister was not guilty of betraying his underlying principles. Heath was not a follower of Hayek and Friedman in 1970, and he was no socialist in 1972. He was what he had always been – a firm believer in the approach to government which had been dominant in each party since 1945. The dash for growth and the subsidies to industry associated with the 'Barber Boom' were simply designed to stave off a repetition of the mass unemployment which had blighted Heath's early years in the 1930s. The far-reaching nature of Heath's measures, in fact, was not a symptom of a dramatic conversion; rather, it stemmed from a deep and consistent commitment to full employment.

Fittingly, the downfall of the Heath government had little to do with the misunderstood U-turn. Instead, it should be traced to the unnecessary climate of confrontation between the government and the unions, created by the heavy-handed Industrial Relations Act which was arguably the policy which deviated most seriously from the post-war consensual approach. While some Conservatives thought that Heath had failed because he had not stuck to his supposedly hard-line views of 1970, the overwhelming majority of the party recognized that this simply reflected the wishful thinking of the party's ideologues. Heath's fall resulted from a mixture of mistakes, misjudgements and ill-luck; if there was a lesson to be learned from his defeat, it was that he should have presented a more flexible image from the start of his premiership.

# II

When Margaret Thatcher took the party leadership in 1975, most of her shadow cabinet opposed her monetarist ideas. Her victory owed more to a reaction against Heath among the parliamentary party than to general enthusiasm for her beliefs. An authoritative study has estimated that fewer than 10 per cent of Conservative MPs were 'Thatcherites' in 1975.[13] While the Conservatives remained in opposition, it was widely felt that Thatcher was on probation. Although it was recognized that important reforms were necessary if Britain was to remain governable and relatively prosperous, few Conservatives were dreaming of a revolution. If they felt that Mrs Thatcher's zeal was rather too hot, they could console themselves with the thought that in Britain, at least, radicalism rarely survives prolonged exposure to the frustrations of government.

By 1990 the situation was very different. By that time, ministers who continued to disagree with Thatcherism in private felt it prudent to act (and vote) as if she was right. Even if the leader herself was now regarded as an electoral liability (and her flagship Poll Tax as a dangerous navigational hazard) these 'Career Thatcherites' behaved as if there was no viable alternative to her general line of policy. The Labour Party had abandoned the socialist policies of the early 1980s, and was now retreating even from the more cautious priorities of the Attlee governments. Whatever the actual success of her measures, few could dispute that Mrs Thatcher had transformed almost every aspect of British politics.

This is not to say, of course, that she had implemented her ideas in exactly the form she would have wished. No British political leader has been able to do this, for the very good reason that political practice resists ideological blueprints, however popular they might be. Mrs Thatcher did not create a free-market Utopia, where hard work and sloth automatically received their due rewards. This was only to be predicted, given that this ideological vision is contrary to human nature. On a sober view of political realities, the most that can be achieved is to redesign the political 'mind-set' – the assumptions, and even the vocabulary, which underlie public debate. Mrs Thatcher's views had a limited impact on the electorate, which thought that Labour and the

Conservatives were equally extreme.[14] Yet her ideas had something like the desired effect on politicians, even outside her own party. The assumptions and the vocabulary of public debate had been altered by the Thatcherite preoccupations with low inflation, privatization and the 'free' market, based on the ideological premise that the state should liberate the self-interested, rational individual. Even when opinion polls showed that the public refused to accept that post-war priorities should be abandoned, most politicians felt able to ignore them. After Mrs Thatcher's third election victory in 1987 the new mood in Westminster allowed the Poll Tax (which had been scornfully rejected early in her premiership) to be carried through Parliament, despite objections which proved to be very well founded. At the same time, Career Thatcherites were now attempting to win favour with the Prime Minister by appeasing her desire for dramatic changes in the National Health Service, education and social security.

So the claim that ideology was the driving force of Thatcherism is not refuted by the Thatcher governments' failure to satisfy all of the plans dreamed up by economic liberals free from the pressures of office. If complete consistency is required to establish the presence of an ideological commitment, some absurd conclusions would follow: for example, one would have to say that Lenin was not an ideologue because he felt it necessary to introduce the New Economic Policy as a temporary expedient. The Conservative Party under Margaret Thatcher was as ideological as any British political party can be while entertaining any hope of electoral success. During the 1980s, with the opposition hampered by divisions and sour memories of the 1970s, Thatcherites were able to push the tolerance of the electorate further than any British party has been able to do in the democratic era.

Whatever their faults, Conservative post-war governments up to 1979 tried to ensure that no section of the community felt that their interests were ignored: that the British public thought of itself as one nation. Even before 1945 the party included a noisy faction of free-market zealots; to explain the existence of these ideas within the Conservative Party would require a lengthy digression, but the decline of the Liberal Party as an alternative to socialism is probably the most important factor. Until the election of Mrs Thatcher the ethos of the leadership successfully resisted this minority view. By contrast, Mrs Thatcher's administrations willingly surrendered to it. They did nothing to discourage social divisions during the 1980s; if anything, their championship of the self-interested individual acted to stimulate them. When evidence of social fragmentation was presented (even by a former Conservative ally like the Anglican Church), it was either ignored or attacked. Mrs Thatcher's rhetoric of inflexibility might have disguised an occasional willingness to compromise, but her tactical retreats were only made in preparation of future ideological advance.

Nothing exemplifies Mrs Thatcher's 'Two Nations' philosophy better than her taxation policy. While Conservatives agreed that the 1979 rate of income tax at 83 per cent for top earners was too high, they also accept that progressive taxation is essential in an enlightened modern economy. By 1990 the top rate of income tax had been reduced by 43 per cent; the corresponding cut for average earners had been 8 per cent. At the same time, regressive taxes, such as national insurance contributions and taxes on consumption, were increasing. Overall, by 1989 the poorest fifth of the population was contributing 40 per cent of its income to the Exchequer, while the wealthiest fifth paid only 35 per cent.[15] However much the rich had been 'soaked' by Mr Healey in the 1970s, this act of bourgeois vengeance was contrary to the Conservative ethos.

In electoral terms, the policy on direct taxation was an undoubted success; it encouraged the minority which voted Conservative during these years to suppress their misgivings about other Thatcherite initiatives. If this section of the electorate apparently conformed to the economic liberal model of the individual by acting out of self-interest, however, it contradicted another free-market assumption by being less than perfectly rational. The mystique associated with income tax rates seemed to authenticate the idea that the Conservatives were the party of low taxation, but the balance was recouped through higher VAT and increased National Insurance payments (for all except the highest earners). Even those who genuinely felt their pockets bulging have lost out in other ways. The effect on society, while difficult to quantify, was serious. The 1988 budget, which awarded almost half of its £6 billion benefits to the richest 5 per cent of the population, might have been intended to encourage 'work, responsibility and success', as the 1979 manifesto had originally promised. In practice, it fostered a prolonged fit of irresponsible consumption, affecting almost everyone except the 'excluded' unemployed.

While the bulk of the temporary yields from North Sea oil and privatization was being used to produce a 'feel-good factor' in those who already had plenty to be cheerful about, the rest was subsidizing the government's unrivalled performance in job-destruction. Between 1979 and 1988, social security spending rose, in real terms, by about 30 per cent. Most of this increase was due to the increase in unemployment. The fact that some benefits more than kept pace with inflation is commendable. However, by 1989 the poorest fifth of the population were spending 30 per cent of their disposable income in indirect taxes.[16] As the numbers of long-term unemployed rose in defiance of government statisticians, they were constantly exposed to evidence of rising living standards for those fortunate enough to stay in work. 'Relative deprivation' was regarded by government spokesmen as a myth invented by mischievous sociologists, but its effects were real enough, increasing social alienation during the 1980s.

Conservatives believe that absolute economic equality is impossible, if not undesirable. Yet there is a limit beyond which inequality becomes intolerable. Thatcherites, however, seemed to think that it was the poor who should not be tolerated. The attitude of government spokesmen towards the unemployed was often reminiscent of La Rochefoucauld's maxim that we hate people we have injured more than those who have injured us. Nigel Lawson's attack on 'idleness and irresponsibility' in 1985 was typical of the government's sophisticated analysis of the problem.[17] Along with their Two Nation economics, Thatcherites were Two Nation psychologists; while those in highly paid employment needed greater rewards to improve their performance, the jobless should be threatened with loss of benefits in order to make them seek work.[18] Surveys showed that this unlikely theory was a fantasy, but no evidence can shake the faith of ideologues.[19] The inconsistency of the government's attitude did not stop there; by turns, the unemployed were portrayed as shiftless dullards who had to be forced to take control of their lives, then as cunning schemers who were bathing in taxpayers' money.

Conservatives do not believe that all of the unemployed are desperately seeking work, though clearly most of them are.

However, unlike Thatcherites who wish to punish the unfortunate for the sins of an irresponsible minority, Conservatives recognize that there must be a reasonable level of support for all. For Conservatives, the best way of ensuring that all able people take up jobs is to help provide them; even if such policies are ineffectual, they are at least likely to convince individuals that they are part of a collective effort, which is bound to reduce the kind of feelings of despair and neglect which tarnished the 1980s. Knowing that governments are not prepared to leave people at the mercy of so-called market forces also helps to reduce insecurity among those still in work; as the Major government has found, unless consumers feel secure, the national economy will suffer. For Conservatives, Thatcherite policies towards the unemployed were worse than a crime – they were a mistake.

Thatcherites, however, preferred to ignore mistakes rather than to learn from them. By October 1980 there was already strong evidence that the policies were not working, but the Prime Minister told the Conservative Party conference that she was not prepared to change course. Having been dubbed 'The Iron Lady' during her years in opposition, the Prime Minister was more concerned to live up to the nickname than to follow the tradition of pragmatic Conservative leadership. In the following year, widespread rioting in Britain's inner cities provoked Mrs Thatcher to deny any connection between her policies and social discontent. Denouncing the rioters, or blaming the influence of the 1960s, was seen as a more appropriate response than any attempt to remedy urban problems.

For Thatcherites, inflexibility was a test of virility which post-war Conservatives had failed. On this view, previous party leaders had matched their policies to the needs of the time because they lacked Mrs Thatcher's moral and political courage. The point of politics, by contrast, was to force events to adapt themselves to abstract free-market theory. For Conservatives, such inflexibility is actually a sign of political weakness; after all, it takes more political courage to admit failure than to ignore evidence that policies have gone wrong. This was a kind of courage which Mrs Thatcher palpably lacked. Under her premiership, regular complaints that 'the message isn't getting through' were the nearest approaches to confessions of failure; of course, such 'presentational' matters could always be attributed to bias within the BBC. Perhaps Mrs

Thatcher had a partial excuse, because most other media sources constantly reassured her that her policies were either working already, or were on the verge of producing an economic miracle.

The Thatcher governments' obsession with monetarism is the best example of their perseverance with futile causes. As a practical policy, monetarism had two significant flaws; the money supply could not be defined, let alone controlled. In fact, in so far as the money supply can be measured, the Thatcherite experiment proved that it does not affect inflation in the mechanical way predicted by the sages of monetarism. Yet Thatcherites had invested too much in Milton Friedman's theorizing to admit that it could be flawed. Best of all, it fitted their self-serving view that governments should do no more than set a framework for economic activity.

Eventually, even the Thatcher government had tacitly to drop monetarism (in a fanfare of silence). Inflation was temporarily driven out, not by control of the money supply but by the time-dishonoured method of creating mass unemployment. This remedy had been available to all post-war governments; Mrs Thatcher was the only Prime Minister whose electoral circumstances allowed her to escape the proper consequences of applying it. The unemployed and their families were not so fortunate.

British industry was certainly inefficient in 1979, and a shake-up accompanied by some privatization and trade union reform would have been welcome to Conservatives. The problem with Thatcherism was that even when it assaulted the right targets it used inappropriate tactics. Privatization was as ill-planned as state ownership had originally been, and although responsible ministers talked as though the sales would increase competition, in most cases public utilities were simply turned into private monopolies. Instead of 'popular capitalism', with individual shareholders exercising control, the new monopolies were dominated by profit-hungry financial institutions, which had no interest in controlling the inflated management salaries which outraged public opinion after 1990. This pattern was repeated in other areas. After Jim Prior's prudent trade union reforms, the government continued to press for more and more changes, presumably inspired by the need to embarrass the Labour Party more than a desire to promote industrial co-operation. If only because of Arthur

Scargill's political motives, the Prime Minister had to resist the miners' strike; but instead of healing social wounds the eventual victory seemed only to fuel her desire to discover more 'enemies within'. Even the sale of council houses, a well-established Conservative policy originally designed to make people feel that they belonged to their communities, ended up reflecting little credit on the Thatcher governments. The refusal to release receipts from housing sales was part of an unedifying campaign to bully local government. In view of Mrs Thatcher's antipathy towards institutions which dissented from her beliefs, it was fitting that her attacks on Europe and local government provided the most pressing reasons for her party to turn against her at last.

## III

Thatcherism was a complex phenomenon, but despite the subtle differences among its supporters the general outlines are clear, and these were clearly incompatible with post-war British Conservatism. Perhaps it is misleading to place too much emphasis on some of Mrs Thatcher's cruder remarks, but no other Conservative leader would have thought of exclaiming, 'We must have an ideology', as Thatcher did at a meeting of the Conservative Philosophy Group.[20] She normally attributed her beliefs to instinct, mixed with the homespun common sense of her father. While these influences clearly played a part in convincing her that her policies were invariably right, Thatcherite ideology was largely inspired by nineteenth-century liberalism, as expounded (though hardly updated) by American and continental writers, further distilled by the odd assortment of rationalists and communist converts who staffed her favourite think-tanks.[21] In economics, the master-science of Thatcherism, the liberal inspiration is indisputable. The eulogies of the individual entrepreneur, the denigration of state interference and the religious faith in the free market all would have drawn encouraging smiles from Cobden, Bright and Herbert Spencer. The fact that all of these aspirations resulted in a disappointing growth rate (despite North Sea Oil), endemic unemployment, the decimation of manufacturing, widening inequalities, a boom in crime and more than a whiff of corrupt practices, only reinforced what history could have taught the Thatcherites before their bold project left the drawing-board. Hard-line liberalism produced prosperity on paper and widespread misery in practice when it held sway in the nineteenth century. It could hardly have served the country any better after 1979, when Britain's economic status was so different.

Some Thatcherites were coy on the subject, but others made no attempt to disguise the true nature of their creed. Despite occasional attempts to claim allegiance to figures like Burke (and even Disraeli), the Thatcherite pantheon was mostly populated by liberals. Not even Michael Oakeshott, the most prominent of twentieth-century British Conservatives, featured very prominently in the ideological name-dropping of Thatcherites. Milton Friedman and Friedrich von Hayek were acknowledged as mentors (even though neither of these luminaries received this accolade with unmixed pleasure). In financial matters, at least, Nigel Lawson idolized Gladstone, and Sir Keith Joseph famously advised his officials to read Adam Smith (even though the latter's *Theory of Moral Sentiments* showed his distance from Thatcherite individualism). The Institute of Economic Affairs, which constantly provided advice for what it saw as a friendly administration, was dedicated to popularizing the cause of economic liberalism. The moral ideas urged by Mrs Thatcher as an adjunct to her economic experiment came from the identical source; it is often forgotten that 'Victorian values' such as self-help were essential ingredients of nineteenth-century liberalism. Mrs Thatcher's apparent belief that such a moral climate could be recreated by an act of will was another telling symptom of her distance from pragmatic Conservatism.

The identification of Thatcherism as a member of the liberal (or perhaps neo-liberal) family is hotly denied by some of her supporters, who realize that political brand-loyalty makes the name of Conservatism a useful asset in electoral struggles. Others (notably David Willetts) have argued that economic liberalism is quite compatible with a Conservative outlook.[22] Willetts is a skilful advocate, but he cannot make this synthesis seem plausible even on paper. After all, Roger Scruton (another admirer of Mrs Thatcher) had previously identified liberalism as 'the principal enemy of conservatism'.[23] A more subtle line of analysis agrees that the economic agenda of Thatcherism was liberal, but suggests that its emphasis on law and order places it within the Conservative fold. Thatcherism, for these observers, was an ideological cocktail, composed of rather ill-matched ingredients.[24]

Although this argument is associated with some very astute analysis of Thatcherism, it cannot be accepted. The notion that Thatcherism consisted of a belief in both a 'free economy' and a 'strong state' is very true, but belief in a strong state is not exclusive to Conservatives. Conservatives believe in a strong state because they think that human nature is unpredictable; as such, they also advocate economic intervention by the state, which should step in when social cohesion is endangered by mass unemployment. By contrast, the Thatcherite self-denying ordinance in economic matters meant that in certain respects the frontiers of the state had to be rolled forward rather than back. The very nature of the Thatcherite experiment demanded a heavy emphasis on law and order; *laissez-faire* policies which are intended to benefit property-owners at the expense of the poor need an enlarged police force to sustain them. Other reforms, such as the Poll Tax and the changes at Health and Education also caused an increase in bureaucracy; in the absence of popular support, many of these reforms had to be administered by appointed bodies, thus reinforcing the Thatcherite attack on local government. By the end of the Thatcher period the proportion of national income absorbed by the state had not fallen; the only changes were that less government spending had a productive purpose, and an ever-growing proportion of public money was distributed by unelected 'quangos'. Since this revolution in government activity took place in support of economic liberalism, the idea that the associated growth of state power can serve as proof of Mrs Thatcher's residual Conservatism is clearly mistaken.

Thatcherism as a programme for government contradicted the Conservative tradition, but its immediate legacy did offer some consolation to Conservatives. The fall of Mrs Thatcher represented an excellent opportunity for Conservative government to realign itself with the public mood; a period of 'consolidation', with the reversal of some Thatcherite excesses, would almost certainly have won approval after November 1990. At first, some of John Major's rhetoric (and his more emollient personality) seemed to promise a welcome change of direction.

Unfortunately the change did not extend beyond a shuffle of

personnel. As Hugo Young has written, 'the ideological engine could not stop itself going forward.'[25] Having been groomed by Thatcherism, ministers could not break out of the attitudes which they had absorbed before 1990. Since the Thatcher governments were re-elected despite their deep mid-term unpopularity, Conservative ministers began to think that the public would eventually acquiesce in anything they cared to do. Even if they had possessed sufficient imagination to seek out alternative polices, these Career Thatcherites considered that, provided they could get 'presentation' right and distribute tax cuts to the right people, the electorate would continue to re-elect them. In part, this formula seems to have worked in 1992, although Major's victory also owed something to the general gloom, which made voters sceptical about the promises offered by Labour. But while the public might just about accept a prolonged period of skilful rule by one party, they cannot be expected to tolerate indefinitely the hegemony of a single, failed ideology. On present trends, the Conservative Party leadership will only understand this when it is granted a period of reflection in opposition.

## Notes

[1] A. Seldon and S. Ball, 'Introduction', in A. Seldon and S. Ball (eds.), *Conservative Century: The Conservative Party since 1900* (Oxford, 1994), 1.

[2] Conservative Political Centre, *Conservatism 1945–1950* (London, 1950), 14.

[3] R. Blake, *The Conservative Party from Peel to Thatcher* (London, 1985 edn.), 245.

[4] I. Macleod, *Neville Chamberlain* (London, 1961), 170–1.

[5] R. Blake, *Disraeli* (London, 1966), 482.

[6] Speech at Leamington, 1 June 1946, reprinted in Conservative Political Centre, *Conservatism 1945–1950*, 80.

[7] For an excellent discussion of this issue, see A. Haworth, *Anti-Liberalism: Markets, Philosophy and Myth* (London, 1994).

[8] Speech of 5 October 1946, quoted in Conservative Political Centre, *Conservatism 1945–1950*, 80.

[9] Q. Hogg, *The Case for Conservatism* (London, 1947), 284–95.

[10] A. Seldon, 'The Churchill Administration, 1951–1955', in P. Hennessy and A. Seldon (eds.), *Ruling Performance: British Governments from Attlee to Thatcher* (Oxford, 1987), 65.

[11] As the Institute of Economic Affairs complained in 1977, 'none of the

three political parties questioned the fundamental economic *rationale* of state welfare financed substantially by taxes' (R. Harris and A. Seldon, *Not from Benevolence* (London 1977), 41).

[12] For a characteristic version of the myth, see N. Tebbit, *Upwardly Mobile* (London, 1989), 134–5.

[13] I. Crewe and D. Searing, 'Ideological Change in the British Conservative Party', *American Political Science Review* 82 (1988), 371. For the strength of economic liberalism within the party under Heath, see P. Norton, *Conservative Dissidents: Dissent within the Parliamentary Conservative Party, 1970–74* (London, 1978).

[14] See, for example, I. Crewe, 'Values: The Crusade that Failed', in D. Kavanagh and A. Seldon (eds.), *The Thatcher Effect: A Decade of Change* (Oxford,1989), 239–50.

[15] I. Gilmour, *Dancing with Dogma* (London, 1992), 152. See also Daunton, ' "A Kind of Tax Prison": Rethinking Conservative Taxation Policy, 1960–1970' in this volume.

[16] Gilmour, *Dancing with Dogma*, 152.

[17] Ibid., 153.

[18] Similarly, while business leaders were to be freed from the menace of 'red tape', the paperwork confronting benefit claimants continually increased.

[19] See P. Riddell, *The Thatcher Era and its Legacy* (Oxford, 1991), 221.

[20] Quoted in H. Young, *One of Us* (London, 1990 edn.), 406.

[21] For interesting (though largely uncritical) accounts of Mrs Thatcher's ideological allies, see R. Cockett, *Thinking the Unthinkable: Think-Tanks and the Economic Counter-Revolution* (London, 1994), and J. Ranelagh, *Thatcher's People* (London, 1991).

[22] D. Willetts, *Modern Conservatism* (Harmondsworth, 1992).

[23] R. Scruton, *The Meaning of Conservatism* (Harmondsworth,1980), 12.

[24] This approach is best exemplified by A. Gamble, *The Free Economy and the Strong State* (Houndmills, 2nd edn. 1994).

[25] H. Young, 'The Prime Minister', in D. Kavanagh and A. Seldon (eds.), *The Major Effect* (London, 1994), 22.

# Part Two

# Identity

# The Conservatives in Wales, 1880–1935

### FELIX AUBEL

The history of the Conservative Party in Wales has undeniably been one of consistent electoral failure throughout most of the Principality. The *South Wales Daily News* of 27 January 1874 made the retrospectively accurate prophetic comment that 'Welsh Toryism is only a dumb dog that cannot bark', while ten years later the *Pall Mall Gazette* observed that Conservatism was but 'a rare exotic in the Principality'.[1] One can largely account for the Tory electoral failure during the period 1880–1914 by the fact that the party was uncompromisingly opposed to Church disestablishment, a movement supported by a clear majority of Welsh people, who were overwhelmingly Nonconformist.[2] An anonymous 'Tory Churchman' conceded as much in July 1892 when he claimed that 'so long as the question of Disestablishment stood in the way the Welsh Conservative Party would only be knocking its head against a stone wall'.[3] This assessment was also supported by Austen Chamberlain in 1921 when, speaking not long after the disestablishment of the Anglican Church in the Principality, he asserted that 'across every political issue for a hundred years in Wales has come the question of the Church'.[4] Nevertheless, the solving of this problem did not lead to 'the steady emergence from a dark eclipse' of the Welsh Tories, as somewhat optimistically predicted by the *Western Mail*, since the party's electoral performance showed no significant overall improvement when the Principality as a whole is taken into consideration.[5]

In order to try to explain why the Conservative Party in Wales largely failed to benefit from the ending of the disestablishment controversy, undoubtedly its Achilles' heel during the pre-war years, one has to undertake a general appraisal of Welsh Toryism. This study will therefore commence with an examination of the Conservative Party's record in parliamentary elections, with particular emphasis being given to its significant support in the anglicized regions of the Principality, especially in some of the boroughs and several counties adjacent to the English border. Welsh county council results are then analysed in an attempt to deduce whether Tory support ran on lines broadly parallel on local and national issues. Unfortunately, however, this assessment of the county council returns does not extend into the inter-war era, because the formation of so-called 'anti-Socialist' electoral groupings to try to combat 'the rise of Labour' makes it exceedingly difficult to locate with any degree of accuracy the overall numerical strength of the specifically Conservative representatives throughout the Principality. The organization and leadership of Welsh Toryism is then discussed, with particular emphasis being given to the comparatively narrow socio-economic composition of the party hierarchy including the members of Parliament. There follows a conclusion which provides an overview of the Conservative Party's position in Wales.

# I

The general election results in Wales during the period appear to confirm the Liberal hegemony established in the Principality in 1880, when the Conservatives were reduced to a mere four members of Parliament out of a total of thirty-four.[6] The Tories' average percentage of the votes cast between 1885 and 1910 was only 37·7 per cent, and the party only ever came reasonably close to sending double-figure parliamentary representation to Westminster in 1886 and 1895 when seven and nine members respectively, including a solitary Liberal Unionist on each occasion, were elected. The nadir in Welsh Tory fortunes was, however, reached in the 'Liberal landslide' of 1906 when not a single Conservative was returned from the Principality. This often abysmal Tory election performance is illustrated in table 1 which outlines the party's fortunes between the general elections of 1885 and 1910.[7] Thus the Conservatives won a mere thirty-four triumphs at general elections in Wales during this period, which amounts to only one eighth of the overall parliamentary representation.[8]

Table 1

| Year | Candidates | Unopposed | Elected | Total votes | % | Seats |
|------|-----------|-----------|---------|-------------|-----|-------|
| 1885 | 29 | 0 | 4 | 79690 | 38·9 | 33 |
| 1886 | 24 | 2 | 7 | 60048 | 46·1 | 33 |
| 1892 | 29 | 0 | 3 | 78038 | 37·2 | 33 |
| 1895 | 31 | 0 | 9 | 103802 | 42·2 | 33 |
| 1900 | 21 | 1 | 6 | 63932 | 37·6 | 33 |
| 1906 | 20 | 0 | 0 | 65949 | 33·8 | 33 |
| 1910(J) | 33 | 0 | 2 | 116769 | 31·9 | 33 |
| 1910(D) | 20 | 0 | 3 | 81100 | 33·8 | 33 |

Average % 37·7

In spite of this generally lacklustre Tory election performance, both in terms of actual victories at the polls and to a considerably lesser extent in the aggregate popular vote, the Conservatives achieved significant levels of support in no fewer than eight of the eleven borough constituencies in Wales. On the other hand, the Conservatives only ever won on at least one occasion four out of the twenty-two Welsh county constituencies between 1885 and 1910.[9] Indeed, Radnorshire was strictly speaking the only unitary county gained by the Tories, the remaining three being individual divisions of larger shires.[10]

To explain why no fewer than twenty-two of the thirty-four Conservative election victories in Wales, excluding by-elections, between 1885 and 1910 were achieved in the eleven borough constituencies in the Principality, one has to take into account a number of socio-economic factors which may have assisted the Tory cause. Ever since the Middle Ages many of these boroughs, with their castles and fortified town walls, had been 'the outposts of English influence in Wales', which could well have contributed towards making their general voting behaviour more akin to that of England.[11] Their often cosmopolitan populations, the comparative weakness of the Welsh language and of religious Nonconformity, made most of these boroughs highly marginal divisions. With no apparent 'built-in' Liberal hegemony, as was the case in the rest of Wales, the Tories were able to gain election victories, albeit narrow ones.[12]

By contrast, the unitary Welsh county constituencies, the sole exception being Radnorshire, were overwhelmingly 'electoral deserts' for the Tories. The existence of large Welsh monoglot populations acted as a barrier to anglicizing influences, while the preponderance of a usually Welsh-speaking religious Nonconformity ensured that the issues of Church disestablishment and disendowment dominated the political agenda in these areas from the 1880s onwards.[13] Tensions between a socially anglicized, largely Conservative-orientated landowning class, compounded by their general adherence to the Established Church, and their almost invariably Welsh-speaking, frequently Nonconformist, and Liberal-inclined tenantry, only worsened matters, particularly when the memory of the 'evictions' of 1868 contributed extensively towards the formation of much of the latter's political ethos.[14] Also, Welsh farms were generally considerably smaller than their English counterparts, thus further highlighting the social divide between landlord and tenant; the payment of the tithe by the latter to the 'alien' Church and their continuing grievances over 'security of tenure' only entrenching the Radical cause in these places.[15] In Radnorshire, conversely, over 90 per cent of the population were monoglot English-speakers, 19,884 people against only 1,128 bilinguals in 1911. Similarly, there were said to have been 3,885 Anglicans in comparison to 4,861 Dissenters in 1905, by far the largest percentage for the former anywhere in Wales, with the exception of Flintshire. In addition, agricultural holdings, which dominated Radnorshire, tended to be larger and more prosperous, all factors shared to varying degrees by the significantly anglicized county divisions of South Monmouthshire and South Glamorgan, where the Tories also gained several election triumphs.[16]

The electoral boundary changes of 1917–18, together with the extension of the franchise, largely confirmed the seemingly permanent relegation of Welsh Conservatism into a minority political cause during the inter-war years. The Tories only ever secured thirty-seven election victories, excluding by-elections, in the thirty-six Welsh constituencies between 1918 and 1935. Although in terms of seats won this was a considerable improvement on the pre-war era, the Conservative percentage of the vote actually fell to 21·4 per cent during these years. The advent of three-party politics on a national scale, together with the formation of anti-Socialist agreements with Liberals in an attempt to halt the general advance of the Labour Party in Wales, were probably responsible for this decline.[17]

*Table 2*

| Year | Candidates | Unopposed | Elected | Total votes | % | Seats |
|------|-----------|-----------|---------|-------------|------|-------|
| 1918 | 8 | 0 | 4 | 59592 | 11·3 | 36 |
| 1922 | 19 | 1 | 6 | 190919 | 21·4 | 36 |
| 1923 | 19 | 0 | 4 | 178113 | 21·1 | 36 |
| 1924 | 17 | 0 | 9 | 224014 | 28·4 | 36 |
| 1929 | 36 | 0 | 1 | 289695 | 22·0 | 36 |
| 1931 | 14 | 0 | 6 | 240861 | 22·1 | 36 |
| 1935 | 14 | 0 | 6 | 204099 | 23·4 | 36 |

Average % 21·4

The Conservatives, moreover, narrowly failed to continue their pre-war tradition of performing considerably better in the borough constituencies than in the counties, the post-war totals, excluding by-elections, being eighteen to nineteen in favour of the latter.[18] Thus, while the division of Cardiff Boroughs into three seats appears to have assisted the Tories, and the broad continuation of Monmouth Boroughs under the name of Newport ensured that the comparatively strong Conservative tradition there was carried on into the post-war era, there were also adverse effects in the boundary changes. The abolition of the primarily Tory Denbigh and Montgomery borough constituencies undoubtedly weakened the Conservatives in north Wales where the party only won seats in 1924 and 1935. Similarly, the incorporation of significantly, if not predominantly, Tory Pembroke Boroughs into the surrounding county seat may well have contributed towards the reduction of the Conservative representation at Westminster.[19]

The county constituencies were extensively rearranged into twenty-five divisions, if the new single-member Welsh University seat is included with them.[20] Among the unitary counties, Flintshire was actually won on two occasions by the

Conservatives, their only victories throughout north Wales during the inter-war period. Though the Tories had never won this seat between 1885 and 1910, the generally 'English' character of much of the area, together with the relative strength of the Anglican Church, had probably been responsible for some fairly close election results, particularly in Flint Boroughs.[21] Similarly, Pembrokeshire, with its quite strong Conservative tradition in the Pembroke Boroughs and also in the 'Little England Beyond Wales' southern portion of the county, went Tory in 1924, and might well have done so again in 1931 had not the Liberals allegedly persuaded the Labour Party to refrain from contesting on the eve of nomination day.[22] On the other hand, the abolition of the pre-war Radnorshire division must surely have been detrimental to the Conservatives, since its absorption into much larger Breconshire, which although sometimes polling quite strongly at parliamentary level during the pre-war years never actually returned a Tory member, made the new constituency generally less favourable.[23] The increased post-war Conservative strength in the Welsh counties is, however, mostly accounted for by the fact that the new Monmouth seat proved to be, with its overwhelmingly anglicized and primarily rural composition, an impregnable Tory fortress. Similarly, the Boundary Commission's removal of the coal-mining components of South Glamorgan made the new Llandaff-Barry division much more fertile electoral territory for the Conservatives.[24]

## II

The first Welsh county council elections results of January 1889 were to prove to be yet another significant reversal in the fortunes of the Conservative Party in Wales. Many of the landed gentry who had ruled the countryside for centuries as justices of the peace, were defeated at the polls by usually middle-class Nonconformist Liberals.[25] Indeed, every Welsh county with the exception of Breconshire was captured by the Radicals, mostly by large electoral majorities, the Liberals winning no less than 215 of the 330 seats in south Wales and 179 out of the 264 in the north. Table 3 provides a detailed breakdown of the performances of the parties in the triennial contests of 1889 and 1892.[26]

*Table 3*

| Parties | Year 1889 | % | Year 1892 | % |
|---|---|---|---|---|
| Con., Un., Ind. | 200 | 33·7 | 194 | 32·7 |
| Lib., Rad. | 394 | 66·3 | 400 | 67·3 |
| Total | 594 | | 594 | |

In spite of the negative outcome of the first two county council elections as far as the Conservative Party in Wales was concerned, one must remember that the Tories, together with their Unionist and Independent allies, gained 33.7 per cent and 32.7 per cent of the overall political representation on the thirteen local authorities in 1889 and 1892 respectively, a phenomenon very broadly repeated in the triennial contests up to 1913.[27]

In the overwhelmingly Welsh-speaking, largely Nonconformist and primarily rural heartlands of Wales, such as Anglesey, Cardiganshire, Carmarthenshire and Merioneth, the Tories had been relegated to a marginal irrelevance, thereby simply confirming their generally abysmal parliamentary election results.[28] Moreover, in a heavily industrialized county, with still a significant Welsh-speaking population like Glamorgan, the Conservative councillors nearly all hailed from the area's most anglicized regions like the Vale of Glamorgan, the outskirts of Cardiff and the Gower peninsula, where religious Dissent seems to have been weakest.[29] A similar pattern of voting behaviour may well have existed in significantly anglicized Denbighshire and Pembrokeshire, where the Tories actually gained control of the former county council in 1895 and the latter in 1898. The Conservatives were, however, generally strongest at this level of government, as was frequently the case in parliamentary contests, in the parts of counties directly adjacent to England: Flintshire, Denbighshire, Montgomeryshire, Radnorshire, Breconshire and Monmouthshire. Indeed, the Tory strength in the eastern portions of Breconshire and Radnorshire probably made a decisive contribution to enabling them to obtain electoral majorities on these local authorities on several occasions from 1889 to 1913, while Flintshire was actually won outright by the party in 1910. In addition, the heavily anglicized enclave of east

Monmouthshire had arguably the highest Conservative county council political representation anywhere in the Principality, insufficient, however, to counterbalance the overall Radicalism of the industrial regions of the shire.[30]

# III

There can be little doubt that the Welsh Conservatives were in practice generally very poorly organized throughout most of the Principality, the *Western Mail* of 28 November 1893 going as far as to assert that except in a few towns like Cardiff, Newport and Swansea, the party's apparatus 'rarely appears in evidence except on state occasions'. Captain R. W. E. Middleton, the chief Tory agent at Central Office, conceded as much during the annual meeting of the National Union at Cardiff the same month, adding that unless the Conservative machinery in the Principality was greatly improved the party would be 'doomed' to continued electoral failure.[31] In his *Memories*, published in 1925, Sir A. S. T. Griffith-Boscawen, the former Coalition Minister of Agriculture and Fisheries, also testified to the perilous condition of Conservative organization in much of the Principality. This Wrexham-born son of an anglicized landlord conceded that 'the Welsh Conservatives are not good organizers. They have tremendous demonstrations and deliver magnificent speeches, and then nothing more happens until the next demonstration!'[32] Another retrospective account claimed that during the years prior to 1918, there were only 'about six' qualified party agents in the Principality, and 'in many constituencies' no active divisional associations were in existence. This unfavourable position was contrasted with the situation in 1928 when it was stated that there were now twenty-four full-time agents, covering twenty-eight seats, out of a total of thirty-six, and six part-time officials.[33]

From the mid-1880s until after the general election of 1906 the Conservative Party in Wales was organized into three provincial divisions of the National Union, these being the South Wales, North Wales, and Western division.[34] After the 1906 election defeat H. M. Imbert-Terry's decentralization scheme of party organization at Conservative Central Office was applied to Wales. This resulted in Glamorgan and Monmouthshire being made into separate provincial divisions. In the remainder of the Principality, the North Wales provincial division was left unaltered, while the remaining south Wales constituencies outside Glamorgan and Monmouthshire continued under their pre-1906 administrative grouping.[35] These general arrangements continued to operate during the inter-war era.

In October 1921, the Wales and Monmouthshire National Conservative Council was established. This organization was intended to co-ordinate the activities of the four existing provincial divisions, and enable the Tories to speak with a more unified voice on political issues specifically affecting the Principality. This body consisted of 392 members, including the officials of the provincial divisions, representatives, male, female and junior, from each of the thirty-six Welsh constituencies, party agents, club officials, parliamentary candidates, together with Conservative members in both Houses of Parliament hailing from the Principality. To oversee this new organization an executive committee numbering 117 people was also established, with a central core of twelve members to deal with 'matters of special importance'.[36]

A further development occurred in October 1923 when the annual meeting of the Wales and Monmouthshire National Conservative Council agreed to form an associated women's section for the Principality.[37] The first official gathering of the Welsh Conservative National Women's Council was held at Newport on 7 May 1924 when it was reported that the organization now had 17,000 subscribing members, the strongest branches being located in the Monmouth, Llandaff-Barry and Cardiff seats.[38] In 1925 the women's annual meeting was informed that there were twenty-eight central constituency ladies' Tory associations in existence out of a possible thirty-six, the eight exceptions being the four 'hopeless' mining divisions of Aberdare, Abertillery, Bedwellty and Merthyr Tydfil, together with overwhelmingly Welsh-speaking Caernarvonshire and Cardiganshire, and also diverse Montgomeryshire and the University of Wales. In addition, the women had supervised the establishment of forty-seven branches of the Junior Imperial League and fourteen unspecified 'juvenile' organizations, possibly embryonic groups of Young Britons, throughout the Principality.[39]

There seems to have been a further improvement in 1926, since not only had women's central committees been formed at

Aberdare and Abertillery, but the overall female membership was said to have increased by 'nearly 5,000' in south Wales and Monmouthshire, and by 'nearly 3,000' in north Wales, thereby making an overall addition of 'over 7,000' to the 1924 figure.[40] Indeed, such was the alleged success of the Junior Imperial League under the guidance of the women's association that it was permitted to establish its own organization for south Wales and Monmouthshire in May 1928, and for north Wales in August 1929.[41] The next located membership figures for the women's Conservative organization in Wales are those issued in April 1932, which claim that the number of adherents now 'exceeded 37,000' an increase of 'nearly 2,000' on 1930, with a central association now established in every Welsh constituency, apart from the University of Wales.[42]

None the less, there appears to have been an overall decline in the numerical strength of the Welsh Tory women from late 1932, possibly accounted for by the depth of the economic depression. Table 4 shows how the total had dropped since 1932.

*Table 4*

| Year | Membership |
| --- | --- |
| 1933 | 34356 |
| 1934 | 35122 |
| 1935 | 35133 |

Similarly, the annual meeting of the women's Conservative organization was informed in June 1936 that although the number of Young Britons branches in the Principality had increased from the previous year's total of twenty-eight to the current thirty-three, the overall membership of the ladies' association had remained static, and there had been a significant decline in the annual subscriptions received from £1,200 to only £821.[43]

# IV

One of the greatest obstacles faced by the Conservative Party in Wales was its perceived identification with 'Englishness' and

'English interests', a factor undoubtedly accentuated by the anglicized nature of its leadership.[44] The Revd J. V. Morgan, by no means a wholly unsympathetic Welsh Nonconformist minister, writing in 1914, summarized matters most accurately with the comment that 'Conservatism in Wales has never had a leader of the type of Mr Lloyd George'. Morgan then proceeded to claim with much plausibility that the social exclusiveness of the leadership of Welsh Toryism, largely restricted as it was to the English-speaking, English-educated and Anglican landlord class, was a virtually insurmountable obstacle to the emergence of populist Welsh Conservative orators who could communicate effectively with the still significantly monoglot Welsh-speaking masses.[45]

Some Tories such as the self-styled 'J.A.S.', writing in the National Union Conference handbook for 1908, claimed that the party had been severely handicapped in general elections owing to its selection of candidates who had been 'unfamiliar with Welsh conditions'.[46] J. V. Morgan was, however, at liberty to be even more critical about the unsuitability of the majority of the Tory standard bearers selected for Welsh seats:

> Conservative candidates of the aristocratic type proceed in their luxurious motor cars, smoking their Havanna cigars, to a meeting held in a small schoolroom in a country parish, then speak a language foreign to the natives . . . their candidature is nothing less than an insult to the community.[47]

An analysis of the background of those fifteen Tory members elected to Westminster between 1918 and 1935 demonstrates that they frequently hailed from the landowning and commercial classes. Moreover, every member, with the exception of Gwilym Rowlands, were non-Welsh speakers, and were elected in those divisions within the Principality where the greatest anglicization had taken place. Table 5 lists these members, the constituencies held by them, the duration of their representation, and their occupations.[48]

In attempting to summarize the reasons for this almost invariably unfavourable Tory electoral position in Wales, one can state that the social exclusiveness of the leadership of Welsh Conservatism, its association with perceived 'English' interests, particularly the Anglican Church, and the generally poor

Table 5

| Name | Constituency | Duration | Occupation |
|------|-------------|----------|-----------|
| R. G. Clarry | Newport | 1922–9, 1931–45 | Gas engineer |
| C. K. Cook | Cardiff East | 1924–9 | Barrister |
| William Cope | Llandaff-Barry | 1918–29 | Company director |
| J. H. Cory | Cardiff South | 1918–23 | Shipowner |
| H. A. Evans | Cardiff South | 1924–9, 1931–45 | Businessman |
| C. L. Forestier-Walker | Monmouth | 1918–34 | Company director |
| J. C. Gould | Cardiff Central | 1918–24 | Shipowner |
| W. D. Hall | Brecon and Radnor | 1924–9, 1931–5 | Landowner |
| J. A. Herbert | Monmouth | 1934–9 | Landowner |
| Lewis Lougher | Cardiff East | 1922–3 | Shipowner |
|  | Cardiff Central | 1924–9 |  |
| O. T. Morris | Cardiff East | 1931–42 | Barrister |
| Patrick Munro | Llandaff-Barry | 1931–42 | Diplomat |
| C. W. M. Price | Pembroke | 1924–9 | Solicitor |
| E. H. G. Roberts | Flint | 1924–9 | Barrister |
| Gwilym Rowlands | Flint | 1935–45 | Coal merchant |

organization of the party throughout most of the Principality were responsible for the Tory failure to capitalize on the dramatic political upheavals within Liberalism which occurred during the inter-war years. In the 1920s the Conservatives performed little better in the Principality than before the First World War, and occasionally they did worse. Apart from the most anglicized portions of Wales, like Cardiff, Llandaff-Barry and Monmouth, where some middle-class Liberals defected to the Tories during the 1920s and 1930s in an attempt to combat the rising tide of socialism, a phenomenon sometimes repeated in the mining valleys, many traditional Radicals found their new political home in the Labour Party.[49]

As regards Welsh-speaking rural Wales, the Conservative Party's failure to exploit socio-economic developments in the countryside to its own electoral advantage led to it being continually marginalized in the politics of these areas. In his analysis of Welsh politics, T. H. Davies clearly demonstrated that, prior to 1914, the tenant farmer and agricultural labourer had both regarded 'the big Tory landowner as the tyrant'. However, by the 1920s, many tenant farmers had become landowners themselves and the gulf between them and their workers was widening.[50] There was thus an increasing common interest between the old landlord class and the new property-owning democracy, accelerated perhaps by the decline in religious sectarianism as a consequence of disestablishment being finally achieved in 1920. This could have benefited the Conservatives electorally, if only they had become more populist and sympathetic to Welsh sentiments. In the final analysis, the Liberals were able to occupy this 'conservative' ground in Welsh politics only because of the failure of the Conservative Party to acquire a truly Welsh electoral appeal.[51]

## Notes

1  All references are taken from F. F. E. Aubel, 'Welsh Conservatism 1885–1935: Five Studies in Adaptation' (unpublished Ph.D. thesis, Wales, 1994); *South Wales Daily News*, 27 January 1874; *Pall Mall Gazette*, 17 October 1884.
2  *The Cambrian*, 30 April 1880; *South Wales Daily News*, 2 July 1892; *Barry Dock News*, 6 June 1913.
3  *Western Mail*, 18 July 1892.
4  *Glamorgan County Times*, 17 December 1921.
5  *Western Mail*, 21 September 1929.
6  J. P. Jenkins, *A History of Modern Wales 1536–1990* (London, 1992), 330; A. J. James and J. E. Thomas, *Wales at Westminster: A History of the Parliamentary Representation of Wales 1800–1979* (Llandysul, 1981), 69. Merthyr Boroughs returned two members.
7  F. W. S. Craig, *British Electoral Facts 1832–1987* (Aldershot, 1989), 13–20; M. Kinnear, *The British Voter: An Atlas and Survey since 1885* (London, 1981), 13–32.
8  H. M. Pelling, *Social Geography of British Elections 1885–1910* (London, 1967), 358
9  James and Thomas, *Wales at Westminster*, 206–7.
10 Pelling, *Social Geography of British Elections*, 363; F.W.S. Craig, *British Parliamentary Election Results 1885–1910* (Aldershot, 1989), 467–88.
11 Pelling, *Social Geography of British Elections*, 357–8.
12 M. Pugh, *The Tories and the People 1880–1935* (Oxford, 1985), 134–5.
13 Pelling, *Social Geography of British Elections*, 368; K. O. Morgan, *Rebirth of a Nation: Wales 1880–1980* (Oxford, 1981), 40–1; *Western Mail*, 15 January 1910.
14 D. W. Howell, *Land and People in Nineteenth-Century Wales* (London, 1978), 42, 85, 89; D. N. Cannadine, *The Decline and Fall of the British Aristocracy* (New Haven, 1990), 59; *Welsh Gazette*, 13 January 1910.

[15] Pelling, *Social Geography of British Elections*, 348; J. Davies, 'The End of the Great Estates and the Rise of Freehold Farming in Wales', *Welsh History Review* 7 (December 1974), 186–211.

[16] K. O. Morgan, *Wales in British Politics 1868-1922* (Cardiff, 1980), 315–16; G. E. Jones, *Modern Wales: A Concise History c. 1485–1979* (Cambridge, 1984), 249.

[17] F. W. S. Craig, *British Electoral Facts 1832-1987*, 21–33; D. E. Butler and G. Butler, *British Political Facts 1900–1985* (London, 1986), 230–1.

[18] James and Thomas, *Wales at Westminster*, 208–9.

[19] F. W. S. Craig, *British Parliamentary Election Results 1918-1949* (Glasgow, 1969), 533–70.

[20] James and Thomas, *Wales at Westminster*, 209.

[21] Pelling, *Social Geography of British Elections*, 351–67.

[22] *South Wales Daily News*, 14 April 1892; *Western Mail*, 17 October 1931.

[23] Pelling, *Social Geography of British Elections*, 363–4.

[24] *Boundary Commission (England and Wales) 1885*, I:122, 69; *Boundary Commission (England and Wales) 1917*, II:56, 54.

[25] Morgan, *Rebirth of a Nation*, 52.

[26] *Caernarvon and Denbigh Herald*, 1 February 1889, 11 March 1892 .

[27] *South Wales Daily News*, *Western Mail*, January 1889, March 1892–1913.

[28] Jenkins, *History of Modern Wales*, 331.

[29] *South Wales Daily News*, 21 January 1889.

[30] *Western Mail*, 11 March 1892, 9 March 1895, 5 March 1910, 11 March 1913; *Star of Gwent*, 15 March 1895.

[31] *Western Mail*, 28–9 November 1893; *Who Was Who*, I: 1897–1915 (London, 1920), 359.

[32] A. S. T. Griffith-Boscawen, *Memories* (London, 1925), 57, 64; *Who Was Who*, IV: *1941–1950* (London, 1952), 473.

[33] *Western Mail*, 28 February 1928.

[34] *Western Mail*, 23 November 1893, 13–16 February 1897.

[35] *Who Was Who*, III: *1929–1940* (London, 1941), 689–90; *Western Mail*, 1–3 November 1911.

[36] *Western Mail*, 26 October 1921; *Glamorgan County Times*, 22 and 29 October 1921; *Monmouthshire Beacon*, 16 December 1921.

[37] *Western Mail*, 6 October 1923.

[38] *Glamorgan County Times*, 10 May 1924.

[39] *Western Mail*, 14 May 1925.

[40] *Glamorgan County Times*, 2 October 1926.

[41] *Western Mail*, 10 May 1928, 2 August 1929; *The Imp*, July 1929.

[42] *Western Mail*, 22 April 1932.

[43] *Western Mail*, 18 May 1935, 27 June 1936.

[44] *The Cambrian*, 30 April 1880; *Carmarthen Journal*, 22 July 1892; *Western Mail*, 23 November 1893, 30 May 1929; Morgan, *Rebirth of a Nation*, 46; Jenkins, *History of Modern Wales*, 327–8.

45 J. V. Morgan, *The Philosophy of Welsh History* (London, 1914), 162.

46 'J.A.S.', 'The Welsh Nation and the Conservative Party', in *The National Union of Conservative and Constitutional Associations: Souvenir of the Forty-Second Annual Conference* (Cardiff, 1908), 9–11.

47 Morgan, *Rebirth of a Nation*, 161–2.

48 M. Stenton and S. Lees (eds.), *Who's Who of British Members of Parliament*, III: *1919–1945* (Sussex, 1979); B. Jones, *Parliamentary Elections in Wales 1900–1975* (Talybont, 1977).

49 M. Kinnear, *The Fall of Lloyd George: The Political Crisis of 1922* (London, 1973), 177–9.

50 T. H. Davies, 'Politics 1914–1933', *Welsh Outlook* 20 (December 1933), 341.

51 A. B. Philip, *The Welsh Question: Nationalism in Welsh Politics 1945–1970* (Cardiff, 1975), 312; F. F. E. Aubel, 'Cardiganshire Parliamentary Elections and their Backgrounds 1921–32' (unpublished M.Phil. thesis, Wales, 1989), 232–3.

# Scottish Conservatism and Unionism since 1918

### RICHARD FINLAY

The object of this chapter is to give a brief overview of the development of the Conservative Party in Scotland since 1918. In particular, it will focus on how Unionists, as Conservatives were called in Scotland until 1965, maintained a distinctive Scottish political identity north of the border and how the party responded to the particular challenges and changes to the Anglo-Scottish Union in this period.

The Scottish Unionist Party emerged in good shape after the First World War. The rise of the Labour Party, industrial militancy, middle-class fears of 'Bolshevism' and the seemingly intractable difficulties faced by a divided Liberal Party, all provided an excellent opportunity for the Scottish Unionists to assert themselves as the dominant anti-socialist force in Scottish politics.[1] While much scholarly attention has been focused on the 'Red' Clyde and the extent to which it was a genuine revolutionary moment, the fact remains that in the contemporary Scottish middle-class imagination, Red Clydeside was no myth.[2] Just as the working class began to flex its political muscles, the middle class mobilized more rapidly and thoroughly in response to the dangers of socialism. The Middle Class Union, the Junior Imperial League and the Young Unionists were formed or reformed to combat the spread of socialism and working-class militancy. In the strikes of 1919, middle-class volunteers turned out to do their bit to keep the country running.[3] A point often neglected in Scottish historiography is how effective and cohesive the Scottish middle class remained in the face of the Labour challenge which in 1918 witnessed a landslide for the Coalition. The general election result of 1918 was a good one for the Unionists, especially given their pre-war weakness. Thirty-two candidates were returned against their pre-war total of eleven. The intervention of the Labour Party had the effect of dividing the progressive vote, which meant that out of Scotland's seventy-two seats, only eight Liberals were returned without the Coupon, while Labour won seven.[4]

The general election of 1918 had shown how powerful the anti-socialist lobby was in Scotland, and Unionist policy was aimed at capturing this. Yet, the Unionists had to compete with the Liberal Party which preached class conciliation and whose pre-war message still had a powerful resonance in Scottish politics.[5] Furthermore, both the Unionist and the Liberal commitment to the cause of anti-socialism was powerful enough to override conventional party politics. Indeed, one of the hallmarks of post-1918 Scottish politics was the tendency of local Unionist and Liberal constituencies to agree to stand down if it was thought that the anti-socialist vote was in danger of dividing to let in a Labour candidate. Scottish Unionists and their Liberal allies were the most vociferous defenders of the Coalition and in the general election of 1922 the pact was maintained to cover almost two-thirds of all Scottish constituencies. Informal pacts between Unionists and Liberals still continued in the election of 1923.[6] Given that the local elections following the Coupon Election showed a steady rise in Labour support and lingering working-class militancy, it is not surprising that an anti-socialist bloc should find so much favour north of the border. Whereas many in the Tory heartlands of the south were insulated from the socialist advance, Scottish Unionists felt themselves to be on the front line and, as the general election of 1922 graphically illustrated, when Labour broke through to gain twenty-nine seats, their scalps were ripe for the taking.

The long-drawn-out disintegration of the Liberal Party prevented the Unionists from monopolizing the anti-socialist vote until 1924. Given that the presence of a sitting candidate was of paramount importance in dictating the anti-socialist campaign in a particular constituency, Unionists found that this often meant using the constituency machine to support a sitting Liberal.[7] Unionist fortunes took a turn for the better after the 1923 election, although the election result was not particularly good. The Liberals were united around the old shibboleth of free trade which still managed to strike a chord in Scottish society. Also, the Labour Party made further progress and the prospect of a Labour government looked like a distinct possibility which further raised anti-socialist hackles.[8] Asquith's decision to support the minority Labour government sounded the death knell of Liberal anti-socialist pretensions. His decision horrified business leaders in his Paisley constituency, all of whom pointed out that maintaining his anti-socialist credentials were essential to Liberal Party fortunes in Scotland.[9] The Unionist press had a field day, denouncing Liberal claims of class conciliation as class capitulation.[10] In the almost hysterical anti-communist fever of the 1924 general election, the Unionists were able to parade their unblemished anti-socialist credentials to good effect and put in their best electoral performance in Scotland since 1900 by capturing thirty-eight seats with over 40 per cent of the vote. The party was now the undisputed champion of anti-socialism in Scotland.

The realignment on the right of Scottish politics was not simply due to Liberal weakness, although the party's deep-seated divisions and its failing organization meant that it was unlikely to be able to sustain an important role in Scottish politics.[11] Unionist organization, however, was overhauled, with membership in Glasgow alone increasing from 7,000 in 1913 to 20,000 in 1922 and 32,000 in 1929.[12] The young, women and farming interests were targeted. Throughout village halls, women were warned by Lady Baxter of the 'horrors of Bolshevism and that it was neither wise nor kind to protect them from such knowledge, however unpleasant'.[13] The rural vote proved susceptible to the Unionist message. The break-up of great estates and the purchase by tenant farmers of their own farms during and after the war created a ready-made clientele for the Unionist Party. Liberal policy was tainted with anti-landlord sentiment and Labour's policy of land nationalization left the Unionists as the natural party of the farmers. Furthermore, increasing unionization of farm labour exacerbated class tensions in the countryside. In the 1924 general election, the Unionists were able to capture twenty-two county seats from the Liberals, clearly illustrating that the rural anti-socialist bloc had coalesced around the Unionist Party.[14] In the towns and cities, the Unionists were sharpening up their message to claim the anti-socialist inheritance. The abandonment of protection in 1924 removed a major stumbling block to the wholesale conversion of the middle class to Unionism in the west of Scotland.[15] Also, the party began to shed its 'die-hard' image, with some progressive Conservatives such as Noel Skelton, John Buchan, Walter Elliot and Bob Boothby coming increasingly to the fore. The removal of the Irish question in Scottish politics, likewise, gave the party's hard-liners less opportunity to air their extremist 'no surrender' views. The close and often turbulent relationship with the proletarian and unrespectable Orange Order was no longer deemed to be a priority as the party focused its attention almost exclusively on middle-class concerns. Even during the height of Protestant extremism during the inter-war period, the Unionist Party was careful to distance itself from sectarian rabble rousers.[16]

Scottish politics in the 1930s was dominated by the impact of the Great Depression and the resultant economic and social dislocation which followed in its wake. Statistic after statistic showed that the Scottish economy was more adversely affected than the south, and social indicators such as unemployment, infant mortality, health and housing all illustrated the extent to which Scotland was trailing the United Kingdom in terms of life chances.[17] Although the political crisis of 1931 and the ensuing general election had left the Unionist Party in Scotland with an unassailable hegemony, the persistence of endemic social and economic problems gave rise to widespread dissatisfaction as to the government's handling of the crisis, and increasingly such grievances were taking on a nationalist air.[18] Whereas nationalism in the 1920s was associated with the left and consequently of little concern to Unionists, in the 1930s, however, nationalist discontent was emanating from traditional middle-class quarters. Normally quiescent Unionist allies in the Scottish press were highlighting how government policies were tapered for the economy of the south of England and that these often worked to the detriment of the Scottish economy. According to one Glasgow businessman: 'Scotland has her own particular problems and we will never make much progress until masters and men alike realise that what applies to England does not necessarily apply here.'[19] A flood of publications appeared, mostly written from a centre-right perspective, bemoaning the fate of Scottish society, economy and culture. For many it seemed that the nation was locked into a spiral of decline. Opinion polls showed support for some measure of Home Rule to be on the increase and the Scottish Unionists suffered a nationalist secession in Cathcart. The Scottish National Party appeared to be attracting moderate opinion and while most Unionists did not endorse Scottish nationalism or Home Rule, they openly acknowledged that it was founded on legitimate grievances.[20] The nationalists, according to John Buchan, were driven by an 'honourable fear' and furthermore, most Unionists were convinced that unless the problems of the Scottish economy were rectified, the nationalists would emerge as a major force in Scottish politics.[21]

The fundamental problem facing Unionists was to reconstruct and adapt their ideology to the changed circumstances of the 1930s. Pre-war Unionism was founded on the premise that Scotland was an equal partner with England in the imperial mission.[22] Scottish soldiers, generals, missionaries, colonial governor generals, emigrants and businessmen, it was argued, had helped to build and sustain the Empire. The Scots prided themselves on being a 'race of Empire builders'. Scottish economic prosperity was based to a large extent on imperial trade and Glasgow flourished as the 'Second City of the Empire'. Scottish soldiers and generals had proved the martial prowess of the Scottish nation in imperial campaigns. Emigrants proved the drive and entrepreneurial vitality of the Scots, and products of the Scottish education system played a large part in imperial administration. These factors and others were fundamental pillars of Scottish national identity before 1914, and pre-war Unionism was confident and strident in these assumptions. No political party had a monopoly over Unionism and these values were equally endorsed by the Liberal Party. Ironically, the pre-war Scottish Unionist Party was more interested in the Irish Union than the Scottish one.[23] The inter-war period witnessed a crisis of national identity in Scotland as the fundamental pillars of Scottish middle-class imperial identity were swept away by the dislocations following the First World War. Militarism was no longer held in such high esteem, Scotland was no longer the workshop of the Empire, the flood of emigration was evidence of poor opportunities at home, and in a mass democracy few were interested in the appointment of another Scottish colonial governor general.[24]

The dislocations following the war challenged many of the pre-war assumptions regarding the efficacy of the Union and the Unionist Party was forced by the mounting discontent to address this.

Historically, the Unionists had always acknowledged the legitimacy of Scottish national sentiment and had often used it to good effect.[25] The problem facing Unionists in the 1930s was twofold. Firstly, how to acknowledge the legitimacy of nationalist sentiment without encouraging political separatism, and secondly how to solve the structural deficiencies of the Scottish economy which were giving rise to nationalist sentiment in the first place. The Scottish Unionist Party had two camps of thought about the economic problems: class warriors and class conciliators. The class warriors were associated with the western Scottish industrialists who adopted a 'wait and see' attitude to the problems of economic dislocation. They were reluctant to diversify away from the heavy industries in the expectation that things would pick up again and their solution to the problem of overcapacity was defensive amalgamations, which had the effect of more tightly interlinking the Scottish economy under a self-contained industrial oligarchy.[26] Class warriors such as Sir James Lithgow, Sir Steven Bisland, John Craig, J. P. McLay and Sir Robert Horne were unremitting in their hostility to trade unions and working-class political organizations. The Economic League was used to identify left-wing agitators, and the industrialists gave solid support to the organization in its anti-socialist crusade.[27] Also, they were equally hostile to state expenditure on social welfare. According to Lithgow: 'There is a large body which appears to expect everything from the state but is prepared to give nothing in return.'[28] Furthermore, he argued, there ought to be a 'judicious pruning, in the interests of industry, of social services which had out-stripped the bounds of healthy growth'.[29] Class warriors, however, were not against state intervention in the economy, if it suited their own interests. Given that they were heavily dependent on government orders for warships, the industrial wing of the party openly welcomed state subsidies for shipbuilding.[30] Also, the industrialists dominated the quasi-official agencies which had the remit of inquiry into Scottish economic problems, such as the Scottish Development Council.[31] Given the reluctance of Scottish industrialists to instigate any fundamental reforms of the Scottish economy, the endemic structural faults would remain and recovery was only possible due to rearmament in the late 1930s, which further increased the power of the industrialists in the economic life of the nation. Yet, as the Scottish Secretary of State, Walter Elliot, conceded in 1937, without solving the fundamental social and economic problems, the 'dissatisfaction and unease amongst moderate and reasonable people of every rank – a dissatisfaction expressed in every book written about Scotland now for several years' would remain.[32]

Class conciliators, such as Walter Elliot, argued for greater state intervention to improve social conditions. Numerous committees were established to examine the problems of the Scottish economy and make suggestions as to how it could be revitalized.[33] The prime motivation behind this, however, was to give the appearance of action, because such bodies lacked any real power and offered no real solutions. The Scottish Economic Committee, the Special Areas Reconstruction Association, the Glasgow Empire Exhibition and the Hillington Industrial Estate were all designed to promote new industries and employment opportunities, but only dented the surface of the problem.[34] At times, Unionist frustration at the seeming intractability of the problems, combined with Whitehall indifference, boiled to the surface. Walter Elliot could not contain himself over the decision to scrap the Cunard cruiser in 1932:

> The question is not so simple from the point of view of workers on the Clyde. Government can scrap cruisers and claim the money for something else. But the people of Scotland know that officials are too apt to spend money saved on bridges in London, and carrying out other work in England, while there is more than enough unemployment in Scotland.[35]

Robert Boothby, caught on an off-guard moment, claimed that 'the real interests of Scotland have been sacrificed to those of England'.[36] Class conciliators were well aware that a policy of inaction would fuel increasing nationalist resentment and were prepared to make maximum use of the limited powers of government available to them. Unfortunately, they could only offer piecemeal solutions to the problems of mass unemployment. However, widespread circulation of proposals such as giving free milk to needy school children illustrated a concern to do something to alleviate the impact of poverty.[37]

The nature of Unionism as a political philosophy underwent a radical change in the 1930s in response to the perceived upsurge in Scottish nationalist sentiment. The confident and strident notions of pre-war 'imperial Scotland' were replaced with a negative and defeatist approach to the difficulties of economic dislocation. Scottish nationalism was countered with arguments of Scottish dependency. Sir Robert Horne berated his fellow countrymen for abandoning their usual canny approach to fiscal matters:

> The Welsh are showing the kind of wisdom that is generally attributed to the Scots, because, knowing that the amount of their unemployment is so much greater than elsewhere, probably they realise that they would find great difficulty in providing unemployment benefit by themselves, and they are wise to rely on the richer country than to seek separation.[38]

Industrialists warned that any move towards separation would have disastrous economic consequences. The message was clearly relayed that if people thought things were bad at the moment, the creation of a Scottish parliament would make things worse.[39] Time and again, it was emphasized that Scotland needed England to survive. Unionism increasingly degenerated into nothing more than a sentimental appeal to past imperial achievements. 'What was the parrot cry of home rule', asked Bob Boothby, when compared to 'our phenomenal control over a world-wide empire that has made the name of Scotland famous, admired and respected in every quarter of the globe'.[40] The Glasgow Empire Exhibition in 1938 was an attempt to utilize imperial sentiment to inject a 'feel-good' factor in Scottish politics.[41] Unable to offer a practical solution to the difficulties of the Scottish situation, Unionism increasingly retreated into negative and defeatist national self-effacement.

Increasingly Unionists found that the only way to appease Scottish sentiment was through gesture politics. The relocation of the Scottish Office to Edinburgh, following the publication of the Gilmour Report in 1937, was an attempt to bring Scottish government closer to the people and satisfy nationalist sentiment by providing a symbolic figurehead to the distinctiveness of Scotland's position within the United Kingdom. Administrative devolution, it was hoped, would circumvent the demand for Home Rule by giving the Scots better government, as opposed to more government.[42] Unlike the reforms of 1928, the relocation of the

Scottish Office was carefully packaged to give the impression that the Scots would enjoy more 'administrative autonomy' and would be able to deal with their own problems in their own way without interference from Westminster.[43] The number of royal visits was increased, more money was found for Scottish libraries and museums, records removed from Scotland in the reign of Edward I were returned as a gesture of good will, and the Glasgow Empire Exhibition of 1938 made great play of Scotland's role as a mother nation of the empire.[44] All were designed to reinforce the notion that Scottish nationality could be accommodated within the Union. However, as most were prepared to admit, the only long-term guarantee for the security of the Union and the well-being of the Unionist Party lay in a fundamental restructuring of the Scottish economy.

The Second World War and the ideological triumph of corporatism provided a much needed ideological boost for Unionism in Scotland because it provided the necessary apparatus to remedy the endemic social and economic problems which had plagued Scottish politicians in the inter-war era. The feeling of helplessness in the 1930s had softened up many Scottish Unionists to accept that corporatism and government intervention was the only possible option to regenerate the Scottish economy and solve the desperate social problems. Unionists played a major part in formulating post-war reconstruction policy through the Committee of Ex-Secretaries of State, which was set up by the Labour Scottish Secretary of State, Tom Johnston.[45] While there has been a tendency to represent the government of Johnston as a new departure in Scottish politics, it should be noted that in style and substance it was very similar to the various committees which were formed in the 1930s. The wartime quangos were following established practice and the only real difference was that the pale was extended to take in the representatives of organized labour.[46] The demand-managed economy was also attractive to the industrial wing of the party who saw the opportunity for guaranteed orders.[47] The creation of the welfare state in Scotland was designed to ensure that administration would remain within the control of the Scottish Office.[48] The wholesale devolution of administrative power to Scotland during the war was favourably endorsed by Scottish Unionists because it ensured that important decisions were taken by the Scottish political élite themselves, and it had the added bonus that it was not democratically accountable. Corporatism was finally able to plug the vacuum created by the collapse of imperial prosperity.

While Scottish Unionists acquiesced in the building of the welfare state, they used a distinctive Scottish dimension to criticize the policies of the Attlee government, in particular nationalization, because it meant removing control of key Scottish industries to London. Unionists in Scotland made political capital out of the attack on centralization which, they claimed, harmed Scottish interests and undermined the notion of 'an equal partnership with England'. Socialism was denounced more for its tendency to remove industrial control to England than for its attack on the rights of property. Demands were made for separate Scottish authorities to control nationalized industries in Scotland.[49] The Balfour Commission was denounced because it referred to Scotland as a 'region' and the Unionists used the Scottish flag in their election campaigns of 1951 and 1955. The early 1950s witnessed an upsurge of Scottish national unease, most of which came from the middle class and was exemplified over concerns about nationalization, and the use of the numeral 'II' at the coronation of Queen Elizabeth; it expressed itself in the Scottish National Convention, the stealing of the Stone of Destiny and the blowing up of postal boxes with the offending 'II'.[50] The extent to which nationalist sentiment played a major role in Scottish political development at this time is a debatable point. However, there was a perception at the time, and one which still largely holds today, that the Unionist success in the 1955 general election, in which they secured just over half of the total votes cast in Scotland, owed a significant part to their ability to capitalize on Scottish national concerns. The important point to be emphasized here is that the Conservatives maintained a distinctive identity north of the border in the 1950s.

While Unionist policy eschewed political devolution in the 1950s, sympathetic noises were made towards the principle of greater administrative autonomy in Scotland. Just as Labour attitudes towards Scottish Home Rule were hardening in the wake of nationalist flirtations with the Conservatives, particularly at the Paisley by-election of 1948, Scottish Tories found that nationalist overtures and 'playing the Scottish card' afforded them a distinctive edge in their policies north of the border. The

Conservatives made much of the claim that they were out to protect the interests of Scotland while projecting Labour as the party of centralization and 'London' government:

> Union is not amalgamation. Scotland is a nation . . . It is only since 1945, under the first socialist majority, that we have seen the policy of amalgamation superseding that of Union. This must inevitably result from the fulfilment of the socialist creed, which is basically one of amalgamation and centralisation. To this policy we are fundamentally opposed.[51]

The principle that the Union was a partnership of two distinctive nations was trumpeted in contradistinction to Labour's message of British uniformity, especially as in 1957 it abandoned any pretence of support for a Scottish parliament.[52] In other words, the electorate was told that if they wanted Scotland to remain distinctive, they should vote Unionist. Given such leanings, Heath's 'Declaration of Perth' in 1968, in which the party endorsed political devolution, need not be interpreted as such a radical departure from previous policy. The Conservative Party in Scotland had always accepted the principle of a distinctive national dimension in Scottish politics, and as a consequence of this there was always the potential for acknowledging this within the framework of political devolution. However, Heath's intention was to impose modernization on the party from above in response to the rise of the Scottish Nationalist Party which he believed was the new coming force in British politics.[53] However, the leadership underestimated the latent hostility to devolution within the rank and file and it never enjoyed total support. Ideologically, Scottish Unionists have been conditioned to accept that Scottish nationality is not dependent on separate political representation. Devolution officially remained part of the Scottish Conservative Party's manifesto until 1979.

In spite of these tartan trappings, Scottish politics in the period from the early 1950s to the late 1960s was mainly determined by the British political agenda. The main ebbs and flows of the British electoral system were also experienced in Scotland.[54] In terms of percentage votes, the period from 1945 to 1959 was one of remarkable stability with the vagaries of the British electoral system responsible for the movements in numbers of MPs. Although the decline of the Unionist Party in Scotland is dated from the early sixties, some caution ought to be exercised here. Firstly, Conservative support hovered just under the 40 per cent mark in general elections until 1970. Secondly, although the tally of Scottish MPs was hardly impressive, this was due to vote inefficiency. For example, in 1970 with 38 per cent of the vote the Conservatives won twenty-three seats compared to Labour which won forty-four seats with 44·5 per cent of the vote. It is worth pointing out that the situation in Scotland was the reverse of England, where the Tories enjoyed high vote efficiency and Labour low vote efficiency. Also, in the mid-1970s when Conservative support fell due to the rise of the SNP, it is worth stressing that Labour support fell by a similar amount, although Labour vote efficiency prevented any substantial drop in the number of MPs elected. A case could be made that the Conservative decline before 1974 in Scotland was rather more apparent than real. There is no doubt that the Unionists were losing support in the 1960s and early 1970s, mainly because of the decline of the tradition of working-class Unionism which had based much of its appeal on popular Scottish Protestantism.[55] Indeed, the party changed its name to the Scottish *Conservative* and Unionist Party in 1965 to bring it more in line with the English party. Labour's ability to present itself as the champion of the corporate state cost the Tories traditional west-coast Protestant, working-class support. However, given that the Conservatives were the party of the middle class (and it has to be remembered that the middle class formed a smaller proportion of society in Scotland than was the case in England, with only 26 per cent of the population owner-occupiers in 1970), it is clear that the Conservatives were not only holding the middle-class vote but were still able to retain a significant part of the working-class vote throughout the 1960s. Even during the low ebb of the mid-1970s when support dropped to only 25 per cent of the electorate, by the general election of 1979 this had improved to 30 per cent.

The advent of Thatcherism marks an important watershed in Scottish political history and it is really from this point in time that the Conservative Party begins to experience real difficulty north of the border. Indeed, it has been the decline of the Conservatives which has marked the political divergence of Scotland and England (though not Wales). The following reasons may be suggested. Firstly, the attack on corporatism was not widely endorsed by the Scottish middle class. Indeed, to some extent, corporatism had become part and parcel of Scottish middle-class values, as many had benefited substantially from these policies in the past. The attack on corporatism was perceived as an attack on Scottish political culture *per se*. Secondly, the Conservatives were unable to promote a distinctive Scottish dimension, and the party was increasingly seen as the party of middle England. The vacuum in Unionist ideology which had been plugged with corporatism reappeared and exposed significant contradictions in Conservative philosophy. In England the message was independence and self-reliance; the state would take a back seat. In Scotland it was a return to the message of the 1930s that the Scots were subsidized and dependent on government expenditure. As the opposition parties put some form of self-government at the centre of their Scottish policies the Tories increasingly used the argument of dependency in defence of the Union. Apart from saying different things in Scotland and England, the dependency argument is not one that readily appeals to the traditional middle-class voter. Unionism was negative and defeatist and in spite of the recent *Taking Stock* exercise which attempted to promote Scotland as a nation within the Union (the decision to host the European Summit in Edinburgh as a European capital in 1993 is a good example of the attempt to regenerate Scottish nationality within the Union), the Conservatives in Scotland lacked the vital Scottish dimension which the opposition parties had. The third and final reason concerns British identity in Scotland. Corporatism and the welfare state were instrumental in making the Scots feel that the Union with Britain was worth something. The welfare state and the managed economy were vital in promoting a new sense of Britishness in Scotland after 1945, and by and large this held good until 1979. However, the Thatcherite attack on consensus values robbed the Scots of an acceptable vision of Britain, and paradoxically the upsurge in Scottish nationalism has been fuelled by a desire to preserve what are fundamentally British institutions such as the health service and comprehensive education. The Scots have painted the ideology of welfare statism tartan and called it their own.[56] The point to be stressed is that in fundamentals, the English nation changed its political values in 1979 more than the Scots or the Welsh, and, in this context, Conservatism and the Conservative governments have been interpreted as *English* and alien. It is this cultural perception, more than anything, which explains recent Scottish political behaviour and the decline of Conservatism.

## Notes

[1] See I. G. C. Hutchison, *A Political History of Scotland, 1832–1924: Parties, Elections and Issues* (Edinburgh, 1986), 309–33; I. McLean, *The Legend of Red Clydeside* (Edinburgh, 1983), 111–39; R. J. Finlay, 'Continuity and Change: Scottish Politics, 1900–45', in T. M. Devine and R. J. Finlay (eds.), *Scotland in the Twentieth Century* (Edinburgh, 1996); and J. Melling, *Rent Strike* (Edinburgh, 1983).

[2] See T. Brotherstone, 'Does Red Clydeside Matter Any More?', in R. Duncan and A. McIvor (eds.), *Militant Workers: Labour and Class Conflict on the Clyde 1900–1950* (Edinburgh, 1992), 52–80.

[3] Hutchison, *Political History*, 309–18.

[4] Ibid.

[5] Ibid.; Finlay, 'Continuity and Change'.

[6] Hutchison, *Political History*, 318–21.

[7] Ibid., 320–3.

[8] See I. S. Wood, 'Hope Deferred: Labour in Scotland in the 1920s', in I. Donnachie, C. Harvie and I. S. Wood (eds.), *Forward! Labour Politics in Scotland 1888–1980* (Edinburgh, 1989), 30–48.

[9] C. MacDonald, 'The Radical Thread: Paisley Politics, 1880–1924' (unpublished Ph.D. thesis, University of Strathclyde, 1995), chapter 8; and Hutchison, *Political History*, 326.

[10] *Daily Record*, 20 December 1923, and *Glasgow Herald*, 18 January 1924.

[11] Hutchison, *Political History*, 321–8.

[12] C. Harvie, *No Gods and Precious Few Heroes: Scotland 1914–1980* (London, 1981), 90.

[13] Quoted in Hutchison, *Political History*, 317.

[14] Ibid., 319–21.

[15] Ibid.

[16] S. J. Brown, 'Outside the Covenant: The Scottish Presbyterian Churches and Irish Immigration, 1922–38', *Innes Review* LXII (Spring 1991), 19–45; and R. J. Finlay, 'Nationalism, Race, Religion and the "Irish Question" in Inter-War Scotland', *Innes Review* LXII (Spring 1991), 46–67.

[17] See R. J. Finlay, 'National Identity in Crisis: Politicians, Intellectuals and the "End of Scotland", 1920–39', *History* 79 (1994), 242–59.

[18] Ibid., 248.

[19] *Glasgow Chambers of Commerce Journal* (August 1932).

[20] R. J. Finlay, *Independent and Free: Scottish Politics and the Origins of the Scottish National Party, 1918–1945* (Edinburgh, 1994), 156–73.

[21] See in particular HC Deb 5th ser, vol.272 (22 November 1932).

[22] R. J. Finlay, 'Imperial Scotland: Scottish National Identity and the British Empire, 1850–1914', in J. M. MacKenzie (ed.), *Scotland and the British Empire* (Manchester, forthcoming).

[23] R. J. Finlay, *A Partnership for Good? Scottish Politics and the Union since 1880* (Edinburgh, 1996), ch.2.

[24] Finlay, 'National Identity in Crisis'.

[25] Finlay, 'Continuity and Change', 1–6.

[26] R. J. Finlay, 'In Defence of Oligarchy: Scotland in the Twentieth Century', *Scottish Historical Review* LXXIII (April 1994), 109.

[27] See A. McIvor and H. Paterson, 'Combating the Left: Victimisation and Anti-Labour Activities on Clydeside, 1900–39', in Duncan and McIvor, *Militant Workers*, 129–55.

[28] Speech at the International Engineering Congress in Glasgow, 21 July 1938, quoted in the *Glasgow Herald*.

[29] Ibid.

[30] T. Burns, *The Real Rulers of Scotland* (Glasgow, 1940), 17.

[31] Ibid., 20.

[32] Scottish Records Office, DD 10/175, 'Memorandum on the State of Scotland 18 December 1937'.

[33] Finlay, 'National Identity in Crisis', 258.

[34] Ibid.

[35] *Daily Record*, 12 February 1932.

[36] *Glasgow Herald*, 20 June 1931.

[37] Ibid., 18 March 1932.

[38] HC Deb, vol.272, col.341 (22 November 1932).

[39] Finlay, 'National Identity in Crisis', 256–7.

[40] *Scots Independent*, January 1930.

[41] Finlay, 'National Identity in Crisis', 258–9.

[42] See I. G. C. Hutchison, 'Government in Twentieth Century Scotland', in Devine and Finlay, *Scotland in the Twentieth Century*.

[43] J. Mitchell, *Conservatives and the Union: A Study of Conservative Party Attitudes to Scotland* (Edinburgh, 1990), 17–38.

[44] Finlay, 'National Identity in Crisis', 258.

[45] R. H. Campbell, 'The Committee of Ex-Secretaries of State for Scotland and Industrial Policy, 1941–45', *Scottish Industrial History* 2 (1979).

[46] Finlay, 'In Defence of Oligarchy', 110.

[47] J. Mitchell, 'Scottish Politics since 1945', in Devine and Finlay, *Scotland in the Twentieth Century*.

[48] Ibid.

[49] *Scottish Control of Scottish Affairs: Unionist Policy* (Glasgow, 1949).

50 J. Brand, *The National Movement in Scotland* (1979), 249–68.

51 *Scottish Control of Scottish Affairs*, 1.

52 Mitchell, 'Scottish Politics since 1945'.

53 Mitchell, *Conservatives and the Union*, 56.

54 J. Kellas, *The Scottish Political System* (Cambridge, 1984).

55 G. Walker, 'Varieties of Protestant Identities in Twentieth Century Scotland', in Devine and Finlay, *Scotland in the Twentieth Century*.

56 For a recent treatment of these themes see D. McCrone, *Understanding Scotland: The Sociology of a Stateless Nation* (1992).

# The Construction of a National Identity: Stanley Baldwin, 'Englishness' and the Mass Media in Inter-War Britain

## SIÂN NICHOLAS

'He interpreted the essential spirit of England': thus *The Times* in 1947 described the enduring appeal of Stanley Baldwin through-out the inter-war period.[1] This 'Englishness' became the defining characteristic of a politician who, while Prime Minister for only eight years, dominated the political culture of inter-war Britain. The nature and significance of Baldwin's 'Englishness', a topic which obsessed contemporary commentators, has become a recurrent theme among historians of the Conservative Party and of British national culture and identity.[2]

Why was 'Englishness' such a potent image of inter-war Conservatism? And how was this image of Baldwin as the archetype of Englishness created and sustained in the public mind? A number of writers have discussed how Baldwin's 'Englishness' reflected wider national and cultural assumptions in the inter-war period, but few have considered how this 'English' persona came to be so successfully projected, beyond reference to Baldwin's public speeches and skills as a political communicator. This chapter investigates both these questions.

The ways in which the Conservative Party – and specifically Baldwin and his political allies – used the media played an essential part in securing both his and the party's claims to represent 'the nation' in this period. Baldwin's rise coincided with the consolidation of a mass electorate and the development of the 'new' mass media; indeed, he was the first modern British politician whose persona was mediated through and by the media.

But Baldwin and his party had another advantage. Baldwin's 'English' Conservatism accorded with the very character and nature of the new media whose rise to prominence paralleled his own.

# I

The popular obsession in the inter-war years with ideas of 'England' has recently attracted considerable interest. The replacement of the conventional imperial patriotism of late-Victorian and Edwardian Britain by a self-consciously insular and backward-looking construction of the nation, based on a mythic rural English past, can be traced to a variety of sources, from the late Victorian nostalgia for a pre-industrial way of life and the searing impact of the First World War, to the economic and political uncertainties of the 1920s and 1930s.[3] What Potts has described as a 'nationalist ideology of pure landscape'[4] adapted an idealized vision of patchwork fields, thatched cottages and village greens into a visual shorthand for the nation.

Literature as diverse as H. V. Morton's best-selling *In Search of England* (1927) and the *Shell Motoring Guides to Britain* testify to the romanticization of the English landscape. Landscape became the reference point for a wider focus on 'Englishness' that embraced the whole of English culture: 'Georgian' literature, the music of Vaughan Williams and Ireland, even the 'avant-garde' art of Nash and Piper. Mock-Tudor was the architectual style of choice in the new suburbs. Underpinning it all was that elusive creature, the 'English character'. While Morton wrote of his search for the 'true nation' in the villages, towns and cathedral cities of England, A. G. Macdonell's (Scottish) hero in *England, Their England* (1930) conducted a parallel fictional search among country-house parties and cricket matches for the key to the English character, and found it in the 'kindly laughter-loving warrior poets' represented by Shakespeare and his greatest English creation, Falstaff. While the square-jawed 'clubland heroes' of Sapper and Dornford Yates maintained imperial traditions of nationalistic heroism, the amiable country-house eccentrics of P. G. Wodehouse appealed to a newly nostalgic age.

Yet this imagery – both a middle-class defence against suburbanization and a marketing strategy by the English tourist industry – was inherently contradictory. The conception of Englishness as a 'beautiful reticence' was as self-absorbed as it was self-effacing. Meanwhile, it was politically a flexible – even consensual – construction of the nation, subscribed to by such disparate characters as radical progressive Herbert Read and fascist Henry Williamson. It was the socialist J. B. Priestley ('a city-bred northerner but a resident by choice of Deep England') who maintained in the preface to *The Beauty of Britain* (1935) that the 'typical' English countryside was the true emblem of Englishness, since its appearance of 'compromise between wildness and tameness, between nature and man' mirrored the 'happy compromises that make our social and political plans so irrational and yet so successful'.[5]

It was in the speeches of Stanley Baldwin above all other inter-war politicians that the 'England' of H. V. Morton and his like could be most clearly recognized. Baldwin's celebrated speech, 'England', at the annual dinner of the Royal Society of St George on 6 May 1924, incorporated all these themes: a celebration of the English character (anti-intellectual but full of genius, phlegmatic, resilient, kindly, individualistic) resting on a tribute to England's history, traditions – and landscape:

> To me, England is the country and the country is England . . . the hammer on the anvil in the country smithy, the corncrake on a dewy morning . . . the sight of a plough team coming over the brow of a hill . . . for centuries the one eternal sight of England.[6]

This speech became one of the most frequently quoted statements of his political and patriotic philosophy. Baldwin himself hoped it might be adopted for use at public school speech days.[7] But whereas inter-war 'Englishness' took much of its strength from its inclusiveness and cross-political nature, Baldwin was able to embody this construction in a way that effectively marginalized his political opponents of both the left (the Labour Party) and the right (the die-hard element in his own party), while setting out a challenge to his political nemesis, Lloyd George.

## II

Baldwin's predecessor as party leader and Prime Minister, Andrew Bonar Law, might justifiably be credited with first elaborating a political persona based on ordinariness, trustworthiness and a 'moderate and commonsense patriotism'.[8] However, Baldwin above all became the political incarnation of 'Englishness'. When Baldwin delivered his 'England' speech this English identity was already well established. When he became Prime Minister for the first time in 1923 the *Daily Telegraph* described him as the most 'thoroughly English Englishman in the House of Commons'. From the first, Conservative Party literature focused on the new premier's sturdy English qualities. By the time Wickham Steed's biographical 'investigation' *The Real Stanley Baldwin* appeared in 1930, he was conventionally regarded as 'the most typical Englishman of his day'.[9] Englishness became Baldwin's essential political tactic: a simple appeal to political certainties, with himself, the 'Worcestershire countryman', pipe in hand, conciliator and consensus-builder, at its heart.

Baldwin's public persona, as expressed in his public addresses, his highly successful published collections of speeches, and in the literature disseminated by Conservative Central Office, accorded precisely with the conventional inter-war archetype of the ideal Englishman.[10] He was plain-speaking and without guile ('I am not a clever man. I know nothing of political tactics').[11] He believed in fair play and conciliation, most notably in his withdrawal of Macquisten's anti-trade union bill, against the wishes of much of his party, with the plea 'give peace in our time, O Lord'. He was modest and public-spirited, not only in words ('I have only one interest – to see that every effort is made to help the people of this country')[12] but in actions: his anonymous donation of a fifth of his wealth to the nation in 1919 was soon widely known (the exact proportion having increased in the public mind in the mean time).[13] He had an unshakeable faith in the nobility of his race, in the 'spirit of co-operation' and responsible political outlook inherent in the English people ('ordered liberty will never perish from the earth so long as Englishmen are the guardians of their liberties').[14] Even his relationship with Rudyard Kipling (they were cousins) 'proved good English stock' – although for Baldwin 'Kiplingesque' ideas of Empire had lost their aggressive edge ('In our thought of Empire today there is nothing in the nature of flagwaving', rather, a humble pride in the 'spiritual inheritance which we hold in trust').[15] And above all else, he was trustworthy: 'I would sooner go out of office than deceive the elector with promises incapable of fulfilment.'[16]

Baldwin's political philosophy was more sophisticated than a mere obsession with national stereotypes, and his 'Englishness' was certainly magnified in the public mind at the expense of other aspects of his character.[17] But it was the persona rather than the constitutional theory that took centre stage. This image was reassuring. It was also, superficially at least, almost completely uncontroversial. Neither aggressive nor exclusive, it appeared to celebrate the best features of 'Englishness' without obviously casting aspersions on 'Welshness', 'Scottishness' or 'Irishness' (indeed, Baldwin personally seems to have appealed to Scottish and Welsh voters at a time when the Conservative Party itself was held in little regard). It was sufficiently protectionist to keep at least moderate Conservatives content; yet in a wider context consciously laid claim to Britain's 'liberal inheritance'.[18] But the message was also politically barbed. 'Englishness', handled with care, served to marginalize Baldwin's political opponents as anti-patriotic and anti-English.[19] In the 1920s 'Englishness' became the basis of a sustained attack on socialism and the Labour Party that explicitly developed themes of subversion, unconstitutionality and class violence. In party literature Labour's allegiance to the Red Flag was contrasted with the Conservative Party's loyalty to the Union Jack, Baldwin's high moral tone offsetting the more aggressive red-baiting of his party colleagues.[20] During the 1929 general election, Baldwin's Englishness was used to attack Lloyd George, English neither in origins nor temperament. Lloyd George's dynamism was countered by making a virtue of Baldwin's steadiness ('I have been much criticised . . . on the grounds that I cannot really be in earnest unless I froth at the mouth. But I am an Englishman of an ordinary pattern and the more in earnest I am the more calm and restrained I feel') and probity ('Why is it that so many of Mr Lloyd George's former Colleagues and supporters have ceased to trust him?').[21]

Baldwin thus embodied the compleat English politician. That he was not, as his critics often pointed out, a countryman (a third-generation industrialist, his money deriving from his family's iron foundry), and not even strictly English (his father was part-Welsh, his mother half-Welsh, half-Scottish), was irrelevant – as Ball suggests, since inter-war 'Englishness' was to such an extent a suburban invention, who better to embody it than a romantic industrialist?[22] Neither did he create this persona alone. His scriptwriters included, at various times, not only Sir Patrick Gower, chief publicity officer at Conservative Central Office, but Arthur Bryant (a notable exponent of 'Englishness'), Thomas Jones (Welsh, and a Fabian socialist) and Sir John Reith (a Scot, whose commitment to the concept of public service was matched by a strong authoritarian streak).[23] And he relied as no previous politician on the mass media to project this persona to the country at large.

# III

The Conservative Party has conventionally been considered as enjoying a sustained advantage over its rivals in the media. However, developments in the media in the inter-war years necessitated a complete reappraisal of the nature and character of political publicity.[24] The Conservative Party's success in coming to terms with both the old and the new media was a key factor in their wider political success in the period. Yet again, Baldwin and his English persona were the essential elements in this success.

Although the mainstream press was predominantly conservative (indeed Conservative) in orientation, the political allegiance of Fleet Street was increasingly complex. The inter-war popular press was difficult to influence: 'unreliable', opportunistic in the causes and policies it espoused, populist rather than political.[25] Unlike other Conservative leaders this century, Baldwin therefore could *not* rely on the popular press for support. Moreover, the *Daily Express* and especially the *Daily Mail* were far more anti-Baldwin than anti-Conservative, with Lords Beaverbrook and Rothermere conducting a concerted vendetta against Baldwin in their flagship newspapers. Party publicists felt this keenly; party chairman J. C. C. Davidson believed that Beaverbrook was conniving with Rothermere to destroy Baldwin and put Lloyd George into office.[26] The *Mail* and *Express*'s antagonism towards Baldwin reached a peak during the 'Empire Crusade' years of 1929–31, when the press barons sought to undermine his leadership of the

'betrayal' by the electorate that personally devastated him), he was sufficiently convinced of the strength of his support in the nation at large to fend off calls for his resignation. By 1931 and the formation of the National Government Baldwin was the only party leader who could plausibly sustain the claim to be 'above politics'. The next years saw the apotheosis of Baldwin the 'national statesman', on film, over the air, even in the press. He could afford to ignore the unpopularity of the National Government within his party; publicly it stood as a vindication of Baldwin himself. As the *Star* (a Liberal paper) wrote in July 1934:

> In many ways Mr Baldwin holds an unique position in our political life. He is regarded as epitomising nearly all the best qualities of the parliamentarian. His own plea that he is a plain honest countryman is generally accepted because it has been found by experience that Mr Baldwin possesses these qualities and that if he is cautious in his promises, these promises are always liquidated. Broadly, the country feels it can trust Mr Baldwin.[44]

## V

However, Baldwin's affinity for the new media went deeper than personal contacts and individual skill. If the new media were easier to handle than the old media, their relationship to the world of politics also differed profoundly from that of the newspapers. The press dealt in political controversy and open partisanship. For different reasons, neither radio nor newsreels were in the business of critical editorializing.

First, the inter-war newsreels were not, and were not likely to be, agents of political debate. Although they fulfilled a complex political role, they belonged more to the world of entertainment than journalism, and made no serious attempt to present the complexities of party politics.[45] They played up 'the ordinary, the orderly, the well-arranged aspects of the society around them . . . the points of consensus rather than conflict . . . the basic decencies'.[46] They were under no statutory obligation to avoid controversy, but controversy took too long to expound successfully. Newsreels were quick-cutting, sharply edited, avowedly superficial sources of news, dealing in a shorthand of ideas and responses. The most persuasive messages were the straightforward, the informal and the non-partisan; Baldwin, with his (or his scriptwriters') knack for what might be termed 'sound-bite' political debate, was the ideal political messenger.

Radio's relationship with politics was more complex. Unlike the newsreel companies, the BBC acknowledged a sense of profound responsibility to its audience. Indeed, one of the more remarkable consequences of the institution of a 'public service' ethos in British radio was the extent to which *what* was broadcast assumed a peculiar importance, the integrity of the broadcast word explicitly contrasted with the tainted authority of the printed word.[47] Hilda Matheson, BBC director of talks from 1927 to 1932, believed that 'The microphone has a curious knack of showing what is real and what is unreal, . . . what is sincere and what is an appeal to the gallery' (thus 'broadcasting might have a profound influence on the type of political leader which emerges . . . the influence of broadcasting will be definitely against the demagogue and in favour of the thoughtful statesman').[48]

Despite the party managers' fears that the BBC was not manipulable, one might argue that they were missing the point. As Conservative MP Ian Fraser more perceptively observed:

> The Tory case is more reasonable than emotional . . . consequently our case stands a better chance through the microphone than does that of either of the two other parties. I am sure that Mr Baldwin cannot realise the extraordinary effect of his voice and the intimate personal touch which he creates with the ordinary listener at home. He has the knack, which few have learned, of talking to a million individuals personally, rather than to an imaginary audience of a million. It must never be forgotten that wireless listeners are not a congregation, and are not subject to the mass psychology of the ordinary audience. Mr Lloyd George and Mr Ramsay MacDonald do not appreciate this.[49]

The original Charter of the BBC explicitly prohibited 'political controversy'; thus the rules governing political broadcasting were complex. Although equal access for different viewpoints was theoretically assured, as the Ullswater Committee on Broadcasting (1936) noted, the party in government was inevitably accorded more prominence on the air than the party in opposition.[50] Meanwhile, these 'different viewpoints' were defined entirely in party terms, and it was left to the parties themselves to nominate speakers. Baldwin and his political allies effectively controlled the radio image of his party, ensuring that party mavericks never got the opportunity to air their political differences. He himself was the only politician of any party who habitually broadcast twice in a general election campaign. Since the newsreel proprietors simply did not consider internal Conservative Party disputes as newsworthy, Baldwin's critics in his own party – such as Winston Churchill – might receive publicity in the press but suffered a virtual news blackout on radio and the newsreels.[51]

Above all, the BBC had a unique place in the national culture of inter-war Britain. If newspapers 'fuelled controversy and played upon public anxieties', broadcasting, by contrast, sought to unify and integrate. Despite the best endeavours of some of its staff (and indeed Reith in the early days), the inter-war BBC was resolutely apolitical. Although the formal ban on 'controversial broadcasts' was lifted in 1928, the BBC remained hamstrung by the 'fourteen-day rule' which prevented the discussion of any topic within a fortnight of its being raised in Parliament. Most of the BBC's 'political' output was therefore pitched at a more abstract level, 'an education for citizenship' rather than an interrogation of current controversies, centred on implicitly celebratory expositions of national institutions that isolated examples of social criticism did little to undermine. As Scannell and Cardiff have detailed, in the 1930s radio transformed the relationship between the individual and the nation. The broadcast celebration of religious festivals, civic ceremonies, national days of remembrance and sporting events consolidated a sense of 'national' culture and an image of the 'nation' itself as rational, consensual, even 'arcadian'. Broadcasting, according to one contemporary investigation, was above all else an 'equalising and unifying factor in national life'.[52] Despite the aura of subversion that some claimed pervaded the BBC, this unifying function – indeed, everything implied in the term 'Reithian values' – was inherently conservative.

Reith notoriously stated during the General Strike that 'Since the BBC was a national institution and since the Government ... were acting for the people ... the BBC was for the Government.'[53] This can be extended to the newsreel companies, to whom the government of the day and the 'nation' were effectively synonymous. Newsreels projected representations of the nation, the government represented the nation, therefore the newsreels projected the government. Thus during the 1931 and 1935 elections British Movietone and Gaumont-British threw themselves behind the National Government. In 1931 an estimated 25 million people watched films of the three leaders of the National Government, in which MacDonald and Samuel singled out Baldwin for particular praise. For the 1935 general election campaign, as Ramsden notes, Baldwin was filmed in a set 'appropriate to a Prime Minister', Attlee in a set 'appropriate to the leader of the opposition': Baldwin thus appeared confident and authoritative, Attlee a nervous outsider.[54] The 'Baldwinite Conservatism' embodied in the National Government, understated, self-affirming, conciliatory and diffuse, was the ideal political reflection of the new media.

# VI

Despite the periodic internal challenges to Baldwin's leadership and the disdain in which many within his own party held him,[55] Baldwin remained the essential public face of Conservatism throughout the inter-war years. This public face was above all 'English'. His popularity was indisputable, if not necessarily with the party faithful in the constituency associations or the newspaper proprietors, then with the 'ordinary' voter on whom the authority of the National Government was seen to rest. His opponents, both within and without his party, found themselves fighting on his terms. The extent to which Baldwin's 'Englishness' was simply a contrivance was something widely discussed during his political lifetime, but the much-remarked 'enigma' of his political career was always that commentators could never decide whether he was 'the luckiest of incompetent politicians or the subtlest of competent statesmen', and that the public seemed not to care.[56] Using the new mass media, Baldwin maintained a national persona of imperturbable trustworthiness at a time when the main popular newspapers were branding him a fool or an incompetent. His advantage was that he embodied so many shared assumptions about 'Englishness': he was honest, stolid, affable, fair-minded and proud of his country, and his political competitors all suffered by comparison. And for all the nostalgic impulses he invoked, he was an adept in the most modern publicity techniques.

Even his sternest critics were unable to escape using the language of national identity when attacking him. To one hostile biographer in the mid-1930s, Baldwin's remarkable powers of political survival could be attributed to the national character of the electorate itself: the fact that 'England loves . . . [someone] who muddles through. We are so proud of this national characteristic; it assures us that we are chosen people since not even the worst mistakes of politicans or generals can defeat us'. The irony was that if the electorate's allegiance to Baldwin could be explained by national character, the key to Baldwin's own character lay elsewhere: 'Beneath that simple stolid English exterior . . . there really moves a tortuous, complacent, self-deceiving Celtic brain.'[57] Those who dared attack Baldwin risked having their own patriotism impugned. When a story spread in July 1936 that Baldwin was preparing to resign, a letter to the press from a group of pro-Baldwin MPs concluded that such rumour-mongering was 'as un-English as it is unsportsmanlike'.[58] Only in the years after his retirement from politics, when his reputation suffered a startling collapse, was his Englishness more generally dismissed as artificial, stultifying and parodic.[59]

Yet the most intriguing aspect of Baldwin's appeal remains the way in which his public image corresponded to the character of the new mass media: the message and the medium in unusually close harmony. Unlike the press, both radio and newsreels maintained a deferential relationship to the government of the day, but particularly to the Conservative (or Conservative-dominated) governments of which Baldwin was the chief spokesman. The new media's support for 'Baldwinite Conservatism' had deep causes. Their function was to unite, not to challenge or divide. In the inter-war years the BBC sustained a national identity based on common cultural assumptions, traditions and ceremonies in which England and Britain became largely synonymous. The newsreels, for more prosaic reasons, similarly traded in common assumptions and received wisdoms. In the years after the Second World War this media consensus would increasingly be challenged. But in the inter-war years these media drew on and embellished those shared conceptions of the nation and national identity that Baldwin had done so much to embody in words and manner. He was thus a 'natural' broadcaster in more ways than one.

*Notes*

I am especially indebted to David Jarvis for his comments and advice on this chapter.

1  Lord Baldwin, *A Memoir* (London, 1947), 21.
2  See J. Ramsden, *The Age of Balfour and Baldwin* (London, 1978); P. Williamson, 'The Doctrinal Politics of Stanley Baldwin', in M. Bentley (ed.), *Public and Private Doctrine* (Cambridge, 1993), 181–208; B. Schwarz, 'The Language of Constitutionalism: Baldwinite Conservatism', in [Formations Editorial Collective], *Formations of Nation and People* (London, 1984), 1–18. For Baldwin and national identity see M. Wiener, *English Character and the Decline of the Industrial Spirit, 1850–1980* (Cambridge, 1981); H. Cunningham, 'The Conservative Party and Patriotism', in R. Colls and P. Dodd (eds.), *Englishness: Politics and Culture 1880–1920* (London, 1986), 283–308.
3  See A. Potts, '"Constable Country" between the Wars', in R. Samuel (ed.), *Patriotism, III: National Fictions* (London, 1989), 160–88; M. Chase, 'This is No Claptrap: This is Our Heritage', in C. Shaw and M. Chase (eds.), *The Imagined Past: History and Nostalgia* (Manchester, 1989), 128–46; A. Howkins, 'The Discovery of Rural England', in Colls and Dodd (eds.), *Englishness*, 62–88; see also Wiener, *English Culture*; A. Calder, 'Deep England', in his *The Myth of the Blitz* (London, 1991). One might also add the conclusion to W. C. Sellar and R. J. Yeatman's *1066 and All That* (London, [1930] 1960): 'America was thus clearly top nation, and History came to a .'.
4  Potts, '"Constable Country"', 166.
5  Ibid., 175; Calder, *Myth of the Blitz*, 185; Priestley, quoted in Potts, 174.
6  S. Baldwin, *On England* (London, 1926), 6–7.
7  T. Jones, *Whitehall Diary*, II: *1926–1930*, ed. K. Middlemas (London, 1969), 13.
8  Ramsden, *Age of Balfour and Baldwin*, 92; Cunningham, 'Conservative Party and Patriotism', 292.
9  *Daily Telegraph*, May 1923, quoted in W. Steed, *The Real Stanley Baldwin* (London, 1930), 14; ibid., quotation from dust jacket to first edn.
10  In addition to Baldwin's *On England*, see his *Our Inheritance* (London, 1928), *This Torch of Freedom* (1935) and *Service of our Lives* (1937).
11  Speech to Conservative Party Conference, Plymouth, 25 October 1923, Conservative Party Archive, Harvester Microfiche (hereafter CPA) MFC 1, 'Pamphlets and leaflets', Box 3, 1923/123.
12  Speech at Manchester, 2 November 1923, CPA MFC 1 Box 3, 1923/123.

[13] Baldwin's donation was first made public by the *Birmingham Post*, 29 November 1923; see Ramsden, *Age of Balfour and Baldwin*, 194 n.16. During the 1929 general election campaign Austen Chamberlain referred to Baldwin donating a *third* of his wealth to the nation (Daily Notes, 27 May 1929, CPA MFC 1 Box 4, 1929/201).

[14] Speech at Osmaston, 16 June 1934, CPA MFC 1 Box 4, 1934/27.

[15] *Morning Post*, 24 November 1923; Empire Day broadcast, 24 May 1927, BBC Written Archive Centre, Caversham (hereafter BBC WAC), Talks Scripts.

[16] Broadcast, 8 November 1935, BBC WAC, Talks Scripts.

[17] See Williamson, 'Doctrinal Politics' for extended discussion of Baldwin's political philosophy; S. Ball, *Baldwin and the Conservative Party: The Crisis of 1929–1931* (New Haven and London, 1988), 9.

[18] D. Smith, 'Englishness and the Liberal Inheritance after 1886', in Colls and Dodd (eds.), *Englishness*, 254–83.

[19] See Cunningham, 'Conservative Party and Patriotism', 294–5. Even Baldwin's 'England' speech included a sideswipe at that 'certain section of our people who regard every country as being in the right except their own' (Baldwin, *On England*, 4).

[20] Election pamphlet, CPA MFC 1 Box 3, 1925/58. McKibbin's assessment of Baldwin's 'class-harmonious rhetoric' as unrepresentative of inter-war popular Conservatism is only part of the story; rather, Baldwin provided the essential moral underpinning to the rest of the party's attacks on Labour. See R. McKibbin, 'Class and Conventional Wisdom: The Conservative Party and the "Public" in Inter-War Britain', in his *The Ideologies of Class* (London, 1990), 292; also Williamson, 'Doctrinal Politics', 183, 195.

[21] Broadcast, 22 April 1929, BBC WAC Talks Scripts; election pamphlet, CPA MFC 1 Box 4, 1929/54.

[22] Ball, *Baldwin and the Conservative Party*, 9–10.

[23] See Thomas Jones: it was 'the Englishness of SB that emerges [in *On England*] . . . and I think (for a Welshman) I've played up to that very well' (Jones, *Whitehall Diary*, II: 11).

[24] R. Cockett, 'The Party, Publicity and the Media', in A. Seldon and S. Ball (eds.), *Conservative Century: The Conservative Party since 1900* (Oxford, 1994), 549–64, provides a useful summary (though his discussion of the BBC is perfunctory). See also, C. Seymour-Ure, 'The Press and the Party System between the Wars', in G. Peele and C. Cook (eds.), *The Politics of Reappraisal* (London, 1975), 232–57; T. Jeffery and K. McClelland, 'A World Fit to Live In: The *Daily Mail* and the Middle Classes 1918–39', in J. Curran, A. Smith and P. Wingate (eds.), *Impacts and Influences: Essays in Media Power in the Twentieth Century* (London, 1987), 27–52; J. Curran and J. Seaton, *Power without Responsibility: The Press and Broadcasting in Britain* (London, 1991 edn.), passim.

[25] Seymour-Ure, 'Press and Party System', 251.

[26] S. Koss, *The Rise and Fall of the Political Press in Britain* (London, 1990), 907.

[27] T. Stannage, *Baldwin Thwarts the Opposition: The British General Election of 1935* (London, 1980), 196; see 191–2 for newspapers' party allegiances during the election.

[28] A. J. P. Taylor, *Beaverbrook* (London, 1972), 227–8.

[29] See P. Williamson, *National Crisis and National Government: British Politics, the Economy and Empire 1926–1932* (Cambridge, 1992), 130, 187–90.

[30] See Stannage, *Baldwin Thwarts the Opposition*, 205.

[31] Press circulation figures from Seymour-Ure, 'Press and Party System', 237; radio audience figure is Reith's own: see Reith to Baldwin, 14 April 1929, BBC WAC Reith Scrapbooks S60/6/5; cinema attendance from N. Pronay, 'British Newsreels in the 1930s: (1) Audiences and Producers', *History* 56 (1971), 412.

[32] See T. Hollins, 'The Conservative Party and Film Propaganda between the Wars', *English Historical Review* 96 (1981), 359–69; and J. Ramsden, 'Baldwin and Film', in N. Pronay and D. W. Spring (eds.), *Politics, Propaganda and Film 1918–1945* (London, 1982), 126–43. For instance, Sir Albert Clavering, honorary director of the Conservative and Unionist Films Association (CUFA), was a close friend of Isidore Ostrer, president of Gaumont-British. His brother was director of Pathé. A director of British Movietone, Sir Gordon Craig, was on the CUFA central committee. The film-makers Michael Balcon and Alexander Korda acted as CUFA advisers.

[33] C. Stuart (ed.), *The Reith Diaries* (London, 1975), 105 and passim.

[34] CPA MFC 2, 'Minutes of National Unionist Executive Committee to Central Council', 8 March 1932; Hollins, 'Conservative Party and Film', 363.

[35] Ramsden, 'Baldwin and Film', 136–7.

[36] See Cockett, 'Party, Publicity, and the Media', 557–8.

[37] For Baldwin's first broadcast see A. Briggs, *The Birth of Broadcasting* (London, 1961), 271; *Reith Diaries*, 90; Ramsden, 'Baldwin and Film', 130–2.

[38] See K. Middlemas and J. Barnes, *Baldwin* (London, 1969), 412–14; and compare with I. McIntyre, *The Expense of Glory: A Life of John Reith* (London, 1993), 143–4. Middlemas and Barnes also date the broadcast incorrectly.

[39] Draft, BBC WAC Reith Scrapbooks, S/60/6/4; see also *Reith Diaries*, 102, 124n.

[40] Broadcast, 16 February 1931, BBC WAC Talks Scripts.

[41] A. Briggs, *The Golden Age of Wireless* (London, 1965), 141.

[42] *New Statesman*, 9 November 1935.

43  Williamson, 'Doctrinal Politics', 190.
44  *Star*, 9 July 1934, quoted in *Country First Always: Mr Stanley Baldwin – The Man*, CPA MFC 1 Box 4, 1935/55. Gaumont-British's report of the 1935 general election result follows the same editorial line: after replaying Baldwin's campaign affirmation, 'I think you can trust me by now', the caption flashed up ' . . . And You Do!!' (Ramsden, 'Baldwin and Film', 137).
45  Hollins, 'Conservative Party and Film', 367.
46  N. Pronay, 'British Newsreels in the 1930s: (2) Their Policy and Impact', *History* 57 (1972), 67.
47  'Broadcasting . . . is bound to be truthful, whereas the newspapers . . . distort and colour their presentation of the case' (Ian Fraser to Baldwin, 3 February 1927, Baldwin Papers, Cambridge University Library, 65/38–41).
48  H. Matheson, *Broadcasting* (London, 1933), 99, 100.
49  Ian Fraser to Leo Amery, 19 November 1928, Baldwin Papers 65/55–6. Fraser was blind, and claimed a special empathy with wireless listeners. I am grateful to David Jarvis for providing the Fraser references.
50  Stannage, *Baldwin Thwarts the Opposition*, 184.
51  See J. Seaton, 'Reith and the Denial of Politics', in Curran and Seaton, *Power without Responsibility*, 131–50; though cf. P. Scannell and D. Cardiff, *A Social History of British Broadcasting*, I: *Serving the Nation* (Oxford, 1991), 57 and passim.
52  See P. Scannell and D. Cardiff, 'Broadcasting and National Unity', in Curran, Smith and Wingate (eds.), *Impacts and Influences*, 158–66; and *Serving the Nation*, passim; Stannage, *Baldwin Thwarts the Opposition*, 183–90; Wiener, *English Culture*, 74–5; H. Jennings and W. Gill, *Broadcasting and Everyday Life* (London, 1939), 40.
53  See Reith note for Davidson, 6 May 1926, BBC WAC Reith Scrapbooks S/60/6/4 – though, as McIntyre notes, with the High Court having declared the strike illegal (and the BBC's charter not yet granted), it is not clear what else the BBC could have done (McIntyre, *Expense of Glory*, 146). See also Lord Reith, 'Forsan . . .', *Parliamentary Affairs* 17 (1963/4), 30.
54  Ramsden, 'Baldwin and Film', 136–7.
55  See Ball, *Baldwin and the Conservative Party*, 30–96 for attitudes of party faithful.
56  Lord Baldwin, *A Memoir*, 14.
57  B. Roberts, *Stanley Baldwin, Man or Miracle?* (London, 1936) 273–4.
58  See Roberts, *Stanley Baldwin*, 249–50.
59  See, for instance, Movietone's newsreel obituary of Baldwin, screened in December 1947 ('a sustained piece of character assassination' – Ramsden, 'Baldwin and Film', 138). When in April 1940 Baldwin

offered his services to the BBC, Controller of Programmes Basil
Nicolls noted 'we could bear him in mind for some honorific occasion
where he can talk about England or the Empire or something like that';
the BBC's subsequent invitation to give a talk on the British way of life
on the BBC Overseas Service was (perhaps unsurprisingly) declined.
BBC WAC Rcont1: Stanley Baldwin, correspondence 3 April–15 May
1940.

# The Conservative Party, Immigration and National Identity, 1948–1968

## STEPHEN BROOKE

On 20 April 1968, Enoch Powell appealed to a white population who 'found themselves made strangers in their own country' by non-white immigration.[1] The notorious 'rivers of blood' speech was unreservedly racist in its articulation of the threat that such immigration posed to white Britons, whether over specific issues or the essential character of the nation: 'they found their wives unable to obtain hospital beds in childbirth, their children unable to obtain school places, their homes and neighbourhoods changed beyond recognition; their plans and their prospects for the future defeated.'[2] Though it earned Powell dismissal from the shadow cabinet, the speech met with overwhelming public approval; 74 per cent of those polled by Gallup agreed with Powell's remarks. By February 1969, Powell was the most admired public figure in Britain.[3]

Much has been made of the importance of this episode to the breakdown of 'consensus' politics and the radicalization of the race question in the post-war period.[4] With reference to the latter, for instance, it certainly became easier for politicians to use racially charged language after Powell, such as Margaret Thatcher's 1978 remark that Britons felt 'swamped by people with a different culture', and to proceed with even more rigorous restriction on entry and citizenship, such as the 1971 Immigration Act and the 1981 British Nationality Act.[5]

The relationship between this turning point and the broader question of Conservative thinking on immigration has been less explored. What is perhaps forgotten about the episode, for instance, is not the extent to which Powell's arguments were disowned by the Conservative leadership, but how much their general substance, rather than style, was reluctantly acknowledged. A few days after the speech, Edward Heath told the *Daily Express* that the Conservatives supported strong immigration controls, and that, in this, there was no difference of policy between Powell and the leadership: '[t]he reason I dismissed Mr Powell from the shadow cabinet was not for stating these policies. It was because of the way he did it.'[6] The following September, Heath accepted with regret the legitimacy of the public's response:

> They felt that here was a situation out of hand, which would work to the detriment of their children and of future generations. That here was a crisis unresolved, which could change their way of life and the very nature of society in their own native land.[7]

The play between Powell's speech and Heath's response articulated, in very different tones, a traditional, if of course somewhat misplaced, view of the nation, one of a uniracial and homogeneous community, a white Britain. The Immigration and Nationality Acts passed by Conservative governments in 1971 and 1981 and the response to the problem of Hong Kong after the Tiananmen Square massacre further underlined such a view. To some degree, the admittedly limited historiography of the relationship between the Conservative Party and immigration since 1945 has supported both the continuity and inevitability of this vision of national identity, an orthodoxy in which all roads lead to Powell. This can be perceived in the work of Anna Marie Smith, whose position begins with Powell, or the varying perspectives of D. W. Dean, Bob Carter, Clive Harris and Shirley Joshi, which suggest that a clearly anti-immigrant position based upon racialism was taken up soon after the Conservatives came to power in 1951, constrained only by external concerns for protecting the Commonwealth and domestic worries about creating a partisan issue out of race.[8] What such accounts miss, first of all, is the possibility of a broader and more complex context of Conservative discourse on national identity and race, a complexity caught in the difference of tone between Heath and Powell in 1968.

The emphasis upon the bipartisan character of political responses to immigration in the post-war period has similarly blurred the possibility of differences of approach between the two major parties.[9] This is not, of course, to suggest that Labour and the Conservatives did not share similar reservations and aims about non-white immigration. Despite enactment of the 1948 British Nationality Act, which formalized the 'open-door' policy for all Commonwealth and colonial subjects, as early as 1950 a Labour government sought means to 'check the immigration into this country of coloured people'.[10] Having opposed the Macmillan government's 1962 Commonwealth Immigrants Act while in opposition, Labour accepted, once in government after 1964, that 'a strict control should be kept while these immigrants were absorbed fully into the community'.[11] In 1968, the Wilson government passed its own immigration control Act. It could be argued, however, that post-war immigration still posed different problems to the two major parties, differences inevitably rooted in their respective contexts and histories. Labour's tradition was at least superficially internationalist and anti-imperial, the Conservatives' imperial and anti-cosmopolitan. Accepting that there was broad agreement between the two parties on the end-point of immigration policy in the post-war period should not obscure the idiosyncratic qualities of their respective positions.

The present chapter attempts to bring out the complexity of Conservative reactions to immigration after the Second World War, a complexity suggested by the dialogue between Powell and Heath in 1968. Instead of accepting 1968 or 1951 as the watersheds in the development of such debates, it focuses upon the planning and enactment of the Commonwealth Immigrants Act of 1962. The controls set out by the Act rested upon a voucher system, one which gave priority to those with skills or who held guaranteed places in employment; a limited number of vouchers would be issued to those who could satisfy neither category.[12] Clearly, such categories tended to work against the kind of immigrant coming from colonies or countries of the New Commonwealth, generally unskilled labour. This not only demonstrated the abandonment of Britain's 'open-door' immigration policy, but also formalized a turning point in the Conservative approach to the question and, more broadly, to the party's conception of national identity. The debate within the

Conservative Party over immigration and race reveals much about the party's approach to the broader question of national identity in the post-war period.

The Conservatives have been seen and have seen themselves as defenders of the nation and Empire since the late nineteenth century. As some have shown, this political identity was vigorously and often effectively constructed in the pre-1939 period.[13] Part of that construction was an admittedly sometimes conflicting relation between external and internal national identities, between the imperial and the domestic. Post-war, non-white immigration posed a problem of much different magnitude, enveloping the question of national identity with more explicit concerns about race and colour. Its resolution effectively split the ideals of Empire and nation. There emerged, in the post-war period, an unbridgeable dichotomy between defending and promoting the Empire-Commonwealth and defending the traditional nation. In 1960–2, the period leading up to the Commonwealth Immigrants Act, the former was abandoned.

Despite this shift, it cannot be argued, however, that the Conservatives defined the traditional nation with much force, confidence or clarity. Indeed, if there is an inextricable link between 'nation' and 'narration', then we might remark that, at least until 1962, the Conservatives told that story in a halting voice.[14] Bob Carter, Clive Harris and Shirley Joshi have maintained that between 1951 and 1955, the Conservative government constructed 'an ideological framework in which Black people were seen to be threatening, alien and inassimilable'.[15] It is important to accept as well, though, that there also existed support for multiracialism within the party, sometimes driven by external concerns, sometimes by domestic hopes. The difference was in terms of definition. Articulating what national identity has represented in the political sphere since 1945 remains problematic. In post-war Britain generally, national identity has usually been defined negatively, against Europe, against America and against immigrants, with more knowledge of the limitrophes between cultures than of the actual quality of the subject or the 'other'. There have been few successful attempts to present a contemporary version of either Disraeli's Crystal Palace Speech or Baldwin's pastoral homilies of the 1930s. Powell's contribution was, of course, effective, but it was rooted in resistance and defensiveness. What one can see in the party's engagement with immigration after 1945 is a movement from one positively articulated post-imperial identity to another more exclusive and negatively articulated post-imperial identity. In the examination of this movement, however, we should not forget the space in between the two positions, a space suggested as much by the regret in Heath's voice in 1968 as by the defiance in Powell's.

As this chapter will demonstrate, in the 1950s the Conservative response to non-white immigration was neither uniform nor homogeneous. Opposition to non-white immigration of course existed, at the level of cabinet, party and rank-and-file, but it was matched by visions of a multiracial presence abroad and, more tentatively, a multiracial nation at home. If not submerged, defensive articulations of a traditional nation were subdued. The turning point for the party was after 1960, when rising concern with the level of immigration gave increased weight to defensive voices from below, revealed through discontent among Conservative supporters, to which the Macmillan government responded reluctantly with the 1962 Commonwealth Immigrants Act. This movement may have been likely, but it was not simply inevitable; it was hastened by a failure to define domestic multiracialism in the way that external multiracialism had been defined. If we can speak of the relationship between party and nation as one at least partly constructed by political actors, the question of post-war immigration suggests a point where construction was abandoned in the face of instinct, or, to put it another way, when the failure to construct an effective language of multiracialism left the instincts against such change dominant.

# I

Offering the Conservatives' support for the 1948 British Nationality Act, which formalized free access to the United Kingdom for all colonial subjects, David Maxwell Fyfe looked forward to making them 'as privileged in the United Kingdom as the local citizens'.[16] This support was not idly proffered; indeed, for the Conservatives, there was an important advantage to be gained from extending British citizenship and promoting the idea of the 'mother' country welcoming her numerous children.

If, as is sometimes suggested, the history of post-war immigration and national identity is the obverse of imperial history, then it is important to review Conservative thought on Empire and Commonwealth after the Second World War. The need to frame a new imperial identity for Britain infused Conservative thinking on the Empire-Commonwealth after 1945. In 1948, for instance, the party conference adopted a commitment to 'a new conception of Commonwealth relations by which the British peoples, working together for the common benefit, will become closely integrated into one great strategic and trading unit'.[17] The progress towards colonial self-government and the need to face down communist or nationalist advances in the Third World simply intensified the need to maintain British influence through good will rather than formal rule. 'It is', remarked the Conservative Commonwealth Council in 1955, 'the special quality of positive friendship which is needed most at the awkward stage', a view commonly expressed at the level of leadership and party conference.[18] The monthly party journal of the 1950s, *Onward*, continually pressed this view, stressing, as the Colonial Secretary Oliver Lyttelton wrote in 1954, that '[h]appily for us in Britain and the Colonies, there is no conflict of true interest between us'.[19]

Support for multiracialism was, of course, at the heart of this ideal and intent. In 1960, for instance, a party pamphlet acknowledged that 'the Commonwealth is clearly not a unitary society', but, despite this:

> The Commonwealth is a multiracial society and it is in this that its unique opportunity of serving the world and the greatest single peril to its survival both consist. The problem of reconciling races is therefore, we believe, the central problem of Commonwealth policy.

To this end, British policy rested upon 'a deliberate and irrevocable rejection of the idea of racial segregation', an approach which imbued Harold Macmillan's 'wind of change' speech of 1960: 'in countries inhabited by several different races, it has been our aim to find the means by which the community can become more of a community, and fellowship can be fostered between its various parts.'[20] 'Multiracialism' was, of course, an ideal which could both assure black nationalists in Africa and protect the political position of white communities in Africa. What one can see in this is a reconception of imperial relationships, less forceful, perhaps, than that in the late nineteenth and early twentieth centuries, but broader in its view of race.[21]

To borrow the phrase used by Powell in 1968, 'the cloud no bigger than a man's hand' was, of course, multiracialism within Britain itself.[22] As Conservative ministers were to argue later, it was difficult to plump for multiracialism abroad, while at home supporting restrictions on immigration focused almost entirely upon race. An article in the Conservative Political Centre's journal, *Objective*, argued, for instance, that the Commonwealth was 'a multiracial community, and our concern is with making more and more multiracial communities', but spoke in terms of Singapore and Canada, South Africa and Kenya, not the metropolitan, omitting Britain entirely.[23]

Concerns about the potential disruption of multiracialism in Britain were soon voiced within the Conservative government of 1951, if not in the same breath as support for external multiracialism, at least in abrupt and often discordant counterpoint. In early 1954, Churchill told his cabinet that 'the rapid improvement of communications was likely to lead to a continuing increase in the number of coloured people coming to this country, and their presence here would sooner or later come to be resented by large sections of the British people'.[24] These were concerns echoed by other ministers, such as the Marquess of Salisbury, the Lord President, Lord Swinton, the Secretary at the Commonwealth Relations Office, Oliver Lyttelton, David Maxwell Fyfe, the Home Secretary, and Gwilym Lloyd George, Home Secretary after 1954. An immediate response to the problem was the establishment in January 1953 of an official working party on 'Coloured People Seeking Employment in the United Kingdom'. Its brief was explicit: to explore 'methods whereby coloured people could be stopped or deterred from coming to the United Kingdom in order to find employment'.[25] The progress of this working party between 1953 and 1955 and its successor between 1960 and 1961 provided a dry run for the framing of immigration legislation in 1962. In this, a language of racial difference and fear was the prevailing tone of discussion, providing the sole justification for the restriction of immigration. Arguments for closing the door could not, for instance, rest upon factors such as unemployment, or the disproportionate abuse of social services by immigrants or their flouting of the law, for the simple reason that none of these arguments was credible. The empirical evidence, assiduously gathered from the police, local authorities and social services, offered no support for restricting immigration. A police report on immigrant communities commissioned by the Home Office in 1954 concluded, for instance, that there were no particular problems with immigrant communities in terms of law, order or national assistance. Predictably, the trouble lay with the fears of cultural and economic dislocation simmering within the white population.[26] Such reports did not, however, prevent officials from promoting or constructing a schema of 'otherness' based upon racial stereotype, often contradicted by evidence from the police and the social services.[27] As late as 1961, the Treasury continued to stress the economic benefits of unrestricted immigration in a period of full employment, easing bottlenecks in labour supply, offering a pool of low-wage labour, and serving the cherished aim of a high-growth economy.[28] From empiricism, it seems, the tendency was still to slip into a clichéd language emphasizing 'otherness'.

As Dean has shown, concerns about the effect upon Britain's standing in the Commonwealth and the politicization of the race question prohibited movement on the issue in the 1950s.[29] Dean has written persuasively of the external constraints working against the enactment of immigration legislation up to 1961. What needs to be examined in greater depth are the currents of feeling within the Conservative Party in the same period. It is clear from even a cursory review of opinion outside Whitehall or the cabinet that, first of all, Conservative views of immigration were not uniform and, secondly, that the government responded as much to a change in attitudes within its own party as to the growing levels of immigrants.

## II

Between 1948 and 1960, immigration did not monopolize the Conservatives' attention. Only in 1958, for instance, did the party conference accept a resolution supporting the revision of immigration laws.[30] Through the period 1951–60, Conservative Party opinion on non-white immigration must be characterized as passively rather than actively defensive of the traditional nation.

Die-hard opponents of non-white immigration tended to be found on the margins. More liberal views provided a counterbalance to such views, though they remained undeveloped.

In 1952, for instance, the Bow Group published *Coloured Peoples in Britain*, written for the most part by Anthony McGowan, a report which stressed the changes in attitude required of the white population by multiracial immigration:

> it lies with the English working man not merely to work amicably alongside him, but to break down the social barriers . . . we oppose continual harping on the 'colour problem' in that it makes us unconsciously think of these men and women as 'other people'. If we have to fix our minds on problems, let us think rather of the personal problems of people who happen to be constructed a little differently from ourselves. Education, the schools, the Press, radio, television, greater social contact, all should combine to make us understand these people, eradicate from our minds wrong ideas about them, and in time break down our prejudices. We place the greatest emphasis on greater social contact and we call on all Conservatives to give the lead in this matter.[31]

That the work was republished in 1955 by the Conservative Political Centre as part of a collection entitled *The New Conservatism* suggests the forward-looking aspect to such arguments. Similarly, the party journal *Onward* featured a number of articles on immigrants, at one point, for instance, offering a photograph of black and white children at a sports day in London to underline an offering from Viscountess Davidson on 'Young Britons: A Chance for Children to Learn about the Empire, Citizenship and Patriotism'.[32] More controversial was an article entitled 'The Ebony and Ivory' on the situation of a Jamaican immigrant in Liverpool. The author did not shy from discussing one of the most sensitive of all issues, miscegenation:

> Mr Wynter asked me to be frank and I then sought his opinion about mixed marriages and the children which resulted, which many white people could not reconcile themselves to. He reminded me again that their emotions of love were not different to those of white people. He himself married a white woman.

The article ended on a positive note:

> I came away from Liverpool's Harlem pondering many things. I had conversed with coloured men whose mental ability was far in advance

of many of my compatriots, and yet by accident of birth they were
forced to resort to labouring to make a living. Undaunted, they carry
on, taking every opportunity to advance their education, regarding it as
their sword in the crusade for equality. In all justice, who shall say that
they do not deserve to succeed.[33]

The article provoked one very negative response, surprising in
itself for an official Conservative publication, but perhaps
instructive in showing the growing restiveness of the Conservative
rank-and-file on this issue as the decade wore on. A Mrs Laurie
Williams wrote that the 'whole tone of the article is unsavoury',
promoting the 'misery caused by inter-racial marriage'.[34] An
important lacuna which this minor exchange illustrated was a
perhaps inevitable failure even by proponents of a liberal view of
multiracialism to understand the implications of non-white
immigration, whether 'integration', 'assimilation' or 'coexistence',
a gap which was never satisfactorily reconciled by either party.

As will be suggested, there was a marked shift in Conservative
opinion on race and the apparent threat to national identity posed
by non-white immigrants. Perhaps the most important sphere of
such change was within the Conservative parliamentary party.
This comprised a movement less from the acceptance of non-
white immigration to rejection, but rather from a state of
unfocused disquiet, albeit one which allowed liberal voices and
marginalized outright opponents of immigration on racial
grounds, to one which brought the latter clearly into the mainstream of Conservative thinking.

Discussions on immigration occurred within the Commonwealth Affairs Committee in the 1950s. Generally, this group
reflected racially based reservations about non-white immigration,
but such concerns were not yet shaded in tones of urgency. In
April 1954, a subcommittee produced a memorandum which was
overwhelmingly critical of the immigrant population, particularly
with respect to their perceived work habits ('[t]hey do not take
readily to discipline . . . they are irresponsible and unreliable . . .
[t]hey are quarrelsome . . . [t]hey are lazy') and the 'widespread
racket' of immigrant housing strategies to take over houses
('[d]ropping a rock on floor to disturb people below . . . [p]laying
a musical instrument all night long'), all of which spoke to
conventional wisdom, rather than empirical evidence.[35] The letter
sent to the Home Secretary, David Maxwell Fyfe, was studiously

moderate, however, proposing that legislation had to be non-racial in appearance and, ideally, bipartisan, but warning at the same time that 'colour consciousness' would 'undoubtedly grow if the coloured community here increased in size'.[36] There was some restiveness when, by the end of 1954, 'no satisfactory reply' had been received from Maxwell Fyfe, but the issue was buried by the election of 1955 and the Suez crisis.[37] In 1957, more impatience over the failure to impose immigration controls emerged, with one MP remarking that '[i]t was no good relying on the good offices of Commonwealth countries. It was up to us to move.'[38] Until 1960, no movement occurred, nor, importantly, was pursued. This inertia was not due simply to the external constraints of concern for the Commonwealth.

The Commonwealth Affairs Committee was not, first of all, without supporters of non-white immigration. Patricia Hornsby-Smith, MP for Chislehurst and Joint Under-Secretary of State at the Home Office, noted that 'we owed some gratitude to West Indians when manpower had been short'. The member for Surbiton and Lloyd George's PPS at the Home Office, Nigel Fisher, was a consistent opponent of restrictions on immigration, arguing its importance for the Commonwealth and the domestic economy.[39] If concern about the impact of non-white immigration may have occasionally surfaced in the 1950s, it did not yet dominate Conservative thinking on immigration.

Indeed, up to 1960, only two Conservative MPs stood out publicly as fervent opponents of non-white immigration: Cyril Osborne, member for Louth, and Norman Pannell, who sat for the Liverpool seat of Kirkdale. Both consistently raised the question in the Commons. In 1955, for instance, Osborne attempted unsuccessfully to pass a private member's bill controlling immigration. He claimed that his objection to immigration was non-racial and that he was simply arguing for a recognition of the difficulties with housing, employment and, not least, the outmoded imperial role the Conservatives had given Britain: '[t]he imperialists would like to maintain the age-long policy of free immigration to the "mother" country, but we are no longer the metropolitan centre in the old sense. Britain is now merely the oldest among equals.'[40] None the less, he was also clear, as he told the *Daily Mail*, that '[t]his is a white man's country and I want it to remain so'.[41]

What is most instructive is the treatment accorded Osborne and Pannell by the parliamentary Conservative Party in the 1950s. In January 1955, for instance, only one MP, David Renton (later Under-Secretary at the Home Office between 1958 and 1961), attending the joint Commonwealth and Home Affairs Committee meeting supported Osborne's bill. The majority of Conservative MPs at the meeting objected strongly to ending the open-door policy:

> However well-presented, [it] would degenerate into colour-bar wrangle, with the Government in position of wishing to lower the status of its coloured colonial subjects . . . Such a Bill would lower the Mother Country's traditional status in the Commonwealth . . . Unfortunate timing that, in the year marking Jamaica's 300th anniversary under British rule, an 'Anti-Jamaican' Bill (for so it would inevitably appear) should be passed, or even introduced in the life of a Conservative administration . . . Why should mainly loyal and hard-working Jamaicans be discriminated against when ten times that quantity of disloyal [*sic*] Southern Irish (some of them Sinn Feiners) come and go as they please? . . . A heaven-sent opportunity for the Socialists to shuffle off some of their difficulties on to us.[42]

Osborne recognized himself that he was seen within his own party as a 'crank who has got a bee in his bonnet'.[43]

Whether at the level of cabinet or backbench opinion, therefore, the Conservative Party demonstrated competing views of the relationship between immigration and national identity. This is not to suggest that the defensive view of a uniracial nation, or, to put it another way, the language or instinct of racial difference, was not powerful. It was certainly more consistently present and more forcefully articulated than a more open vision of multiracialism at home. None the less, both coexisted at this time. A memorandum on 'Questions of Policy', drafted for candidates at the 1955 election by the party's Colonial Affairs Committee caught both sides:

> Question: What is the candidate's attitude to the growing influx of immigrants from the Colonies, particularly the British West Indies?
> Suggested Replies: I know and share the concern which the large number of immigrants is causing. We must remember that all these people are British subjects. The problem is therefore one of great complexity . . . The Government have been watching the situation most carefully. This is not a matter which should be allowed to become an issue of Party controversy. My own view is that the best course might be to hold a full inquiry to bring out all the facts.

Question: Are many of these immigrants of an undesirable type?

Suggested Reply: The majority are law-abiding citizens, but if some are not this is true of all communities.[44]

In July 1961, however, a majority of members of the Conservative parliamentary Commonwealth and Home Committees thought 'action to control immigration should be taken urgently'.[45] Within six months, the Conservative government had pledged itself to bring in restrictive legislation. It seems that, as Nigel Fisher himself acknowledged, the difference was the perception of constituents' opinion. Most of those supporting legislation did so as an 'unfortunate necessity' in the face of negative public feeling. It was clear, as well, that this meant an abandonment of one shared assumption of the Conservatives' support for an imperial identity, as revealed in a discussion within the Commonwealth Affairs Committee in November 1961: 'SIR LEONARD ROPNER feared the possible effect on the Commonwealth but said that the conception of Empire had gone. It was no longer a case of Britain acting as "mother" to her Commonwealth "daughters".'[46]

# III

What changed, of course, was the level of public concern over immigration perceived by the Conservatives, not only in public opinion polls, but also through the mail-bags of Central Office and Conservative MPs. An immediate cause was the rise in immigration rates from the New Commonwealth from 1960,

*Table 1: Main Sources of Immigration into the United Kingdom 1956–1962*[47]

| Year | West Indies | India | Pakistan |
|------|-------------|-------|----------|
| 1956 | 26400 | 5600 | 2100 |
| 1957 | 22500 | 6000 | 5200 |
| 1958 | 16500 | 6200 | 4700 |
| 1959 | 20400 | 2900 | 900 |
| 1960 | 52700 | 5900 | 2500 |
| 1961 | 61600 | 23750 | 25100 |
| 1962 | 35000 | 22100 | 24900 |

though the causes of this increase may well have been in anticipation of an immigration restriction bill (see table 1).

A wide range of Conservative constituencies and MPs received anti-immigrant letters in the period 1960–1, not limited to areas such as Birmingham, Liverpool and London, but including Bedford, Esher, Abingdon, Stratford and Harrogate.[48] For instance, W. R. Van Straubenzee, MP for Wokingham, noted the novelty of such concern in his constituency:

> for the first time I am starting to receive from my constituency letters revealing anxiety about coloured immigration into the United Kingdom. I realise that this is an exceptionally thorny problem but undoubtedly it is becoming one in which the general public are getting increasingly restive.[49]

The vast majority of letters received by Conservative MPs such as J. Watts, Gerald Wills, Christopher Soames and John Profumo were critical of the 'open-door' policy. A typical example was one received by Profumo:

> What *is* the matter with the Conservatives they don't face up to this matter [*sic*]? I woul'nt [*sic*] have voted, nor worked for the Conservatives had I known they would allow things to drift as they are. 'Wind of Change' indeed. It is a wind of change for England + unless something is done England will not remain England for long . . . There is the utmost danger of this country being so swamped we shall not be masters in our own land.[50]

In the spring of 1961, the Birmingham Immigration Control Association was established. Though explicitly non-political, its membership boasted an executive drawn from local Conservative voters such as W. J. McIntyre and John Sanders.[51] The following July saw a rent strike begin among 600 white Smethwick municipal tenants objecting to the admission of a Pakistani immigrant to a council maisonette.[52] In August, there were race riots in Middlesbrough.

Public restiveness was reflected in Conservative ranks at Westminster. Cyril Osborne and Norman Pannell's steady pressure on the government met with growing support from the Conservative backbenches. In July and November 1960, deputations of Conservative MPs, mostly from Birmingham, lobbied the Colonial Office for restrictive legislation.[53] *The Times* could remark in December 1960 that 'Conservative members in the Commons are virtually united in the belief that the present uncontrolled inflow of immigrants should not be allowed to continue'.[54] Increasingly, more liberal voices, such as Nigel Fisher, were marginalized in their argument for keeping the open-door policy as 'one of the few cohesive ties that remain' in the Commonwealth.[55] Earlier that year, as noted above, the Conservatives' parliamentary Home Affairs committee had met to discuss the issue. As Nigel Fisher reported to Iain Macleod, the Colonial Seretary, that sentiment was now overwhelmingly towards the abandonment of the open-door policy:

> There is no doubt the majority of Members present at the very well-attended Home Affairs meeting on Thursday were against leaving the problem as it is and in favour of some new legislation. This is the opposite of the majority view when the matter was discussed by the same Committee about two years ago and reflects, of course, the change in attitude due to the steep increase in the immigration figures for 1960.[56]

In July, the majority of the same committee and the Commonwealth committee 'considered that action to control immigration should be taken urgently', not on economic grounds, but social grounds: '[t]he test which should be applied was whether the intending immigrant would be easily assimilated into our population'.[57] Such concerns were much in evidence at the party conference of October 1961, with one delegate remarking, for instance, '[t]hese immigrants are not necessarily inferior to us but they are different – different not only in colour but in background, tradition and habit.'[58]

## IV

Throughout 1960, the Macmillan government refused to abandon unrestricted immigration.[59] In February 1961, it was still the cabinet's view that 'there was no need to decide at once whether legislation should be introduced to control immigration'.[60] The officials' working party could see no legitimate grounds for restriction apart for concerns about white opinion: '[t]he case for restriction on social grounds cannot at the present moment be related to health, crime, public order, or employment.'[61] Though recognizing that there had been a 'startling increase in the number of coloured immigrants' in the first five months of 1961, the cabinet still refused to announce a commitment to restriction in May 1961, pending a report on possible legislation.[62]

In the autumn of 1961, however, admitting the 'growing public anxiety about the position and mounting pressure from government supporters for some measure of control', immigration controls were reluctantly taken up by the government on 10 October. It was agreed that criticism from Commonwealth countries was 'preferable to the continuing risk of ill-feeling over incidents in this country involving coloured Commonwealth immigrants'.[63] The decision was announced, appropriately enough, to the Conservative Party conference meeting in Brighton on 11 October.[64] As the West Indian Prime Minister suggested to Macmillan after the announcement, the older quest for imperial or Commonwealth identity had been abandoned: '[i]t will in future be difficult for any person from the Commonwealth to accept unreflectingly the oft-repeated assertion of multiracial partnership.'[65]

The shape and justification for the bill were predictable. The latter rested entirely upon the question of colour and the protection of white identity, while the shape, based upon an employment voucher system, was consciously intended to mask the racial basis of the bill, as the Home Secretary, R. A. Butler, recognized, 'although the scheme purports to relate solely to employment and to be non-discriminatory, its aim is primarily social and its restrictive effect is intended and would in fact operate on coloured people almost exclusively.'[66] An important omission from the bill, proving this bias, was the exemption granted to immigrant workers from Southern Ireland.

In the Commons, the government faced rancorous criticism from Labour on the racial basis of the bill. Patrick Gordon Walker noted the change in Conservative attitudes to national identity: 'Conservatives pride themselves on being the party of the Commonwealth. I am beginning to think that they and the Ministers on the Front Bench do not know the first thing about the Commonwealth today.'[67] Conservative opinion was more muted. During the Second Reading, Conservative speakers, like Cyril Osborne and Harold Gurden from Birmingham, pressed hard-line support for immigration controls, citing crime and problems of housing, and touching as well on the revision of the imperial relationship, even in a peculiar fashion:

> Going back to the metaphor of the Mother Country and the case of the parent and the child . . . the child is not entitled to come in and turn the parents out of the house. The child is not allowed to come in and should not be allowed to come and take the bathroom door and do things of that kind.[68]

Only Nigel Fisher offered a critical view of the bill from the Conservative backbenches. Fisher dismissed economic concerns surrounding immigration as fallacious and the problem of social tension as simply an excuse for racism. Most importantly, Fisher pointed out the abandonment of the Conservative commitment to Commonwealth not only because:

> it brings to an end the long tradition of free entry for all Commonwealth citizens, but because I believe it to be quite inimical to our whole concept of a multiracial Commonwealth. Here we are, the leaders of the greatest association of nations – many of them coloured – that the world has ever known, legislating against the entry of our own fellow citizens into our own country. In so doing, we must inevitably weaken the rather slender ties which still bind the Commonwealth together. By this Bill, we are cutting yet another Commonwealth cord of unity and cohesion . . . I would add that it seems strange to me that in Africa we attack *apartheid* and preach partnership, but in the United Kingdom we are today taking powers to exclude coloured British citizens.[69]

Fisher abstained on Second Reading; with Lord Balniel (Hertford), he was only one of two Conservative abstentions. The government won a majority of 200 on Second Reading.

Despite the criticism of the Opposition benches, elements of the Conservative press and backbenchers like Fisher, the Conservatives enjoyed enormous popular support for the bill;[70] in November 1961, 76 per cent of those polled approved of the measures to control immigration, with only 12 per cent disapproving and 12 per cent undecided.[71] Though Gallup indicated that the immigration issue was unlikely to shift voters between parties in a profound way, it did come at a time when the Conservatives were very close to Labour in the polls. Butler noted some confidence at the second cabinet committee meeting on the popularity of the bill: 'the Opposition grossly underrated public opinion on the Bill as a whole, since there could be no doubt that the Government had the country solidly behind them on the principle of controlling Commonwealth immigration.'[72]

## V

After 1962, the starting point for Conservative Party discussions on immigration and race was the acknowledgement that no further large-scale, non-white immigration could be permitted, even in the face of economic need.[73] The dramatic ousting of Patrick Gordon Walker by the Conservative candidates in the Smethwick and Leyton elections of 1964 and 1965 amid a welter of racist rhetoric revealed the depth of white feeling on immigration. Within the Conservative Party, one might also note the spilling over of concern over non-white immigration into other domestic spheres, marking, one might argue, the further internalization of the race question.

Education was one example. In April 1964, for instance, Arthur Tiley, MP for Bradford, noted that there was a feeling that 'coloured children swamp certain schools', lowering standards, also noted by Edward Boyle.[74] The party's Immigration Policy Group accepted the need for American-style busing to ensure a ceiling of 30 per cent immigrant children per school.[75] This provoked some disquiet with figures such as Heath and Selwyn Lloyd, who feared a racialist stigma being attached to specific figures, but none the less accepted the need for the '*even* distribution of immigrant school children'.[76]

In circles of liberal Conservative opinion on immigration, the tone was one of regret, tinged with the growing realization that both the battle and the war had been lost. Writing in *Crossbow* after Peter Griffiths's successful racist campaign in Smethwick, for instance, Malcolm Rutherford lamented the loss of the Conservatives' 'old, moderate, enlightened line'. He argued that the real failure had been that a multiracial view of the nation had not accompanied post-war immigration, in the way that a multiracial view of the Empire-Commonwealth had accompanied the reconception of post-war imperial relations:

Neither Smethwick, nor anywhere else in Britain, had been asked to accept a multiracial society. Such places had just been expected to receive varying numbers of coloured immigrants without being given any clear lead as to how they should cope with them. 'Multiracial' in fact was a theoretical term adopted by the British Government in an effort to fulfil its commitments to the white minorities in Africa at the same time as granting the Africans independence. Nobody had ever defined whether it meant that the minority races should ultimately be absorbed, assimilated, or just integrated, or whether like federation, it was a term used as a smokescreen to cover the fact that the Government was simply leaving the problem to someone else.

Probably without realizing it, Griffiths had put his finger on just this intellectual muddle. 'Smethwick rejects the idea of a multiracial society' was a statement neither Wilson nor Home were capable of answering, simply because neither of them had worked out what it was Smethwick was supposed to accept.[77]

Rutherford evoked both the loss of an external post-imperial identity for Britain and the failure to develop an internal post-imperial identity, that of multiracialism. In 1968, the tone of Heath's response to Enoch Powell was an implicit acknowledgement of this loss and failure. In 1905, in the midst of another period of anti-immigrant sentiment, both Conservative and Liberal politicians had, according to David Feldman, perceived an opportunity to use the affirmation of national identity, 'home and country', in order to unify disparate strata of Edwardian society.[78] The public response to Powell's speech painfully demonstrated the continuing importance of race in politics. National identity or 'home and country' was, however, a much more complex cipher for the Conservative Party after the Second World War than it had been in 1905. The difference between the two periods lies not only in the understandable reluctance of Conservatives to rely only upon a defensive and often racist instinct, but also in their reluctance to construct and promote an effective alternative vision of national identity in post-war Britain.

*Notes*

Acknowledgement is made to the generous research funding provided by the Social Science and Humanities Research Council of Canada. The author is also grateful to Amy Black for her invaluable assistance with research.

1 Bodleian Library, Oxford, Conservative Party Archives [hereafter CPA], CCO 505/4/63, text of speech at Wolverhampton made by Enoch Powell, 20 April 1968.

2 Ibid.

3 See G. H. Gallup, *Gallup International Opinion Polls*, II: *Great Britain 1965–75* (New York, 1976), 984, 1037.

4 See, for instance, D. Kavanagh, *Thatcherism and British Politics: The End of Consensus?* (Oxford, 1987) and A. Gamble, *The Free Economy and the Strong State* (Durham, NC, 1988).

5 *Daily Mail*, 31 January 1978.

6 *Daily Express*, 25 April 1968.

7 E. Heath, *Immigration and Racial Harmony* (London: Conservative Political Centre, 20 September 1968), 2.

8 See A. M. Smith, *New Right Discourse on Race and Sexuality* (Cambridge, 1994); D. W. Dean, 'Conservative Governments and the Restriction of Commonwealth Immigration in the 1950s: The Problems of Constraint', *Historical Journal* 35 (1992), 171–94; B. Carter, C. Harris and S. Joshi, *The 1951–55 Conservative Governments and the Racialisation of Black Immigration* (Warwick: Centre for Research in Ethnic Relations, Policy Papers in Ethnic Relations 11, October 1987).

9 See Z. Layton-Henry, *The Politics of Immigration* (Oxford, 1991); J. Solomos, *Race and Racism in Post-War Britain* (London, 1987); C. Holmes, 'Immigration', in T. R. Gourvish and A. O'Day (eds.), *Britain since 1945* (London, 1991), 209–31.

10 Public Record Office, Kew [hereafter PRO], CAB 128/19, CM (50) 37, Cabinet Minutes, 19 June 1950; see also K. Paul, '"British Subjects" and "British Stock": Labour's Postwar Imperialism', *Journal of British Studies* 34 (1995), 233–76.

11 PRO, CAB 128/39, CC (64) 6, Cabinet Minutes, 5 November 1964.

12 See *Parliamentary Debates* (Commons) 350 (16 November 1961), 696.

13 J. Lawrence, 'Class and Gender in the Making of Urban Toryism, 1880–1914', *English Historical Review* 108 (1993), 629–52; R. I. McKibbin, 'Class and Conventional Wisdom', in *Ideologies of Class* (Oxford, 1991), 259–93; H. Cunningham, 'The Conservative Party and Patriotism', in R. Colls and P. Dodd (eds.), *Englishness: Politics and Culture 1880–1920* (London, 1986), 288–321.

14 For discussions of the theory of 'nation' and 'narration', see H. Bhabba (ed.), *Nation and Narration* (London, 1990).

15 Carter, Harris and Joshi, *The 1951–55 Conservative Governments and the Racialisation of Black Immigration*, 1.

16 *Parliamentary Debates* (Commons) 453 (7 July 1948), c.403.

17 Conservative Party, *Annual Conference Report* (1948), 64.

18 Conservative Commonwealth Council, *Colonial Rule: Enemies and Obligations* (London: Conservative Political Centre, no.141, March 1955), 5; see also Marquess of Salisbury, *Commonwealth and Empire* (London: Commonwealth Series no.1, 24 April 1955), 4.

19 Oliver Lyttelton, 'The Colonies Step Forward', *Onward* 1/6 (March 1954), 10.

20 *Wind of Change* (London: Conservative Political Centre, April 1960), 16, 29; *The Times*, 4 February 1960.

21 See E. H. H. Green, *The Crisis of Conservatism: The Politics, Economics and Ideology of the British Conservative Party 1880–1914* (London, 1995), 199–201.

22 It is ironic that at the same time, the Macmillan government was willing to expend considerable funds on the Commonwealth Scholarship Scheme to bring students to Britain.

23 C. F. Carrington, 'The Multiracial Community', *Objective* 23 (June 1956), 3.

24 PRO, CAB 128/27, CC (54) 7, Cabinet Conclusions, 3 February 1954; this was accompanied by criticism offered by the popular press; see, for instance, D. Divine, 'From Tiger Bay', *Sunday Graphic*, 26 October 1952.

25 PRO, CO 1028/22, CWP (53) 1, Working Party on Coloured People Seeking Employment in the United Kingdom, Minutes, 30 January 1953.

26 PRO, PREM 11/824, Home Office, Police Report, 12 October 1954.

27 PRO, CO 1028/22, CWP (53) 15, 'The Employment Position of Coloured Workers: Note by the Ministry of Labour', 28 September 1953; CWP (53) 10, 'Information Obtained by the Police about Coloured Communities in the United Kingdom', 11 July 1953.

28 PRO, CO 1032/304, 'Economic Effects of Legislation into United Kingdom: Memorandum by Treasury', n.d. [July 1961].

29 See Dean, 'Conservative Governments and the Restriction of Commonwealth Immigration in the 1950s'.

30 Conservative Party, *Annual Conference Report* (1958), 149–51.

31 Bow Group, *Coloured Peoples in Britain* (1952), republished in Conservative Political Centre, *The New Conservatism* (London, 1955), 150.

32 Viscountess Davidson, 'Young Britons: A Chance for Children to Learn about the Empire, Citizenship and Patriotism', *Onward* 1/7 (April 1954), 9.

[33] Stanley Rowland, 'The Ebony and the Ivory', *Onward* 2/2 (November 1954), 4–5.

[34] *Onward* 2/3 (December 1954), 15.

[35] CPA, CCO 507/1/1, Commonwealth Affairs Committee, 'Coloured Immigrants', 14 April 1954.

[36] CPA, CCO 507/1/1, Commonwealth Affairs Committee, B. Braine to D. Maxwell Fyfe, 20 April 1954.

[37] CPA, CCO 507/1/1, Commonwealth Affairs Committee, Minutes, 1 November 1954.

[38] CPA, CCO 507/1/1, Commonwealth Affairs Committee, Minutes, 15 July 1957.

[39] Ibid.

[40] *The Times*, 10 February 1955.

[41] *Daily Mail*, 7 February 1961.

[42] PRO, PREM 11/824, Conservative Parliamentary Party, Commonwealth and Home Affairs Committee Meeting, Minutes, 27 January 1955.

[43] PRO, CO 1032/298, C. Osborne to R. A. Butler, 4 August 1960.

[44] CPA, CCO4/6/33, Colonial Affairs Committee, 'General Election 1955: Questions of Policy: Colonial Immigrants', n.d. [1955].

[45] PRO, 1032/304, Conservative Parliamentary Party, Commonwealth and Home Affairs Committee Joint Meeting, Minutes, 6 July 1961.

[46] CPA, CCO 507/1/2, Commonwealth Affairs Committee, West Indies Subcommittee Minutes, 13 November 1961.

[47] From D. E. Butler and G. Butler, *British Political Facts 1900–94* (London, 1994), 327.

[48] Among the Conservative MPs receiving letters were Michael Hughes-Young (Wandsworth), Robert Matthew (Honiton, Devonshire); Airey Neave (Abingdon, Berkshire); Richard Nugent (Guildford, Surrey); Edith Pitt (Edgbaston, Birmingham); John Profumo (Stratford, Warwickshire); James Ramsden (Harrogate, Yorkshire); William Robson-Brown (Esher, Surrey); William Roots (South Kensington); Christopher Soames (Bedford); James Watts (Moss Side); W. R. Van Straubenzee (Wokingham, Berkshire); Gerald Wills (Bridgwater). See PRO, CO 1032/298, 299 and 300.

[49] PRO, CO 1032/299, W. R. Van Straubenzee to H. Fraser, 18 May 1961.

[50] PRO, CO 1032/298, W. M. Taylor to J. Profumo, 23 July 1960; see also CO 1032/299 and CO 1032/300.

[51] See Birmingham Immigration Control Association, 'Statement', n.d. [1961].

[52] See *The Times*, 24, 25, 26, 27 and 29 July 1961; given later developments, it is worth noting that Peter Griffiths, the successful Conservative candidate in the infamous contest of 1964 did not

support the rent strike when serving as leader of the Conservative group in the council.

53  See *The Times*, 14 July 1960; PRO, CO 1032/302, Minutes of Meeting with Deputation of Birmingham Conservative MPs, 15 November 1960.

54  *The Times*, 16 December 1960.

55  *The Times*, 18 February 1961.

56  PRO, CO 1032/298, N. Fisher to I. MacLeod, 6 February 1961.

57  PRO, CO 1032/304, Minutes of the Joint Meeting of the [Conservative Parliamentary] Home Affairs and Commonwealth Committees, 6 July 1961.

58  Conservative Party, *Annual Conference Report* (1961), 30.

59  See, for instance, comments made by Iain Macleod, *The Times*, 22 April 1960.

60  PRO, CAB 128/35, CC (61) 7, Cabinet Minutes, 16 February 1961.

61  PRO, CO 1032/305, CWP (61) 20, Working Party, 'Report to Ministerial Committee', 17 July 1961.

62  PRO, CAB 128/35, CC (61) 29, Cabinet Minutes, 30 May 1961.

63  PRO, CAB 128/35, CC (61) 55, Cabinet Minutes, 10 October 1961.

64  Conservative Party, *Annual Conference Report* (1961), 26–33.

65  PRO, PREM 11/3238, Prime Minister, West Indies, to Macmillan, 17 November 1961.

66  PRO, CAB 129/107, C (61) 153, 'Commonwealth Migrants', Memorandum by the Home Secretary, 6 October 1961.

67  *Parliamentary Debates* (Commons) 350 (16 November 1961), 712.

68  Ibid., 768.

69  Ibid., 778.

70  See *The Times*, 17 November 1961.

71  Gallup, *Gallup International Public Opinion Polls: Great Britain*, 610–11.

72  PRO, CAB 130/180, Commonwealth Immigrants Bill Committee, 2nd Meeting, Minutes, 28 November 1961; see also PREM 11/3238, I. Macleod to H. Macmillan, 15 November 1961.

73  CPA, CRD 3/16/1, PG/9/65/21, Immigration Policy Group, Manifesto Points, 7 July 1965.

74  CPA, CRD 3/16/1, A. Tiley, 'Bradford's Immigrant Problem', 26 April 1965; CPA, CRD 3/16/1, PG/9/65/10, Immigration Policy Committee Minutes, 30 April 1965.

75  CPA, CRD 3/16/1, PG/9/65/13, Immigration Policy Committee Minutes, 19 May 1965; see also *Immigration and the Commonwealth* (London: Conservative Political Centre, June 1965), 20–1.

76  CPA, CRD 3/16/2, 'Party Policy on Immigration and Race Relations', n.d. [June 1965]; see also S. Lloyd to E. Heath, 10 June 1965; E. Heath to S. Lloyd, 14 June 1965.

77  M. Rutherford, 'Sentence on the Immigrants', *Crossbow* 9/33 (October–December 1965), 15–16.

[78] See D. Feldman, 'The Importance of Being English: Jewish Immigration and the Decay of Liberal England', in G. Stedman Jones and D. Feldman (eds.), *Metropolis: London* (London, 1989), 56–84.

*Part Three*


*Gender*

# The Conservative Party and the Politics of Gender, 1900–1939

## DAVID JARVIS

I ask the Government to remember that we women of the Unionist Party have to fight a great battle, there are so many men who say such amazingly stupid things about women in our party.

Nancy Astor, 9 February 1927.[1]

With the flappers' vote playing an important part in the result, and the inevitable new batch of women members coming into the Commons, I find myself in a reposeful state of mind, and able to quote:

> From toilsome days and tiresome ways
> Good fortune sets me free
> From all great guns, and women's tongues
> Good God delivers me.

Sir Warden Chilcott, MP, on his decision to leave the House of Commons, 5 March 1929.[2]

The history of the Conservative Party and the study of gender have rarely crossed paths.[3] Historians have only recently begun to examine how assumptions about differential sex roles and gender identities have helped to shape the form and content of Conservative politics. This approach has scarcely been applied at all to the early twentieth-century period,[4] even though the suffrage campaign and subsequent parliamentary enfranchisement of women made the politics of gender at this time both fluid and controversial.[5] Scholarly neglect of the inter-war period is particularly surprising in view of the number of recent psephological studies suggesting that the 'gender gap' in British voting habits was already evident in the 1920s.[6] Several studies of women's involvement in the early twentieth-century Conservative Party do exist,[7] but they generally concentrate on the experience of women as a discrete group rather the wider party's reaction to women. Such research has undoubtedly advanced our understanding of the scale and importance of female political activity. It is dangerous, however, to infer from the success story of Conservative women's organizations that the fluidity of gendered identities in this period posed no threat to the Conservative Party. Conservatives may have increasingly believed that they had answers to the 'woman question', but many of them also feared that such a response would in turn throw up a 'man question' that might prove altogether more intractable. Fully to understand the implications of female enfranchisement for Conservatism, it is therefore essential to recognize that the party's problem was one of gender, and not just of 'women'.[8]

This point becomes clearer on examining Conservative beliefs about the needs and desires of women as active political agents. Although the prospect and subsequent arrival of female suffrage prompted many Tories to lament the uncertainty of future politics, there was remarkable agreement within the party about the existence of a specifically female political agenda.[9] Conservatives of both sexes generally assumed that women favoured 'domestic' political issues, with a particular emphasis on matters affecting women and children and on social reform.[10] Similarly, women were generally believed to have a high moral stance politically, especially on the temperance issue.[11] In terms of international politics, women were believed to be imperially minded in a practical sense, and keen on the idea of the Empire as a family.[12] The more aggressive and jingoistic connotations of Empire were, however, considered anathema to women, because of their sympathy for international co-operation and peace initiatives. Vacuous appeals to the glories of imperialism,[13] anything approaching sabre-rattling and any policy adversely affecting household expenditure were therefore to be avoided as far as possible, even when otherwise in the national interest.[14] Some of these assumptions evolved over time – most obviously in relation to female imperialism – but little seems to have happened by 1939 to make Tory strategists doubt this general order of female priorities, and party propaganda aimed at women voters faithfully reflected them.[15] Few Conservatives doubted either what women wanted from party institutions. They sought a congenial social environment, meetings timed not to clash with domestic responsibilities,[16] freedom from boisterous masculinity, and a smoke-free, alcohol-free and obscenity-free atmosphere.[17]

Albeit with some grousing, Conservatives could and largely did seek to address these needs. After 1928, women formed the majority of electors, and by the early 1930s, there was growing evidence of their reliability as Conservative voters.[18] Almost all Conservative campaigners also acknowledged that since the war Tory women had been far more active on the party's behalf than their male colleagues. It is therefore all too easy to present the Conservative response to female enfranchisement as a straightforward success – another feather in the cap of popular Toryism. In this chapter, I offer an alternative and more equivocal assessment, informed by evidence of profound disquiet within Conservative ranks about the 'feminization' of politics from 1900 onwards. Many Conservatives feared that the party was paying an unacceptably high price for women's support, and thus jeopardizing both the future of its existing institutions and its traditional electoral support. I will focus here on two particularly common complaints: first, that women were ruining the ambience and effectiveness of Conservative constituency organizations, and second, that women's growing influence was undermining the 'manly' conduct of politics more generally.

I

We should divest our minds of prejudice and accept the fact that sooner or later the masculine element will be a minority on the Register and in the associations, and that no fictitious safeguards will prevent the women having their way if they want it . . . We must show the courage of men, and not be terrified by the bogey of female domination. It is not that sort of woman who joins our party.

Leigh Maclachlan, June 1920.[19]

Historians of Conservative women's organizations have tended to stress the continuity between pre- and post-war political practice. According to Martin Pugh, for example, 'In view of their extensive traditional role as allied forces of the party in bodies such as the Primrose League and the Tariff Reform League it is not surprising that Conservative women adapted to th[e] post-war system with little friction.'[20] It is important to stress, however, that whatever the political utility of Conservative women before 1918, their activity was recognized for what it was: ancillary to the main institutions of the party. Representative Conservative bodies remained as exclusively male as the parliamentary electorate. Praise of female workers and canvassers cost constituency officials little, since women had yet to 'invade' the central institutions of the party.[21] Equally, however positive Conservatives were about women's political influence, their enthusiasm remained tempered by a due sense of its irrelevance, while women lacked the parliamentary vote. In such circumstances, to proselytize among women was to neglect the primary purpose of party politics, as J. H. Bottomley reminded canvassers in 1912: 'DON'T be satisfied with seeing the wife. She may talk, but remember the husband is the voter. See him.'[22]

Many party workers therefore believed the experience of Edwardian politics irrelevant to post-war conditions in terms of mobilizing and organizing women. One delegate warned the 1917 National Union conference:

> What an absurdity for us to endeavour to organize women for future political purposes if we are to look at this question from the old land marks and to gauge women's organisations by the women's organisations which, all honour to them, have done the work in the past. They have done their work in conjunction with us to get the male voters to the poll, to educate, to trace and to help the men.[23]

Most constituency associations seem to have recognized the force of this argument, although consensus on the necessity of reform did not extend to the nature of the reform required. At issue was the principle of integrating women's organizations into the main constituency bodies. The proponents both of integration and of continued separation received influential backing, although the general trend between the wars was towards integration.[24] At the same time, the party's rules were revised to allocate women at least one-third of the places on all representative bodies in the National Union.[25] Judging by the expansion of female membership of the party and the effectiveness of Conservative women's political work, these developments were undoubtedly successful.[26] Their repercussions on the wider party, however, produced considerable debate.

By the early 1920s the reliance of Conservative constituency associations on their female members had become a truism within the party. Almost all agents, MPs and candidates acknowledged that women were outdoing men in terms of canvassing, propaganda work and fundraising. As early as 1919 for example, Glasgow Conservatives were attributing critical significance to their work:

> Too much credit for any success we have achieved could not be given to the women. All over the country the women's influence was great and good, but we wish to give particular credit to our women members for their untiring efforts . . . their work meant the difference between victory and defeat.[27]

Underlying the generous recognition of female work, however, lay widespread concern about the changing character of popular Conservatism. A good index of this feeling was the attitude of male Conservative agents. Although they were probably the most vocal section of the party in their recognition of women's constituency work, they also betrayed considerable misgivings about its wider repercussions. This ambivalence was neatly summarized by the columnist 'Ubique' in the 1926 *Agents' Journal*:

> most agents adopt the true philosophical attitude towards women, which is a mingling of fear and affection. They admire the limitless energy and devotion displayed by women in political work, but they have an uneasy sense that the feminine tide may sweep everything before it.[28]

Most at threat from this 'feminine tide' apparently were the party's organization of men and the traditional culture of masculine conviviality within Conservative institutions.

The first fear reflected the belief that official encouragement of Conservative women and the visible success of their organizations were undermining the main constituency associations, which tended in practice to be the 'men's' organizations.[29] In part, this was because men were believed to be resting on their laurels while women kept constituency activity going.[30] More worryingly, constant praise of women's superior efforts on the party's behalf was alleged to be undermining male activists' morale. One agent warned ominously in 1936 of the need 'to see that the men are not sickened by always hearing that they do nothing'.[31] By the mid-1930s, Central Office identified the need for the party to increase its male membership as a major priority.[32] The general director, Sir Robert Topping, reminded agents in his New Year's Message for 1935 that this was a 'matter . . . of vital importance'. Subsequent responses in the *Agents' Journal* optimistically claimed that women's membership had peaked and that 'a political issue which will excite men is inevitable, and when that issue does come the constituency which organized its men will stand the best chance of victory'.[33] Though unproven, the inverse correlation between the membership of male and female branches of the party was taken for granted by most contributors to this discussion, thus casting a significant shadow over Tory women's achievements.

Agents' resentment at female 'intrusion' into male political preserves was even more marked. The National Society of Conservative and Unionist Agents was the focus of considerable controversy throughout the inter-war period concerning the admission of women agents and 'women's organizers' as members. Failure to resolve the issue satisfactorily led to the creation in 1927 of the rival National Association of Conservative and Unionist Women's Organisers, and relations between the two bodies remained frosty well into the 1930s.[34] At a personal level, too, it seems that women organizers often experienced ill-disguised hostility from male colleagues. At the 1922 party conference dinner they were reportedly consigned to their own table 'as though they all had the measles'.[35] Many agents evidently resented the novel experience of dealing regularly with women to conduct constituency business, accusing 'party women' of spite, fussiness and hysteria.[36] Several also complained that women organizers in their constituencies were not co-operating with the main association or were otherwise subverting the agent's authority.[37] Temporary returns to an exclusively male environment were therefore much in demand. One West Midlands agent confessed in 1935 that the main attraction of a recent party training course was that it was spent in sound male company, with the wiles of political ladies far behind us. For one week in the year, we are taken back to the atmosphere and cheery companionship of lots of men doing the same job, which was such a feature of the Army courses now so many years ago.[38]

Agents were by no mean alone within the party in their desire to protect 'male space'. In the 1920s, for example, this issue strongly influenced debates about the role of the Conservative club movement. Even before the war, the future of Conservative workingmen's clubs had been uncertain, as Jon Lawrence has shown in his excellent study of popular Toryism in the West Midlands. Lawrence identifies a growing tension in the Edwardian period between the clubs' celebration of a predominantly masculine popular culture centred on 'the pub, the racecourse and the football terrace' and the 'home and hearth' Toryism of the Primrose League.[39] Women's higher political profile after the war exacerbated this tension. Long-standing male members recognized that women would not take kindly to the 'three Bs' of existing clubs – billiards, bar and bridge[40] – but most hoped that women would set up their own clubs rather than insist on joining existing ones.[41] In 1922, the secretary of the Conservative Clubs Association ridiculed the idea of mixed clubs:

> The tastes of men and women from the club standpoint are utterly and entirely different. Immediately there would be friction; feathers would fly, and the club would 'bust up', the men going off to some place where they could breathe, call a spade an 'adjectival shovel' if they wanted to, and have 'one over the eight' if possessed of an acute thirst, without being subjected to feminine observation and strictures.[42]

In practice many agents favoured allowing women into the clubs, no doubt because they believed the beer and billiards to be largely antithetical to useful political work. Male activists did not, however, give up their search for a space apart from female colleagues resented as 'prigs' and 'bores'.[43] It is interesting that the Unionist Labour Committees, designed to promote working-class representation within the party and an important symbol of its democratization, were reputed to attract men because they did not admit women:

> It is the only committee inside the association upon which women are not eligible for membership. Not that any untoward language is never

used [*sic*], but it may be that members feel a certain freedom of speech can be indulged in without the necessity for that care and restraint which must be remembered when the fair sex are in evidence.[44]

Other self-consciously proletarian offshoots of the party such as the pseudo-Masonic National Conservative League in the north-east also excluded women and celebrated the virtues of brotherly bonding in a congenial atmosphere. As Alan Hand waxed lyrical to fellow agents in 1925:

> You know that every man in the room has become your brother, and that you can count on him, and he on you. Would not this make you realise that you were part of a living force, and that your faith was worth fighting for?[45]

Another area of conflict concerned the party's youth organizations. Before the war, most youth organizations were exclusively male, and they celebrated a robust and no-nonsense masculine political culture. The chairman of the Junior Imperial League, for example, urged his members in 1910 to take stern action against 'radical hooliganism':

> Our party, who never countenance the disturbance of Radical meetings, must be prepared to protect their own and deal out summary justice to Radical rowdies who frequently are imported into a constituency simply for the purpose of noisy obstruction. Surely there is sufficient athletic vigour in the ranks of the Unionist juniors to render such manoeuvres unpleasant to those who indulge in them.[46]

Similar sentiments seem to have animated local youth movements, such as the 'Flying Brigade' in Birmingham. They catered for a perceived need among young men for political 'action' and excitement, although their primary service to the party was long-term: as a means of attaching future political activists to the Conservative cause.

The 1918 Representation of the People Act and the 1928 Equal Franchise Act significantly raised the profile of youth organiza-tions. Universal suffrage at twenty-one prompted considerable Conservative discussion of the 'youth vote'.[47] Many activists believed young voters of both sexes particularly vulnerable to socialist idealism, and therefore placed new emphasis on the political education of youth.[48] Concerns about political immaturity also fuelled fears that even more extreme political forces might capture the nation's young voters. The threat of communism originally dominated this discussion, but growing evidence of Conservative youth's flirtations with fascism soon broadened the terms of debate.[49]

In the immediate aftermath of the war, the party prioritized the resocialization of returning soldiers within party institutions. This led in practice to great flexibility over age restrictions within local Junior Imperial League branches, so that demobilized troops would not be prevented from rejoining their old organizations.[50] Simultaneously, of course, the arrival of partial female suffrage after 1918 and the imminent prospect of equal suffrage concentrated Conservative minds on the need to recruit young women. Contrary to Martin Pugh's bizarre assertion that the League remained 'adamantly male',[51] it actively encouraged female membership from the early 1920s.[52] By 1924, the continuing refusal of the Lancashire and Cheshire Federation to admit women merely isolated them from the rest of the country.[53] Officially, this new obligation to cater for both men and women presented few problems. Sir Henry Imbert-Terry noted in the 1921 annual report:

> The inclusion of women in the work of the League has proved of the greatest value, both in increase of numbers – many branches having more than doubled their membership – and in efficiency . . . in no case has any difficulty arisen through the inclusion of female members.[54]

In practice, however, several difficulties seem to have presented themselves.

The most intractable problem for party youth organizers was that the political and social needs of male and female youth were assumed to be to a large extent incompatible. Young women were believed to want outings, rambles and debating classes. 'Healthy lads', many of whom would have seen action in the war, were still believed to want 'adventure', confrontational politics and even the prospect of violence. This tension is reflected in the wide range of branch activities reported in the *Junior Imperial League Gazette* (later *The Imp*). These included speaking contests, day-trips, mixed sports and even a mock Ku Klux Klan raid on West Bromwich in full costume.[55] The attempt to make the League attractive to young women, particularly through the greater provision of purely social functions, led some senior Conservatives to question its usefulness to the party.[56] Such misgivings grew in the 1930s in tandem with the perceived threat to Conservative youth from fascism. Young men in particular were reputedly attracted to the BUF because it offered a more aggressive and exciting political approach than the Conservatives could offer.[57] In 1934 the Conservative Research Department's Cabinet Committee set out to address this problem as part of a general survey of political youth movements. Committee members were anxious to harness 'the urge for physical improvement' to party ends,[58] and researched similar experiments in Italy, Czechoslovakia and Germany.[59] The initiative ultimately came to nothing, but the anxiety to provide an outlet for youthful, and particularly masculine, energy persisted.

Local youth organizations wrestled with similar problems. The Flying Brigade in Birmingham, for example, seems to have run into problems when it admitted women after the war. Arthur Steel-Maitland, MP for Erdington, feared that the Brigade's new tone was losing young men to the party. In 1927 his secretary reported Steel-Maitland's conversation with an ex-member of the brigade, 'a very big strong fellow' who had told the MP 'that he preferred the fascisti as he thought that there might be more incidents in working for them'. Steel-Maitland was anxious to keep such men interested in the party, and suggested inviting some fascists into local Conservative branches 'to put some life into them'.[60] Specifically, he identified a major role for them in the stewarding of party meetings. As I will argue in the next section, this strategy became a popular means within the party of reasserting the masculine character of popular politics.

Although the major charge levelled at women's activity within Conservative institutions was that it undermined and antagonized their male colleagues, some critics also challenged the received wisdom that women's political work was of critical importance to the party. Bazaars, fêtes, whist drives and cottage meetings were all very well, the argument ran, but they could scarcely deal with the socialist threat. Agents encouraging such activity were merely running away from the fight:

> Look at any constituency . . . The Labour Party's local agent is a fighter, with fist and tongue, who really believes in his cause . . . The

Conservative agent . . . objects to 'too much activity, because it only stirs up opposition'. The form of Conservative activity most popular with him is whist drives.[61]

Mr L. C. Hands, Conservative agent for Loughborough, developed this theme in 1936 by stressing the essentially peripheral influence of women's work:

Whereas the women's branches do undoubtedly, by publicity, do more for our cause than the efforts of the men's branches, nevertheless men, by their greater interest in political questions and the opportunities they make for discussing, arguing etcetera, have the greater influence on the result of the polls.[62]

This implicit juxtaposition of the central 'manly' political struggle based on conflict and argument with an ephemeral womanly fixation with good works and socializing implied that the quality of men's political activity more than made up for what it lacked in quantity. Such criticism of women's political work in many ways echoes the contempt of some male social commentators, such as Orwell and Priestley, for the 'feminization' of mass leisure and consumption patterns between the wars. In politics no less than in popular culture, women's influence was accused of promoting the ephemeral, the superficial and the decorative at the expense of more important concerns. In identifying conflict as a criterion of political effectiveness, Conservative women's detractors were also looking to the political world beyond the party.

## II

The nicest and best balanced individuals each have a bit of both sexes in their composition. The physically strong, muscular man with a keen intellect is all the better for a sympathetic intuition, which makes him as unselfish as a good woman; and the gentle, refined sympathetic woman is none the worse for the broadminded, courageous outlook attributed to men, with the stronger physique and interest in the larger questions of life, as well as the more domestic atmosphere of home.

*Popular View*, October 1921[63]

Edwardian debates about the consequences of women's suffrage focused as much on the future conduct of politics as on its likely substance,[64] and post-war Conservatives shared this preoccupation. Many constituency activists feared that women's 'civilizing influence' would dilute the healthy conflict they believed to be the stuff of politics. In 1920, for example, Glasgow Conservatives' annual report claimed: 'during a time marked by increasing unrest and instability, when nothing seems fixed or sacred, a strong and virile membership . . . should surely be the aim.'[65] Such sentiments were not symptomatic of a crude desire to exclude women – Bradford Conservatives in 1920 celebrated the progress of the 'strong and virile branches' of their Women's Unionist Association[66] – but rather a reaffirmation of established norms of political conduct now seen to be under threat. A major problem in the immediate post-war years of coalitionism, as to a lesser extent in the 1930s, was the suspension of normal party conflict. This supposedly took the fight out of politics and diminished its attraction, particularly to young men. North Cornwall constituency association's annual report for 1921 noted:

> We are still waiting for the return of our young men to the old interest in party movements and party affairs. The reaction from the war spirit has left them without clear or fixed ideas as to their duty to the public life of the country . . . Young men are naturally fighters, and the give and take conditions inevitable and necessary in a coalition arrangement leave them somewhat cold and indifferent.[67]

In such examples, the 'man's way' in politics involved a clear conflict, preferably between just two fighters. When proposing the fusion of the Conservative and Liberal parties against Labour, Gerald Howard declared: 'Let us throw aside our petty prejudices and stand forward . . . It is the British way, it is a man's way, and if carried out with courage and sincerity will save the principles of representative democracy.'[68] In the same vein, many Conservatives celebrated the vehemently anti-socialist election campaign of 1924 as a 'manly fight' and relished industrial conflict as the ultimate form of political confrontation.[69] Interestingly, military metaphors for political conduct recurred frequently during such crises, at a time when their resonance remained particularly poignant. Henry Page Croft, for example, likened Central Office to 'GHQ' during the 1924 campaign, while Lord Londonderry characterized the Miners' Federation in late 1926 as 'one of the powerful army corps in the field against us'.[70]

Another sign of Conservative desire to maintain manliness in politics is the representation of individual political role models. Masculinity was very prominent in Conservative idealizations of leadership. Party literature portrayed Baldwin as St George fighting the dragon of unemployment, and as a figure of rocklike strength combined with reassuring male authority.[71] The man himself also often went out of his way to stress his capacity to fight 'to the end' if so required.[72] Conversely, Central Office often satirized Labour leaders, and particularly Ramsay MacDonald, as a female figure – unattractive, shameless and with a difficult brood of children.[73] Conservative parliamentary candidates also elevated 'masculine' virtues, most notably courage and fighting qualities, to a measure of fitness for office. Many posed for their election address photographs in military uniform, sometimes reinforcing their image by references to their decorations or courage in action. Captain Erskine-Bolst, for example, told South Hackney electors: 'I took part in much hard fighting with the "boys". I was twice wounded, was badly gassed, suffered from trench fever, and on one occasion was buried alive with three comrades.'[74] Typically, this unimpeachable masculinity was juxtaposed with his opponent's record as a conscientious objector. By-election leaflets during the contest quoted from the Labour candidate's tribunal evidence in 1916 and pointedly asked voters: 'Whom do you Prefer for your Member? A Conscientious Objector or a Man who Did his Bit?' Central Office led the propaganda assault on the unmanly war record of Labour candidates, ridiculing the discharge of one MP under the headline 'Mother fetched him home'.[75]

These attitudes were clearly also held privately. Matthew Dillon, Conservative agent for the Seaham division of Durham, wrote to the seat's ex-candidate advertising the credentials of his successor:

> Two of his brothers won the VC. One attained the rank of Brigadier-General, and they have two military crosses in addition, so that apart from the fact that he is a well-known cricketer and footballer he has much to recommend him to the Electors, a good deal more than a person like Sidney Webb, who has never done a useful day's work in his life and could not fight a cat.[76]

Women's reactions to this adulation of masculinity in campaigning are more difficult to gauge, but Margaret Beavan's unsuccessful candidature in the Everton division of Liverpool in 1929 is suggestive. The choice of Beavan to fight the Everton division, where election contests were renowned for sectarian violence, was controversial among other leading Liverpool Conservatives. Sandeman Allen MP praised Beavan's qualities but warned Lord Derby, 'I hope they will select a strong man, it will be a hard fight.'[77] Beavan herself, although previously the city's mayor, confessed to Derby pre-hustings nerves that she attributed to her sex: 'I go through agonies of shyness – so am a woman after all despite a brief masquerade as "m'lord"!'[78] Subsequently, in the aftermath of defeat she declined to contest the seat again, explaining to Derby:

> It is to some extent a question of physical strength. I have to admit that I have not the physique to battle, as I had to battle, with excited and sometimes angry crowds, to push my way through to meetings and to stand the nervous strain of constant attempts to break up meetings; and sometimes the use of physical violence. I honestly do not think that Everton is the type of Ward where a woman could contest unless she be a much stronger and more forcible woman, both mentally and physically than I am.[79]

Although it is always difficult to read too much into single episodes, particularly in such an untypical city, several points of interest emerge from this. It seems that Conservative women sometimes internalized gendered constructions of a masculine, confrontational model of campaigning to which  women were supposedly unsuited – despite the rollicking electioneering style pioneered by Nancy Astor.[80] Beavan's choice as candidate in such an untypically violent constituency also reinforces the possibility that female candidates were often set up to fail by selection committees. The reaction of her male colleagues meanwhile confirms the impression that despite indignant official denunciations of socialist electoral violence, the 'rough and tumble' of street politics served the useful purpose of reinforcing the case against female candidates.[81]

Ambivalence about election violence was widespread within the party, and surfaced throughout this period. Levels of Conservative outrage depended not merely on the party allegiance of the perpetrators, but more importantly on the sex of the alleged victims. Conservative magazines before the war, for example, affected considerable indignation at alleged Liberal brutality towards suffragettes.[82] One columnist vehemently denounced the Asquith government in 1910 for having 'locked up over one thousand little suffragettes'.[83] Similarly, post-war party literature made great play out of all violent incidents attributable to Labour supporters in which women could be presented as victims.[84] In February 1924, under the headline 'Samples of Socialism. Free Speech Denied: Women Kicked!', the *Popular View* fulminated with typical indignation:

> The Socialist party stands for the equality of the sexes. The rowdies proved it by treating women candidates and political workers as vilely as they did its men opponents. In Glasgow, Miss Robertson . . . was kicked so badly that the doctors ordered her to abandon her campaign. Lady Eustace Percy was mobbed and injured at Hastings and struck by a broken cup. At Newport, Monmouth, Mrs Clarry . . . was pelted with mud and kicked.[85]

Such high-minded self-righteousness, however, coexisted in the Conservative press with an often explicit nostalgia for a lost Edwardian world of gentlemanly 'fisticuffs' at the hustings. Socialist 'Yahoos' stood condemned not so much for their resort to violence *per se*, but for its uncouth character. Thus the *Sheffield Daily Telegraph* observed wistfully in 1929:

> The fact is that the old rivalry between the Conservative and the Liberal which worked peace-loving citizens to a pitch of violence – both of language and action – does not now exist. The picturesque scenes of the old days when eminently respectable citizens were discerned in fiery altercation with equally well known public men have passed. Men in those days were inspired by party fervour, and were terribly in earnest. But fair play was a jewel. There were no fanatics to make a nightly practice of breaking up meetings for the love of destructiveness.[86]

To some extent such sentiments reflected simple Conservative distaste for the lower social tone of the post-1918 electorate, but the more prominent public role of women in campaigning was also important in making electoral violence less acceptable. Consequently, women were often blamed for the excessive dullness of inter-war elections, most notably when the notoriously anti-flapper *Daily Mail*[87] bemoaned the quiescence of the 1929 election campaign: 'Can it be that the excessive dilution of the electorate – with millions of new voters who have literally had the vote forced on them – and the apparition of the flappers as a deciding factor on the scene have destroyed the old rough and tumble spirit of a British election?'[88]

As the earlier discussion of party youth organizations highlighted, such Conservative enthusiasm for 'rough and tumble' largely reflected the desire to maintain young men's interest in politics after the war. In this context, problems of electoral violence, and particularly the difficulties of maintaining public order at political meetings, presented an ideal opportunity to keep young Conservative men occupied. Organized socialist disruption of Conservative meetings caused considerable discussion within the party. Because the demonstrators were normally young and male,[89] few Tories had any scruples about dealing with them roughly. Contributors to the *Agents' Journal* were as keen to use force against hecklers as they had been to rough up peace demonstrators during the war.[90] In areas affected by persistent disturbances, party youth organizations mobilized for action. Kilmarnock Junior Imperialists, for example, 'formed a squad to act as a bodyguard' to the Conservative candidate and 'intended to be present at every Labour meeting to take part in heckling'.[91] In Birmingham Conservative stewards received direct instructions to rough up Labour hecklers, as the city's chief agent made clear:

> In the case of men it was necessary that they should be taught a lesson or two before we could expect quiet meetings. We concluded that efficient stewarding was desirable to remove disorderly persons and that the stewards need not be given instructions to carefully handle such persons. If one or two of these gentlemen were hurt in the process of being removed, it might prove a salutary lesson.[92]

In this way Conservative fears about the need to harness youthful virility found a perfect solution: 'stout young men' could again get a kick out of politics while solving a major practical problem.

## III

This chapter has only scratched the surface of this subject, and there is enormous scope for further research. It would be

extremely useful to know more, for example, about the experience
of women organizers, female candidates and candidates' spouses.
Historians also need to analyse the gendered construction of
public policy in Conservative discourse, particularly in relation to
discussions of the state and of economic issues. The limited
material here does, however, point to two interesting conclusions.
Within the Conservative Party, women clearly encountered
considerable resentment from male colleagues who disliked their
intrusion into a previously masculine domain. This hostility
reflected both a reluctance to adapt long-standing models of
behaviour and a belief that the new feminine style of politics was
insufficiently confrontational to mobilize voters. Such attitudes
suggest that the contrast between Conservative Party institutions
and the stereotype of macho, union-dominated Labour organizations may have been less stark than previously implied,[93] and thus
an inadequate explanation of the Tories' greater success in
mobilizing women. It also seems clear that Conservative
constructions of gender identity informed both the content and
style of popular politics. In particular, hostility to the coalition,
anti-socialism and local electioneering strategy all to some extent
reflected a desire to reassert the essential masculinity of the
political arena. Ironically perhaps, the increasing Conservative
adulation of Empire shoppers and 'domestic Chancellors of the
Exchequer' after 1900 seems to have reinforced the party's need
for real men in politics.

## Notes

1. Press cutting from the Commons debate on the Address, Reading
   University Library, MS Astor 1416/1/263.
2. Chilcott to Derby, 5 March 1929, Liverpool City Library, MS Derby
   17/6/8.
3. On gender as a category of historical analysis, see J. W. Scott, *Gender
   and the Politics of History* (New York, 1988). For its relevance to political
   conservatism, see M. Groot and E. Reid, 'Women: If not Apolitical,
   then Conservative', in J. Siltanen and M. Stanworth (eds.), *Women and
   the Public Sphere: A Critique of Sociology and Politics* (London, 1984) and
   P. Norris, 'Conservative Attitudes in Recent British Elections: An
   Emerging Gender Gap?', *Political Studies* 34 (1986), 120–8.
4. A valuable recent exception in this respect is J. Lawrence, 'Class and

Gender in the Making of Urban Toryism, 1880–1914', *English Historical Review* 108 (1993), 630–52.

5 See, for example, S. Kingsley Kent, *Making Peace: The Reconstruction of Gender in Interwar Britain* (Princeton, 1993).

6 J. Rasmussen, 'The Political Integration of British Women: The Response of a Traditional System to a Newly Emergent Group', *Social Science History* 7 (1983), 61–95; J. Turner, 'Sex, Age and the Labour Vote in the 1920s', in P. Denley and D. Hopkin (eds.), *History and Computing* (Cambridge, 1988), II:203–23; *idem, British Politics and the Great War* (New Haven and London, 1992), 390–436.

7 L. Walker, 'Party Political Women: A Comparative Study of Liberal Women and the Primrose League, 1890–1914', in J. Rendall (ed.), *Equal or Different? Women's Politics 1880–1914* (Oxford, 1987), 165–91; M. Pugh, *The Tories and the People, 1880–1935* (Oxford, 1985) and *idem, Women and the Women's Movement in Britain, 1918–59* (London, 1992).

8 The implications of this distinction are explored at length in J. W. Scott, *Gender and the Politics of History* (New York, 1988), 28–50.

9 For a comprehensive discussion of a female Conservative agenda, see the Duchess of Atholl, *Women and Politics* (London, 1931).

10 Astor to Baird, 14 December 1923, Cambridge University Library, MS Baldwin, 35/129; editorial, *C[onservative] A[gents'] J[ournal]*, (January 1918), 6–8.

11 Neville to Ida Chamberlain, 12 May 1923, Birmingham University Library, MS Chamberlain, NC/8/1/394; Amery diary, 10 November 1924, in J. Barnes and D. Nicholson (eds.), *The Leo Amery Diaries,* I: 1896–1929 (London, 1980), 356; Steel–Maitland to Dallas, 12 October 1925, Scottish R[ecord] O[ffice], MS Steel-Maitland, GD 193/118/3/369.

12 E.g. *Popular View* (April 1930), 4.

13 Memorandum, M. Fraser to A. Chamberlain, 30 December 1921, MS Chamberlain, AC 32/4/16.

14 National Union Eastern Area executive committee meeting, 16 June 1924, Bodleian Library C[onservative] P[arty] A[rchives] ARE 7/1/7; Sir D. Keymer to Baldwin, 11 December 1923, MS Baldwin, 35/122–3.

15 These themes are discussed at greater length in B. Campbell, *The Iron Ladies: Why Do Women Vote Tory?* (London, 1987) and D. Jarvis, 'Mrs Maggs and Betty: The Conservative Appeal to Women Voters in the 1920s', *Twentieth Century British History* 5 (1994), 129–52.

16 *CAJ* (April 1923), 84.

17 See above, 180–2.

18 For example Speech of Mr Matthews to the Sheffield Junior Imperial League, reported in the *Sheffield Daily Telegraph*, 15 January 1932; Bridgeman diary, October 1931, in P. Williamson (ed.), *The*

*Modernisation of Conservative Politics: The Diaries and Letters of William Bridgeman, 1904–35* (London, 1988), 250.

[19] L. Maclachlan, 'Women's Organisation', *CAJ* (June 1920), 6–7.

[20] Pugh, *Women and the Women's Movement*, 124–5.

[21] Walker, 'Party Political Women', 179. Even before the war, however, some hostility was evident, e.g. Lane-Fox to Sandars, 1906, quoted in Campbell, *Iron Ladies*, 47.

[22] J. H. Bottomley, *Our Flag* (July 1912), 111.

[23] Speech of Lieut. Connell, NU conference minutes, 1917, p. 45, CPA. See also R. Topping, 'Women's Organisation: A Plea for Joint Associations', *CAJ* (July 1920), 7–10; M. Maxse, 'Women's Organisation', ibid. (June 1924), 138–9.

[24] J. Lovenduski, P. Norris and C. Burness, 'The Party and Women', in A. Seldon and S. Ball (eds.), *Conservative Century: The Conservative Party since 1900* (Oxford, 1994), 611–35.

[25] Pugh, *Tories and the People*, 187.

[26] Idem, *Women and the Women's Movement*, 124–9.

[27] Shettleston C[onservative] A[ssociation] annual report, 24 January 1919, N[ational] L[ibrary] of S[cotland] acc. no. 10424/25. Cf. Penryn and Falmouth CA, A[nnual] G[eneral] M[eeting], 16 October 1929, speech of Mr Barclay, Cornwall RO, DDX 551/10; 'Vade Mecum', *CAJ* (August 1920), 16.

[28] *CAJ* (November 1926), 343.

[29] M. Maxse, 'Women's Organisations', *CAJ* (November 1927), 302.

[30] E.g. Stockton W[omen's] CA executive meeting, 20 February 1929, Durham RO D/X/322/10.

[31] L. C. Hands, 'Controversial and Otherwise', *CAJ* (January 1936), 9.

[32] Pugh, *Women and the Women's Movement*, 126.

[33] R. Topping, *CAJ* (January 1935), 2; anon., 'The Organisation of Men', ibid. (February 1935), 33–4.

[34] A. Fawcett, *Conservative Agent* (Driffield, 1967), 23–6.

[35] *CAJ* (October 1922), 26.

[36] Dillon to Ross, 21 May 1925, quoted in Jarvis, 'Mrs Maggs and Betty', 137; Briggs to Astor, 16 January 1922, MS Astor 1416/1/1/1734; *CAJ* (October 1926), 303.

[37] For example Flintshire CA management committee, 4 September 1930, Clwyd RO, D/DM/307/8. See also Lovenduski et al., 'The Party and Women', 621.

[38] 'The Agent's Course, 1935', *CAJ* (July 1935), 166.

[39] Lawrence, 'Class and Gender', 643–9.

[40] E. J. Forster, 'Women's Conservative Clubs: Are they Useful?', *CAJ* (March 1926), 66.

[41] On the case for and against mixed clubs, see for example Cornwall North CA AGM, 25 February 1919, Cornwall RO, Acc. no.1581,

DDX 381; Lt. Col. Walter à Beckett, 'Women's Political Clubs', *CAJ* (February 1926), 49–50.

[42] *CAJ* (April 1922), 8.

[43] Cuthbert Headlam diary, 4 February 1925, in S. Ball (ed.), *Parliament and Politics in the Age of Baldwin and MacDonald* (London, 1992), 52.

[44] *CAJ* (November 1923), 257.

[45] A. Hand, 'The National Conservative League', *CAJ* (May 1925), 93.

[46] H. Imbert-Terry, 'The Young Brigade', *The Conservative and Unionist* (May 1910), 118.

[47] E.g. Dawson to Hacking, 29 November 1923, Lancashire RO PLC 3, p. 73; speech of Major Davey, National Union Yorkshire agent, reported in *Sheffield Daily Telegraph*, 25 March 1925; speech of Lady Maureen Stanley to Stockton CA AGM, 26 February 1931, Durham RO D/X/322/10. The reasons for the party's preoccupation with youth are discussed at greater length in D. Jarvis, 'The Shaping of Conservative Electoral Hegemony, 1918–39', in J. Lawrence and M. Taylor (eds.), *Party, State and Society: Electoral Behaviour in Modern Britain* (Aldershot, 1996).

[48] C. W. P. Selby, 'The Rising Generation', *CAJ* (December 1924), 276; ibid. (March 1926), 67.

[49] E.g. Junior Imperial League executive committee minutes, 14 October 1925, CCO 506/1/3, 197–9; *CAJ* (June 1935), 153 – report of East Midlands Agents' Association AGM.

[50] Lieut. Connell to Robert Topping, 2 April 1920, CPA CCO 506/1/2.

[51] Pugh, *Tories and the People*, 180 and 183.

[52] For appeals for new members of both sexes, see for example, the *J[unior] I[mperial] L[eague] G[azette]* (June 1921), 1.

[53] *JILG* (April 1924), 16.

[54] Ibid. (April 1922), 1–2.

[55] Ibid. (August 1923), 16.

[56] For Sir Robert Topping, 11 July 1934, CPA CRD 1/60/2, folder 1.

[57] *CAJ* (August 1934), 169.

[58] J. Ball to N. Chamberlain, 13 July 1934, CPA CRD 1/64/1 8(b).

[59] Conservative consultative committee, 16 March and 1 June 1934, CPA CRD 1/64.

[60] D. A. Logan to Beardsmore (agent), 9 February 1927, MS Steel-Maitland GD193/118/3/205; Steel-Maitland to Beardsmore, 14 December 1927, ibid., 193/118/3/7–8.

[61] *CAJ* (February 1927), 37–9.

[62] Ibid. (January 1936), 9.

[63] 'J.M.H.', 'Home Maker and Home-Comer', *Popular View* (October 1921), 21.

[64] See, for example, S. Kingsley Kent, *Sex and Suffrage in Britain, 1860–1914* (Princeton, 1987), chapter 7.

[65] Maryhill CA AGM, 23 January 1920, NLS 10424/85, p.152.

[66] Bradford CA AGM, 5 April 1921, Bradford RO 36D78/5, p.263.

[67] N. Cornwall CA AGM, 29 June 1921, Cornwall RO DDX 381, acc. no 1581.

[68] *CAJ* (May 1921), 7.

[69] For example Camborne CA annual report, 1924, Cornwall RO DDX 387/1606, pp.101–3.

[70] *Morning Post*, 11 October 1924; Londonderry to Churchill, 2 November 1926, quoted in M. Gilbert, *W. S. Churchill*, V: *1922–39* (London, 1976), 217.

[71] 'I Need More Weapons', *Popular View* (December 1923), 2; 'The Rock', *Man in the Street* (June 1926), 5; 'Putting Him on the Right Road', *Popular View* (November 1923), 5.

[72] E.g. *The Times*, 25 June 1930; *The Times*, 18 December 1930.

[73] *The Wallflower*, N[ational] U[nion] leaflet no.2119 (1922); 'The Women's Verdict – "Impossible"!', *Home and Politics* (November 1924), 1; *Mummy's Little Trials*, NU leaflet no.2880 (1929).

[74] Erskine-Bolst scrapbook, 1922–5, election address, 24 July 1922, Lancashire RO PLC 5/14/1.

[75] *Socialists and Ex-Servicemen*, NU leaflet no.2512 (1923).

[76] Dillon to Captain Norton, 24 October 1922, Londonderry MSS, Durham RO D/Lo/C 277.

[77] Sandeman Allen to Derby, 5 April 1929, MS Derby DER 17/6/3.

[78] Beavan to Derby, 14 April 1929, MS Derby 17/6/6.

[79] Beavan to Derby, 10 December 1929, MS Derby 17/6/6.

[80] Pugh, *Women and the Women's Movement*, 173–4; B. Harrison, *Prudent Revolutionaries. Portraits of British Feminists between the Wars* (Oxford, 1987), 81–2.

[81] The problems facing prospective women candidates since 1918 are discussed in Lovenduski et al., 'The Party and Women', 625–30.

[82] E.g. *The Conservative* (March 1906), 15.

[83] *The Conservative and Unionist* (August 1910), 137.

[84] Jarvis, 'Mrs Maggs and Betty', 144.

[85] *Popular View* (February 1924), 12. See also Lord Birkenhead, 'The Dictatorship of the Hooligan', *Daily Mail*, 22 October 1924.

[86] *Sheffield Daily Telegraph* press cutting (November 1922), Sheffield Citizens' Association Minute Book, Sheffield City Library, LD 2110, 65–6.

[87] Strictly speaking, the *Mail* is hard to classify as a Conservative paper in 1929, because of Rothermere's violent hostility to Baldwin – 'independent Conservative' is perhaps the most accurate description of its politics.

[88] *Daily Mail*, 23 May 1929, 10 (my italics).

[89] Undated memo (1917), W. M. Fison (Conservative agent, Chelmsford),

MS Steel-Maitland, GM 193/202/82–6; Western Division of Scottish CA, council meeting 5 June 1929, NLS Acc. no.10424, pp. 131–2, speech of Mr Bloch (Gorbals).

90 *CAJ* (January 1927), 11; ibid. (January 1917), 1.

91 Western Division of Scottish CUA, council meeting, 6 November 1929, NLS Acc. no.10424, pp.152–4.

92 Edwards memorandum to Steel-Maitland, 31 December 1928, MS Steel-Maitland GD 193/209/271–3.

93 E.g. Pugh, *Women and the Women's Movement*, 126.

# Explaining the Gender Gap: The Conservative Party and the Women's Vote, 1945–1964

## INA ZWEINIGER-BARGIELOWSKA

This chapter examines gender differences in voting behaviour between 1945 and the 1960s based on Gallup polls. These polls show a gap of up to 17 points in male and female voting behaviour and a strong female preference for the Conservative Party.[1] As Perry Anderson put it in the mid-1960s, 'If women had voted the same way as men, the Labour Party would have been uninterruptedly in power since 1945.'[2] Or, to reverse the point, if men had been disenfranchised, the Conservatives would have won all elections apart from 1945 and 1966. These gender differences in voting behaviour have been virtually ignored in the mainstream literature despite the fact that Conservative success among women voters goes a long way towards explaining the party's victories during the 1950s.

In the Nuffield election studies and elsewhere attention centres on class. The link between voting and class is of course critical during the period but class-based analysis is problematic. In the first place, Labour won a small majority of the working-class vote, and the party's share among middle-class voters stood at between one-eighth and one-quarter.[3] However, the Conservatives drew considerable support from all classes including the bulk of votes among higher social groups as well as a large chunk of the working-class vote (between one-third and 44 per cent). The persistence of working-class Tories provides a challenge to class-based analysis which has never been fully addressed. Second, classification is difficult since class, a 'most elusive concept',[4] could be defined in terms of 'income, occupation or ownership of capital'[5] as well as 'consciousness' and 'collective identity'.[6] Conventionally, occupation is used to define classes with salary earners counted as middle class and wage earners included in the working class; the respective percentages in the 1951 census among occupied males are 22 and 78.[7] There are considerable differences in income and status within these strata and it is virtually impossible to define the boundaries between middle and working class. There is also a marked disparity between objective and subjective class identities.[8] According to a Gallup poll conducted in 1948, 47 per cent described themselves as middle class and only 46 per cent as working class.[9] Finally, it is difficult to fit women into essentially male categories based on income and employment patterns, and the practice of classing women with the male head of household is highly questionable.[10] Gender-based analysis does not suffer from these problems and associated sampling difficulties. Of course, the gender gap was smaller than the class gap but it was certainly sufficient to make a difference, especially when the results were close and the political implications of narrow majorities were further exaggerated by the first-past-the-post electoral system.

Conventional accounts of female Conservatism are based on simplistic notions of female domesticity. Women's political behaviour differs from that of men because of their relative isolation from the formative world of work and trade union, and their seclusion in the private sphere predisposes women towards apathy and deference. Another approach sees greater female Conservatism as a cohort factor since women who acquired the franchise in the inter-war years voted for the dominant Conservative Party and continued to support the party for habitual reasons in the post-war period.

There is no innate tendency among women to vote Conservative, and this chapter shows that these structural explanations are flawed. The gender gap is not static but changed over time. In 1945 and 1966 a majority of women supported Labour, since 1970 differences in male and female voting behaviour have narrowed and in 1983 as well as 1987 the gender gap was no longer significant.[11] In 1992 the Conservatives again did better among women and Labour 'suffered from the gender gap being its widest for any of the four elections since 1979'.[12] The cohort analysis is little more than a circular argument which fails to examine why women were more attracted to Conservatism in the inter-war years. Both approaches are based on static notions of femininity and masculinity as well as a gender-blind conceptualization of political behaviour which have been criticized by feminist historians.

Women's preference for the Conservatives is understood from a historical perspective focusing on the post-war Conservative Party's distinctive appeal to women electors in their endeavour to rebuild an electoral majority after 1945. The Conservative Party made a considerable effort to win over female support both in terms of organization and policy. This includes Conservative exploitation of female discontent with Labour's policy of austerity which was contrasted with the promise and later delivery of affluence. The Conservative appeal to women went beyond consumerism, and the women's charter *A True Balance: In the Home, in Employment and as Citizens*[13] contained feminist demands such as equal pay and equal citizenship. These policies were continuously pressed by Conservative women, and a number of important reforms were indeed implemented in the 1950s. The Conservatives introduced equal pay in the public sector in 1954 in a deliberate attempt to gain an electoral advantage over Labour, and the party was also responsible for the admission of women to the House of Lords in 1958. By contrast, Black and Brooke argue that '[a]t best, Labour was baffled by questions involving gender. At worst, it was indifferent or hostile.'[14] Labour propaganda was based on the assumption that women's interests could be conflated with those of their menfolk. Women were almost exclusively addressed as wives and mothers, and the Attlee government failed to act on equal pay, despite cross-party support for the reform. From the late 1940s onwards, Labour women's loyalty to the Labour government gained priority over their desire for equal pay, which was no longer discussed.

Instead of trying to explain away female Conservatism, it is in fact possible to make out a very positive case for it during the particular circumstances of the early post-war years. In the British context the relationship between women's concerns, feminism and the left–right political cleavage is complex. Certainly, right-wing voting does not imply female submission to patriarchy or unquestioning acceptance of the traditional domestic role. Rather,

Conservative voting denotes women's preference for that party which appreciated the importance of gender difference in political mobilization.

I

Gallup polls based on quota samples were conducted immediately before or after the day of a general election. Gallup polls were the only polls available until 1959 and, according to Henry Durant, the director of Gallup, were fairly accurate in the early post-war years. Between 1945 and 1964, 'the Gallup Poll has forecast the distance between the two parties with an average error of 1.9 per cent . . . it has always forecast the winner correctly.'[15] The record of opinion polls deteriorated from 1970 onwards when the margin of error increased and polls predicted the wrong result, for instance, in 1970 and 1992.[16] Figure 1 and table 1 show a cyclical trend in the voting patterns of both sexes, with a narrowing gap in 1950 and again in 1959. The most important point of figure 1 is the consistent and, at times, large Labour lead among men, which stands in stark contrast with the Conservative lead among women, especially during the 1950s. Figure 2 illustrates the male

**Figure 1**

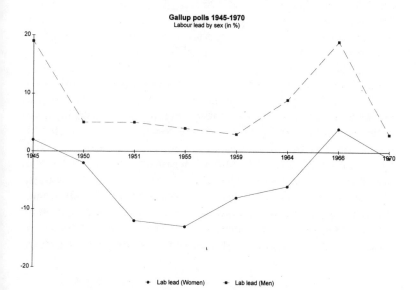

Gallup polls 1945-1970
Labour lead by sex (in %)

Table 1: Sex differences in voting behaviour (Gallup polls, 1945–1970)

| Men | | | | | | | | |
| --- | --- | --- | --- | --- | --- | --- | --- | --- |
| Party | 1945 | 1950 | 1951 | 1955 | 1959 | 1964 | 1966 | 1970 |
| Cons. | 35 | 41 | 46 | 47 | 45 | 40 | 37 | 46 |
| Lab. | 54 | 46 | 51 | 51 | 48 | 49 | 56 | 49 |
| Lib. | 11 | 13 | 3 | 2 | 7 | 11 | 7 | 5 |
| Lab. lead | 19 | 5 | 5 | 4 | 3 | 9 | 19 | 3 |
| | | | | | | | | |
| Women | | | | | | | | |
| Party | 1945 | 1950 | 1951 | 1955 | 1959 | 1964 | 1966 | 1970 |
| Cons. | 43 | 45 | 54 | 55 | 51 | 45 | 44 | 46 |
| Lab. | 45 | 43 | 42 | 42 | 43 | 39 | 48 | 45 |
| Lib. | 12 | 12 | 4 | 3 | 6 | 16 | 8 | 9 |
| Lab. lead | 2 | -2 | -12 | -13 | -8 | -6 | 4 | -1 |

Source: see fig.1.

preference for Labour and female preference for the Conservatives in more detail. It supports the argument that if women had been disenfranchised, Labour would have won every general election between 1945 and 1970. Equally, if men had been excluded, the Conservatives would have won every election apart from 1945 and 1966. Labour won by a narrow margin in 1950 and 1964 and especially in 1950 the gender gap was small. In 1964 the Conservatives were penalized by a steep increase in the female Liberal vote. Hence, Labour needed the female vote to win a working majority while the Conservatives were able to offset their poor performance among men with a disproportionate share of the female vote between 1951 and 1959.

The cyclical nature of the female vote, with a majority of women voting Labour both at the beginning and towards the end of our period, points towards the inadequacy of structural explanations of female Conservatism. Neither female employment patterns nor the age of the female electorate can explain why 43 per cent, 55 per cent and 44 per cent of women voted Conservative in 1945, 1955 and 1966 respectively. Parties have to mobilize their potential support and painfully construct coalitions of interest groups. It is inappropriate to conceive of the electorate divided into social blocs which will vote in a particular way with parties as passive beneficiaries of socio-economic change.[17] Rather, there is a dynamic relationship between political parties

# Figure 2

## (a)

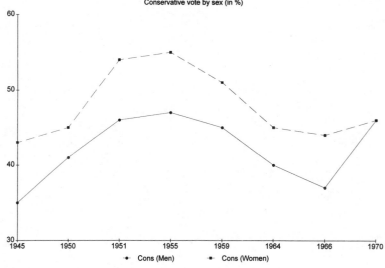

**Gallup polls 1945-1970**
Conservative vote by sex (in %)

## (b)

**Gallup polls 1945-1970**
Labour vote by sex (in %)

**(c)**

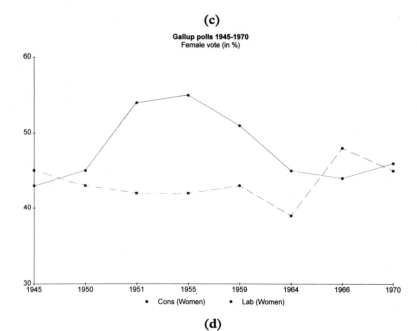

**(d)**

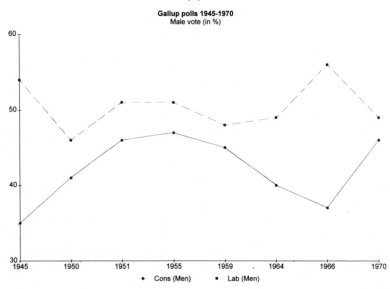

and the electorate and this process is historically contingent. The relative success, or otherwise, of a political party in mobilizing its potential support changes over time, depending on the conjunction of a whole range of variables such as organization, policy and rhetoric. For instance, the Conservative recovery after 1945 and their success in the 1950s was partly the result of a distinctive appeal to women discontented with austerity.[18]

James Hinton rejects the suggestion of female disillusionment with Labour and stresses the greater deterioration in male Labour support. By contrast, Labour held onto women and especially working-class women well in 1950.[19] From a methodological perspective, it is doubtful how much weight can be attached to opinion polls between elections since there was in fact considerable movement in party fortunes.[20] The class breakdown, especially among women, fails to consider the problems of classification raised earlier, and Hinton also uses somewhat different figures.[21] Most importantly, of course, Labour won in 1950, even if its majority was much reduced, and therefore the 1951 general election was critical. In 1950 Labour held on to female support better than that of men; Labour lost 8 per cent among men and only 2 per cent among women. It is perhaps more significant that this deterioration in the female vote obliterated Labour's lead among women and the Conservatives moved slightly ahead, whereas the male Labour lead, while narrowed, remained fairly secure at 5 per cent (see table 1). According to an internal Labour memorandum, Labour obtained 52.5 per cent of the male working-class vote but only 44.5 per cent among working-class women, an 8 per cent gap in support.

> As 8 per cent of working class women represents 3 per cent of the total electorate, or almost exactly one million voters, it is easy to picture the happy results that would follow if working men could only persuade their womenfolk to share their opinions.[22]

In 1951 there was a large swing towards the Conservatives among women while male support for Labour actually increased and the gap between Labour and Conservatives among men remained identical at 5 per cent. Hinton's argument is valid for the period 1945–50 but not for the period 1945–51. Therefore, the female Conservative preference in 1951 goes a long way towards explaining the Conservative victory. Similar factors were at work in 1955 when Labour support among men actually increased but these gains were offset by a further rise in Conservative female support. In 1959 and especially 1964 the Conservatives suffered from a female drift towards the Liberals and only in 1966 did Labour obtain a majority of the female vote again.

## II

Gender differences in voting behaviour have been virtually ignored by mainstream psephology and electoral sociology. In the Nuffield election studies as well as the work by Benney and Abrams the focus is on class.[23] The lower middle and higher working classes are the battle ground in a dominant two-party system. This approach, which was conceptualized during the heyday of the two-party system between 1945 and 1970, has been criticized more recently. From the 1970s onwards class voting declined and by 1979 the class-model explained less than half of all votes.[24] Similarly, Goldthorpe and Lockwood's influential 'affluent worker' project which set out to study the *embourgeoisement* of the working class against the background of Labour's poor electoral performance in the 1950s ignored that section of the working class who were above all responsible for the Conservative victories, namely working-class women. The research focused on male workers.[25]

Butler, Goldthorpe and others are gender-blind. There is little sign that the notion of a male norm in political behaviour was ever questioned, and these commentators fail to acknowledge the difficulties associated with fitting women into sociological and political categories such as class which are conceptualized on the basis of male employment patterns. Women's political behaviour, if it is not ignored altogether, is problematized since it deviates from the male norm. Butler and Stokes highlight women's active involvement in the Church of England, which helps explain their greater Conservatism. Further, there is a cohort factor since many female Conservatives were attracted to the party during the Conservative-dominated inter-war years, but the circular nature of this argument is ignored.[26] For MacKenzie and Silver, Conservatism among working-class women is rooted in their isolation from industrial society which predisposed especially older, poorer women towards deference and adherence to dominant value systems.[27]

The theme that female political consciousness was under-developed (analogous to that of the working-class Tory) is developed by Anderson. He draws attention to the low female support for Labour. This is due to a 'vast silence' with regard to women's condition:

> The premature death of the suffragette movement . . . left women in a position of social inferiority . . . They are, on average, more ignorant, worse paid, less respected, and employed in duller work than men. An immense burden of mystification adapts them to their predetermined roles, and renders them the most passive, most prejudiced, most ill-informed citizens in society. In effect, the whole horizontal class system is cross-structured by a deep vertical system of sexual inequality and infantilism. Women are, then, inevitably far more subject than men to the magical aspects of Conservatism – the mystique of deference, the worship of ceremony and hierarchy.[28]

It is inappropriate to lament working-class women's failure to behave as Marx had predicted. The starting point should not be a perception of women as isolated from the formative world of work and trade union and therefore in need of education to develop their political consciousness fully. Rather, it is necessary to analyse what left-wing ideology has to offer to women and to appreciate that socialism in general and the Labour Party in particular originated primarily in furthering the interests of organized male labour. Despite the importance of the welfarist agenda with undoubted benefits for women and children, which was promoted by Labour women,[29] as Pat Thane acknowledges, their achievement was 'minimal'. 'There was a fundamental difference' between Labour women and men; 'when they collided the male vision generally won' and female ambitions were 'blocked by the crude exercise of male power'.[30] Socialist discourse frequently assumes that female interests are identical to those of the male breadwinner but in view of the unequal division of resources in the working-class household Labour politics had little to offer to those women whose poverty was primarily due to a meagre housekeeping allowance.[31] During the inter-war years Conservative propaganda aimed to capitalize from this 'female alienation from a "beer and butty" culture of Labour and trade union politics [which] equated socialism with machismo and the unacceptable face of male aggression'.[32]

The revival of feminism since the late 1960s has produced an increasingly influential critique of many basic tenets of social science. Similarly, the emergence of a distinct women's history has drawn attention to the significance of gender differences in life style, attitudes and political behaviour. Gender is no longer relegated to the status of a minor background variable. Rather, in order to understand historical processes it is necessary to adopt a gendered perspective. According to Joan Scott, 'gender is the social organization of sexual difference.' It is impossible to generalize about men and women and 'gender is the knowledge that establishes meanings for bodily differences . . . [which] vary across cultures, social groups, and time.'[33] For example, the notion of citizenship developed in the eighteenth and nineteenth century was based on gendered assumptions which determined franchise and property rights. Thus the citizenship of the male independent artisan and sole breadwinner implied a dependent wife.[34] This distinctive perception of masculinity was crucial in the development of mass political culture and became the basis of political rhetoric. This was not a natural, ahistorical phenomenon but socially constructed within the specific context of the late nineteenth century. Therefore, the notion of a rational, male citizen in the public sphere is as much a social construct as his antithesis, the emotional, female non-citizen whose life was largely confined to the private sphere. These ideals, which always fell short of reality, were extremely influential and persistent in the perception of gender identities. With the rise of the women's movement from the late nineteenth century onwards, gender identities have been contested and are continuously redefined.

From a political-science perspective Charlot, Evans and a collection of papers edited by Siltanen and Stanworth question negative stereotypes about female political behaviour. These are that women are more apathetic and less committed or sophisticated than men, that they passively follow the male example and that they are more Conservative.[35] The notion of greater female apathy is largely due to a narrow masculinist definition of politics and, with regard to turnout, education and class are more important than sex. These commentators highlight the contradiction that, on the one hand, women passively follow the male lead (female influence on men is rarely considered) but, on the other, frequently are more right-wing. Charlot cites evidence of conjugal independence and when there was agreement between husband and wife this was not due to male dominance but to common values. Greater female Conservatism, of course, changes over time, and Norris highlights the reversed gender gap in both Britain and the USA in recent years.[36] Finally, Goot and Reid deplore that female loyalty to one party is dismissed as habitual and conservative either with a capital or, indeed, a small 'c' while women who switch parties are 'fickle' and 'immature'.[37]

Hence, female attitudes to politics should not be compared with a male norm and found wanting, but rather have to be understood in distinctive feminine terms, as male attitudes should be analysed with regard to equally contested and ambiguous notions of masculinity. Female Conservatism is not deviant but has to be explained in terms of women's own priorities rather than their failure to behave like men. Jon Lawrence argues that female Conservatism does not 'denote something fundamental about the nature of women'. Rather, the answer to questions why the Conservative Party has done better among women and Labour among men has to focus

> not on the peculiarities of men and women, but on the peculiarities of political parties. That is, we should analyse the gendered language and practice of political parties in an attempt to understand why they should have appealed differentially to men and women.[38]

This approach has informed the writings of nineteenth- and early twentieth-century historians but has been neglected by post-war historians despite the fact that gender differences in voting behaviour were politically most significant after 1945.

# III

The franchise reforms of 1918 and 1928 presented a challenge to the major political parties which had formally to incorporate politically active women and win over the mass of the female electorate.[39] Labour and the Conservatives appealed to women within the traditional female sphere of concern about home, family and welfare matters. Both parties emphasized different issues as female voters were integrated into existing ideologies. Labour called for a family wage to relieve women from the double burden as well as social reform to raise the working-class standard of living. These policies would benefit working-class women and children. The Conservatives highlighted their commitment to freedom, defence of the family and social stability as well as women's role as consumers who benefited from low prices and taxes. Neither party was particularly pro-feminist and the notion that women were more sympathetic to Labour is not borne out by the inter-war evidence. There was tension in the Labour Party between the claims of feminists and male trade unionists, and the Conservatives did more to redress gender inequalities in society, especially during the Conservative-dominated 1920s when a whole string of reforms was introduced.[40]

From the establishment of the Primrose League in the late nineteenth century onwards, the Conservatives were highly successful in mobilizing women.[41] After 1918 women were allocated at least one-third representation on all party bodies and equal representation after 1928, all party vice-chairmen[42] were women from 1930 onwards and women acted as chairmen of the National Union for about one year in three between 1926 and 1957.[43] At a lower level of the party organization, women increasingly formed the backbone of the Conservative Party, making a major contribution to voluntary work.[44] Female membership stood at about 1 million in the late 1920s and early 1930s, when Labour organized between 250,000 and 300,000 women, although there were also approximately 1 million female trade unionists, and it appears that the Conservatives gained a slight electoral advantage from the female franchise during the inter-war years.[45]

No systematic figures of the gender breakdown of Conservative Party membership are available but a range of evidence suggests that at least half of the party's members were female.[46] Conservative Party membership in the 1950s reached an all-time high of 2·8 million, which means that up to 1·5 million women were members of the Conservative Party during the early post-war years.[47] Labour's female membership was rather lower with 364,000 individual members in 1950 and more in the trade unions, although the overwhelming majority of the 5 million trade union members were male.[48] In Greenwich three-quarters of

Labour Party members were male, as were 86 per cent of delegates at the 1970 party conference.[49] It would be misleading to argue that women played an equal role in the higher reaches of the Conservative Party, and they did not do very well in getting female candidates adopted. Indeed, while women remained a tiny minority with less than 5 per cent of MPs, Labour did slightly better in this respect.[50] Conservative women frequently called for more female candidates and MPs, and in 1952 Evelyn Emmet, chairman of the party's women's organization, deplored the fact that

> an intelligent woman, desirous of taking up a political career, has a better chance under the Socialist banner than under the Conservative, because our Party, for some obscure reason, is apathetic, if not slightly hostile towards the efforts of women to enter public life.[51]

There was no change in this respect but the greater female presence in the Conservative Party was important with regard to both organization and policy.

In the early post-war years the party was conscious of the need to appeal to and mobilize women. In the files of the influential Central Women's Advisory Committee (hereafter CWAC), in organization files as well as the Public Opinion Research Department the importance of women to the party is continuously highlighted.[52] For instance, in February 1949 the CWAC, discussing a Central Office memorandum, stressed that 'it was of the utmost importance that the women's organizations should be encouraged and strengthened at all levels'.[53] In July 1951, Emmet stressed that it was 'essential to win the support of the women . . . before the next General Election, in view of a) their numbers, and b) their influence'.[54] This policy was extremely successful and there was an unprecedented increase in membership by about 2 million from 700,000 in 1946 to 2.8 million in 1953. At least half of the new members were women, posing a challenge to the party organization. After 1953–5 the momentum was lost and membership declined to 2.2 million in the late 1950s.[55] In autumn 1957, Emmet, in correspondence with Edward Heath, the chief whip, and Viscount Hailsham, the party chairman, claimed that women 'got us in on both the last elections'. While male members of the party 'may be able to do without the vote' of women MPs 'we cannot do without the woman voter in the country'. Emmet and Marjorie Maxse, the party's vice-chairman between 1944 and 1950, having built up the women's organization after the war, which contributed towards winning two general elections, were now concerned about declining female support. Emmet demanded a working party at prime ministerial level on women but her proposals were rejected.[56] However, a lower-level working party had considered the issue since the summer, and a series of conferences and new propaganda material helped to revitalize the women's organization.[57]

With regard to policy, the battle for the female vote focused on what could be called the consumption agenda, which need only be summarized briefly here.[58] The persistence and indeed intensification of rationing and austerity policies after the war was controversial, and shortages of food and consumer goods became a major area of political debate which had wider implications in terms of economic policy and civil liberties. Labour's argument was that post-war shortages were inevitable, that the government was doing a good job in difficult circumstances and that the maintenance of fair shares coupled with full employment, food subsidies and the creation of the welfare state amounted to a significant improvement in working-class living standards compared with the bad old days of the 1930s. The Conservatives claimed that austerity was due to Labour mismanagement and incompetence rather than post-war dislocation. They held that living standards had declined and in order to restore the ample supplies of cheap consumer goods available during the 1930s, it was necessary to eliminate wartime controls and introduce free market principles into economic management. *Labour Woman*, the party's journal for women members, and the Labour Party women's conferences in the late 1940s wholeheartedly endorsed government policy. There were repeated calls for loyalty to the government in difficult times, the gains for women and children were emphasized and Labour women disparaged the irresponsible Tory campaign aimed at disgruntled housewives.[59] By contrast, Conservative propaganda was critical of the whole culture of austerity, and from the mid-1950s onwards the party celebrated the ending of austerity and return to prosperity. For example, the party magazine *Onward* featured a torn ration book and a full bag of shopping on the front cover in April 1954. Housewives, 'shopping extra' with more choice and better quality, could finally celebrate 'Victory Day' in contrast with empty shops and black markets under socialism.[60]

The battle over consumption and living standards was not only critical during the general elections of 1950 and 1951[61] but the 1955 general election was again fought on the issue. Conservative propaganda contrasted the return to freedom and prosperity since 1951 with Labour's policy of rationing, controls and crises with slogans such as 'Housewives choice: . . . queuing for bread and potatoes in peacetime: will you ever forget it?'[62] The Conservatives suggested that Labour's policy to bring back government trading and price controls would mean a return to rationing, forcing Labour to issue a denial.[63] A leaflet featuring a crossed-out ration book read, 'Nail this Tory lie!' Stressing that Labour 'started derationing as supplies improved', this 'deliberate Tory lie' or 'Ration book stunt' was compared with Churchill's 'gestapo' speech of 1945.[64] Throughout the 1950s the Conservatives underlined their achievements by invoking the language of austerity. 'More liberty for you', the 'freedom to earn all you can and buy what you like' was contrasted with 'rationing, austerity, shortages, queues, "snoopers", and black markets' which were accepted as inevitable under Labour.[65] By the early 1960s the theme was still used but had become rather tired and dated.[66]

During the 1950s, Labour's attitude towards the swift dismantling of wartime controls was indeed ambivalent. As Attlee put it in 1955, the

> Conservative government, by the abolition of subsidies, has brought about untold difficulties. I realise that the rationing of foodstuffs was not popular, but at least it enabled people to obtain fair shares at reasonable prices. Nowadays . . . the shops [are] filled with articles at prices which the ordinary man and woman cannot afford.[67]

The party never really came to terms with its defeats in the elections of 1951 and 1955 which were explained in terms of voters being fooled by false Tory promises and superior Conservative organization.[68] A rare exception was a resolution discussed at the 1952 women's conference which suggested that Labour's defeat in 1951 was due to inadequate education and propaganda in the face of the Tory campaign aimed at housewives. However, the resolution was defeated since it was 'unfairly critical' of the party, which had polled the largest number of votes and thereby earned a moral victory.[69] It was only after the 1959 defeat that there was a major overhaul of policy and the party became revitalized and rejuvenated.

The Conservative appeal to women went beyond this consumption agenda and, indeed, during the early post-war years it was the Conservatives and especially Conservative women who appealed to the female electorate, building on the traditions of the women's movement. Conventionally, it is argued that the women's movement was defunct from the late 1930s to the 1960s with the equal-rights tradition not only dead but outmoded after the Equal Franchise Act of 1928. The new woman-centred feminism associated with Eleanor Rathbone focused on a welfare agenda, and by the 1940s feminism had become submerged in Labour's welfare policy.[70] This chronology is based on the assumption that feminism is ideologically on the left. A recent issue of *Gender and History*,[71] focusing on women and the right, aims to understand why women support right-wing ideologies, which is equated with female endorsement of patriarchy and acceptance of women's traditional role. There is no contribution on Britain in the volume and the possibility that women on the right can be more progressive in terms of feminist demands than those on left is not really considered. In the British context, the relationship between women's issues, feminism and the left–right dichotomy is far from simple, and the notion that the left was more sympathetic to feminist demands is not borne out by the evidence.

The Conservatives' feminist agenda is exemplified in *A True Balance: In the Home, in Employment and as Citizens*, the party's 'charter' for women, published in 1949.[72] Conservative women laid claim to the traditions and achievements of the women's movement and highlighted reforms introduced by Conservative governments. Acknowledging the changing role of women in society and particularly their contribution in the recent war effort, the pamphlet deplored the continuing discrimination against women and demanded that 'women should play an equal part with men as citizens' and that domestic life should be based on partnership and joint responsibility. To further this end 'the United Nations Charter to . . . "promote and encourage respect for human rights and for fundamental freedoms for all, without distinction of race, sex, language, or religion"' is invoked. The section on women in the home emphasizes the importance of family life, demanding adequate housing and labour-saving devices to ease the heavy burdens placed upon the housewife. The section on employment, recognizing women's increased participation in the labour market, calls for equal opportunities and, crucially, 'the rate for the job'. Equal pay in central and local government service was a topic of considerable debate in the early post-war years and a Royal Commission on Equal Pay reported in 1946.[73] *True Balance* agreed that wages in industry should be settled by free collective bargaining but recommended 'that the next Conservative Government should proceed with the application of this principle of the Rate for the Job during the period of its first Parliament'. This commitment was incorporated into *The Right Road for Britain*, election manifestos and other propaganda material.[74] With regard to citizenship, there was a call for equality and greater representation of women 'who should have a proper share in the government'. Specific demands included admission of women to the House of Lords on the same terms as men, ending of discrimination against married women with regard to domicile laws, income tax and post-war credits as well as reform of the laws of solicitation to punish male co-offenders equally.[75]

*True Balance* was presented to the Conservative Party's women's conference in May 1949. The resolution that 'this conference approves the recommendations of the report on women's questions, and requests that these be embodied in the policy on which the party will fight the general election' was carried overwhelmingly with only four votes against. The report was sent to Churchill and at least 250,000 copies were sold.[76] The CWAC was unanimously in favour of the 'excellent' report, it received a largely favourable reaction in the areas[77] but *True Balance* and, particularly, the commitment to equal pay was controversial among women voters and male party members. Apparently, the report was 'wholly rejected by most Members on the Front Bench . . . in the most scornful terms' and an inquiry in 1954 showed that many older housewives and all men were against equal pay although younger women were predominantly in favour.[78] The CWAC was committed to the report and the committee which had drawn it up met in July 1951, stressing the need to 'assure the electorate of our sincerity . . . to implement what has been said in

our manifesto . . . and *A True Balance*'.[79] The CWAC parliamentary subcommittee went back to *True Balance* in December 1951 in
order to 'bring forward recommendations'.[80] Whatever the views
of the male front bench, the report was taken very seriously by
leading Conservative women and the issues raised were discussed
throughout the 1950s.

Looking at Labour Party propaganda during the period nothing
of the status of *True Balance* was published. There are only a few
publications directly addressed to women or focusing on women,
and Mary Sutherland's call in 1944 for a 'charter' for housewives
and mothers was never followed up.[81] Labour's document *Is a
Woman's Place in the Home?*, published in 1946, demanded equal
pay and equal opportunities for women as well as better welfare
provision to improve the position of women in the home.[82]
However, this pamphlet was only intended for use by constituency
discussion groups, and its arguments were not translated into
official policy statements. Most Labour propaganda material
specifically aimed at women, the focus of discussion in *Labour
Woman* and at women's conferences, addresses women in their
role as wives and mothers. Labour's women's sections met the
'trade union needs of the women in the home' and a 1949 leaflet,
entitled 'There is a place for every woman in the Labour Party',
claimed that 'no government has done more for women in such a
short period', highlighting family allowances, the NHS, food
subsidies and fair shares as well as full employment.[83]

The contrast between Labour and Conservative women's policy
is illustrated by looking at the equal pay issue. In 1944 the House
of Commons passed an amendment to the Education Bill granting
equal pay to female teachers. It was moved by the Conservative
MP Thelma Cazalet-Keir but overturned by Churchill on a vote of
confidence.[84] This vote forced the appointment of a Royal
Commission on Equal Pay and resulted in the launch of the
feminist Equal Pay Campaign Committee (hereafter EPCC). The
committee was closely associated with Conservative female MPs
such as Irene Ward and discreetly supported by leading members
of the CWAC such as Lady Davidson and Evelyn Emmet. The
first chair was Conservative MP Mavis Tate, and after her death in
1947 it was run by Cazalet-Keir who had lost her seat in 1945.
However, the EPCC was a cross-party organization which
received support from Labour MPs such as Barbara Castle and

Edith Summerskill. Over fifty women's organizations and trade unions were affiliated to the committee, and the range of propaganda material produced included the film *To Be a Woman*, directed by Jill Craigie, financed by the affiliated organizations.[85]

The Royal Commission reported in 1946. It approved of equal pay in government service but there was no agreement with regard to private industry. In 1947 Dalton, the Chancellor of the Exchequer, announced the government's position on equal pay:

> 'The Government accept, as regards their own employees the justice of the claim' but they assert that in incurring additional expenditure the Government must be the judge of priorities, and they will not apply the principle at the present time on the ground that 'it would be wholly inflationary in its results'.[86]

This was Labour's policy until the party lost office in 1951. Labour women were strongly in favour of equal pay, and the 1947 women's conference welcomed government recognition of the justice of the claim in principle despite disappointment at the delay in implementation. In 1948, Labour's Joint Standing Committee of Working Women's Organizations, following the chancellor's refusal to implement equal pay in view of the wage freeze, accepted that implementation should be delayed until 'the economic situation seemed to warrant it'. Despite many resolutions demanding equal pay in 1948, loyalty to the government took priority over the desire for equal pay, Conference endorsed the Joint Standing Committee's view, and after 1949 the issue was no longer discussed.[87] A press cutting from the *Daily Herald* which, under the headline 'Labour women will wait', noted 'solid backing for the government', as well as the report of the conference in *Labour Woman*, are included in the EPCC files in the Conservative Party archive. A hand-written comment dated 20 October 1948 by Marjorie Maxse reads, 'I feel we ought to be able to make capital out of the Equal Pay backsliding.'[88]

After the election of the Conservative government, Conservative women continued to press the demand for equal pay. In February 1952 the CWAC's parliamentary subcommittee considered equal pay 'to be the most vital issue' to be discussed with Butler, the chancellor, and Maxwell Fyfe, the party chairman. In view of the economic situation the immediate demand was for equal increments as a 'most important first step'.[89] Butler, who was in fact sympathetic towards the claim and perceived the electoral advantage of action on equal pay, did nothing, but at least he kept the women talking.[90] Another ally was the Minister of Education, Sir David Eccles, who had signed the questionnaire in support of equal pay sent to MPs in 1950 and 1951 and whose wife was a member of the CWAC responsible for the equal pay campaign in the late 1940s.[91] The pressure of the campaign intensified during 1953 and 1954. In March 1954 two petitions containing 680,000 signatures were presented to the House of Commons by the EPCC and trade unionists. Ward, Summerskill and Castle as well as EPCC members were driven in horse-drawn carriages 'decorated with rosettes in the white and green common to the suffrage organisations'. The first was 'driven by Mr David Jacobs who drove Dame Millicent Fawcett and Mrs Emmeline Pankhurst about London when they were campaigning for votes for women before the First World War'.[92] Faced with Labour's recent commitment to implement the policy immediately if they won the next general election, Butler finally convinced the cabinet to proceed towards equal pay in the civil service by seven increments, a decision announced in the budget speech.[93] Teaching quickly followed suit and in November 1955 the EPCC under the chairmanship of Cazalet-Keir hosted a celebratory 'Milestone Dinner' at the Savoy Hotel attended by Butler and Eccles as principal guests, sympathetic Conservative and Liberal MPs, representatives from the wider feminist movement including Philippa Strachey and Lord Pethick-Lawrence, and of course Conservative women such as Emmet, Davidson, Eccles and Ward.[94]

The importance of party political considerations in the implementation of equal pay in 1954 is rightly highlighted by Smith but I would go further in emphasizing the role of Conservative women in continuously pressing for the reform from the late 1940s onwards. Other successes of Conservative women include the admission of women to the House of Lords in 1958 and the ending of discrimination against female housebuyers.[95] However, in areas such as fair treatment with regard to income tax or equal retirement nothing was achieved in the 1950s. From the early 1960s onwards, Conservative women were engulfed in the wider crisis of growing disillusionment with the Conservative Party. The rhetoric of Conservative affluence and peace in contrast with Labour's austerity appeared dated in opposition to Wilson's dynamic and forward-looking Labour Party. With regard to party organization, the expansion and drive of the early 1950s was replaced by malaise and unease about falling membership, which was perceived to be ageing, but efforts to recruit younger women were not successful.[96]

By contrast, from the early 1960s onwards there is evidence among Labour women of revival and renewed confidence after a prolonged period of low morale and despair. In the wake of the third successive general election defeat, a National Labour Women's Advisory Committee document highlighted that Labour had done worse among women in certain areas, and the party decided to look 'at new ideas, methods and activities' in order to expand the women's organization.[97] Many new women's sections were set up, a membership drive was launched following Wilson's election as party leader and sales of *Labour Woman* increased.[98] The 1964 Labour women's conference congratulated the TUC on their 'charter for women' which advocated equal pay and equal opportunities for women in industry. Resolutions supported equal wages and called on the NEC 'to draw up a programme to provide greater opportunities for . . . women [and] to remove the considerable disadvantages and injustices'.[99] In the 1960s Labour women were again in the forefront of the battle for equal rights. Labour's new approach to women was not without success and a report on the 1966 general election noted with pleasure that the party had 'for the first time, obtained a majority of the female vote, and it would be very satisfactory if we could retain it'.[100] In 1964 and 1966 a new generation of women MPs was elected and promoted to ministerial jobs; Labour's nineteen female MPs dwarfed the rump of only seven women on the Conservative side and Labour stars such as Castle, Williams and Hart became the role model of the female politician.[101]

# IV

Gender differences in voting behaviour are a critical and neglected factor in understanding the general election results of the early post-war period. These differences are not static indicating a mechanical predilection among women towards Conservatism and among men towards the Labour Party, but rather contingent and historically determined. While Labour polled the majority of the female vote in 1945 and 1966, between these years and especially in the 1950s the Conservatives were able to achieve a clear lead among women voters. This female preference for Conservatism was not due to ignorance, deference or lack of sophistication among women voters. Rather, it was the result of a sustained effort by the Conservative Party in general and Conservative women in particular to recruit and integrate women into the party organization as well as to appeal to the mass of the female electorate with a set of policies which recognized the importance of gender difference. The politics of affluence appealed to women in their role as homemakers and consumers. Yet, the Conservative Party went beyond the confines of women's traditional role and in *The True Balance* called for equality for women as workers and citizens. These feminist policies were certainly not implemented in their entirety, but the Conservative Party was more sympathetic than Labour towards women's demands for greater equality, most notably with regard to equal pay, during the early post-war years. Building on the traditions of the women's movement, Conservative women could take pride in reducing gender inequalities in Britain during the 1950s.

## Notes

An earlier version of this paper was presented at the ICBH Summer School, 'British History 1945–95: The State of the Art', July 1995. I am grateful for comments received then as well as at Gregynog. Special thanks are due to Stephen Brooke, Martin Francis, David Jarvis, Kevin Jefferys, Duncan Tanner and Pat Thane.

[1] H. Durant, 'Voting Behaviour in Britain, 1945–64', in R. Rose (ed.), *Studies in British Politics* (London, 1966), 125, tab.; The Gallup Poll, 'Voting Behaviour in Britain', in *idem*, 3rd edn. (London, 1976), 211, tab.

[2] P. Anderson, 'Problems of Socialist Strategy', in P. Anderson et al., *Towards Socialism* (London, 1965), 276.

[3] See figures 1, 2 and table 1.

[4] A. M. Carr-Saunders, D. Caradog Jones and C. A. Moser, *A Survey of Social Conditions in England and Wales* (Oxford, 1958), 115; P. Joyce (ed.), *Class* (Oxford, 1995).

[5] P. Summerfield, 'The "Levelling of Class"', in H. L. Smith (ed.), *War*

and *Social Change: British Society in the Second World War* (Manchester, 1986), 179.

[6] R. S. Neale, *Class in English History, 1680–1850* (Oxford, 1981) quoted in Summerfield, '"Levelling"', 179–80.

[7] Carr-Saunders, *Survey of Social Conditions*, 114.

[8] Ibid., 115.

[9] R. Lewis and A. Maude, *The English Middle Classes* (London, 1949), 17–18; A. Marwick, *British Society since 1945* (London, 1982), 48.

[10] See e.g. F. Zweig, *Women's Life and Labour* (London, 1952), 121–3. His respondents who disliked being labelled 'working class', emphasized respectability and status rather than occupation and income.

[11] M. Charlot, 'Women and Elections in Britain', in H. R. Penniman (ed.), *Britain at the Polls, 1979* (Washington and London, 1981), 245, fig.; J. Lovenduski et al., 'The Party and Women', in A. Seldon and S. Ball, *Conservative Century: The Conservative Party since 1900* (Oxford, 1994), 614; I. Crewe et al., *The British Electorate, 1963–1987: A Compendium of Data from the British Election Studies* (Cambridge, 1991), 6, tab.

[12] D. E. Butler and D. Kavanagh, *The British General Election of 1992* (Basingstoke, 1992), 279, 277, tab.

[13] Conservative and Unionist Central Office (hereafter CUCO) (London, 1949).

[14] A. Black and S. Brooke, 'Labour and the Problem of Gender, 1951–1970', forthcoming.

[15] Durant, 'Voting Behaviour in Britain, 1945–64', 122.

[16] D. E. Butler, *British General Elections since 1945* (Oxford, 1989), 106–7, tab.

[17] J. Lawrence, 'Class and Gender in the Making of Urban Toryism, 1880–1914', *English Historical Review* 108 (1993), 630–2; S. O. Rose, 'Gender and Labour History', *International Review of Social History* 38 (1993), Supplement 1, 159–91; J. Curtice, 'Political Sociology 1945–92', in J. Obelkevich and P. Catterall (eds.), *Understanding Post-War British Society* (London, 1994). These arguments are further developed in J. Lawrence and M. Taylor (eds.), *Party, State and Society: Electoral Behaviour in Modern Britain* (Aldershot, 1996).

[18] I. Zweiniger-Bargielowska, 'Rationing, Austerity and the Conservative Party Recovery after 1945', *Historical Journal* 37 (1994), 173–97.

[19] J. Hinton, 'Women and the Labour Vote, 1945–50', *Labour History Review* 57 (1992), 59–66; J. Hinton, 'Militant Housewives: The British Housewives' League and the Attlee Government', *History Workshop Journal* 38 (1994), 129–30.

[20] Zweiniger-Bargielowska, 'Rationing', 184, fig.

[21] Hinton's figures for February 1950 and October 1951 are based on the *Gallup Political Index* 49 (February 1964), used by Anderson,

'Problems' and N. Hart, 'Gender and the Rise and Fall of Class Politics', *New Left Review* 175 (1989), 21. These figures are somewhat different from the gender breakdown in Durant's original article and Rose's later editions as well as the piece by Charlot. I use these latter figures which are more widely cited and strengthen my argument. According to the other figures there was a smaller swing to the Conservatives among women between 1950 and 1951.

22 Labour Party, RD 350, April 1950, General Election 1950: notes on the findings of opinion polls. This quotation again indicates Labour's masculinist approach by suggesting that female voters could be reached through Labour's male working-class supporters whereas the Conservative appeal to the working man was often through his wife.

23 Gender is conspicuous by its absence (apart from an occasional reference to female candidates) in the Nuffield studies, R. B. McCallum and A. Readman, *The British General Election of 1945* (London, 1947); H. G. Nicholas, *The British General Election of 1950* (London, 1951); D. E. Butler, *The British General Election of 1951* (London, 1952); D. E. Butler, *The British General Election of 1955* (London, 1955); D. E. Butler and R. Rose, *The British General Election of 1959* (London, 1960); D. E. Butler and A. King, *The British General Election of 1964* (London, 1965); D. E. Butler and A. King, *The British General Election of 1966* (London, 1966); D. E. Butler and M. Pinto-Duschinsky, *The British General Election of 1970* (London, 1971); M. Benney and P. Geiss, 'Social Class and Politics in Greenwich', *British Journal of Sociology* 1 (1950), 310–27; M. Abrams and R. Rose, *Must Labour Lose?* (Harmondsworth, 1960).

24 For a good summary of the literature on 'class voting', including the recent critique, see R. Waller, 'Conservative Electoral Support and Social Class', in Seldon and Ball, *Conservative Century*, 592–602.

25 J. H. Goldthorpe et al., *The Affluent Worker in the Class Structure* (Cambridge, 1969), and J. H. Goldthorpe et al., *The Affluent Worker: Political Attitudes and Behaviour* (Cambridge, 1971). The neglect of women is highlighted by Hart, 'Gender', 20–1, 26–7; and M. Pugh, 'Popular Conservatism in Britain: Continuity and Change, 1880–1987', *Journal of British Studies* 27 (1988), 280–1.

26 D. E. Butler and D. Stokes, *Political Change in Britain* (London, 1969), 63, 107–8, 129.

27 R. McKenzie and A. Silver, *Angels in Marble: Working Class Conservatives in Urban England* (London, 1968), 187–90, 261.

28 Anderson, 'Problems', 276–7.

29 J. Mark-Lawson et al., 'Gender and Local Politics: Struggles over Welfare Policies, 1918–1939', in L. Murgatroyd et al., *Localities, Class and Gender* (London, 1985), 195–215.

30 P. Thane, 'Women of the British Labour Party and Feminism', in H. L.

Smith, *British Feminism in the Twentieth Century* (Aldershot, 1990), 140–1.

[31] Hart, 'Gender', 28–37, 41–6; see also L. Oren, 'The Welfare of Women in Laboring Families: England, 1860–1950', *Feminist Studies* 1 (1973), 107–25; C. Blackford, 'Wives and Citizens and Watchdogs of Equality: Post-War British Feminists', in J. Fyrth (ed.), *Labour's Promised Land? Culture and Society in Labour Britain, 1945–51* (London, 1995), 58–72.

[32] D. Jarvis, 'Mrs Maggs and Betty: The Conservative Appeal to Women Voters in the 1920s', *Twentieth Century British History* 5 (1994), 144.

[33] J. W. Scott, *Gender and the Politics of History* (New York, 1988), 2.

[34] K. McClelland, 'Some Thoughts on Masculinity and the "Representative Artisan" in Britain, 1850–1880', *Gender and History* 1 (1989), 164–77; Rose, 'Gender', 147–56; S. O. Rose, *Limited Livelihoods: Gender and Class in Nineteenth Century England* (London, 1992).

[35] Charlot, 'Women'; J. Evans, 'Women and Politics: A Re-appraisal', *Political Studies* 28 (1980), 210–21; J. Siltanen and M. Stanworth (eds.), *Women and the Public Sphere: A Critique of Sociology and Politics* (London, 1984).

[36] P. Norris, 'Conservative Attitudes in Recent British Elections: An Emerging Gender Gap?', *Political Studies* 34 (1986), 120–8.

[37] M. Goot and E. Reid, 'Women: If not Apolitical, then Conservative', in Siltanen and Stanworth, *Women and the Public Sphere*, 130–2.

[38] J. Lawrence, 'Party Politics and the Politics of Gender in Modern Britain' (unpublished paper, 1993), 13–14.

[39] On franchise reform see M. Pugh, *Women's Suffrage in Britain, 1867–1929* (London, 1980); B. Harrison, 'Women's Suffrage at Westminster, 1866–1928', in M. Bentley and J. Stevenson (eds.), *High and Low Politics in Modern Britain: Ten Studies* (Oxford, 1983), 80–122. On the political integration of women during the inter-war years see M. Pugh, *Women and the Women's Movement in Britain 1914–1959* (London, 1992); M. Pugh, 'Women, Food and Politics, 1880–1930', *History Today* 41, 3 (1991), 14–20; P. M. Graves, *Labour Women: Women in British Working-Class Politics, 1918–1939* (Cambridge, 1994). On the relationship between feminism and politics see Smith, *British Feminism*.

[40] Thane, 'Women of the British Labour Party'; Pugh, *Women and the Women's Movement*, 101–3, 120–4.

[41] M. Pugh, *The Tories and the People* (Oxford, 1985), 27, 47–56.

[42] I am here deliberately using 'sexist' terminology since this language was used by the women themselves at the time.

[43] J. Ramsden, *The Age of Balfour and Baldwin 1902–1940* (London, 1978), 250–1; Conservative Party Archive, Bodleian Library, Oxford (hereafter BLO), CCO 500/9/7, Women in Politics 1960: Some Facts and Figures.

[44] S. Ball, 'Local Conservatism and the Evolution of Party Organisation',

in Seldon and Ball, *Conservative Century*, 272–3, 290–6; Lovenduski et al., 'The Party and Women', 617, 624.

45 Pugh, *Women and the Women's Movement*, 124–30, 145–51.

46 Ball, 'Local Conservatism', 265; Lovenduski et al., 'The Party and Women', 623; Pugh, 'Popular Conservatism', 266; and M. Benney et al., *How People Vote: A Study of Electoral Behaviour in Greenwich* (London, 1956), 46–7.

47 For membership figures see Zweiniger-Bargielowska, 'Rationing', 189–90.

48 Labour Party, *Annual Conference Report* (1951), 36.

49 Benney, *How People Vote*, 46–7; J. Lovenduski and P. Norris, *Gender and Party Politics* (London, 1993), 40–1.

50 F. W. S. Craig, *British Parliamentary Election Statistics, 1918–1970* (Chichester, 1971), 69–70, tabs.; J. Hills, 'Candidates, the Impact of Gender', *Parliamentary Affairs* 34 (1981), 221–8.

51 Archives of the Conservative Party, Harvester MFL 48, Minutes of the Central Women's Advisory Council (hereafter CWAC), Parliamentary Subcommittee, memo, 20 March 1952.

52 BLO, CCO 500/9/2, CCO 500/9/7, Organization Department files relating to women; Public Opinion Research Department, CCO 4/3/249, March 1950, Confidential Supplement to Public Opinion Survey No.14, and CCO 4/4/267, April 1951.

53 BLO, CCO 170/1/1/3, 10 February 1949.

54 BLO, CCO 4/4/328, 12 July 1951.

55 BLO, CCO 500/11/7.

56 BLO, CCO 4/7/444, correspondence 14 September to 16 October 1957.

57 BLO, CCO 500/9/2, Report of Working Party on Women's Organisation, 4 July 1957.

58 See Zweiniger-Bargielowska, 'Rationing'; I. Zweiniger-Bargielowska, 'Consensus and Consumption: Rationing, Austerity and Controls after the War', in H. Jones and M. Kandiah (eds.), *The Myth of Consensus* (Basingstoke, 1996).

59 *Labour Woman* (March and November 1946, January 1947, January and September 1948, July–August and December 1950); Archives of the Labour Party: Harvester Microfiche, MFC 6, Labour Party Pamphlets and Leaflets, 1949/1, Agenda for the twenty-seventh National Conference of Labour Women, 27–9 September 1949.

60 CUCO, *Onward* 1, 7 (April 1954); Archives of the Conservative Party, Harvester Microfiche, MFC 1, Conservative Party Pamphlets and Leaflets, 1954/26, Westminster News: Housewives are 'Shopping Extra', 1954/24, Westminster News: End of Rationing; see also 1954/6, Food Rationing Ends: The Conservatives get Things Done!, 1954/33, Ration Book 'Good-bye-ee'.

[61] See Zweiniger-Bargielowska, 'Rationing'; Zweiniger-Bargielowska, 'Consensus'.

[62] Harvester Microfiche, MFC 1, 1955/128, Popular Record: Voters' Choice: with the Conservatives: Peace and Plenty, with the Socialists Controls and Crisis; see also 1955/7, Conservative Key Points. Freedom, 1955/80, The Choice!, 1955/84, Is this Honest? . . . Don't Swap Tory Plenty for Labour Scarcity, 1955/111, Conservative Key Points. The Housewife.

[63] Ibid., 1955/20, Westminster News: Labour's 'Back to Queues', 1955/35, Labour's New Policy: Shopping Orders to the Housewife, 1955/83, Under Labour, Rationing. Under the Conservatives, Freedom of Choice, 1955/127, Labour's Bluff.

[64] Labour Party, Nail this Tory Lie! (London, 1955), National Library of Wales, Aberystwyth, Labour Party, misc. literature; *Labour Woman* (December 1954).

[65] Harvester Microfiche, MFC 1, 1958/35, see also 1958/28, Better Living for You, 1958/39, This was Your Life . . . Seven Years Ago!

[66] Ibid., 1961/116, Do you Remember Life Ten Years ago?, 1964/63, The Conservatives Believe in Prosperity, 1964/121, Prosperity – Just Look around You.

[67] *Labour Woman* (January 1955). See also Harvester Microfiche, MFC 6, 1954/18, Is it really Good-Bye to Rationing?, 1955/4, And so the Poor Housewife has None!, 1956/31, Housewives Choice?, deploring the end of fair shares and the Tories' policy of 'rationing by purse'.

[68] *Labour Woman* (January, May and September 1952, July and December 1955).

[69] Harvester MFC 37, Labour Party Women's Organisation, Women's Conference, 22–4 April, 1952, 12–13.

[70] O. Banks, *Faces of Feminism* (Oxford, 1981), 163–79. For a critique see Smith, *British Feminism*, especially the contribution by Lewis; Blackford, 'Wives', 58–72.

[71] Vol.3 (1991).

[72] CUCO, February 1949. *True Balance* was drawn up by the Conservative and Unionist Committee on Women's Questions, chaired by Malcolm McCorquodale, whose members included leading Conservative women as well as male MPs.

[73] See H. L. Smith, 'The Politics of Conservative Reform: The Equal Pay for Equal Work Issue, 1945–1955', *Historical Journal* 35 (1992), 401–15.

[74] F. W. S. Craig, *British General Election Manifestos 1900–1974* (Chichester, 1975), 143, 191 (election manifestos of 1950 and 1955); CUCO, *The Right Road for Britain* (London, 1949), 42–4; CUCO, *The Campaign Guide 1950* (London, 1949), 663–4; CUCO, *The Campaign Guide 1955* (London, 1955), 157–8, 297–8.

[75] This issue is discussed by M. Francis in the present volume.

[76] Harvester MFL 48, CWAC General Purposes Committee, 28 March 1949; BLO, CCO 170/1/1/4, CWAC, 28 April 1949; CCO 4/3/311, correspondence, 18 and 28 July 1949.

[77] BLO, CCO 170/1/1/3, CWAC, 16 March 1949; in other areas there was strong opposition to equal pay, CWAC, 17 April 1947.

[78] BLO, CCO 4/4/35, Correspondence Hornsby-Smith to Lady Maxwell Fyfe, 27 July 1951; CCO 4/6/109, Memo on Equal Pay, 1 April 1954.

[79] BLO, CCO 4/4/35, 12 July 1951; see also CCO 170/1/1/4, CWAC, 6 September 1951.

[80] Harvester MFL 48, CWAC Parliamentary Subcommittee, 4 December 1951 and 11 November 1953.

[81] *Labour Woman* (February 1944).

[82] Labour Party, *Is a Woman's Place in the Home?*, Labour Discussion Series no.9 (London, 1946).

[83] *Labour Woman* (February 1945); Harvester MFC 6, 1949/40.

[84] See Smith, 'Politics of Conservative Reform'; A. Potter, 'The Equal Pay Campaign Committee: A Case-Study of a Pressure Group', *Political Studies* 5 (1957), 49–64; P. Thane, 'Towards Equal Opportunities? Women in Britain since 1945', in T. Gourvish and A. O'Day, *Britain since 1945* (London, 1991), 183–91; Blackford, 'Wives and Citizens', 64–7.

[85] CCO 3/2/38, EPCC, minutes, 22 November 1949, Newsletter no.11 (May 1950), minutes, 22 November 1950; a circular (n.d.) in this file lists the supporting societies, which include women's trade unions in teaching, civil service and local government, feminist societies such as the Six Point Group and the Open Door Council as well as party political bodies including the National Union of Conservative Associations, the Fabian Society (Women's Group) and the Women's Liberal Federation.

[86] BLO, CCO 3/1/14, EPCC, *Equal Pay for Equal Work: A Black Record* (London, 1949).

[87] *Labour Woman* (October 1948); Harvester MFC 6, 1948/1, Agenda for twenty-sixth National Conference of Labour Women; 1949/1, Agenda for twenty-seventh National Conference of Labour Women.

[88] BLO, CCO 3/1/14, EPCC, includes cuttings from the *Daily Herald*, 1 October 1948 and *Labour Woman* (October 1948).

[89] Harvester MFL 48, Reel 4, CWAC Parliamentary Subcommittee, 13 February and 20 March 1952.

[90] Smith, 'Politics of Conservative Reform', 403–6; Harvester MFL 48, Reel 4, CWAC Parliamentary Subcommittee, 17 July 1952 and 12 February 1953; BLO CCO 3/4/53, EPCC, 5 February 1954.

[91] BLO CCO 3/4/53, List of Conservative MPs supporting equal pay, Press statement from the Ministry of Education, 14 February 1955; Harvester MFL 48, CWAC Parliamentary Subcommittee, 15 January 1947.

92 *The Times*, 9 March 1954.

93 Smith, 'Politics of Conservative Reform', 409–14.

94 BLO CCO 3/4/53, Correspondence and accounts of Milestone Dinner, 10 November 1955; *The Times*, 11 November 1955. The EPCC, having campaigned for immediate implementation of equal pay, was divided over the question of increments, seven members of the committee boycotted the dinner and the EPCC was wound up early in 1956; Potter, 'Equal Pay Campaign Committee', 53; Smith, 'Politics of Conservative Reform', 414. I suspect that the Conservative tone of the dinner may have been an added reason for the split.

95 CUCO, *The Campaign Guide 1955*, 297–8; CUCO, *The Campaign Guide 1959* (London, 1959), 355–6; Harvester Microfiche, MFC 1, 1959/21, Extracts from a speech by Harold Macmillan at a mass meeting following the Conservative women's conference, 25 June 1959.

96 BLO, CCO 500/9/7, Women in the Party Organisation, Progress Report, November 1961; CCO 500/9/9, reports, 13 February 1963 and 25 September 1963.

97 Harvester Microfiche, MFC 6, 1960/55, National Labour Women's Advisory Committee: Expansion of Women's Organisation and Activities; 1960/71, Report of thirty-seventh Women's Conference, April 1960, 38–40.

98 Ibid., see annual reports in 1961/3, Agenda for thirty-eighth Women's Conference, March 1961, 1962/1, Agenda for thirty-ninth Women's Conference, May 1962, 1963/1, Agenda for fortieth Women's Conference, April 1963, 1963/86, *Labour Woman* (March 1963), 1964/1, Agenda for forty-first Women's Conference, March 1964.

99 Ibid., 1964/1, Agenda for forty-first Women's Conference, March 1964, 1964/5, The Charter of Rights; Harvester Microfiche MFC 17, Archives of the Trades Union Congress: pamphlets and leaflets, 1963/16, Six-point Charter for Women at Work.

100 Labour Party Archives, Home Policy Committee, Re20, 'The 1966 General Election', July 1966.

101 BLO, CCO 500/9/9, Women in Politics in 1966 which, in marked contrast with the 1960 version (CCO 500/9/7), is now dominated by Labour women.

*Part Four*


*Policy*

# The Conservative Party, the State and Social Policy, 1880–1914

## E. H. H. GREEN

In 1892 Lord Salisbury, commenting on a set of social reforms proposed by Joseph Chamberlain, told Arthur Balfour, 'these social questions are destined to break up our party.'[1] Salisbury's remark was informed by his characteristic pessimism, but in many respects his concern was both understandable and justifiable, for 'the social question' and the role of the state in addressing it were issues which posed significant problems for the Conservative Party in the late nineteenth and early twentieth century.

The Conservatives' concern with the social question began in earnest in 1884 – there had been *sporadic* interest before but it was the mid-1880s which witnessed the development of a more systematic level of debate. The electoral reforms of 1884–5 provided the main impetus for this interest in social issues. The extension of the franchise in 1884 had added 1.76 million new voters to the electorate, and it had ensured that, for the first time, working-class voters predominated in both town and country. Conservative assumptions about the *nature* of this new mass electorate shaped their perception of the political implications of the franchise extension. Writing in 1883 Salisbury had described a democracy as 'consisting of men who are ordinarily engrossed by the daily necessities of self support',[2] alluding to the cross-party consensus that a mass electorate could but be an impoverished electorate. Salisbury's view that this posed a *particular* difficulty for the Conservatives stemmed from his assumption that material considerations would matter more to the poorer elements of society than attachment to established institutions, and that an improvement in their standard of living would be their main priority. In this respect Salisbury agreed with the Fabian Society that the political enfranchisement of the masses would be followed by a demand for their social and economic enfranchisement. What Conservatives saw as threatening in this was that the poor masses would seek to gain material improvement at the expense of the better-off. The spectre haunting Salisbury and his party in the early 1880s was the radical demagogue exploiting the privations of the poorer classes of elector and 'impressing upon them that the function of legislation is to transfer to them something . . . from the pockets of their more fortunate countrymen'.[3] Hence, somewhat ironically, Joseph Chamberlain appeared to symbolize the dangerous potential of the new politics when he fused his belief that 'the future of politics are social politics' with his demand to know what 'ransom' property would pay to preserve its privileges.[4] From 1884 a central assumption of British politics, which the Conservative Party did not dispute, was that finding an answer to the social question was bound to be an electoral imperative. In turn this meant that the Conservatives, like their political opponents, had to define, or perhaps more accurately redefine, the boundaries of the state.

The social question posed two distinct but related practical problems for the Conservative Party. First, there was the question of whether they could satisfy the desire of the mass electorate for material betterment. Second, there was the issue of whether they could do this without injuring other elements of society. But both these issues necessarily raised the more abstract problem of the role of the state. On a general level, securing material improvement for the masses posed questions about the boundaries of state action – the proper function of the state, and its relationship to civil society and the individual were major ethical issues in this context. On a more specific level there was the problem of who was to pay for any state action to improve the lot of the poorer classes – the proper function of the state in securing social and especially distributive justice. This last issue was particularly problematic given the fiscal climate of the late nineteenth and early twentieth century. The seemingly effortless budgetary surpluses enjoyed by mid-Victorian governments had given way to a growing 'fiscal crisis' of the British state, with both central and

local government budgets under increasing strain.[5] By the late
1880s it was evident that any new bold social policy initiative
involving significant new expenditure by the state would require
new sources of revenue – for the first time since the 1840s the
nature and legitimacy of Britain's tax regime was being
scrutinized.[6] The Conservatives thus faced both ethical and
economic problems concerning the role of the state, and, what was
equally important, had to confront the relationship between the
two.


# I

In examining the Conservative position on the role of the state it is
perhaps worth emphasizing at the outset that this was an issue
which prompted a great deal of Conservative *thought*. The
historiography of the late nineteenth and early twentieth century is
brimful with works devoted to developments on the left of British
politics which have stressed, indeed foregrounded, the role of
socialist and Liberal intellectuals in helping to shape their parties'
approaches to social policy and state intervention. Equally
important, these works have eschewed the redundant (and
epistemologically dubious) dichotomy between political thought
and action in favour of an examination of how intellectuals,
journalists, economists and practising politicians, operating within a
common frame of ideological reference points, were seeking to
define recognizably 'Liberal' or 'Labour' answers to the social
question and the role of the state. By way of contrast the
Conservative position on these issues has tended to be seen as
*political* in the narrowest usage of that word. However, the fact is
that for Conservatives, no less than for Liberals or socialists, the
role of the state was a problem of ideas, for Conservatives too were
seeking to define a recognizably *Conservative* answer to the social
question. Indeed, if one wishes to understand the controversies
which racked the Conservative Party in the early twentieth century,
then one must grasp that the tensions in the party were in large part
symptomatic of a conflict between differing conceptions of what
constituted a proper Conservative position on the role of the state.

From the outset Conservatives were not united on their stance
on the role of the state. Rather there was a variety of Conservative

positions. The first, which may be termed 'libertarian', viewed extensions of the state's functions with suspicion and/or downright hostility. The most extreme libertarian stance was most closely associated in the 1880s and 1890s with Lord Wemyss and his fellow members of the Liberty and Property Defence League, whose Spencerian opposition to state intervention led them not only to oppose such mild reforms as half-day holidays and seating for shop assistants, but also to denounce Salisbury himself as a 'socialist' for promoting slum clearance and schemes for rehousing the working class in the mid-1880s.[7] In the early twentieth century these extreme libertarian ideas were promulgated by members of the British Constitutional Association[8] and by prominent Conservative free-traders. The junior Conservative MP for the City of London, Sir Frederick Banbury, produced the most forthright parliamentary statements of the extreme libertarian view, but the editor of the Conservative free-trade journal *The Spectator*, John St Loe Strachey, was perhaps the most eloquent spokesman for this position. For example, in 1907 Strachey argued that 'a bad proposal like old age pensions is not improved by calling it social reform instead of Socialism',[9] and in 1908 he denounced both the Liberal government for enacting social reforms like pensions and the Conservative Party for not opposing them.[10] A milder form of libertarian thought was articulated by Lord Hugh Cecil in his book *Conservatism* and in his less well-known Herbert Spencer lecture, published in 1910 as *Liberty and Authority*. Cecil accepted that it was legitimate for the state to act to help the poor and needy – he did not, for example, attack old age pensions as *necessarily* bad. But Cecil was insistent that the state should confine its acts of charity to those 'unable' to help themselves, such as women, children and the aged, and he was hostile to any intervention that benefited adult working men, such as the regulation of hours and conditions of work.[11] Cecil's grounds for objection to any more sweeping intervention by the state was based on what came to be known by the late twentieth century as the theory of 'dependency culture'. In *Liberty and Authority* Cecil stated that

> If we enfeeble human nature by removing from it the discipline of liberty, then certainly we shall be wandering astray; and while we use the machinery of the State to get, as we think, somewhat nearer the

solution of this problem or that, we shall all the time be destroying that on which the State itself depends, that from which any real and permanent good can come – the individual character.[12]

Likewise in *Conservatism* he underscored the view that state intervention robbed individuals and social groups of the positive, educative benefits of self-achievement. An example he chose to illustrate his case was state action to regulate hours and wages, specifically the Trade Boards Act of 1909 and the Mines Act of 1912. These measures, he contended, weakened both employers and more especially employees by obviating the necessity for collective bargaining and destroying the learning experience that would have been gained by voluntary organization and negotiation – 'character is strengthened by the effort to find a way out of difficulty and hardships, and is weakened by the habit of looking to the State.'[13] Cecil felt that state intervention was almost always debilitating, and that it was preferable that 'each man look for help and progress to himself . . . trained by self-discipline and self-control, and not to the State's enervating hand'.[14]

Cecil's concerns about state intervention were not, however, confined to his fear of its debilitating effects on character. He was also very keen to limit the justification for and thereby the *extent* of state action. As noted above, Cecil had no objection to the introduction of some state social reforms, such as pensions. But he was clear that, for example, the aged poor had no *right* to receive assistance, and that the provision of pensions was not a matter of *justice*. Rather he stated that such relief was acceptable only if conceived as *national charity*.[15] Cecil's position here was that if one accepted state intervention on grounds of social justice this would open the door to Socialism. According to Cecil the language of social justice would allow the state to indulge in sweeping intervention, and in particular justify state action to 'rectify' social inequalities. This he deemed wrong on the grounds that, as James Meadowcroft has pointed out, there was no ethical element in economic processes.[16] If the state acted to 'correct' the market it could, Cecil contended, only act unjustly, in that it would attack benefits that had already been established by open economic processes, and thereby inflict undeserved injuries on innocent parties.[17] It was in this context that Cecil raised the taxation question. Taxes for the common good, such as raising revenue for defending the community against external aggressors, were, Cecil argued, wholly justifiable, but taxes raised from one person or group for the benefit of another were unjust. The state, Cecil stated, was the community's 'trustee', and hence it could not 'inflict injustice in the interest of those for whom it acts';[18] it was Cecil's view that 'a pecuniary fine does not cease to be an injustice because it is called a tax or a readjustment of property'.[19]

Cecil's position on the state is more nuanced than is often recognized, and he should not be lumped in with extreme libertarians like Herbert Spencer and the Liberty and Property Defence League, for he certainly left the state much more room for manœuvre than Spencer and Wemyss.[20] However, it is not difficult to see why the subtleties of Cecil's logic are often overlooked. To begin with, although Cecil was not unequivocally individualist or anti-statist, his insistence that the state was 'the sum of the individuals that make it up'[21] placed him, in purely intellectual terms, in antagonism to those who saw the state as an organism, most obviously New Liberals and Socialists but also a substantial number of prominent Conservative thinkers and politicians.[22] Equally important, Cecil's main political allegiances in the Edwardian period were the British Constitutional Association and the Conservative free-trade cause, the two homes of libertarian Conservatism in its most extreme manifestations. That Cecil should have been drawn to these 'Men Versus the State' owed less perhaps to Cecil's logic than to the logic of the situation, in that developments within Conservatism left little room for Cecil's moderate libertarian position.

That Cecil should have found his only congenial political home amongst the more extreme libertarians was due to the way in which libertarian positions of all forms were increasingly marginalized in British politics in general and Conservative politics in particular in the late nineteenth and early twentieth century. The Conservative position on the social question and the role of the state was dominated by, broadly speaking, two strands of thought, one of which was ascendant during the 1880s and 1890s, and the other in the Edwardian era. In the late nineteenth century the dominant position was what is best described as Quietism. Embodied in the outlook of Salisbury himself the Quietist stance was prepared to accept that state action was helpful to social problems, but on a piecemeal basis, with

proposals being assessed on their individual merits. This approach
can be read as simply political pragmatism, and this was certainly
how Salisbury was wont to describe it, with his characteristic
question of *all* policy proposals – 'is it practical politics?' – the
epitome of cautious empiricism. But as with all supposedly
empirically based arguments the Quietist approach carried some
important implicit theoretical assumptions.[23] Most important of
these was that a case-by-case assessment of social policy
represented a denial of the need for a systemic approach to the
social question. The Quietist presupposition was, in effect, that
wherever possible the agencies of civil society were the best
mechanisms for dealing with social ills, and that they were to be
supplemented rather than supplanted by limited state action. At
first glance this may seem to be little different from a moderate
libertarianism. However, there was a key difference in the
underlying assumptions, in that the Quietists had no objection *in
principle* to state action, whereas all libertarians, whether moderate
or extreme, were predisposed to oppose state intervention on the
grounds that it was more likely to be a substitute for rather than a
supplement to the agencies of civil society.

The Conservative approach that became dominant in the
Edwardian period was explicitly collectivist. In contrast to their
libertarian colleagues, Conservative collectivists did not see
extensions of the state as either actually or potentially socialist, but
insisted that state-sponsored social reform was the best antidote to
socialism. Likewise they differed from Quietists in accepting the
case for a systematic approach to the social question. The
spokesmen for this brand of Conservatism rejected the idea that
the state was simply the sum of its individual parts and insisted
that there could be no antagonism between the interests of the
individual and those of the state. Like many New Liberal and
socialist thinkers, Conservative collectivists drew on an organic
conception of state–society relations, with the Conservative
economist William Cunningham arguing that

> The State is the embodiment of what is common to the different
> persons in the nation, it expresses the spirit which each shares . . . we
> cannot represent the State as an abstract entity that is antagonistic to
> the individual citizens. The State is concerned with the general interest
> – with what is common to all.[24]

Conflict between common and individual interests only arose, Cunningham stated, because future prosperity could be sacrificed by individuals whose desire for immediate gain led them to overlook longer-term prospects. 'In the eager competition of individuals with one another, Cunningham wrote,

> public objects of general good and for the common advantage, may be overlooked. It is necessary that they should be consciously and deliberately taken in hand by public authority; and there must be some interference with private interests favourable to some and unfavourable to others . . . In so far as the national resources and the aggregate of individual wealth are distinct, it is desirable that the public authority should occasionally interfere.[25]

In short, to ensure that the interest of the whole community, which included the long-term good of the individual, was protected it was necessary that the state regulate economic and social processes. Such an outlook was clearly antagonistic to even the mild libertarianism of Hugh Cecil, let alone the Spencerian visions of the Liberty and Property Defence league. For Cunningham economic processes had an evident ethical content, the state was *not* the sum of individuals and it was legitimate for the state to take action harmful to some and beneficial to others. It was precisely this kind of thinking which, in the Edwardian period, informed the activities of the Unionist Social Reform Committee as it sought to construct a clear, positive Conservative social policy to offer as an alternative to the 'Socialistic' schemes of the Liberal government. The committee's document on *Industrial Unrest*, published in 1914, made explicit its dismissal of libertarian assumptions, stating that

> we have . . . outlived that curious philosophic conception of relations between the State and the individual which finds its origin in Rousseau and its most powerful exponents on this side of the channel in Bentham, the two Mills, Herbert Spencer and Cobden.

Indeed, it went on to argue that

> the view of the modern as of ancient Toryism is that the interests of the State and of the community must at all costs be safeguarded, but that the interests of the worker must not be sacrificed in the process, for the worker is an integral part of the State.

For Conservative collectivists the state was the key instrument in the monitoring and preservation of national well-being, and this meant ensuring the health and vitality of 'all physical objects which may be used for sustaining and prolonging national life'.[26] The main target of the collectivist Conservatives was evidently libertarian social philosophy, but the willingness to encompass 'all physical objects' also indicated a break from the case-by-case approach to social issues that had characterized the Salisburyan era.

## II

If in the realm of political thought Conservatives were, from the late nineteenth century, engaged in an ongoing debate as to how best to define and delimit the social and economic functions of the state, they were similarly engaged in the realm of policy. Indeed, the two things were part of the same process – two sides of the same coin – whereby Conservatism sought to adapt to the demands of a mass electorate within a maturing industrial society.

The Conservatives' need for a new praxis was made very clear by debates over various social policy issues in the 1890s. The kind of problems they faced are illustrated very well by the proposals that emerged for regulating the hours of labour in various industries, in particular the mines, that were brought forward on a number of occasions in the early 1890s. In a memorandum on 'The Eight Hours Question', written as a briefing document for Arthur Balfour in March 1891, J. S. Sandars argued that an eight-hour day in mining and other industries would raise wages and other employer costs. In some circumstances, Sandars contended, such increased costs could be borne without complaint, but were insupportable in the 1890s because of the intensity of foreign competition.[27] The case against such legislation was put even more strongly by the Conservative MP for Dover (and Balfour's sometime parliamentary secretary) George Wyndham. Writing to his father in May 1892 Wyndham noted that 'the theory of that measure [the Eight Hours bill then before Parliament] is unassailable so long as you exclude foreign competition from the problem'.[28] Over the rest of the decade this argument was wheeled out by many industrialists when any industrial legislation was in the pipeline, and it undoubtedly inhibited Conservative action in this area.[29] The case against such legislation was straightforward – that it would produce increased costs at a time when many British industries were already worried about their international competitiveness. At the same time there were obvious concerns about the electoral and broader social consequences of disappointing the demands of organized labour. The issue of reconciling particular interests with the general interest of the community was inseparable from the problem of reconciling elements of what were regarded as core Conservative constituents (employers) with a wider potential constituency (employees). That this could be successfully achieved through positive state action was illustrated by the Workmen's Compensation Act of 1897. Statutory compensation for industrial injury was welcomed by employees and, for the most part, by employers, for it effectively superseded the Employers' Liability legislation of 1881. Employers' Liability had allowed for litigation to secure compensation for injury at work, but it required often lengthy and costly legal processes, the outcome of which was uncertain. A major complaint against this procedure was that it encouraged an adversarial view of industrial relations by setting employer against employee in the context of legal proceedings. Workmen's Compensation allowed for a form of 'no-fault' procedure which was speedier, cheaper and less stucturally adversarial. The 1897 legislation thus seemed to provide a model whereby the state could act as a broker between the two sides of industry and reconcile their respective interests with the broader interest of the community in social and industrial peace.

In the early twentieth century the Conservative search for an alternative, constructive vision of the state intensified. There were two interrelated reasons for this. In the first place the Conservatives' electoral position deteriorated markedly after 1900. In particular the traumatic defeat of 1906, which saw the Conservative parliamentary contingent reduced to its lowest-ever level, produced reverberations in the Conservative ranks that were not to be felt again until 1945. But as was to be the case in 1945, the key point about the 1906 defeat was the Conservative interpretation of what had occasioned their downfall.

Conservative debate on the 1906 defeat was dominated by the impact of Labour – the twenty-nine Labour MPs elected were, paradoxically, regarded as more important than the 399 Liberals.[30] The significance of Labour was that it was seen to herald a transformation in the nature of British politics, in so far as it indicated that there was 'a new distinction of forces between the Pro-Socialists and the Anti-Socialists'.[31] Over the next three years this new 'socialist challenge' was seen by the whole spectrum of Conservative opinion to be growing stronger and more threatening. The reason for this was the development of the Liberal government's social and fiscal policies. The introduction of free school meals in 1906 and old age pensions in 1908, the trade boards legislation of 1909 and the development of labour exchanges were all indicative of a Liberalism no longer wedded to *laissez-faire*. More worrying still for the Conservatives was the fact that the 'statist' New Liberals were prepared to finance these initiatives with a radical fiscal strategy based on steeply graduated, progressive taxation and additional burdens for, in particular, landed wealth, with the 'People's Budget' of 1909 being seen as the culmination of this new departure.

The direction of British politics in and after 1906 appeared to Conservatives of all hues to bring a delayed confirmation of Salisbury's fears in the 1880s, namely that the forces of radicalism had found a way to mobilize popular opinion on the basis of electoral bribery funded by a 'confiscatory' tax regime. The question the Conservatives faced was how best to combat these now very real problems. For both extreme and mild libertarians the answer was to resist and oppose the Liberal social and fiscal initiatives, but, given the apparent electoral success of those advocating social reform – and, perhaps inaccurately, Labour's emergence was seen as symptomatic of this trend – this seemed an electorally implausible approach. For the same reason the Salisburyan Quietism that had served the party so well in the 1890s also appeared to have lost its electoral purchase. Hence the party sought to discover, with increasing urgency, positive social and fiscal initiatives of their own in order to counter the appeal of the New Liberalism's 'socialistic' strategy.[32]

It is this search which helps to explain the Conservatives' increasing commitment to tariff reform through the Edwardian period, for tariffs marked the point at which the theory and practice of a collectivist Conservative approach to social policy came together. As a revenue measure tariffs promised to spread the burden of increased taxation across all of society, thereby avoiding payment for social reform through openly class-biased taxation. Social reform may have been *directly* aimed at and beneficial to particular sections of society, but the rationale for them was that they would increase the health and efficiency of the nation considered as a whole – and hence it was right that the nation as a whole should pay. As a protective measure tariffs were to secure British productive enterprise, and hence British jobs, against foreign competition. State regulation of trade would thereby ensure general prosperity, stabilize employment and thus reduce poverty. The argument that the revenue and protective aspects of tariff reform were contradictory was dispatched with the argument that if tariffs protected British industry, and thereby increased prosperity, then the taxable capacity of the nation would increase and compensate the Exchequer for any lost earnings from the Customs House.[33] Equally important in this context, protective tariffs were to provide employers with compensation for the costs of other social policies. Here it is noteworthy that the Conservatives not only raised no objections to old age pensions in 1908, but also supported the Trade Boards Act to regulate wages in the sweated trades in 1909, voted *for* National Insurance in 1911, and, on more than one occasion, provided support for the principle of minimum wages in various industries.[34] At the same time, however, the Conservatives insisted, in the words of the Conservative National Union Executive Committee, that 'the[se] new burdens placed upon industry' simply brought home 'the necessity of putting British industries on a par with their foreign competitors by imposing some moderate duties, which should be equivalent to the increased charges'.[35] Tariffs through their various functions enabled the Conservative Party to square the circle of the distributive problems of social policy, by holding out the possibility of a harmony of interests under the umbrella of an active, producers' state. State intervention on social issues, which had seemed to pose so many dangers to the Conservative Party in the late nineteenth century, had to the bulk of the party come to seem like the best answer to the problem of how to equip Conservatism to deal with the challenges of the mass electorate, socialism and the modern industrial world.

## Notes

[1] Salisbury to Balfour, 26 July 1892, Balfour papers, British Library, Add. MSS, 49690, ff. 65–6.

[2] Lord Salisbury, 'Disintegration', in P. Smith (ed.), *Lord Salisbury on Politics* (Cambridge, 1974), 347.

[3] Ibid., 343.

[4] J. Chamberlain to E. Russel, 22 January 1882, cited in R. Jay, *Joseph Chamberlain* (Oxford, 1981), 73. For the 'doctrine of ransom', see Chamberlain at Birmingham, 5 January 1885, in C. Boyd (ed.), *Speeches of the Right Honourable Joseph Chamberlain*, 2 vols. (London, 1913), I:131–40.

[5] For general discussions of the emerging budgetary problems see A. Offer, *Property and Politics* (Cambridge, 1981) and J. Cronin, *The Politics of State Expansion* (London, 1991).

[6] For a discussion of the general historical importance of this question for Conservatives see the chapter by Daunton in this volume.

[7] For the views of this group see N. Soldon, 'Laissez-Faire as Dogma: The Case of the Liberty and Property Defence League', in K. D. Brown (ed.), *Essays in Anti-Labour History* (London, 1974); E. Bristow, 'The Liberty and Property Defence League and Individualism', *Historical Journal* 18 (1975); M. W. Taylor, *Men Versus the State* (Oxford, 1992).

[8] For this group see Taylor, *Men Versus the State*.

[9] Strachey to Lady Londonderry, 8 October 1907, Strachey papers, House of Lords Record Office, S/9/15/3.

[10] See for example Strachey to Lord Wellby, 29 June 1908, Strachey papers, S/16/2/31, and for a more general discussion see A. J. L. Morris, 'John St Loe Strachey and *The Spectator*'(unpublished Cambridge University Ph.D. thesis, 1984).

[11] H. Cecil, *Conservatism* (London, 1912), 188–90.

[12] Cecil, *Liberty and Authority*, 64–5.

[13] Cecil, *Conservatism*, 189.

[14] Cecil, *Liberty and Authority*, 17.

[15] Cecil, *Conservatism*, 183–8.

[16] See J. Meadowcroft, *Conceptualizing the State* (Oxford, 1995), 96.

[17] For a discussion of Cecil's position here see ibid., 95–8.

[18] Cecil, *Conservatism*, 165.

[19] Ibid., 166.

[20] This point is established at length by James Meadowcroft's work, see n.15.

[21] Cecil, *Conservatism*, 162.

[22] See below for a discussion of Conservative organicists.

[23] This case-by-case approach was in fact the position adopted by the marginalist economist W. S. Jevons.

24  W. Cunningham, *Politics and Economics* (London, 1885), 135.
25  W. Cunningham, *Political Economy and Practical Life* (London, 1893), 24.
26  Unionist Social Reform Committee, *Industrial Unrest* (London, 1914), 2.
27  J. S. Sandars to Balfour, n.d. [March 1891], J. S. Sandars papers, Bodleian Library, Oxford, MS Eng. Hist. c. 724, ff. 152–88.
28  G. Wyndham to C. Wyndham, 22 May 1892, in J. Mackail and G. Wyndham, *Life and Letters of George Wyndham*, 2 vols. (London, 1925), I:260–1.
29  See E. P. Hennock, *British Social Reform and German Precedents* (Oxford, 1987), 140–1, 174–5, 188–95 for examples.
30  For a full discussion of the Conservative response to Labour see E. H. H. Green, *The Crisis of Conservatism* (London, 1995), 136–40.
31  W. Lawler-Wilson, *The Menace of Socialism* (London, 1909), 17.
32  For further discussion of this development see Green, *Crisis*, 148–52.
33  For this argument see 'tariff reformer' (L. S. Amery) to *The Times*, 28 March 1908.
34  For a detailed discussion of these developments see Green, *Crisis*, 242–66, 285–94.
35  National Union Council, 'Report' to National Union Conference, 14 November 1912, National Union Conference Minutes, 1912, Conservative Party Archive, Bodleian Library, Oxford.

# The Cold War and the Santa Claus Syndrome: Dilemmas in Conservative Social Policy-Making, 1945–1957

## HARRIET JONES

It would be a mistake to underestimate the impact of the Second World War on British society and politics. The war transformed the economic position of the country and, internationally, led to the rise of a new world order in which Britain's role was much less certain. In domestic terms, it culminated in the election of a Labour government with a solid majority and a mandate to undertake the peacetime transformation of the country through the continuation of an expanded role for the state in the direction of the economy and the provision of social services. Conservatism was thrown into a profound crisis as a result of these developments, and lurched uncertainly for several years afterwards. Indeed, Churchill's return to power in October 1951 represented a remarkably swift recovery for a party so thoroughly defeated just six years previously. Over time, however, there has been a tendency in the historiography to assume that a sea-change in values accompanying the experiences of the Second World War and demonstrated in the results of the 1945 general election led to a golden era of consensual politics. What happened after 1945 has often been described as basically the consolidation of élite opinion around a set of values which emerged out of the Home Front, values which entailed an acceptance of this new framework of state intervention.[1] It is almost as if nothing of any real interest happened in Britain until the 1970s, when the settlement which arose out of the war was wholly bankrupt and discredited by stagflation, rising unemployment, acrimony in industry, and relative international decline.[2] According to this view, the agenda for social policy (the construction of a 'welfare state') was settled in the Ministry of Reconstruction from the autumn of 1943. Although there were still details of policy to be hammered out between the two major parties, no fundamental issues divided them. The story of Conservative social policy between 1945 and 1957, in this paradigm, is one in which the party comes to terms with and learns to accept and embrace a 'modern ideal of welfare'. It suggests a transformative process within the party between 1943 and 1951 which laid the foundation for a post-war settlement.[3]

But the changes associated with the 'people's war', far-reaching as they undoubtedly were, have often dwarfed the significance of subsequent events. For although histories of the period have tended to see these shifts as setting the framework for the next generation of policy developments in Britain, the fact remains that the early post-war period was not dominated by reforming socialist governments, but rather by a long and successful period of Conservative administration after 1951. That is, post-war Britain has been guided largely by Conservative policy-makers, and it was a Conservative vision of society which (with the exception of those six years immediately following the cessation of hostilities) determined social policy up to 1964. The exciting thing about so much of the new research on contemporary British history is that it suggests that the early post-war period is in fact much more interesting and significant than has previously been acknowledged. In the past few years a new interpretation of the 1940s and 1950s has begun to emerge, in which factors other than the Second World War are given equal weight in explaining politics and policy-making in this critical period. Some have argued that there was in fact no consensus,[4] others that consensus was derived from sources other than the Second World War.[5] These new interpretations all suggest, however, that a closer look at the archives now available support revisionist assertions that the genesis of post-war debates cannot be explained exclusively by reference back to the wartime coalition.

This is certainly the case with Conservative social policy-making. The usual narrative, in which the party is seen as undergoing a transformative process as a result of the war and electoral defeat, is not borne out by the archives. Instead, it has become clear that internal policy debates within the party continued throughout the period – and that the 'left', or 'Tory' or 'progressive' wing of the party did *not* hold the balance of power within the leadership by the end of the 1940s. On the contrary, it was the articulation and leadership of a reinvigorated neo-liberal Conservatism which led the party through the 1950 and 1951 general elections.[6] In this sense, the return to power of the Conservatives in 1951 can be interpreted as having been of equal – and arguably, of even greater – significance than the election which returned Labour in 1945. The 1951 election becomes a watershed because it signifies the end of a socialist experiment which attempted to extend and to make permanent some of the features of wartime society,[7] and the beginning of Conservative attempts to steer British welfare away from the trend towards universalism and egalitarianism apparent in Labour initiatives. That does not necessarily mean, however, that 1951 entailed some sort of restoration of the pre-war status quo, although in some fields – housing for example – policy was returned to a pattern more closely resembling the pre-war period. But the Conservatives came to power determined to safeguard private enterprise and to reject the use of the state as an agency of egalitarian strategies in social policy. What needs explaining, therefore, is not how the party reinvented itself around the acceptance of a new ideology of equality, but rather how the party responded to the threat of socialism, how it generated popular consent for the reassertion of a capitalist economy so soon after the defeat of fascism in Europe, and the influences which determined social policy after 1951 and prevented a more radical shift away from the Attlee years. The development of party social policy during the period under consideration here confronted Conservatives with a series of dilemmas, for short-term policy decisions taken in the interest of maintaining popular support for a free-enterprise system lodged in a Western alliance often conflicted with the narrower economic and social goals of the party, fomenting internal debate and tension underneath a veneer of unity and consent. Conservative behaviour in these years can only be explained by understanding not just the impact of the Second World War, but by placing policy developments into the context of two powerful forces which limited the extent to which the party leadership was prepared to pursue the narrow ideological objectives of neo-liberal Con-servatism: the generation of national unity necessitated by the

Cold War, and the related electoral imperative of maintaining the allegiance of important groups of voters who benefited from the social reforms put in place between 1945 and 1951.

At the beginning of the 1950s Conservative propaganda promised to 'set the people free' from the controls inherent in socialist management of the economy, and at the same time to maintain the 'welfare state', a term which was left intentionally vague. It was a rash pledge, and one which precipitated almost a year of crisis within the cabinet after October 1951. The contradictions involved in promising to unleash consumer demand while maintaining the basic framework of the social services as they had evolved since the war, moreover, became the constant headache of successive Conservative administrations until 1964, most publicly demonstrated in the cabinet row which led to the resignation of Macmillan's Treasury team in January 1958. The Conservatives, in short, contracted a disease which can be called the 'Santa Claus Syndrome', a flippant phrase first coined in Britain by no less a figure than Beveridge himself,[8] used derisively after the war by the prominent backbencher Richard Law during the years of opposition,[9] and one which actually describes the dilemma which characterized Conservative social policy after 1945 rather neatly. It is a complaint which was characterized by the need to avoid terminal decline through the failure to get elected, while at the same time guiding policy along lines compatible with the broad aims of Conservatism: a free-enterprise economy which maintains incentives for individual achievement, the maintenance of the institutions of the state, Church and family, and the defence of the existing social and economic hierarchy. The Santa Claus syndrome reached its peak during the 1951–64 administrations in an age where full employment and high rates of growth enabled Conservative policy-makers to deliver presents in the form of continuing high rates of public expenditure and consumer choice, without having to make the painful policy decisions which would have been necessary in a harsher economic climate. That is, the party was able to postpone a confrontation over welfare in the 1950s, and by limiting public spending cuts to areas such as investment in services, was never forced to develop a coherent general strategy for change. This was only possible, of course, because of the improvement in international economic conditions from the end of 1952, when a period of high growth enabled the government to manage a high level of public spending alongside growing consumer affluence. The Conservatives found themselves after the war in a position where it would have been politically unthinkable not to have taken advantage of this opportunity, and to that extent it is wise to remember that British Conservatism was faced from 1945 with a set of challenges which, ironically, were the legacy of its own past success.

First and foremost, it should be remembered that the Conservative defence of free enterprise was really thrown off course by 1945, when popular acceptance of collectivist solutions to social problems was at its height. This was a crisis which had been brewing since 1917; economic crisis following the First World War had been met on the continent of Europe by the rise of radical forms of political organization: fascism and communism. At home, Britain had managed to avoid these extremes in the inter-war period, but, as a result, memories of mass unemployment and hardship were subsequently associated in the public mind with Conservatism, which continued to dominate politics in the years of the Great Depression. This contrasted sharply with the wartime experience, in which direction of the economy at home was generally believed to have been instrumental to the war effort. Widespread admiration of the Soviet system, actively promoted by the government during the war, was reinforced by 'war communism' on the home front.[10] The direction of labour was accompanied by a significant change in the nature of the social services. The Beveridge proposals can hardly be described as revolutionary, but the principle of 'fair shares for all' and of universalism in the social services represented a profound shift in the public perception of the relationship between the citizen and the state. These developments were viewed with dread amongst Conservatives during the war, and the party's internal debates before 1945 were focused on strategies to ensure that such changes would be limited to the duration.[11] Indeed, Beveridge was widely resisted within the party, partly because of the expense involved, but also because it was thought that a system of 'social security' was fundamentally incompatible with capitalism: it would rob the individual of the incentive which was the vital ingredient of the free-enterprise system.[12] Wealth creation and economic growth were seen as the nation's clear priorities at the end of the war. The 'welfare state' – even Beveridge, much less the socialist model – was not just expensive, it was corrupting, and would obstruct the great task of economic reconstruction. So while the party was in favour of an extension and rationalization of the social services after the war, such reforms were interpreted in the tradition of Chamberlainite reform. Social policy was necessary either to provide a safety net – in the residual sense – or to extend opportunities and as a spur to incentives – in the sense of the 1944 Education Act. But a redistributive or egalitarian social policy was never on the party's agenda, and its vision of the welfare state was distinctly Conservative, if not always coherently set out.

The Conservatives fought the 1945 election on a platform which called for the reduction of taxation and a return to free enterprise, alongside the rationalization and extension of the social services, contingent upon financial circumstances. Although the mood of the electorate at the end of the war has been subjected to some debate recently,[13] Labour was elected with a majority large enough to be taken as a mandate to undertake a programme which set out profoundly to redistribute wealth through the agency of the state. Helen Mercer, commenting on industrial policy, has argued that 'the world situation looked exceptionally threatening for the future of private property in 1945'.[14] In her view, an élite consensus emerged at the end of the war on the organization of industry; large-scale production in a capitalist framework was the aim of both Labour and Conservative élites. Mercer's work rejects the notion that consensus was the product of a war-inspired collectivism, and suggests that its origins should be sought over the wider issues surrounding the struggle between capitalist and communist patterns of ownership. It is certainly the case that after the war, the first and most radical policy statement issued by the party was *The Industrial Charter* of 1947, which proposed a 'new deal' in industrial relations reminiscent of continental Christian Democracy.[15] Labour initiatives in social policy, however, were viewed with mounting anxiety after 1945, and came to dominate policy development after 1947. By 1949, the party was promoting a reasonably coherent alternative to the Labour model, based on a residual pattern which would shift the focus of provision from universalism to means-testing.[16] As Butler would later write in his memoirs, Conservative policy-making in the opposition period set out to convince the electorate that it stood for a 'humanized capitalism'.[17]

To set these developments in a wider context, one should remember that fears on the right over the political strength of socialist and communist parties were widespread throughout western Europe at this time. Clearly the position of unstable tripartite governments in Italy and France, for example, was the cause of a great deal of concern, not only to the Americans, keen to promote the economic containment of the Soviet sphere of influence in Europe, but even for the British Labour government, which dallied with but ultimately rejected the idea of a British-led European 'Third Force' on the grounds that western Europe was not stable enough to provide the basis for a national security policy.[18] Christian Democracy emerged on the continent in response to the urgent need to find a consensual basis for stable politics in a capitalist framework.[19] Western European governments, including Britain, all constructed what can broadly be described as welfare states after the war, in spite of widely varying wartime experiences. But whereas the short-term problems for the continental right were obvious in the late 1940s, it can be argued that in Britain the problem which faced Conservatives was somewhat different, simply because Britain under Labour presented a far more stable and convincing case to the electorate. In West Germany, to take the obvious example, post-war politics was based on a firm rejection of Nazism, shaped largely by the American occupation, and thus embraced individual freedom in the context of Erhard's social market. In Britain, however, where politics before the war had been dominated by Conservatism, the political agenda by 1945 was based on a 'never again' mentality which implied the rejection of free enterprise and the acceptance of an enlarged role for the state.

Conservatism in Britain was thus put on the defensive in a sense which was not true of Christian Democracy on the continent. But a series of events, both internationally and at home, soon worked in the party's favour. A reassertion of free enterprise was led by the United States, which through its economic muscle exerted a great deal of pressure to secure western Europe against socialization. The Truman Doctrine and the Marshall Plan were designed both to secure the economic containment of communism and to promote an economically powerful and integrated, liberal partner in the markets of western Europe. Richard Cockett has recently described the emergence of a 'neo-liberal counter-revolution' in

Britain, marked by the publication of texts such as von Hayek's *Road to Serfdom* in 1944 and the formation of a number of organizations to argue for the virtues of the market.[20] The Labour government found itself confronted with a series of economic crises from 1947, and responded by depressing consumer demand still further in order to minimize cuts to its universalist system of welfare, and taking urgent action to boost the export drive.[21] Meanwhile, the Conservatives refined a series of policies which were influenced by all of these developments. By the 1949 the party was promoting a very clearly articulated programme based on a reassertion of a residual model of welfare and what was termed 'property-owning democracy.' Iain Macleod, whose work with Enoch Powell at the Conservative Research Department after 1948 was crucial in the formation of Conservative strategies towards the welfare state in the run-up to the elections,[22] asserted that there was a 'distinct cleavage of opinion apparent today between the Conservative and Socialist approach to the social services' based around universal and residual models of welfare.[23] Writing to Quintin Hogg, who was drafting *The Right Road for Britain*, he suggested the following passage:

> the Conservative Party does not regard the true function of the social services to be either the provision of an average standard or the redistribution of wealth. It approves the historic function of the social services as the relief of the unfortunate from misfortune, of the sick from ill-health, of the needy from distress.[24]

This approach, combined with promises to cut taxes, to remove controls and rationing as quickly as possible, and to extend property-ownership, formed the basis of the party's domestic strategy at the end of the opposition period.

As Ina Zweiniger-Bargielowska has demonstrated, these promises struck a chord with the electorate at this time, particularly with women and voters from the most affluent constituencies.[25] Voters were presented with a more dynamic and socially conscious Conservatism in 1951, but one which was anti-socialist and distinctly Conservative. The election resulted in only a slim majority, however, and a smaller proportion of the popular vote (48%) than that obtained by Labour (48.9%). When returned to office in the autumn of 1951, the party was pledged to maintain a welfare state – albeit one in which attention would be focused on those in the greatest need. There was no mandate for radical change in that direction, however, given the narrowness of victory. For the party's dilemma was that the middle classes liked the welfare state, and hated high taxation. The electorate wanted to have its cake and eat it, and Conservatism had encouraged the belief that it was possible to do both. Upon election, therefore, the new administration was careful to balance the need to maintain the allegiance of the electorate to its brand of 'humanized capitalism' while steering policy away from the socialist turn it had taken as a result of war and Labour government. This was bound to be an exercise in caution.

It is commonly remarked how little change followed the election of the first post-war Conservative government, and with the benefit of hindsight that does indeed appear to have been the case.[26] On the one hand, there was no overtly drastic departure from previous policy. On the other, we are only beginning to appreciate just how close we came to a full-blown political crisis in the months following the election. The balance of payments crisis with which the cabinet was confronted in October jeopardized the fragile basis upon which the party had regained power, and in the months leading up to the March budget the government considered a range of drastic measures including deep cuts in public expenditure, which would have redrawn the scope of the welfare state, as well as floating the pound under the terms of the ROBOT scheme.[27] That the government ultimately rejected such steps has been taken as an indication of a post-war consensus, but can in fact only be understood in the context of Cold War politics and the slim majority upon which Churchill's power rested. Records of the cabinet discussions on ROBOT, for example, indicate the gravity with which ministers viewed the situation with which they were faced:

> The adoption of the plan would give rise to very great political difficulty. Public opinion in this country was wholly unprepared for such measures. The sudden reversal of the economic policies which had been pursued for the last twelve years, and in particular the abandonment of the objective of seeking stability in internal prices and wages, would come as a severe shock to public opinion. Under democratic government with universal suffrage such violent reversals of policy were hardly practicable. Even if the case for this change were abundantly clear on the merits, there would be very great difficulty in persuading the public

to accept it. Moreover, the adoption of this policy would create an unbridgeable gap between the Government and the Opposition; and, if it were thought possible that an even more grave economic crisis might develop later in the year, it would be unjustifiable to take at this stage a step which might exclude all possibility of forming a National Government to handle that situation.[28]

ROBOT made sense if the Government's only priority was to free the economy of physical controls, and to return to a greater emphasis on the mechanism of the market. Indeed, in their final conclusions to these discussions

> Ministers reaffirmed their desire to dispense as soon as practicable with the system of physical controls and to move, as opportunity offered, towards the restoration of a more free economy in which there would be scope for the operation of the price mechanism.[29]

The fact that cautious heads prevailed, however, is not an indication of ideological opposition within cabinet to free-market principles and the reduction of state intervention, but rather the product of the escalation of Cold War tension in the early 1950s, and the economic and political imperatives dictated by that tension. The adoption of a more radical programme by the government would have led to the collapse of the European Payments Union, a serious rift between Britain and its Commonwealth allies, the disapproval of the United States, and the polarization of domestic politics. It is clear that at this critical juncture, when the prospect of a new war was looming, the narrow ideological considerations of the party had to be set aside in the interests of national and western unity, *just as they had been during the Second World War*. Ideological factors did continue to play in social policy-formulation, particularly from 1953 when the international economic and political climate had eased. But the shift in orientation came gradually and cautiously.[30] The party leadership was keenly aware, of course, of the need to maintain the fragile contract which it had constructed with the electorate, in order to distance Conservatism from memories of the inter-war years.

Consider the case of housing, for example. Towards the end of the opposition period, housing had emerged as the centrepiece of Conservative social-policy proposals, the heart of promises to spread property-ownership and the construction of a 'property-owning democracy'. Under Bevan, housing policy had taken on a universal character based upon need rather than upon the ability to pay; licences to build privately were restricted, and those homes which were built privately were limited in size and standard. The bulk of new housing was provided through the local authorities, and targeted at general needs rather than focused on slum clearance.[31] But congestion and materials shortages in the building industry led to public disaffection with socialist housing policy; this was the weak spot which the Conservatives, promising to unleash the productive forces of the market, hoped to use as a showcase policy to demonstrate the virtues of free enterprise. The 1950 conference pledge to build 300,000 houses a year, which featured so strongly in the subsequent election campaign was, therefore, not simply a Santa Claus gift to the electorate, but one which held an ideological significance as well.[32] Once in office, however, the implication of the decisions taken in cabinet in the early months of 1952 was that controls over imports and the domestic market would need to continue for some time. Ironically, therefore, Macmillan did not achieve his target in 1953 through the privatization of housing policy, but through the machinery of the local authorities. It was only subsequently and on the basis of that achievement that housing provision was shifted towards the private sector; building for home ownership grew as a proportion of total provision from 13 per cent in 1951 to 32 per cent in 1954, and remained a minority of total provision until 1958.[33] In short, although ideological considerations did ultimately guide the direction of housing policy in the long term, the government's immediate priority was the generation and maintenance of broad popular support.

Conservative governments in the 1950s had more scope to influence housing policy, where there was no popular Labour precedent, than was the case with other social policies. Curbing the growth of public expenditure on the social services remained a priority within successive cabinets, but was achieved in a haphazard way, by limiting or postponing investment and by tampering with marginal aspects of policy rather than by seeking a new general settlement for the funding of the welfare state. Thus for example, there was increasing frustration over the cost of the NHS, and it was hoped that the Guillebaud inquiry would pave the way for reform, but when the committee reported in 1956, its findings were precisely the opposite of what the government had hoped to hear.[34] It was cumulative exasperation with this absence of a grand strategy which led increasingly to heated argument in cabinet over the correct approach to the problem of growing expenditure on the social services in the latter half of the decade. Macleod's frustration with the Treasury approach was over the narrowness and incoherence involved in annual fiscal budget-cutting rounds and was already apparent at the beginning of 1957, in his correspondence with the Prime Minister:

> . . . if we can avoid minor irritants and get one big settlement so much the better. We can't get this from the Family Allowance proposal . . . Nor can we abolish the Dental Service . . . Nor is it worth trying to get a couple of million quid from increasing the charges for dentures. It would arouse fury amongst the old age pensioners, it would increase the demand for higher rates of retirement pensions, and it would mean a bitter and controversial piece of legislation for nothing. Superficially, the hospital boarding charge is attractive. In practice, it is not so. 43 per cent of the beds are occupied by mental patients, many of the others by the aged and by children, and we can't tax the old and the young and the mad to help the surtax payers.[35]

Macleod was not concerned merely to defend the spending ministries against the Treasury. He was arguing in favour of a more coherent, and Conservative, approach. In the same memorandum he stresses that 'if we can't produce some incentives and some taxation adjustments in this Budget, our people won't believe in the idea of an Opportunity State'.[36] The whole thrust of his argument at this time was over the need to find a new strategy to guide the party away from its social policy limbo. It is thus from 1957 that new approaches to welfare began to be discussed within the party.[37]

This chapter has argued that the apparent convergence between the two main parties on social policy and the construction of a 'welfare state' after 1945 cannot be explained in terms of the wartime experience alone. Archival evidence and official records make it abundantly clear that the neo-liberal or right wing of the Conservative Party maintained a strong hold on policy-formulation during and after the war; policy developments within Conservatism cannot, therefore, be explained in terms of a leftwards shift in ideological affinity. Instead, it is more fruitful to think in terms of the challenges which confronted a thoroughly defeated Conservatism after 1945: the overwhelming popular support for Beveridge, the popularity of collective approaches to social problems encouraged by the war, public admiration of the Soviet Union before 1946, the instability of western European politics and the construction of a Western, capitalist alliance during the emergence of the early Cold War. In this context British Conservatism, confronting a popular and dynamic reforming socialist government, was faced with an unprecedented set of challenges. The party's policy behaviour in the 1940s and 1950s, therefore, can only be understood in terms of the overwhelming imperative to generate a broad popular consensus around a new 'humanized capitalism' in order to fight the Cold War with as unified and solid a front as possible. Welfare states and mixed economies developed throughout the West in these years in response to this need, and Britain was no exception. In short, policy behaviour was dictated by a peculiar set of international and domestic circumstances, and made possible by the high rates of growth associated with the mid-1950s. Conservatism, however, was not transformed by the experiences of war and electoral defeat in the sense used by many historians. The party merely adopted new tactics in this period to confirm and uphold its traditional and familiar objectives.

## Notes

I would like to thank a number of people for helping me to develop the ideas discussed below, including Martin Francis, Jose Harris, Michael Kandiah, Helen Mercer and Ina Zweiniger-Bargielowska.

1 I am referring, of course, in particular to the seminal text by the historian P. Addison, *The Road to 1945* (London, 1975), which has more than any other text set the agenda for debate on post-war British political history since its publication.
2 It would be grossly unfair to suggest that Addison would go along with such a simplistic description, but readers will undoubtedly be familiar with some of the extremes to which consensus theory can be taken. See, for example, D. Kavanagh and P. Morris, *Consensus Politics from Attlee to Thatcher* (Oxford, 1989).
3 For a classic recent interpretation of this school, see T. Raison, *Tories and the Welfare State: A History of Conservative Social Policy since the Second World War* (Basingstoke, 1990). It is perhaps more surprising that non-partisan authors have often accepted such a straightforward

account; see N. Timmins, *The Five Giants: A Biography of the Welfare State* (London, 1995).

4  For example, K. Jefferys, *The Churchill Coalition and Wartime Politics, 1940–1945* (Manchester, 1991); S. Brooke, *Labour's War: The Labour Party During the Second World War* (Oxford, 1992); H. Jones, 'The Conservative Party and Social Policy, 1942–55' (unpublished doctoral thesis, London, 1992). See in general the variety of essays included in H. Jones and M. Kandiah (eds.), *The Myth of Consensus: New Views on British History, 1945–64* (Basingstoke, 1996).

5  See in particular, H. Mercer, 'Industrial Organisation and Ownership, and a New Definition of the Post-war "Consensus"', in Jones and Kandiah, *Myth of Consensus*.

6  A view first articulated in my dissertation, Jones, 'The Conservative Party and Social Policy', but accepted in subsequent published works: see H. Glennerster, *British Social Policy since 1945* (Oxford, 1995); J. Ramsden, *The Age of Churchill and Eden, 1940–57* (London, 1995).

7  See, for example, N. Rollings, ' "The Reichstag Method of Governing"?: The Attlee Governments and Permanent Economic Controls', in H. Mercer et al. (eds.), *Labour Governments and Private Industry: The Experience of 1945–51* (Edinburgh, 1992). The party was increasingly concerned over the permanent implications of some of the legislation introduced at the end of the 1940s; the Housing bill of 1949 is one example (CPA CRD2/27/2).

8  My thanks to Jose Harris for this information.

9  The papers of Lord Coleraine (private possession), notes for speeches, 1945 and 1946.

10  L. Minkin, *The Contentious Alliance: Trade Unions and the Labour Party* (Edinburgh, 1991), chapter 1.

11  See Jones, 'The Conservative Party and Social Policy', chapter 2.

12  CPA CRD2/28/6, 19 January 1943, *Report on the Beveridge Proposals*.

13  S. Fielding, 'What did "the People" Want?: The Meaning of the 1945 General Election', *Historical Journal* 35 (1992); for a different view, see J. Mortimer, 'The Changing Mood of Working People', in J. Fyrth (ed.), *Labour's High Noon: The Government and the Economy 1945–51* (London, 1993).

14  H. Mercer et al., *Labour Governments and Private Industry*.

15  Conservative Party, *The Industrial Charter: A Statement of Conservative Industrial Policy* (London, 1947).

16  Jones, 'The Conservative Party and Social Policy', chapter 3; see also H. Jones, 'A Bloodless Counter-Revolution: The Conservative Defence of Inequality, 1945–51', in Jones and Kandiah, *Myth of Consensus*.

17  R. A. Butler, *The Art of the Possible* (London, 1971), 134.

18  S. Greenwood, 'The Third Force in the Late 1940s', in B. Brivati and

H. Jones (eds.), *From Reconstruction to Integration: Britain and Europe since 1945* (Leicester, 1993).

[19] The recent publication, D. Hanley (ed.), *Christian Democracy in Europe: A Comparative Perspective* (London, 1994), begins to fill a sad dearth in the English-language literature on this subject.

[20] R. Cockett, *Thinking the Unthinkable: Think-Tanks and the Economic Counter-Revolution, 1931–83* (London, 1974), chapter 2.

[21] See A. Cairncross, *Years of Recovery: British Economic Policy, 1945–51* (London, 1985).

[22] See their joint work *The Social Services: Needs and Means* (London, Conservative Political Centre, 1952).

[23] Conservative Party Archives [hereafter CPA], CRD2/27/5, PMC(49)5, 19 May 1949.

[24] Ibid., 4 April 1949, Macleod to Hogg.

[25] I. Zweiniger-Bargielowska, 'Rationing, Austerity and the Conservative Party Recovery after 1945', *Historical Journal* 37 (1994); I. Zweiniger-Bargielowska, 'Consensus and Consumption: Rationing, Austerity and Controls after the War', in Jones and Kandiah, *Myth of Consensus*.

[26] See, for example, A. Seldon, *Churchill's Indian Summer: The Conservative Government, 1951–55* (London, 1981).

[27] Edmund Dell's new research has rightly pointed to the gravity of the debate: 'Rab and ROBOT', paper presented to the Institute of Contemporary British History, Summer Conference, London, 12 July 1995.

[28] Public Records Office [hereafter PRO], CAB128/40 CC(52)23rd, 24th and 25th Conclusions, 28 and 29 February 1952. This record is a newly released summary of discussions of three cabinet meetings, first available in 1995.

[29] Ibid.

[30] Jones, 'The Conservative Party and Social Policy', chapters 4–7; see also H. Jones, 'New Tricks for an Old Dog? The Conservative Party and Social Policy, 1951–5', in A. Gorst, L. Johnman and S. Lucas (eds.), *Contemporary British History 1931–61: Politics and the Limits of Policy* (London, 1991).

[31] See J. Campbell, *Nye Bevan and the Mirage of British Socialism* (London, 1987).

[32] Jones, 'The Conservative Party and Social Policy', chapter 3.

[33] Ibid., chapter 5.

[34] *Report of the Committee of Enquiry into the Cost of the NHS*, Cmd 9663 (1956).

[35] PRO, PREM11/1805, 31 January 1957, Macleod to Macmillan.

[36] Ibid.

[37] This subsequent period is covered by Lowe's contribution to this volume.

# The Replanning of the Welfare State, 1957–1964

### RODNEY LOWE

In economic policy it has long been recognized that the early 1960s were a period of 'far-reaching reappraisal'. Most of the policies which the Wilson government was later to 'proclaim its own' were, as Samuel Brittan has noted, actually planned 'inside the Treasury and other government departments around 1960–61'.[1] What is less well recognized is that there was a simultaneous and equally far-reaching reappraisal of welfare policy. It is the purpose of this chapter to establish its extent, causes and consequences.

The reappraisal of welfare policy started at an administrative level in 1955 and at a political level on Macmillan's appointment as Prime Minister in 1957. The stimuli were similar: frustration with policy drift under Churchill and Eden; recognition that some permanent increase in state intervention was inevitable after the war; and belief that policies designed, particularly by Beveridge, in reaction to the depression of the 1930s should be adjusted to the needs of an increasingly affluent society. Administrative reform reached its climax with the establishment of the Public Expenditure Survey Committee (PESC) in 1961. This was a Treasury-dominated committee of officials which matched forecasts for future public expenditure against prospective economic resources in order to provide the cabinet, for the first time, with the means of establishing informed, rational and co-ordinated priorities.[2] Political reappraisal was more tortuous. It affected the party at all levels, but it was driven by officials within

the Conservative Research Department (working in particular on
the internal Future of the Social Services and the Tax Policy
Committees) and the two ginger groups chaired by Iain Macleod
(the 1957–9 Policy Study Group and the 1961–3 Chairman's
Committee). It is upon these four committees that this chapter
will largely concentrate.[3]

As with the Treasury, the first instinct of the CRD and the
Macleod groups was to roll back the state in order to reduce
taxation, release initiative and encourage personal responsibility.[4]
The two fundamental goals of a dynamic economy and a healthy
democracy could thereby be achieved. Their views, however,
quickly moderated. The Future of the Social Services Committee
(FSSC) on its own admission had begun 'with a bias in favour of
radical change' but neither its interim report in 1961 nor its final
report in 1963 contained any 'dramatic recommendations'.[5] The
Tax Policy Committee underwent a similar conversion. Committed before 1960 to the traditional Conservative (and Treasury)
belief that tax cuts were sacrosanct, it then began to waver and by
1963 was advising the Chancellor that 'the urgency has gone out
of the demand for the reduction of taxes and many now attach
more importance to increasing expenditure'.[6] This perception was
shared by Macleod. Both his ginger groups had opened with an
attack on universal national insurance by Enoch Powell, his co-
author of the 1952 pamphlet *The Social Services: Needs and Means*
which had first urged a move to greater selectivity. Political and
administrative reality, however, soon intruded with the result that
he rejected both the attacks and, more particularly, the cuts in
welfare expenditure with which they were associated. Alert, for
example, to the Treasury's attempt to use the PESC to effect such
cuts he wrote privately to the Chancellor, Selwyn Lloyd, in
February 1961 warning him of his opposition and then openly
voiced his opposition to Lloyd's successor, Maudling. As he
informed the cabinet in December 1962:

> The steadily increasing level of public expenditure could be justified by
> reference to accepted social principles . . . In his view public opinion
> was ready to accept an increase in the proportion of GNP taken up by
> public expenditure and the consequent high level of taxation.[7]

Such a modification of basic Conservative instincts at both an
official and political level within the party had an immediate

impact on government policy and civil service advice. Persistent demands by the Treasury for cuts in public expenditure were defeated, most dramatically in January 1958 (when the Chancellor, Thorneycroft, and his junior ministers including Powell were forced to resign) and in January 1962 (when Selwyn Lloyd was obliged to break his commitment to the IMF to restrict the annual rise of public expenditure to 2·5 per cent). The immediate cause of both crises was welfare policy: the cabinet's refusal in 1958 to withdraw family allowances from the second child and the threat by David Eccles, as Minister of Education in 1962, to resign if his budget was further reduced. Lloyd's defeat indeed led directly to the 'night of the long knives' in July 1962 and the promotion of a younger generation of politicians (including Macleod, Maudling, Hailsham and Heath) who were more sympathetic to the modernization of Britain through state action. Equally dramatic was the changed tenor of advice emanating from the Cabinet Office. Norman Brook, as cabinet secretary under Macmillan, had consistently endorsed the Treasury's aversion to public expenditure. By increasing tax and crowding out private investment, it was deemed to discourage enterprise, distort the market and thereby hinder economic growth (upon which everyone's welfare ultimately depended). However, by April 1964 Brook's successor, Burke Trend, was advising Douglas-Home:

(a) An increase in public expenditure – and therefore in tax – is not necessarily a bad thing, in so far as it provides better social benefits for the less fortunate members of the community and eliminates the grosser disparities of wealth.

(b) By any reliable criterion of value for money, it is not always public expenditure that needs to be reduced. The private sector, particularly public consumption, may be the villain of the piece; and in so far as an increase of tax on 'luxuries' is unavoidable, it may be preferable to an arbitrary cut in programmes of e.g. new housing and new schools.[8]

So fundamental a reversal of policy and of its underlying assumptions demands an examination of the 'accepted social principles' to which Macleod alluded. How far were they distinctively Conservative? First, however, the extent of the reappraisal at both an official and political level in each area of welfare policy must be established. Is it as true in welfare as in

economic policy that later Labour legislation was dependent upon
it?

# I

There is no agreed definition of welfare policy. Most
commentators agree that at its narrowest it embraces five core
areas: social security, the personal social services, health,
education and housing. More broadly, employment policy was
identified by Beveridge in 1942 as central to any government's
welfare programme for psychological and economic reasons.
Individual welfare is dependent above all on the satisfaction of a
regular, rewarding job and full employment, which, by maximizing
government revenue and minimizing claimants, ensures the
solvency of the overall programme. Titmuss in 1955 extended the
definition further to include fiscal and occupational welfare.
Individual welfare, he argued, was affected as much by how
government revenue was raised as by how it was spent, and by the
granting of tax concessions to industry to subsidize fringe benefits
for its (usually senior) staff. More recent commentators have even
argued that any legislation affecting personal behaviour, such as
abortion or divorce, should also be included on the grounds that it
affects people 'more deeply and personally' than any structural
change to pensions or the NHS.[9] This chapter will take the
broader definition, concentrating first on cash services directed
largely to those in need and then on services in kind.

It was in the related areas of social security, the personal social
services and occupational welfare that the most radical changes
might have been expected to occur, because it was here that the
principles of universalism (as enshrined in the Beveridge Report)
clashed most directly with those of selectivity (as instinctively
favoured by the party). In an increasingly affluent society, could
not and should not people take responsibility for their own welfare
rather than looking to the state? Likewise should not employers –
as recommended in the 1947 *Industrial Charter* and as practised
on the continent – accept direct responsibility for the welfare of
their workforce? Consequently, should not the role of government
be restricted to maximizing the opportunities for personal
initiative whilst targeting help on those in genuine need? Was this

not the most effective way to achieve a competitive, modern economy and a humane, caring society?

Major changes to social security were indeed effected between 1957 and 1964 but their net result was to extend rather than contract the role of government. The Beveridge Report had insisted, for example, on a minimal role for the state's national insurance scheme. It should do no more than provide a minimum subsistence income based on the claimant's physiological needs. 'To give by compulsory insurance more than is needed for subsistence', it warned, 'is an unnecessary interference with individual responsibilities.'[10] In 1958 and 1959, however, the Conservatives raised insurance and assistance benefits higher than was justified by price rises; and in their 1959 and 1964 manifestos they promised first pensioners and then all claimants a 'share in the higher standards produced by an expanding economy'. They therefore embraced the concept of relative poverty, based on the claimant's social need actively to participate in society, before it was popularized by social scientists at the London School of Economics. As a ministerial Social Services Committee had indeed noted as early as 1960:

> There was not necessarily any difference between the concept of need and the concept of sharing in the expanding wealth of the country. There could be no absolute standard of need. It was a constantly changing concept and depended on what was generally accepted by the community at the time as a minimum standard of living. As a society became more prosperous, so did this minimum rise.[11]

In addition, the 1959 National Insurance Act broke new ground in two major ways. It breached Beveridge's principle of flat-rate contributions for flat-rate benefits by introducing for employees on or just above average wages, earnings-related pensions in return for earnings-related contributions. It also established the right to contract-out of the state scheme into a private occupational pension – despite surprisingly fierce opposition from the insurance industry (which feared the conditions to be placed on approved schemes, such as inflation-proofing) and the Treasury (which resented, and continued to resent, lost revenue).[12] This Act was unquestionably less comprehensive and redistributive than Labour's contemporary plans – which significantly remained unimplemented by 1970. It did prepare the way, however, for the universalization of occupational pensions by the third Wilson government in 1975. It also led to the extension of the earnings-related principle to unemployment and sickness benefit, for which detailed planning in Whitehall and with industry had been completed by 1964. Labour capitalized on this planning when introducing the measures in 1966.

Other major changes were debated and planned. Most prominent were the creation of a ministry of social security (as established by Labour in 1966) and a guaranteed income in old age (another unrealized promise in Labour's 1964 manifesto). The amalgamation of social service departments, in order to increase co-ordination and provide a powerful cabinet presence, was a consistent aim of Macleod after 1957; but disagreement over which ministries to merge and whether to bring the National Assistance Board (NAB) under direct ministerial control enabled the civil service to prevaricate. However, Margaret Thatcher and Keith Joseph significantly remained staunch advocates of the option, taken later by Labour, to incorporate NAB into the ministry.[13] A second example of a striking affinity between the Conservative right and Labour was the guaranteed income in old age, the chief advocate of which was Enoch Powell. He was hostile to the contributory National Insurance pension which, he argued, was neither actuarially sound nor adequate; and he wished to replace it with far more generous pensions paid only to those whose income, after a means test, could be shown to be inadequate. As the plan was developed, particularly within the CRD, the reform was to be financed through a payroll (or social security) tax as on the continent with the means test implemented automatically through a tax return from each pensioner.[14] Here was the germ of the 'holy grail' of the 1960s and 1970s, a negative income tax by which benefits could be targeted on those in need without stigma – thereby ensuring full take-up. The plan was seriously considered in the drafting of the 1964 manifesto but was eventually rejected on political, social and practical grounds. It would, it was deemed, disappoint expectations (fostered by insurance contributions), penalize thrift and – as was ultimately to prove the case – be administratively unworkable.

These major reforms were but part of a wide-ranging policy review. Other detailed proposals, belatedly withdrawn from the 1964 manifesto, included increased family allowances for the fourth child (introduced by Labour in 1967), higher benefits for long-term claimants and attendance allowances for the chronically sick (both introduced in 1970). Each demonstrated a genuine concern for those in greatest need, a concern extended into the field of the personal social services where the first comprehensive plan for community care was published in 1963 (Cmnd 1973). At all levels of the party there was a continuing demand that local government should co-ordinate statutory and voluntary effort so that – in Powell's words – people in the final twenty years of their life should have as comprehensive a range of services as those in their first twenty. In consequence, it was relatively easy for the party to accept the 1968 Seebohm Report (Cmnd 3703) and for Joseph after 1970 to oversee the creation by each local authority of a unified social service department staffed by trained social workers.[15] Lower-paid workers were another underprivileged group whose status the Conservatives sought to raise. A Contract of Employment Act was passed in 1963 to ensure a minimum of job security and in 1964 a Redundancy Payments bill (enacted by Labour in 1965) was in an advanced stage of negotiation with both sides of industry. 'We can no longer accept the difference of status between the wage earner and salary earner', Macmillan argued. The persistence of day contracts in particular was a 'remnant of a medieval system and shameful to a modern society'.[16]

In the three other major areas of welfare – health, education and housing – there was a parallel reappraisal and development of policy. In each, state intervention was initially subject to hostile scrutiny. Following Bevan's supposed extravagance, the NHS was the particular bogey of both Conservative politicians and Treasury officials. To increase its self-sufficiency the Macmillan cabinet immediately raised health insurance contributions and charges (although its objective was never to recoup more than 23 per cent of its total cost, Beveridge's recommended figure). A range of other reforms, including 'hotel' charges for hospitals and the hiving-off of whole areas such as dental and ophthalmic care, was also vigorously advocated until – surprisingly – Powell's appointment as minister of health. The justification for increased payments was that they would reinforce personal responsibility, alert consumers to the true cost of services and strengthen the patient–doctor relationship. Similar arguments were used, remarkably until 1962, to support the introduction of fees into state schools.[17] Some way to reduce rocketing educational expenditure was sought, and fees (whether paid in full by parents or subsidized by a government voucher) provided an answer as well as giving parents both a reason and the means to take a greater interest in their children's education and to counteract the professional power of teachers. It was in housing, however, that the state was most effectively 'rolled back'. On the assumption in 1955 that the post-war housing shortage had been remedied, subsidies to local government were restricted to special needs (such as slum clearance), whilst the 1957 Rent Act decontrolled many private rents and the 1959 Town and Country Planning Act obliged local government to purchase land at its full market value.

Despite such an inauspicious start, however, state intervention expanded rapidly in the early 1960s. This was particularly true of education policy where increased expenditure could most easily be equated with the attainment of two cardinal Conservative goals: greater equality of opportunity and, through the creation of a trained workforce, international competitiveness. Every level of education was affected. The Plowden Commission on primary education was appointed in 1963. On its 1968 report Labour was to base its policy of educational priority areas. In secondary education, a £300m building programme was launched in 1958 with the explicit aim of raising standards throughout the tripartite system to allay misgivings about the 'eleven plus' exam and jealousy of public schools. Comprehensive schools were welcomed and built, wherever deemed educationally justified, and public schools even condemned by Eccles, as minister of education, as a major cause of social inequality.[18] A commitment to raise the school-leaving age to sixteen (postponed by Labour in 1968) was also made in the 1964 manifesto. In further and technical education, there was a major reorganization and an expansion of technical colleges following the 1956 White Paper and the 1959 Crowther Report,[19] whilst the Industrial Training Act was passed in 1964 (to be implemented by Labour) to enable progressive employers to overhaul the apprenticeship system. Finally, there was an unprecedented explosion in higher education with the commissioning of seven new universities even before the publication, and immediate acceptance, of the 1963 Robbins Report (Cmnd 2159) which recommended a further doubling in student numbers within ten years. Even a 'varsity for viewers' (the Open University, as established by Labour in 1968) was actively championed within the CRD.

Expansion was equally dramatic in the two other services despite – or even because of – the appointment of the supposedly right-wing Enoch Powell as minister of health in 1960 and Keith Joseph as minister of housing in 1962. In 1962 Powell launched an ambitious ten-year hospital building programme, costing some £500m, designed to replace the antiquated buildings, inherited from the inter-war years, with a national network of modern district general hospitals. Joseph was responsible for an even more ambitious programme to correct increasingly apparent market failures in the field of housing. It included the reintroduction of general grants and of an annual building target of 350,000 dwellings; the establishment of a National Building Authority to oblige the construction industry to modernize; the drafting of regional plans to determine the pattern of land use, and the release of land, over the following twenty years; and even the reintroduction of Labour's betterment tax because, in Joseph's words, 'no government can close its mind to the possibility of securing for the public some part of the profit flowing from the grant of planning permission'.[20] Such interventionist measures, which were admitted to be 'not particularly Conservative in the usual sense', were allied to more conventional party policy including financial inducements for home ownership (such as the abolition of Schedule A taxation) and the establishment of a Housing Corporation to provide an alternative source of low-cost rented accommodation to local government.

In each of the remaining areas of welfare policy – employment, taxation and social legislation – there was an equally thorough reappraisal. The commitment of the cabinet, and particularly of Macmillan himself, to full employment remained firm. Counter-cyclical measures were taken in the economic downturns of 1958 and 1962, and a more active regional policy adopted in the Local Economy Acts of 1960 and 1963. Macmillan himself chaired an emergency committee over the winter of 1962–3 to modernize the infrastructure of Scotland and the north-east. His objectives were not merely political but also economic and social. He acknowledged that an aggregate unemployment figure of even 2 per cent would be politically damaging if 'the figure was an average of 5 per cent in one place and 1 per cent in another' but he was equally concerned to increase international competitiveness by tapping unused potential and 'to redress the grave social anomalies that are created by the imbalance' between the 'rich' south and the poorer north.[21] For a similar mix of economic and social reasons, the Treasury instigated a fundamental review of the tax system including the optimum balance between direct and indirect tax, the structure of indirect taxation and the advantages of a payroll tax. The redistributive impact of tax changes was also, for the first time, seriously considered in the budgets of 1962–4 and particular reforms implemented, such as a modified Capital Gains Tax (later greatly extended by Labour).[22] Finally, under Butler's influence, a range of liberal legislation on subjects as diverse as prostitution, gambling and probation was proposed. It provided the antidote to less liberal acts, such as the long-resisted 1962 Commonwealth Immigration Act, and thus some foundation for the 'permissive moment' of the late 1960s.[23]

There can be no question, therefore, that there was a comprehensive reappraisal of welfare policy in the early 1960s. Admittedly there were continuing disagreements among and between ministers, CRD officials and civil servants. Some policies (such as a betterment tax) were only tentatively proposed, others (such as community care) tentatively implemented, whilst others (such as a guaranteed income in old age) were eventually vetoed. Nevertheless it is clear that a wholly negative attitude towards state intervention was rejected by an increasing majority at all levels within the party. Thus the more ambitious promises of the 1964 manifesto, as a CRD official argued, were 'not the result of a death bed repentance but grew out of the previous record'.[24] In social security policy a serious debate was enjoined about the respective responsibilities of government, employers and individuals. In other areas such as housing and health, action was taken to correct proven weaknesses in either the market or voluntary provision. The incoming Labour government clearly had differing views on a variety of issues, such as tenants' rights and the pace of comprehensivization. The small print of its legislation and its ideological underpinning may have been different. Particularly where its achievements were substantial, however, it built upon either the earlier achievements or the planning of the Conservatives.

# II

Why was there so comprehensive a reappraisal? There are two possible explanations. The first is that it was a reaction, either enforced or opportunistic, to outside events. The second is that it was a positive, if contested, attempt to adapt Conservatism and the Conservative Party to the reality of an affluent, technologically complex society. The two explanations are not mutually exclusive.

The Conservative governments of 1957–64, like all other governments, were the prisoners of events. These events might be specific such as the sterling crises of 1957 and 1961 (which required a decision on whether welfare expenditure, properly targeted, assisted or impeded economic growth), the application to join the EEC in 1961 (which prompted the review of the tax system) or the establishment of the National Economic Development Office in 1962 (which hastened the consideration of occupational welfare). More importantly, however, the pressures – to which civil servants required answers – were more long-term. In the late 1950s, for example, pensions policy had radically to be reviewed as a result of a decision by the Attlee government in 1948 that those who had made no prior insurance contributions would be entitled to a full pension were they to make regular contributions over the following ten years. By 1958 this entitlement was worth up to ten times the actuarial value of their contributions, and these pensions had to be financed from some source – either the general taxpayer or wealthier contributors through earnings-related contributions.[25] Educational provision and expenditure also had to rise as the children of the post-war 'baby boom' passed successively through primary, secondary and tertiary education. Moreover, in each service there was a legacy of ill-distributed and outdated facilities to be corrected. This brought Powell as Minister of Health into particular disrepute with his former right-wing allies. He continued to argue that the NHS was innately inferior to private medicine but defended his Hospital Plan on the grounds that, since the NHS could not be abolished, the only option was the 'business-like improvement of its efficiency'.[26] Practical problems, in other words, demanded practical answers.

Even 'practical' solutions depend to an extent on political choice, and there were throughout the period two principal

political influences on the timing and content of change. The first
was the need to respond to Labour Party initiatives. This was
particularly true of pensions policy, where serious planning started
after the publication in May 1957 of Labour's superannuation
plans and where Butler typically advised that it should be possible
'not only to steal the Whigs' clothes but to dye them a more
attractive shade'.[27] It was true also of the reawakened interest in
occupational welfare in 1960 and the consideration of earnings-
related short-term benefits in 1962. The more potent influence by
far, however, was the search for electoral advantage. This
permeated Macleod's ginger groups, fed by the increasingly
sophisticated psephological analysis of the CRD.

Convinced by 1962 that welfare policy was the key to electoral
success, Macleod was concerned not to offend trade unionists
(without some of whose votes 'no party . . . could form a
government') and to attract women.[28] This meant, in particular,
no swingeing attack on the 'social wage' or the NHS. The three
groups whose interests were regarded as paramount, however,
were the young, the upwardly mobile and the existing middle class
(broadly defined). It was the perceived acceptance of state welfare
by the first two groups that persuaded the CRD Tax Policy
Committee to alter its views on the respective merits of tax cuts
and increased public expenditure. It also underpinned Macleod's
attack on the Treasury for seeking retrenchment via the PESC. As
he informed the Chancellor in February 1961, he

> did not believe high taxation was a deterrent to increased effort and . . .
> was sure that young people did not think so either. You could not have
> more convincing proof of this than at Saturday's Annual Conference of
> Young Conservatives when they threw out by an overwhelming
> majority a motion which expressed exactly the Treasury point of view
> . . . The speakers were nearly all between 25 and 30 and were precisely
> the type of young executives who were in or going to be in the surtax
> range.[29]

As for the existing middle class, public opinion surveys convinced
Michael Fraser (head of CRD) that it was increasingly appreciative
of state welfare and would tolerate neither its contraction, as
proposed by Powell and initially the FSSC, nor any lowering of
standards. He consequently advised Macleod that the party's right
wing had a very narrow and muddled view of middle-class interests.

'The middle classes in the full sense', he concluded, 'do not pay for health and education and are in fact almost as committed to the Welfare State in its present form as the manual workers. Indeed, in health they have benefited more.'[30] Electoral advantage clearly lay in the expansion, not the contraction, of welfare policy.

To pursue this advantage was not necessarily opportunistic. The future of Britain as a participative and economically competitive democracy, it could be argued, depended as much as the future of the Conservatives on giving the young and upwardly mobile their head. Macmillan was also convinced that modernization could only be achieved through co-operation and not conflict with the trade unions. Hence Thorneycroft's enforced resignation (because the withdrawal of family allowances would have been deemed an attack on the 'social wage' and provoked an industrial reaction) and the attempt to raise the status of workers through improved occupational welfare after 1962. This change of emphasis entailed a bold and bitter battle with the party's right wing. Not only was its opposition to increased public expenditure overruled, but its special demands (such as tax relief on private school fees and free drugs for private health patients) dismissed as socially divisive. What was needed fully to refute charges of opportunism, however, was a consistent and principled pattern to policy. This is precisely what Michael Fraser had called for in 1957 at the start of the policy review.[31]

Consistency and principle required the resolution of two questions. Was public expenditure, or could it be, economically efficient? What was the proper balance of responsibility between government and the individual for personal welfare? Both questions were addressed at a political and administrative level. Powell, as has been seen, rejected the later view of many economists that the collective provision of health care is more efficient than market provision. In other areas, a different conclusion was reached. In response to the Institute of Economic Affairs' *Choice in Welfare*, for example, even Treasury officials concluded: 'a universal state scheme ought to be cheaper to administer and more efficient to operate than a multiplicity of private pension schemes and ought therefore to be better for the economy as a whole.'[32] There was unanimity within the party that high educational expenditure was essential for economic competitiveness, and, as has been seen, market failure in housing necessitated measures that were 'not particularly Conservative in the usual sense'. The innate conservatism of both sides of industry could also only be broken by government action such as the Industrial Training Act (to compel higher standards of apprenticeship) and earnings-related unemployment and redundancy pay (to encourage greater labour mobility). The real battle was joined, however, in February 1961 when Macleod challenged Treasury logic deployed in the draft of the first PESC report. 'The draft should be revised', he insisted, 'to remove the apparent implication . . . that public expenditure was regarded as inherently undesirable. Some kinds of expenditure played an essential part in developing the competitive power of the economy.'[33] Thereafter the draft was modified and Treasury officials even started to acknowledge the indispensability of public expenditure to growth.

The debate was even fuller, especially within the CRD, over the delivery of individual welfare. The foremost objective of government, it was agreed, was the creation of an 'opportunity' state by the maximization of economic freedom and direct encouragement of personal initiative. Traditional welfare measures were not necessarily incompatible with this objective because for many they provided a 'springboard', not just a safety net.[34] A condition of opportunity, however, was responsibility – responsibility for one's own welfare and for those in genuine need. The trouble was that these two types of responsibility were potentially contradictory. The first led logically to the purchase of welfare through the market (assisted perhaps by tax allowances). The second required not only charitable work but also contractual participation in universal services such as National Insurance or the NHS. Such services gave concrete expression to the ideal of 'one nation' though the provision, in modern jargon, of a 'common risk pool'. They also obviated the need for a two-tier, means-tested system and provided an incentive for everyone to ensure their efficient administration. The government tried to square this circle by obliging the more affluent to pay a higher price for universal services – in the NHS, for example, through higher insurance contributions and charges, and in council housing through economic rents. The extra revenue thus generated was to be targeted on those in greatest need, such as the chronically ill, through higher long-term benefits. It was this strategy which ultimately persuaded the FSSC to drop its demands for 'radical change'.

There were, however, distinct limits at both an administrative and political level to the development of this principled new approach. The Treasury's welcome to public expenditure extended mainly to 'economic' initiatives, such as investment in nationalized industries. The virtues of welfare expenditure were more grudgingly acknowledged. 'Some services (e.g. education and health)', officials admitted, 'have a potential contribution to make to growth in the long run, but are in the nature of investments that take a long time to yield a return.'[35] On the pragmatic compromise between universalism and selectivism, even Macleod expressed severe doubts. Was not the move towards an earnings-related system tying the affluent still further to a bureaucratic monster based on the myth of 'actuarial' insurance? Was not this system, moreover, spreading benefits so thinly that those in genuine need were receiving inadequate help? His solution was the establishment of a new Beveridge Committee to resolve the dilemma. It was a suggestion incorporated into the 1964 manifesto but only mutedly so. After all, a fourteenth year in office was hardly the most appropriate time to be reconsidering first principles.

The germ of a new approach to welfare policy was, therefore, developed in the early 1960s as a result not just of administrative pressure and electoral opportunism but of a serious attempt to adjust Conservatism to the realities of a modern, affluent society. Hard decisions, however, were evaded. On the economic necessity for greater state expenditure, the debate rarely moved beyond the aggregate to establish particular priorities in each area of welfare. On the targeting of welfare, there was little consensus on which of the services guaranteeing security and incentives to the middle classes could or should be withdrawn to fund greater discrimination in favour of those in greatest need. The evasion of these fundamental challenges exposed a lack of political leadership at the highest level.

## III

Between 1958 and 1964 there was indubitably a radical reappraisal of welfare policy, which transformed attitudes at both a political and administrative level and led to a series of substantial reforms on which the Wilson government was later to build. This reappraisal, however, coincided with a perceived loss of morale and direction particularly within the constituencies. It was also mounted by a government which in retrospect has been condemned as bordering on socialist. To what extent, then, can it be said to have contributed to a damaging dilution of Conservatism?

Crosland in 1962 still identified 'deep differences' between the Conservative and Labour Parties on welfare policy. They existed, he argued, 'not because the Conservatives are necessarily less humanitarian, but because they hold particular views as to the proper role of the state, the desirable level of taxation, and the importance of private as opposed to collective responsibility'.[36] He was certainly correct to acknowledge the Conservatives' humanitarianism. This was evident in the concern for those in greatest need. However, he was more outdated on the issues of taxation and the state because – as has been seen – there had been a revolution in attitudes towards the virtues of higher taxation and the economic value of government expenditure. This inevitably clouded the distinction between private and collective responsibility. Beneath the froth of adversarial rhetoric, in other words, there was a growing convergence of party views not just on negative issues (such as the unacceptability of high unemployment) but on the positive welfare role of government.

This consensus nevertheless was sufficiently broad to accommodate differences of emphasis. In pensions policy, for example, there was significant disagreement over whether the economic power of occupational pension funds should be exercised by government or the market. In education, Edward Boyle (despite his alleged socialist sympathies) argued forcefully that the ultimate role of government was to encourage individual diversity rather than greater conformity.[37] Whilst addressing problems that had to be resolved in an increasingly affluent and complex society, therefore, the policy reappraisal deliberately sought – and laid the foundations for – a distinctive new Conservatism. That these foundations were not properly built upon, thereby causing a sense of lost direction, was the fault not of the reappraisal itself but of inadequate political leadership. That is why a new planning exercise was initiated so urgently and professionally after 1964 by Edward Heath.

## Notes

I should like to thank the ESRC, the Leverhulme Trust and the University of Bristol for financial support. The research was completed while I was a visiting scholar at St John's College, Oxford, and forms part of the ESRC's Whitehall Programme.

[1] S. Brittan, *Steering the Economy* (Harmondsworth, 1971), 227.
[2] See R. Lowe, 'Resignation at the Treasury, 1955–7', *Journal of Social Policy* 18 (1989), 505–26; R. Lowe 'Milestone or Millstone? The 1959–61 Plowden Committee and its Impact of British Welfare Policy', *Historical Journal* (forthcoming 1997).
[3] The papers of the committees are in the Conservative Party Archives (CPA) at the Bodleian. Those of the Future of the Social Services Committee are at CRD 2/29 and the Tax Policy Committee at CRD 3/7/26/1–3. Those of the Policy Study Group are at CRD 2/53/25–8 and the Chairman's Committee at CRD 2/52/7–9.
[4] See Daunton's contribution to this volume.
[5] CPA, ACP 3/8, ACP (61) 89, *Interim Report*, 40; ACP 2/2, ACP (63) 57th, minute 4.
[6] CPA, CRD 3/7/26/3, TCP (63) 3.
[7] Treasury, 2PIO, 81/01 part A, I. Macleod to S. Lloyd, 27 February 1961; Public Record Office (PRO), CAB 128/36, C (62) 75, 3, 20 December 1962. Government documents cited 'Treasury' are available under the thirty-year rule but had not at the time of writing been transferred to the PRO.
[8] PRO, PREM 11/4778, minute of 8 April 1964. Ironically, Macleod had left the cabinet by then.
[9] Sir William Beveridge, *Social Insurance and Allied Services*, Cmd 6404 (London, 1942), 163–5; R. M. Titmuss, *Essays on the 'Welfare State'* (London, 1958), 34–55; H. Glennerster, *British Social Policy since 1945* (Oxford, 1995), chapter 7.
[10] Beveridge, *Social Insurance*, para. 294.
[11] PRO, CAB 134/2533, SS (60) 7th, minutes for 8 April 1960.
[12] See, for instance, the review of policy on 4 February 1964 in Treasury, 2SS 41/96/01 B: 'the Treasury have no interest in maintaining contracting out and would like to see it abolished.'
[13] For a summary of the campaign, see CPA, CRD 2/52/7, doc. 88; and for the views of Thatcher and Joseph, CPA, LCC (65) 12, p.13. In anticipation of Labour, a change in name from national assistance to 'supplementary allowance' had also been mooted.
[14] The proposal was advanced first by Powell in 1957 in CPA, CRD 2/53/25, PSG (57) 4 and most fully by Peter Goldman in 1963 in CPA,

SC/63/1, SC/63/9. It was finally rejected by Douglas-Home on 19 May 1964, see PRO, PREM 11/4686.

[15] For the fullest exposition of his views, see E. Powell, 'Social Policy', 7 March 1962 in CPA, CRD 2/52/8, CC7. The party welcomed the call in the 1959 Younghusband Report for the greater training of social workers and passed the 1963 Children and Young Persons Act which lifted restrictions on preventive work within families.

[16] PRO, PREM 11/3930, draft of address to cabinet, 28 May 1962.

[17] The latest expressions of these views are in the 1960 Official Committee on Health Service Finance and the 1961 Interim Report of the FSSC. See PRO, CAB 134/2051 and CPA, ACP 3/8, ACP (61) 89.

[18] Eccles justified his views at the height of the battle with Lloyd in 'Education Policy', 4 January 1962, PRO, CAB 129/108, C (62) 5. For a summary of attitudes to the 'eleven plus' and comprehensives, see the letters by Edward Boyle to Macmillan on 3 July 1963 and R. A. Butler on 5 February 1964 in CPA, CRD 2/29/10. Acceptable ways to close down public schools were difficult to identify, as Labour's Public School Commission discovered.

[19] *Technical Education*, Cmd 9703 (1956); G. Crowther, *Fifteen to Eighteen* (London, 1959).

[20] Trinity College, Cambridge, R. A. Butler papers, H52, f.107. The later confession can be found in CPA, CRD 2/52/9, draft minutes of the fourth meeting of the Chairman's Committee.

[21] PRO, CAB 129/111, C (62) 201, H. Macmillan, 'The Modernization of Britain'. For anyone doubting the then moral commitment to full employment, which distinguishes the Macmillan government from later Conservative administrations, it should be noted that the definition of 'full employment' was significantly below that of Beveridge in 1942 (8.5 per cent) and Keynes in the 1940s (5 per cent). Remarkably for any Chancellor of the Exchequer, Amory specified as one of his four principle themes for the 1959 manifesto 'to be sensitive to the evils of heavy unemployment'(PRO, PREM 11/2248).

[22] Treasury, 2PIO 90/155/01 A and Annex; 2PIO 90/144/03. The Central Statistical Office and the Treasury were at the forefront of academic attempts to measure redistribution.

[23] See contributions by Francis and Brooke in this volume.

[24] Butler papers, H5O, B. Sewill to Butler, 22 November 1963.

[25] L. Hannah, *Inventing Retirement* (Cambridge, 1986), 53. The Conservative decision to raise pensions in line with prices also undermined the Fund's finances.

[26] CPA, CRD 2/52/9, draft minutes of the third meeting of the Chairman's Committee, 19 March 1962.

[27] CPA, CRD 2/53/28, minutes of the fifth meeting of the Policy Study Group, 6 May 1957.

[28] CPA, ACP 2/1, ACP (57) 33, 5, minutes of Advisory Policy Committee, 30 April 1958. For his views on the importance of welfare policy, see CPA, CRD 2/52/9, second meeting of the Chairman's Committee, 12 February 1962.

[29] Treasury, 2PIO 81/01 part A, I. Macleod to S. Lloyd, 27 February 1961.

[30] CPA, CRD 2/52/7, M. Fraser to I. Macleod, 29 March 1962.

[31] CPA, ACP 3/4, ACP/57/48, M. Fraser, 'A Forward Look', 9 January 1957.

[32] Treasury, 2SS, 541/106/01. For party unity on educational expenditure, see the summary of the Chequers meeting of 28 April 1963 in CPA, SC 63/1.

[33] Treasury, 2PIO, 81/77/01, MGPE (61) 2nd, 27 February 1961.

[34] Butler papers, G32, f. 132, report by Toby Low, 1958.

[35] Treasury, 2PIO, 81/76/01 part B, MGPE (62) 6, 12 July 1962.

[36] C. A. R. Crosland, *The Conservative Enemy* (London, 1962), 123.

[37] University of Leeds, Boyle papers, 660/22684A, E. Boyle to M. Fraser, 26 February 1964. For the Heath planning exercise, see R. Lowe, 'Social policy', in S. Ball and A. Seldon (eds.), *The Heath Government: A Reappraisal* (London, 1996).

# 'Liberty with Order': Conservative Economic Policy, 1951–1964

## JIM TOMLINSON

At the 1954 Conservative Annual Conference R. A. Butler, the Chancellor of the Exchequer, summarized what he saw as the Conservative approach to economic policy in the following words: 'What we want to achieve in our overseas policy, as in our home, is an approach which combines liberty with order.'[1] In this chapter I want to use that formulation to try and throw some fresh light on the politics and ideology which underlay Conservative economic policy in the 1951–64 period. As a preliminary it is necessary to say something about the existing state of the literature on economic policy in this period, before looking at the possibility of approaching the issues from a rather different angle.

Accounts of the economic policies of these Conservative governments by both political and economic historians have focused on the perceived overarching concern with macro-economic issues, especially full employment, and the balance of payments, at least up until the belated enthusiasm for growth apparently evident in the creation of the National Economic Development Council in 1961/2. Political biographies and autobiographies of ministers concerned have been replete with accounts of the dramatic twists and turns of short-run macro-economic management. On the other hand, since the rise of 'declinism' as the dominant framework for analysing the post-war British economy at the end of the 1950s, both left and New Right critics have portrayed governments in this period as contributing to relative 'decline' by their insouciant disregard for the growing debilitation in the underlying state of the economy.[2]

On the macro-economic side it may well be that both critics and defenders of policy in this period have exaggerated their cases. Whilst committed by electoral calculation, if nothing else, to the pursuit of full employment, the actual impact of economic policy on the maintenance of this objective was probably small, the underlying cause being the investment and trade booms across the industrialized world which caused the prosperity of the period. Policy may have helped expectations about future prospects both by some measures of international liberalization, and domestically by ruling out deflation as a policy option, but the idea of a direct link from Keynesian-inspired fiscal policy to full employment has to be discarded.[3] Just as misleading is the idea that this was a period of mounting fiscal deficits, undermining the stability of the economy. In fact, the government budget showed a consistent current-account surplus. Commitment to full employment, alongside the concern with the balance of payments, led to the much criticized 'stop–go' cycle. But statistical evidence suggests that this policy generated no greater fluctuations in output than occurred in the faster-growing western European economies over the same period.[4] Finally, whilst the concern of governments in this period with the external account is hardly to be doubted, the detrimental impact on performance commonly alleged to follow may again be exaggerated. For example, the view that Britain suffered from a persistently overvalued exchange rate is difficult to reconcile with the buoyant current-account position through most of this period. The Sterling Area, in particular, may have been less of a 'burden' than is normally suggested, with the Sterling balances less volatile than often pictured, the area providing no debilitating 'featherbed' for British exports, nor draining away a significant proportion of Britain's investment funds.[5]

The epithet of 'wasted years' often applied by critics to this period is based on the assumption that these governments were obsessed with macro policies that were detrimental to more rapid growth, and failed to develop much interest in policies aimed at directly improving economic efficiency. A central argument of this chapter is that such a view is incomplete in understanding Conservative approaches to economic policy in this period. Rather, the central theme here is that the Conservatives throughout their period of office both knew about and tried to respond to the mounting evidence of relatively slow economic growth, but were inhibited from any kind of adequate response not so much by macro-economic obsessions as by their ideological inhibitions and political calculations about the feasible policy options.

It needs to be emphasized initially that the Conservatives 'knew' very early in the 1950s that the emerging comparative data from the OEEC and UN showed British performance in a poor light. Across a range of indices, such as share of world trade, productivity, industrial production and national income growth the evident weaknesses of Britain had been acknowledged and discussed amongst senior civil servants and ministers from almost as soon as the Conservatives came to office. Much of this discussion was 'behind closed doors', but it does also appear in public documents, not only those produced by international bodies like the OEEC and UN, but also in government publications like the *Economic Survey* and the *Board of Trade Journal*.[6] To respond to the evidence, however, was a very different matter.

First, of course, it has to be recognized that the evidence of 'decline' had to be interpreted and its significance assessed. Most obviously, the figures given prominence were mainly *rates of change*, whilst the government was aware that British living standards were much higher in absolute terms, and that the gains of countries like Germany and France might just be a once-and-for-all catching-up. Some of the figures could also be seen in both pessimistic and more optimistic light, and there was, for example, considerable debate in the ministries about the importance of the decline in Britain's share of world trade, acknowledged to be apparent from 1952.[7]

Second, even where it was accepted that the figures showed something was going wrong, the incentive to respond in the early and mid-1950s was reduced by both the 'Gift from the Gods' of the improving terms of trade, with their favourable effect on living standards, and the failure of the political opposition to take up the issue. On the other hand, the Conservatives were driven to take the issue of economic growth seriously, as they had from the late 1940s focused their appeal on 'setting the people free' from controls, with the clear presumption that this freeing would unleash a demand for a rising standard of living which the Conservatives were best placed to respond to. This political calculation was initially astute, given the evident problems of the Labour Party in responding to the sustained increase in 'affluence'.[8] Thus the famous talk of doubling the standard of living in twenty-five years in 1954 articulated a belief already implicit in Conservative thinking, that this was a ground upon which they could beat Labour, even if a minority resisted this appeal to the electorate's 'vulgar materialism'.[9]

However, with the sustained 'stop' after the 1955 election coupled to the stabilization of the terms of trade, the promise of a relatively rapid, painless improvement in living standards started to evaporate. From just after the 1959 election not only did Labour start to hitch its electoral fortunes to a declinist critique of the Tories, but bodies like the Federation of British Industry joined the chattering classes in endorsing this dissatisfaction with Britain's economic performance. From then onwards the Conservatives were on the defensive, and felt obliged implicitly to accept the criticism of past policy, and to put forward their own new policy responses.

In understanding the evolution of those policy responses over the whole period of Conservative government, it is necessary to characterize the economic ideology that informed the government's position in this period. This is inherently difficult to do, and common labels such as 'Butskellism' need to be used with care.[10] But if we emphasize the competing goals of liberty and order, this provides a way of trying to make sense of the twists and turns of policy.

The goal of liberty would seem to fit neatly with a neo-liberal perspective on economic issues, in which the level of efficiency is largely a function of the amount of competition in the economy. In this period, it is crucial to note, the Conservatives did not pursue strongly pro-competitive policies. Domestically, the 1956 Restrictive Practices Act, which, as Mercer has emphasized, was by no means the product of a strong governmental commitment to economic liberalism, did have an unexpectedly strong impact on reducing the number of formal agreements on such practices, but many were replaced either by informal arrangements or by mergers of the firms concerned.[11] The banning of Resale Price Maintenance in 1964 probably had comparatively little impact on industrial, as opposed to retailing, efficiency. Both these pieces of legislation stirred up major disputes in the Conservative Party and governments.[12] Broadly speaking, certainly down to almost the very end of their period in office, the Conservatives put more emphasis on the threat to 'order' posed by the prominence given to free competition than its liberalizing advantages.

From a neo-liberal point of view competition in the labour market is at least as important as in product markets. But the Tory leadership in this period largely accepted the political calculation that any attack on collective bargaining and the trade unions was likely to be electorally damaging. Butler defined this approach when he argued that

> [t]he way to deal with the Trade Unions is not to bludgeon them or attack them by resolutions, but for our members to enter their ranks, work with them, treat them as a thoroughly British institution and show them that our way of life is as good as any they have ever thought of.[13]

Such an attitude meant, for example, that whilst attacking union 'restrictive practices' was a staple of Conservative rhetoric in discussions of monopoly in these years, action on this issue was limited to exhortation rather than legislation to try and change union behaviour. There is plenty of evidence of strong anti-union views amongst backbenchers and in the party generally, but this seems to stem more from a hostility to the perceived political success of the unions than from a clear endorsement of neo-liberal views about the need to free the labour market from their embrace.[14]

Equally, as regards the role of competition in this period, it is striking that Britain remained the most protected country in western Europe as regards international trade right through until the mid-1960s, until the Kennedy Round of GATT negotiations. Whilst quantitative restrictions on trade were reduced in line with international agreements, tariffs were cut very cautiously, largely through fear of the balance of payments consequences. The main qualification to this stance of very restricted support for foreign competition comes from the encouragement of inward investment by (largely American) multinationals, a policy pursued for many years prior to the 1950s, and driven at least as much by balance of payments considerations as by the belief that such inflows would stimulate the efficiency of British industry.[15] The only other instance of enthusiasm for reducing protection was the sudden emphasis on the need for industry to be subjected to the 'cold shower of competition' evident in ministerial circles after the rejection of Britain's EC application in 1963.[16]

If their neo-liberal credentials were little evident in their pursuit of competition, the same attitudes led to significant 'interventionist' initiatives where this was deemed politically desirable. One area where government did search from an early date for policies to respond to perceived economic inefficiencies was in the area of 'manpower', especially technically qualified manpower. The Conservatives took over the Attlee government's belief in the need to expand the supply of this resource, and this was turned into policies in education, which did see a significant rise in graduates in this area.[17] But whilst this shows a clear recognition of, and policy response to, a 'supply-side' problem, discussions and actions on this issue actually clearly demonstrate the strength of the political constraints on Conservative economic policy-making. The White Paper on education of 1956 emphasized this 'manpower' issue, and had a rhetoric about the centrality of technical training to Britain's economic future that Harold Wilson in the early 1960s would have envied.[18] This was followed in 1957 by a defence White Paper which argued that the key problem was to deploy this expanding supply of the qualified into economically valuable work by reducing military claims both on manpower in general and on technicians and engineers in particular.[19] Hence the whole nuclear strategy of this defence statement was based on the idea that such a posture would have economically beneficial consequences. But whilst the total manpower in the services did indeed fall over the next few years, the nuclear strategy required *more* not less of scarce trained manpower as R and D activity expanded. The issue then became whether Britain would give up military *commitments* to allow a redeployment of resources to the civilian sector, and the answer, evident in the growth of military expenditure in the early 1960s, was 'no'.[20]

In this crucial example, the problem was not one of ignorance or unconcern with economic performance, but political priorities. Whilst Britain's posture as a world power had been criticized for its economic effects by senior ministers from the time the Conservatives came to power, there was ultimately no willingness to give up that posture, only an ultimately fruitless attempt to try and achieve it on the cheap.[21]

Equally, the well-known enthusiasm for interventionist policies to try and increase growth in the early 1960s, symbolized by the NEDC, has to be seen largely as a response to a threatening political situation, rather than a positive initiative to reposition the Tory approach to economic policy. After the 1959 election, the growing attacks on government policy required some response. In an attempt to appease these critics the NEDC exercise seemed to offer a new framework for achieving long-standing goals like an incomes policy and constraint on public expenditure growth, whilst (fairly cynically) embracing the rhetoric of indicative planning. In this light, claims that 1960/1 should be seen as a major turning point in post-war economic policy should be treated with some scepticism.[22]

The tension between pursuing liberty and pursuing order may also be seen in looking at the key issue of investment. The general assumption of most economists in this period (though with some significant dissenters) was that higher investment was the key to faster growth, and this approach was largely accepted by the government. International comparisons made by the OEEC and UN provided widely cited evidence of Britain's low share of investment in GNP, and in response the government did attempt to encourage investment both by specific tax breaks (inherited from the Attlee government) and general tax cuts.[23]

At one level such a strategy could be seen as politically and ideologically unproblematic for the Conservatives, a policy which would unite neo-liberals and interventionists as well as being likely to prove popular with Conservative voters. But in fact it raised a number of tensions. First, if the general aim of policy was to raise the standard of living as fast as possible, this meant for electoral reasons seeing the expansion of consumption as crucial. But in the short run higher investment had to be at the expense of consumption (given the weakness of the trade balance) so that for all the talk of raising investment, after the surge of the late 1940s, investment's share in British GNP continued to lag behind that in major competing countries.[24] The Conservatives delivered on their promise of lifting the tight controls on consumption of the Attlee period, but the result was that the distribution of national income growth was strikingly less favourable to investment than under Labour.[25]

Second, the tax breaks given to investment had a dual role, both as long-run stimulants and as components of short-term macro-economic management. Their latter role has long been criticized, such variable incentives being seen as part of the much derided stop–go cycle, with inhibiting rather than encouraging effects on investment.[26] But if we look at the longer-run aspect we can also see a major problem, which is that from the mid-1950s these tax breaks were only just enough to offset the decline in the underlying rate of profit, so that, in so far as investment is dependent on rates of return, Conservative policy was doing no more than offsetting the adverse effects of this underlying trend. This should be compared with the late 1940s when, although taxes on profits were much higher, the underlying profit position was very favourable to companies.[27]

Third, policies to raise aggregate investment in practice had to deal with the fact that much of the discussion assumed that it was *industrial* investment which was crucial, but this was, as always, only a small part of the total investment picture. Most investment was in construction, in housing, roads and railways, and in turn much of this was in the public sector.[28] So policies to raise investment inevitably raised issues about the scope and nature of the public sector.

The Conservatives failed to evolve a clear stance on the growth of public expenditure, which fell as a share of GDP until 1958 because of falling defence expenditure and fast GDP growth, but rose thereafter. On the one hand, in the name of liberty, there was a broad ideological opposition to the expansion of the state's role which had occurred in the 1940s, and this view underlay talk of 'setting the people free'. But on the other hand, the commitment to 'order' and social stability, coupled to electoral considerations and demographic trends, combined to reduce greatly the room for manœuvre on social services expenditure. Whilst direct frontal assault on this expenditure was resisted, nevertheless much Conservative discussion continued to assume that expenditure growth was a problem.[29] One result of this dilemma was the attempt to squeeze public expenditure on defence, evident in the 1957 White Paper, but as already noted, this failed in the face of an unwillingness to cut commitments when it became apparent that the nuclear option, coupled to much smaller but professional armed forces, was not the route to financial savings.[30]

Until the end of the Korean War the total level of investment was tightly controlled by physical measures. In 1953 this was replaced by a combination of financial 'guidance' in the private sector, operated through the Capital Issues Committee, and more importantly through bank lending, alongside 'planning' in the public sector. The broad aim was to shift resources from public to private sectors, but this was impeded by (a) the scale of the Macmillan housing boom in the early 1950s; (b) the very low level of investment in health and education under the Attlee government, so that political pressures for improvement in these areas was extremely strong in the 1950s; and (c) the fact that much of the nationalized sector was extremely capital-intensive, and arguably had a key role to play in economic expansion, so that a crude 'public bad/private good' view of investment was patently inadequate. The result of all this was that no clear priorities in investment were sustained, policy lurching from one short-term approach to another. The first public-sector investment pro-gramme was initiated in 1957, and the 1961 White Paper on nationalized industries responded to criticisms of stop–go policies in this sector, but 'short-termism' still dominated.[31]

Perhaps the most obvious period of tension in Conservative policy which can helpfully be understood in the light of the order/liberty dichotomy occurred in the period after the 1955 election. As is well known, after seemingly committing themselves to expansion in 1954, and using fiscal and monetary policy to secure a boom which took them safely through the 1955 election, tight deflationary policies were pursued for several years. The reason for this change of tack was the priority given to defeating inflation. But the interesting question is why so much emphasis was put on this objective. Of course it can be argued that this was simply an economic issue: with a fixed exchange rate, high inflation in comparison with other countries threatened the balance of payments.[32] But it is possible to turn this argument around and say that commitment to a fixed exchange rate was maintained because it provided a discipline on inflation, which was seen as having unfavourable consequences which were fundamentally political. Thus Thorneycroft, as Chancellor of the Exchequer in 1957, spoke of rising prices as 'a social as well as an economic evil. They strike at the pensioner; they hit the saver and they penalise the thrifty.'[33] Ultimately the expansionists won out against those whose fear of inflation, driven by the disorder it purportedly threatened, seemed to be leading into an economic stagnation fatal to Conservative election prospects. But it is important to note that the expansionists were also concerned that faster economic growth should not be too disruptive of social stability. This is very evident in the whole Conservative approach to the labour market, which deserves more attention than it has previously received.

As is well known, and has been reiterated above, the Conservatives in this period took a conciliatory attitude to trade unions. Paul Addison, focusing on the period up to 1955, summarizes the reasons for this approach: 'It was a Government of Tory Wets, for whom social harmony was a higher priority than economic efficiency.'[34] But, especially from the end of the decade, many Conservatives came to believe that greater economic efficiency required substantial changes to the operation of the labour market, and the question was: could this be done without an attack on the role of trade unions? In the event the response that emerged tried to combine a continuation of the conciliatory approach to unions with an attempt to increase labour mobility. This meant not the kind of neo-liberal deregulatory policies in the labour market of the 1980s and 1990s, but an attempt to cushion the financial consequences of mobility for workers by such measures as redundancy payments and higher unemployment pay. By such measures, it was hoped, workers would willingly move to new, higher-productivity jobs. Higher efficiency would then not threaten social stability.[35] In the event, these proposals had to await a Labour government for enactment, but the important point here is that they represented an attempt by the Conservatives to forge proposals which would combine the expansionism deemed electorally necessary with a continuing desire not to confront the population with forced and painful changes in their daily lives.

So far this chapter has suggested that the Conservatives lacked a consistent ideology of economic policy, of either a neo-liberal or interventionist character, but rather should be seen as lurching from expedient to expedient, in part at least because of the competing claims of liberty and order. From such a perspective, does the commonly used epithet 'Keynesian' seem helpful in describing the Conservative approach to economic policy? This term may have some purchase if we use it to describe a combination of belief in macro-management to maintain full employment (but where the economic environment was so favourable as to make the costs of so doing very low), coupled to a broad scepticism about the efficacy of intervention in the market.[36] But such a characterization raises the problem that generally the Conservative governments were *less* neo-liberal than the Keynesian economists who gave them advice, showing a greater interest in *ad hoc* micro-intervention than those economists, and finding the emphasis on competition as a route to efficiency more problematic than text-book Keynesianism suggested. This latter scepticism was, as argued above, because of the Conservative fear that unbridled competition was a threat to stability and order. To characterize policy as 'Keynesian' is therefore only helpful as long as we use that term to suggest a broad ideological disposition to be willing to pursue short-term macroeconomic management, rather than a close attachment to particular economic theories.

This broad stance was compatible with a range of *ad hoc* interventions in industry, but along with political factors it mitigated against intervention in industry where this would involve getting 'inside' the firm. This theme may be illustrated by the fate of the previous Labour government's initiatives on industry, such as the Development Councils which were largely discontinued under the Conservatives, or the British Productivity Council (successor to the AACP), which stumbled from funding crisis to funding crisis in this period.[37] A similar fate befell that other Attlee government creation, the British Institute of Management. Human-relations ideology remained strong in government rhetoric, but little was done to press management to adopt policies which might flow from such a stance. For example, Joint Production Committees, pushed by Labour in the late 1940s, were allowed to wither rapidly away in the face of union and employer indifference.[38] As early as 1954 the government rejected the kind of activist role in trying to raise productivity performed by the Attlee government, and this stance was maintained over the next decade.[39]

If the absence of the kind of detailed interventionism of the Attlee government under the Conservatives is perhaps unsurprising, other features of their policy are less readily explicable. Why, to give one interesting example, was small business (in the manufacturing rather than distribution sector) so neglected? Financial assistance remained limited to that provided by ICFC, whose role was largely independent of policy, no attempt, for example, being made to link its activities to those of CIC or DATAC, though the Radcliffe Committee reiterated the idea of a 'gap' at the lower end of the financial markets.[40] Did this reflect the dominance of business organizations like the FBI by large firms, at a time when the government treated the FBI as the crucial representative of business, or was that problem of representation itself a consequence of the political weakness of this sector? For all the furore over the effects of the abolition of RPM on small retailers, there was little evidence of Conservative disquiet at the growing trend towards the amalgamation and takeover of small industrial firms, especially evident after the 1956 Restrictive Practices Act.[41] Here would seem to lie a striking contrast with other western European countries, where small industrial firms played a much larger economic and political role.

Perhaps the reason for this British peculiarity lay in the faith in scale and technology as the route to economic success, which is surely a striking feature of the thinking of many experts and both political parties through much of the middle years of the twentieth century. Whilst Edgerton has rightly stressed the culture of high technology in Britain in this period, as against the Wiener/Barnett cliché about a culture dominated by classical and literary themes,[42] this perhaps needs to be linked to the widespread belief that such technological imperatives required large-scale industry, an idea which became firmly rooted from the time of the inter-war 'rationalization' movement, and which remained widely prevalent in Britain throughout the 1950s and 1960s.[43]

Overall, this chapter has suggested that the received picture of these Conservative governments may need revising in three main directions. First, that the macro-economic policies about which so much has been written may be rather less important, for good or ill, than commonly supposed. Second, that the 'neo-liberal versus interventionist' approach to understanding economic policy so often adopted may obscure as much as reveal. Third, that a focus on the Conservatives' political objectives, crudely but helpfully summarized as 'liberty with order', can reveal quite a lot about the gyrations through which policy went in these years.

*Notes*

[1] National Union of Conservative and Unionist Associations, *Annual Conference Report 1954* (London, 1957), 65.

[2] The standard economic history works include J. C. R. Dow, *The Management of the British Economy 1945–60* (Cambridge, 1965); S. Brittan, *Steering the Economy* (Harmondsworth, 1971); G. D. N. Worswick and P. H. Ady, *The British Economy in the 1950s* (Oxford, 1962); F. A. Blackaby (ed.), *British Economic Policy 1960–74* (Cambridge, 1978). More recent work is in N. Crafts and N. Woodward (eds.), *The British Economy since 1945* (Oxford, 1991) and R. Floud and D. McCloskey (eds.), *The Economic History of Britain Since 1700*, III: *1939–92* (Cambridge, 1995). The 'classic' contemporary attacks on British 'decline' are M. Shanks, *The Stagnant Society* (London, 1959); A. Shonfield, *British Economic Policy since the War* (London, 1958); N. Macrae, *Sunshades in October* (London, 1963).

[3] R. C. O. Matthews, 'Why has Britain had Full Employment since the War?', *Economic Journal* 78 (1968), 555–69; J. Tomlinson, 'Why was there never a Keynesian Revolution in Economic Policy?', *Economy and Society* 10 (1981), 72–87.

[4] A. Whiting, 'An International Comparison of the Instability of Economic Growth', *Three Banks Review* 66 (1976), 26–46; T. Wilson, 'Instability and the Rate of Growth', *Lloyds Bank Review* 83 (1966), 16–32.

[5] C. Schenk, *Britain and the Sterling Area: From Devaluation to Convertibility in the 1950s* (London, 1994).

[6] J. Tomlinson, 'Inventing Decline', Brunel University Department of Economics Discussion Paper 9501 (Uxbridge, 1995).

[7] PRO, CAB 134/2555, Working Party on UK Export Trends, 1953.

[8] N. Tiratsoo, 'Popular Politics, Affluence and the Labour Party in the 1950s', in A. Gorst, L. Johnman and W. Scott Lucas (eds.), *Contemporary British History 1931–61: Politics and the Limits of Policy* (London, 1990), 44–61.

[9] J. Ramsden, 'From Churchill to Heath', in Lord Butler (ed.), *The Conservatives* (London, 1977), 450, 455.

[10] J. Tomlinson, 'Keynesianism and the Conservatives 1945–64: An Unfortunate Alliance', *History of Political Economy* (forthcoming); N. Rollings, 'Poor Mr Butskell: A Short Life, Wrecked by Schizophrenia?', *Twentieth Century British History* 5 (1994), 183–205.

[11] H. Mercer, *Constructing a Competitive Order: The Hidden History of British Antitrust Policies* (Cambridge, 1995).

[12] N. Harris, *Competition and the Corporate Society: British Conservatives, the State and Industry 1945–64* (London, 1972).

13  NUCUA, *Conference Report 1956*, 49.
14  NUCUA, *Conference Report 1954*, 79–84, 102–7; *Conference Report 1958*, 53–8; *Conference Report 1961*, 109–18.
15  A. D. Morgan, 'Commercial Policy', in Blackaby (ed.), *British Economic Policy*, 515–63; G. Jones, 'The British Government and Foreign Multinationals before 1970', in M. Chick (ed.), *Governments, Industries and Markets* (Aldershot, 1990), 194–214.
16  PRO, CAB 134/1698, President of the Board of Trade, 'Economic Policy after Brussels', 4 March 1963.
17  M. Sanderson, *The Universities and British Industry* (London, 1972), 348–53.
18  Ministry of Education, *Technical Education*, Cmnd 9703 (London, 1956).
19  Ministry of Defence, *White Paper on Defence 1957*, Cmnd 124 (London, 1957).
20  Military spending fell sharply in 1957/8 and slightly in the following two years, but then rose again for the next three years (M. Chalmers, *Paying for Defence* (London, 1985), 68).
21  PRO, CAB 129/52, R. Butler, 'Economic Policy', 17 May 1952.
22  Brittan, *Steering the Economy*, 227; PRO, CAB 134/1689, Economic Policy Committee Minutes, 10 May 1961; CAB 134/1696, 'Economic Growth', 28 June 1962; Conservative Party Archives, Committee on Economic Growth (Chair, Paul Chambers), 1961/2.
23  I. M. D. Little, 'Fiscal Policy', in Worswick and Ady, *British Economy*, 247–9; PRO, T171/595, 'Tax Relief on Industrial Investment', February 1962.
24  This was a persistent theme of OEEC Reports in this period; for example *Fifth Report* (Paris, 1954). In Britain the proportion rose from around 13 per cent in 1952 to 17 per cent in the early 1960s. In the other major western European economies the comparable figures were between 3 and 8 percentage points higher in both periods (OECD, *National Accounts Statistics of OECD Countries* (Paris, annual)).
25  A. Cairncross, *The British Economy since 1945* (London, 1992), 58, 93.
26  C. Bowe (ed.), *The Economics of Investment Subsidies* (London, 1976).
27  M. King, 'The U.K. Profits Crisis: Myth or Reality?', *Economic Journal* 85 (1975), 33–54.
28  Investment in plant and machinery was typically around 30 per cent of total GDFCF (at the peak of Macmillan's housing boom in 1953/4 this category was smaller than investment in dwellings (C. H. Feinstein, *National Income, Expenditure and Output of the UK, 1855–1965* (Cambridge, 1972), table T109).
29  H. Jones, 'New Tricks for an Old Dog? The Churchill Government and Social Policy, 1951–5', in Gorst et al., *Contemporary British History*, 33–43; R. Lowe, 'Resignation at the Treasury: The Social Services

Committee and the Failure to Reform the Welfare State, 1955–57', *Journal of Social Policy* 18 (1989), 505–26; R. Lowe, 'Milestone or Millstone? The 1959–61 Plowden Committee and its Impact on British Welfare Policy' (forthcoming).

[30] Chalmers, *Paying for Defence*, 68–70.

[31] R. Clarke, *Public Expenditure, Management and Control*, ed. Sir Alec Cairncross (London, 1978), 17–19.

[32] It is striking how thin the economic arguments against mild inflation are.

[33] NUCUA, *Conference Report 1957*, 38.

[34] P. Addison, *Churchill on the Home Front 1900–1955* (London, 1992), 387.

[35] PRO, CAB 134/1697, Economic Policy Committee Minutes, 20 June 1963.

[36] P. Hall, *Governing the Economy: The Politics of State Intervention in Britain and France* (Oxford, 1986); Tomlinson, 'Unfortunate Alliance'.

[37] PRO, CAB 134/848, 'Efficiency and Output', 3 December 1953.

[38] PRO, T 228/628, 'British Institute of Management', 1955–8.

[39] PRO, CAB 134/1226, Economic Policy Committee Minutes, 28 April 1954.

[40] Radcliffe, *Committee on the Working of the Monetary System: Report*, Cmnd 827 (London, 1959), paras.932–47; R. Coopey and D. Clarke, *3i: Fifty Years Investment in Industry* (Oxford, 1995) chapter 3.

[41] R. Roberts, 'Regulatory Responses to the Market for Corporate Control in Britain in the 1950s', *Business History* 34 (1992), 183–200.

[42] D. Edgerton, *England and the Aeroplane* (London, 1991).

[43] L. Hannah, *The Rise of the Corporate Economy*, 2nd edn. (London, 1983).

# Easter 2003 Opening Hours

**BATH SPA**
UNIVERSITY COLLEGE

## Newton Park Library

| | |
|---|---|
| Friday 4th April -  Last day of term | 8.15am -  8.15pm |
| Saturday 5th April *(Counter closes 12.30)* | 9.30am - 5.30pm |
| Sunday 6th April  *(Counter closed)* | 1.00pm - 5.30pm |
| Monday 7th to Friday 11th April | 9.00am - 4.45pm |
| Saturday 12th, Sunday 13th April | **Closed** |
| Monday 14th to Thursday 17th April | 9.00am - 4.45pm |
| Friday 18th to Tuesday 22nd April | **Closed** |
| Wednesday 23rd to Friday 25th April | 9.00am - 4.45pm |
| Saturday 26th April *(Counter closes 12.30)* | 9.30am - 5.30pm |
| Sunday 27th April *(Counter closed)* | 1.00pm - 5.30pm |

## Sion Hill Library

| | |
|---|---|
| Friday 4th April -  Last day of term | 9.00am - 8.00pm |
| Saturday 5th, Sunday 6th April | **Closed** |
| Monday 7th to Friday 11th April | 9.30am - 5.00pm |
| Saturday 12th to Tuesday 22nd April | **Closed** |
| Wednesday 23rd, Thursday 24th April | 9.30am - 5.00pm |
| Friday 25th April | Open by appointment only, please ring 01225 875648 |
| Saturday 26th, Sunday 27th April | **Closed** |

**Opening hours as normal from Monday 28th April 2003**

# 'A Kind of Tax Prison': Rethinking Conservative Taxation Policy, 1960–1970[1]

## MARTIN DAUNTON

> One of the clearest contrasts between Conservative and Socialist policy is in the field of taxation. Conservatives believe that high taxation discourages enterprise and initiative, and so tends to impoverish the whole nation . . . By contrast, Socialist policy contains little mention of tax reduction and indeed most Socialists welcome high taxation as a means of achieving their aim of universal equality.[2]

> The contrast that should exist is between the Conservative emphasis on the spread of private ownership and the Socialist emphasis on the concentration of public ownership.[3]

A major achievement of the British state after the reintroduction of income tax in 1842 was the creation of a fiscal system with a high degree of legitimacy and buoyancy. Care was taken that taxation should be neutral between classes, a perception which was successfully renegotiated both in the Edwardian period (with the introduction of a graduated and differentiated income tax) and again after the First World War, with the containment of Labour's demand for a capital levy to redeem the national debt, which threatened to turn taxation into a political fault line. The negotiation of acceptance of the tax system was, to an extent, a rhetorical device which masked deeper inequities in society, but it did prevent the use of taxation in a way which would expose the rhetoric as a sham: care had to be taken that taxation could be realistically portrayed as fair and equitable between classes. The result was to create a high degree of consent to taxation, which was significant for the nature of the British state, helping to define the boundaries between local and central responsibilities, and between market or voluntary and collective solutions. Essentially, the legitimacy of central government taxation led to a reliance on the finance of social services from national taxes rather than local taxation or social insurance contributions through voluntaristic bodies such as friendly societies.

The legitimacy and buoyancy of the fiscal system rested on a shift from indirect to direct taxes for a century after 1842, a trend which was justified on the grounds that indirect taxes fell with particular severity on the poor. Indirect taxes were also linked by Cobdenite and Gladstonian rhetoric with the evils of protection and of warfare, for such taxes were hidden in the price of commodities so that voters were less aware of the costs of military adventurism. Although this rhetoric came under attack from about 1900, the political dangers and administrative difficulties of challenging the 'fiscal constitution'[4] of the nineteenth century remained strong enough to prevent a significant shift to indirect taxation either in the Edwardian period or after the First World War, when a general sales tax was rejected. The introduction of a narrowly based purchase tax in the Second World War did not mark a fundamental alteration in the balance between direct and indirect taxes.[5]

The fiscal constitution forged in the nineteenth century helped to shape the welfare state, and the problem which faced both the Labour and Conservative parties in the 1960s was whether this fiscal constitution could survive the strain of increased costs of welfare, as expectations increased and demographic change placed more strain on the social services. The legitimacy of central government taxation shaped the state in such a way that other means of funding welfare atrophied, with the result that at some point the limits of the fiscal system would be reached. A fiscal system which for so long had seemed to be legitimate, securing a high degree of consent to taxation, could appear rigid and inflexible. A major political problem of the 1960s was how to renegotiate the fiscal constitution, and this was at the centre of discussions within the Conservative Party between 1960 and 1970. The Taxation Policy Committee was largely concerned with immediate pragmatic issues of making recommendations for the next budget between 1959 and 1963, but it did also start to consider general policy in preparation for the next election. The Conservative Parliamentary Finance Committee also established a subcommittee to consider the future structure of direct taxation, which met in 1960 and 1961. The proposals were still tentative in 1964, and a more thorough review was initiated during the years of opposition between 1964 and 1970, when the task of devising a coherent package of fiscal reform fell to the Policy Group on Future Economic Policy, and particularly to subcommittee A on taxation which was formed in 1965. The conflicts over tax policy within the party during the 1960s might appear to be dry and technical but they entailed – as in the 1840s and the Edwardian period – a debate over fundamental assumptions and a battle for the ideological heart of the party.[6]

# I

In January 1960, Brendon Sewill of the Conservative Research Department basked complacently in the satisfaction of nine Conservative budgets which had reduced taxation. Penal rates had been moderated, so that 'the tax structure is very much more sensible and there are no longer any major priorities'.[7] Indeed, the Taxation Policy Committee initially saw little cause for concern, and had no thoughts of a radical agenda for fundamental reform beyond considering where the burden of taxation made the shoe pinch. The conclusion was that the standard of living of the working classes had risen, and that those earning the lowest wages were helped in other ways.

> The worst pinch was in the £1000–2000 a year level, and perhaps a little above. These include a large number of middle-class professional people who have not yet escaped from family responsibilities. In these cases there is not only an actual pinch, but a relative pinch in relation to the big rise in the standard of life of the working population since before the war. For this deserving and important class, a reduction in the standard rate of income tax, and to a lesser extent a reduction in surtax, would be the most useful relief.[8]

The problem, of course, was that it was 'a little blatant' to suggest that those most in need of assistance were people like the members of the committee.[9] Such self-satisfied and self-interested complacency did not survive for long, and in 1960 Edward Boyle accurately predicted to the committee that taxation 'would turn out to be the main bone of contention inside the party during the 1960s'.[10]

The new cause for concern arose from two considerations. One, which was stressed by Boyle, was that reductions in taxation during the 1950s had depended upon special factors which no longer prevailed. A reduction in defence expenditure, and the end of food subsidies and housing grants, allowed a combination of increased social expenditure and tax cuts in the 1950s, but Boyle feared that government expenditure in the future would increase at a faster rate than the gross national product, and he was pessimistic about the possibilities of cutting expenditure or of increasing taxes.[11] There was also an increasing realization that there was a second, and more serious, cause for concern: a crisis in the *structure* of taxation which would require the fiscal constitution to be recast. When Britain was compared with other countries, it was not the high proportion of GNP taken by the government which stood out, but *how* it was taken. On the surface, the British tax system was reassuringly average: the level of taxation was broadly in line with other countries in western Europe, and there was a similar balance between direct and indirect taxes. But the Economist Intelligence Unit argued that it was precisely this 'averageness' which was causing problems and concealing defects in the constituent parts of the tax regime. Indirect taxes were highly selective, falling on a limited range of goods through the purchase tax or excise duties on tobacco, beer and petrol; as a result of this narrow tax base, saturation point was reached more quickly than in countries with a general sales or turnover tax. The result was that increased taxation was more likely to fall on direct taxes which were heavier, over a wider income range, than in other countries in western Europe. Many people had passed through the reduced rates of income tax into the standard rate of tax, so that 'the buoyancy in our tax system is derived from the high marginal rates of direct tax on middle and upper incomes', hence creating the 'pinch' of taxation on middle-class professional families. Further, the contribution of general taxation to welfare expenditure was much greater than elsewhere in western Europe, where social security contributions were more important and funding of social services fell on labour costs rather than taxation of profits and personal income. A further increase in expenditure on welfare would therefore impose strains on a system of general taxation which lacked buoyancy. In a buoyant tax regime, a rise of 1 per cent in national income produces an increase of more than 1 per cent in government revenue, as incomes move into higher tax brackets or more taxed commodities are consumed, so allowing a painless increase in government expenditure or reduction in tax rates. The room for manœuvre was reduced in the 1960s, and the fiscal reforms of Labour after 1964 merely made a bad situation worse, for neither the existing purchase tax nor new taxes such as Selective Employment Tax were capable of restoring buoyancy.[12]

*Table 1   Taxation as a percentage of GNP, 1964*

|  | France | W. Germany | UK |
|---|---|---|---|
| Direct | 10·5 | 13·4 | 15·9 |
| Indirect |  |  |  |
|    (of which sales/turnover tax) | 13·6 (9·3) | 10·6 (5·3) | 10·8 (2·0) |
| Social security contributions | 12·2 | 9·2 | 4·7 |
| Total | 36·2 | 33·2 | 31·4 |

*Source*: CPA, CRD 3/7/26/26, Economist Intelligence Unit Report, 'Comparative Studies in Taxation'.

The growing awareness of a structural problem in the British fiscal system led to a transformation in the debate during the 1960s, which became all the more intense as a result of the innovations of the Labour government after 1964. The Taxation Policy Committee had already realized that something more appealing than a series of 'standstill budgets' was needed to prevent dissatisfaction. It was felt that a fiscal policy must be developed which would appeal to the electorate, and the Committee tentatively hinted at ways in which policy could be changed by shifting the cost of the National Health Service to employees' and employers' contributions, by requiring the nationalized industries to finance more of their development, by encouraging the private provision of welfare services, and by charging tolls on new roads and bridges.[13] Both the Taxation Policy Committee and the subcommittee on direct taxation started to consider proposals for a payroll tax or sales tax, and to discuss reforms of company taxation and the finance of social services.[14] The proposals were undeveloped suggestions, and it was becoming apparent that the party would face difficult decisions over taxation, which would have wide implications for many areas of policy and which would disturb existing electoral alliances. What was needed was not merely tinkerings within the existing fiscal constitution, but a fundamental review of its very basis, which would 'displace income tax from the pinnacle it had occupied for the last 100 years'.[15] The proposed changes needed to be formed into a coherent package which would extend beyond rebarbative technicalities in order to create a new vision of the future of British society.

A fiscal system with a high degree of acceptance since 1842 had resulted in a centralized welfare state which was dependent upon a narrow range of taxes. Although this system was becoming increasingly sclerotic by the 1960s, it would prove to be difficult to rejuvenate, for the tax system rested upon a complex balance of interests which would be politically dangerous to dismantle and reconstruct. There were two equally important requirements. The first need was to articulate a rhetoric which could both justify a major reshaping of the fiscal regime, and re-establish legitimacy and consent on a new basis. The second was to secure the adherence of major interests in order to build a new coalition. Progress was made in constructing a new rhetoric of an opportunity state which promised more rapid growth by offering greater incentives and encouraging efficiency in the use of labour. Everyone would ultimately benefit in the medium to long term, both from the proceeds of growth and from restoring buoyancy to government revenues; in the short term, anyone who suffered should be compensated by improved, selective, welfare benefits. The problem, however, was that the radical proposals emerging from the internal policy debate were not accepted by the leadership as politically expedient. There was a failure to carry through the implications of reforming the tax system into the related area of welfare,[16] and the dangers of alienating existing interests were considered to be too great. There was a large element of political caution in the rejection of the proposals, but it also reflected the way fiscal policy was discussed in Britain. Debates on the fiscal regime were carried out largely behind closed doors, and fiscal policy in Britain was marked by secrecy, so that changes in the tax system were announced as definite intentions in the annual finance bill without prior discussion with interested parties. Such an approach militated against serious long-term reform of the tax structure.[17] The outcome was that the radical proposals for reform were not fully implemented by the Heath government, and it was left to Mrs Thatcher to implement a different – arguably narrower and harmful – version of the rhetoric after 1979.

## II

The contention which emerged was that a crisis in the tax system was blunting efficiency and enterprise. The solution was 'to take the whole tax system to pieces and put it together again in a way that will radically alter the economic climate – the framework of rewards and penalties in which personal and corporate decisions are taken within the economic system'.[18] This was a formidable undertaking which would only make sense if the technicalities of taxation could be linked to a wider rhetoric whose appeal would, it was hoped, permit a greater degree of flexibility and buoyancy in the tax structure by linking fiscal policy to a wider vision of the transformation of British society.

The case was made by William Rees-Mogg, who argued that 'there are two well-established Conservative principles which ought to be applied to personal taxation. One is to improve personal incentives; the other is to encourage the broader ownership of capital.' Conservative governments had, he felt, paid attention to incentives since 1951 but not to property ownership and the encouragement of savings, which required a shift from direct to indirect taxation, and from taxation on income and capital to taxation on expenditure:

> The chief means of encouraging the extension of capital must include the encouragement of home ownership, of the establishment and expansion of small businesses, and of personal saving, particularly through unit trusts . . . For professional men and business managers, there is now great difficulty in forming even quite small capital after tax. Yet capital is usually a stronger incentive than income . . . We are now in a situation where a reasonably successful professional man could well earn £250,000 in his lifetime and yet leave no more than a tenth of that sum on his death. For economic and social reasons this should be put right.[19]

The contention was that high rates of personal taxation prevented salaried and professional men from accumulating capital; if they did save, penal rates of differential taxation on investment income and heavy death duties made their struggles still less rewarding. By contrast, anyone with a large fortune was able to avoid paying taxation by the use of various measures for avoidance, so that 'the present system is weighted against the modest capitalist or would be capitalist compared to the man with a very large fortune'.[20]

High levels of income tax led to a bunching of incomes, so that Britain had a relatively egalitarian income distribution. This was at the expense of incentives to save, which led to a highly skewed distribution of wealth.[21] What was needed, so it seemed, was a tax system which would allow the accumulation of up to £25,000 without tax penalty, so that 'for the first time there will be real and positive encouragement to the acquisition of a modest capital'. The result would, it was hoped, be a transformation of the British economy:

> Economic growth depends fundamentally upon human ingenuity, upon energy, effort and enterprise. These are the true conditions of growth and where they exist the means of achieving the growth will always be found. It is because increasingly as a nation we have lacked these qualities that the British economy has become stagnant and unprogressive. There is no single factor which bears a heavier responsibility for this than our tax system. Too much has been taken and the dice has been too heavily loaded against initiative and enterprise. The proposals we put forward are designed to produce a fundamental change and to recreate in our economy the conditions in which growth will flourish.[22]

Here was the vision, of an opportunity state which would lead to a greater sense of initiative. More problematic was the means by which it should be made reality, and whether any proposals would secure the allegiance of interest groups or the backing of the party leadership. What was needed was simple to define: to find 'so large a revenue raiser that one could take the heat off the income tax'.[23] Agreement on the best alternative was more difficult to secure.

# III

One proposal was to transfer the costs of social services from general taxation to a payroll tax on the lines of West Germany and France, in proportion to the wage and salary bill. The contention was that high direct taxes on profits and personal income were harmful by blunting the incentives of those who paid, and by implicitly subsidizing labour, which weakened the motivation to employers to increase labour productivity and resist wage demands. The existing system of financing social security from general taxation was estimated to be equivalent to a subsidy of £1,000m to labour costs in 1962, or 6·5 per cent of the total wage and salary bill and 29 per cent of taxes on income. A comparison with Germany suggested that a payroll tax to finance social services would save £647m from general taxation, allowing the reduction of income tax by 6*d.* in the £ and the abolition of profits tax. The contention of Arthur Cockfield was that it was 'neither morally justifiable nor economically desirable that those who employed large numbers should be able to shift on to the general body of taxpayers part of the indirect costs of their labour force'. Here, it seemed, was a major reason for the less efficient use of labour than in Europe, and the removal of the subsidy would encourage industrialists to use this scarce resource more effectively and to develop capital-intensive production on which the future prosperity of the country depended. Since revenue from the payroll tax would rise with wages, it would also solve the problem of financing social services and restore buoyancy to the tax system.[24]

There were, however, sceptical . voices. Was it wise to hypothecate taxes by assigning revenue to particular expenditure? Was it advisable to increase costs in labour-intensive industries, with the dangers of increases in prices such as train fares which were politically sensitive? And were the prospects of economizing on the use of labour realistic unless the tax was much higher, particularly in view of the likelihood of hostility from powerful unions? There was no doubt that a payroll tax would increase labour costs and prices in the short run; supporters of the proposal were confident that the results would be beneficial in the long run by shifting the balance between labour- and capital-intensive industries, increasing the incentive to invest, and generating growth. The proposal of the payroll tax was clearly politically sensitive, for it would lead to opposition from employers who faced the prospect of an increase in their labour costs, which were already high, with consequent difficulties in international competition.[25] The immediate political problems were more apparent than the prospects of long-term gains in efficiency and a shift to capital-intensive production. Further, there was uncertainty about how the revenue from the payroll tax would be used. It could pay for higher expenditure on social services; it could reduce income tax; or it could cut company taxation as a compensation for the increased burden of the payroll tax. The group which was considering the reform of the social services abandoned the notion of a social security tax on the grounds that it would merely allow a temporary reduction of other taxes before they returned to their previous level; in effect, there would merely be the imposition of a new tax.[26] The payroll tax was also fatally weakened by Labour's introduction of the Selective Employment Tax in 1964, which the Conservative opposition was pledged to repeal. The logic of the SET was different, based on the assumption that the key to productivity growth was a shift of labour from services into manufacturing, which would be encouraged by a tax on service employment.[27] Nevertheless, it would be politically difficult to repeal the SET and replace it by a general tax on employment. The most that could be advocated was an increase in employers' National Insurance contributions to 7·5 per cent of labour costs, which amounted to a marginal reform of the existing fiscal system rather than a fundamental change in the structure.[28]

Attention turned in another direction: a new indirect tax on sales, turnover or value added. There was initially considerable scepticism, for direct taxes had been reduced by the Conservative governments in the 1950s and early 1960s, so that it could be argued that the balance of taxation was already shifting and incentives being provided. Obviously, an increase in the cost of living would hit the poor and those on fixed incomes, and would provide political capital for Labour to criticize as socially divisive. The existing purchase tax also had the advantage of administrative convenience, for it was collected from 70,000 wholesalers; any replacement would be more complicated and impose strain on relations between the revenue authorities and taxpayers. The simplest tax to administer would be a flat rate duty on sales at the point of final sale, which would involve about 500,000 shopkeepers. Still more complicated was the German 'cascading' turnover tax, which imposed a tax each time a product changed hands throughout its passage from raw material to the final consumer. The disadvantage of such a tax, apart from administrative complexity, was that it would encourage vertical integration and monopoly, for goods were not liable to taxation so long as they remained within a single firm. The alternative was the French system of value added tax which had its own administrative complexities.[29]

No definite decision had been made by the Conservative government about the replacement of the existing purchase tax before its defeat in 1964, when the context was changed both by Labour's radical agenda of tax reform and by the need to find a replacement to the payroll tax in the Conservative 'tax package'. A value added tax offered at least a partial improvement upon reliance on taxation of profits, for it would fall on profits plus labour costs. There was also the advantage that VAT could be refunded on exports, unlike the payroll tax; it would therefore be less harmful to the competitive position of British industry. There was, above all, confidence that a shift in the relative importance of direct and indirect taxes offered the great attraction of restoring buoyancy to the tax system. The argument was that

> increased revenue for bigger public spending would be generated by the buoyancy of taxes which people did not expect to be cut (mainly indirect taxes). At the same time, other taxes (mainly direct) could be cut periodically . . . this would have the effect over the years of shifting the tax burden from direct to indirect taxes.

Moreover, indirect taxes were 'less damaging than the deadening effect of heavy direct taxation on energy, enterprise and efficiency'. The introduction of VAT would therefore provide the basis for a major reform of the rest of the tax system, permitting a reduction in personal and company taxation. The choice of VAT might well have been encouraged by a desire to conform to the tax system emerging in the EEC, but the shift to indirect taxes had domestic origins quite apart from a desire to enter the Common Market. The decision to introduce VAT would also, of course, have a major disadvantage: it would increase the cost of living, and impose a new burden on members of society who would not

benefit from cuts in personal taxes. It was crucial to introduce
further changes to the fiscal system in order to preserve the sense
of equity and justice which underwrote consent and legitimacy. An
opportunity state for some should not entail harm to others.[30]

## IV

The creation of an opportunity state begs an important question:
what were the best incentives to offer, in order to encourage what
type of opportunity? The ability to accumulate a small capital was
seen as a greater incentive than income, and it was necessary to
allow salaried and professional men to accumulate a modest
capital sum. The aim, therefore, was to encourage the
establishment of new, modest fortunes rather than, as at present,
the survival of old money which was protected by trusts. Such a
change in the pattern of wealth distribution, it was assumed,
would release enterprise from the dead hand of accumulated
capital. This ambition was a constant theme in debates on
taxation, and produced a number of divergent, highly contested
solutions.

One proposal had been debated since the reintroduction of the
income tax in 1842 and was finally adopted in 1907: the
differential taxation of unearned income from property and
investments (which arose 'spontaneously' from accumulated
assets) and earned income from trades, professions and
employment (which were 'precarious' and disappeared in ill-
health or unemployment). It was argued that anyone in receipt of
an 'earned' income needed to save in order to provide security for
retirement and for their dependants after their death, unlike
'unearned' income which was based upon an underlying asset
which survived. The advocates of differential taxation of income
were not opposed to the accumulation of capital but aimed to
encourage it on the part of those actively engaged as risk-takers in
trade and the professions.[31] But it seemed to members of the
Conservative tax committees of the 1960s that differentiation was
no longer working: far from encouraging enterprise and
dynamism, it was frustrating risk-takers. High levels of income tax
were held to prevent individuals from exercising their fundamental
right to accumulate capital, which was an integral part of

Conservative philosophy and the best way of creating incentives and enterprise. In order to allow an ever-widening circle of people to acquire capital, it was necessary to reduce income tax and to remove the differential against investment income which 'falls upon the income from savings and thus penalises the very virtues that we seek to encourage'.[32]  This was readily accepted; what was *not* accepted was the proposed means of making good the loss of revenue – an annual tax on wealth or capital which was, in the opinion of Angus Maude, 'really the keystone of the arch'.[33]

It seemed perverse to encourage a wider ownership of capital, and then to tax it. The proposal did, however, have a logic. A report by the National Economic Development Council felt that such a tax 'may have a useful role in a major review of taxation related to a programme of growth'. The case was that a tax on wealth fell on the value of assets rather than their yield, so that it would encourage a shift into higher-risk securities; it would also permit the replacement of the surtax on incomes and provide recipients of earned income with an incentive to greater efforts.[34] This argument appealed to some members of the Conservative committees, who wished 'to tax capital in future, in such a way as to create the conditions for the accumulation of capital', so releasing the incentive to *create* wealth by making it easier to save out of income. The existing levels of income tax were 'near farcical in any system which does not actively regard private incomes as evil', in effect giving an advantage to those who currently held capital which was protected by trusts. The Conservative Party should not, it was argued, merely defend existing wealth. An annual capital or wealth tax would reduce income tax rates and so allow accumulation; other taxes on capital could be moderated by removing the differential against investment income, reducing the capital gains tax introduced by Labour, and reducing death duties. The total burden of taxation on capital would not be reduced so much as redistributed in a way which would encourage accumulation. The wealth tax was also politically necessary in order to offset the concessions to high incomes and *rentiers*. The restructured fiscal regime would, William Clark argued, 'encourage capital to be more productively used' by offering an incentive to invest in high-risk or -yield stock, for the underlying capital would be taxed regardless of its yield, and the income derived from the asset would be less heavily taxed than in the past.

The present structure of tax acted as a disincentive to risk-taking . . . the object of the shift was to place more burden on the static existing accumulations of wealth and thus to avoid the present concentration of the burden of tax on the creation of wealth.

The overall result, argued Nigel Lawson, was a distinct improvement, for 'the present tax structure redistributed wealth but did it illogically. Their proposals would do it logically.'[35]

It was one thing to be logical; it was another to be politically acceptable, particularly when the economic case was open to question. It was doubtful whether a modest reduction in the marginal rate of tax on earned income would affect enough people to make a difference. The impact of the wealth tax on investment decisions was also likely to be small, since most assets were held by the elderly who were more interested in security than risk. Any economic benefits would probably be modest, and could just as easily be achieved less contentiously by ending the distinction between earned and unearned income, or a change in the limit of surtax. The case for a wealth tax made more sense as a measure of social reform designed to reduce the high degree of inequality of wealth and to attack a property-owning gerontocracy.[36] Although some Conservatives supported such reform as a means of generating opportunity, it had a suspiciously socialist tinge. Bruce Millan, a Labour MP, advocated a wealth tax as a means of producing a 'radical distribution of wealth'. Rees-Mogg was horrified, and appealed to William Pitt's maxim that taxation should fall on the fruit and not the tree. Income taxes and the capital gains tax fell on the fruits of property, but a capital tax was

a direct invasion of the right to hold private property without disturbance . . . such a tax goes against what I believe to be an essential element in our Party's character . . . The essence of this tax is that it is an annual capital levy. The Conservative Party has always opposed capital levies and could hardly introduce a regular and progressive one without gross inconsistency.

The capital levy had, of course, been a central plank in Labour policy at the end of the First World War, which aimed to create an alliance of active producers against passive *rentiers*. It had been revived in a muted form by Hugh Dalton in 1947. The measure had dubious antecedents, and Rees-Mogg feared that it 'creates a powerful agency of socialism' and egalitarianism, offering an open invitation to Labour to introduce a more far-reaching socialist fiscal policy. He also doubted the economic benefits of encouraging high-yield, high-risk investment.

> We wanted to encourage people to invest in long term schemes which often involve locking capital up for a considerable time before yielding a return . . . a wealth tax would encourage investment that was highly speculative and encourage people to hold their capital in relatively liquid form switching it frequently.[37]

Certainly, it would be difficult to convince the electorate that the benefits of capital ownership could be extended by the seemingly perverse means of taxing capital. The committee was split, and the shadow cabinet eventually abandoned the wealth tax in 1968. It would, as John Biffen remarked, 'seriously shatter the political morale of a Conservative administration', and Macleod felt that 'the important things on which the Conservative Party ought to be concentrating attention were earning, owning, saving and learning. A proposal to introduce a wealth tax would distract from these objectives.'[38]

The attempt to encourage personal accumulation of modest amounts of capital as a major incentive in an opportunity state came into conflict with the existing structure of company taxation, which dated from Dalton's budget of 1947. A higher rate of tax was imposed on distributed profits, which it was assumed would either be spent on extravagant consumption or accumulated as passive *rentier* capital. Retention of profits could then be encouraged in order to provide funds for investment, which would lead to growth. Taxation was, therefore, biased in favour of companies, for retained profits paid less than dividends in the hands of shareholders, which allowed them to increase their assets and build new plant, unlike individuals who were prevented from accumulating capital by high levels of personal taxation. The policy was open to criticism, for individual incentives were blunted and it was by no means clear that there was a correlation between retention and growth.[39] Distribution was not necessarily harmful, for a large proportion of dividends went to institutional shareholders who reinvested, and retention could lead to the accumulation of assets in large firms which perpetuated old and inefficient industrial concerns and distorted the capital market as an allocator of resources. The technical complexities of company taxation implied a deep divide between two views of society. Labour wished to cut off the flow of income to private owners of assets as a means of preventing the accumulation of large fortunes, and preferred to leave investment decisions to the deliberations of corporate managers rather than to the external market. The introduction of capital gains tax in 1964 complemented the differential taxation of distributed profits, for it taxed any gains realized by shareholders from the sale of shares whose value had risen as a result of the retention of profits. By contrast, the Conservative approach was more inclined to favour allocation by the market, without any attempt to divert the flow of dividends away from shareholders; there was also scepticism about the capital gains tax. Growth was more likely to be encouraged by offering incentives to the accumulation and investment of small amounts of capital, rather than by encouraging retention in existing corporations. The outcome of the debate was to recommend the introduction of the German system of split-rate corporation taxation of 1953, which the Neumark report proposed as the model for the European Economic Community. Undistributed profits should pay a tax of 45 per cent which was equivalent to a rate of 15 per cent on distributed profits and an income tax of 30 per cent in the hands of shareholders. The result would be a reduction in the tax on distributed profits and an increase on undistributed profits, so removing the incentive to plough back earnings into reserves and exposing them to the discipline of the market. A technical change in company taxation was, therefore, an integral part of the vision of an opportunity state which would permit greater incentives and faster growth.[40]

## V

The tax package sought to achieve three aims: a reduction in the proportion of taxation falling on profits and an increase in the proportion on costs in order to increase efficiency; less reliance upon the finance of welfare from general taxation on profits and income which implied a subsidy to employment; and a lower rate of taxation of earnings and distributed profits which discouraged investment. Some of the more radical proposals were abandoned, with the replacement of the payroll tax by higher employers' contributions and the dropping of the wealth tax. Nevertheless, it was hoped that the aims would still be achieved by the introduction of VAT and the removal of differential taxation on investment income and distributed profits, so that it was easier to accumulate and retain a small fortune. Buoyancy would be restored to the tax system, and high marginal rates of income tax reduced in order to encourage incentives. There was, however, a major problem: how to deal with those members of society who would be hit by VAT without benefiting from lower income tax.

The aim was not to favour one class against another, defined in terms of the working class or middle class, but to favour the energetic and enterprising in order to create faster growth which would benefit everyone. The tax package rested upon a desire to change the basis of British society from equality to equity, from stasis to dynamism.

> It is not our aim to favour any single broad section of the community at the expense of another (where the section of community is defined along conventional lines – e.g. middle income earners, pensioners, lower paid workers). Our intention is to favour the energetic, resourceful, enterprising and hard-working against the lazy, cautious and complacent.[41]

It was hoped that such a policy would offer incentives to those who created the nation's wealth in the middle and higher ranges of income. The result would be faster growth so that everyone would be better off in the longer term as a result of a new climate of competition, efficiency and productivity, which was the only way to help people on lower incomes. 'The policy of trying to improve living conditions by a more even distribution of income has, in our view, been pressed over recent years to an extreme at which it becomes self-defeating.'[42]

It was important, however, that no one should suffer in the short term. Price increases would hit everyone, but those who paid little or no direct tax would not have any recompense. There was a serious danger that the tax package was unbalanced as a result of both the replacement of the payroll tax by VAT, which hit the poorest members of society, and the rejection of a wealth tax as compensation for the reduction in direct taxes. In order to preserve some balance in the reforms, it was necessary to offer welfare benefits to those who would be hit by the shift towards indirect taxation, which had major implications for the future structure of the welfare state.

> A package of tax reforms designed to increase incentives to those who produce the Nation's wealth cannot at the same time make adequate provision for those who must receive a greater share than they earn, except through a departure from the principle of universality. The attempt to adjust the balance would otherwise dissipate the very incentives we seek to introduce.[43]

The suggestion that universalism should be replaced by selectivity was crucial to the viability of the scheme: without it there could not be equity for the poor, for compensation by the payment of a higher level of universal benefits would destroy the finances of the tax package.

The package of reforms which emerged by the time of the Conservatives' return to power in 1970 was coherent and comprehensive. It offered an opportunity state based on economic growth and incentives for the accumulation of small capital, in which no one would lose. It claimed to offer an alternative to socialist intervention in the economy through bureaucratic planning; the aim was to change the background against which decisions were taken. Buoyancy and flexibility would be restored to the tax system so that chancellors were freed from the constraints of ever-increasing rates of income tax, which would be demoted from its pinnacle and reduced to a 'smaller, more reputable and less harmful tax'. Growth would be encouraged and buoyancy restored to the tax system so that there could be both reductions in tax rates and a higher level of welfare spending. The result would be beneficial for all:

> This does not mean that in the long run we will be able to spend less on socially desirable objectives. On the contrary, we shall be able to spend more. Once a proper balance can be re-established in the community between the share of our resources taken by the Government and the share which is left for the people, we shall be able to achieve a higher rate of growth. Out of the greater national income generated in this way we shall be able to spend more, not less, without at the same time any of the strains to which the present policy gives rise.[44]

The policy was not, therefore, based upon a crude anti-statism which developed in the 1980s, and it tried – in Rodney Lowe's words – to link competition and compassion.[45] But would the proposals be implemented?

The package started to unravel. Abandonment of the wealth tax meant – as Macleod remarked – that it was not possible to afford all the 'plums' initially proposed (abolition of the differential taxation of unearned income, reduction in death duties and introduction of a split rate of company taxation). The room for manoeuvre was further limited by the pledge to replace the SET, and by a faltering in economic growth. Keith Joseph in particular was alarmed that the revised package of reforms concentrated too much relief on larger investment incomes, with 'very little benefit to the upper-medium earned incomes, which were the ones that affected middle management'.[46] He was concerned that the package would be interpreted as benefiting the wealthy investor, and regretted the rejection of the wealth tax which 'gave a morally defensible package in a way the present package did not'.[47] Joseph had a point, for a computer estimate of the impact of the package commissioned by the Conservative Research Department produced a worrying result: the tax cuts would favour the rich, welfare benefits would assist the poor, but family men on an income of £560 to £1,750 would lose. These middle-class family men were, of course, crucial to the electoral success of the party, and were precisely the group which it hoped to attract to participate in a new, dynamic opportunity state.[48]

The demise of the payroll tax meant an increase in the significance both of VAT and of cuts in government expenditure. The tax system would be less buoyant than anticipated, for VAT would not produce revenue for several years, and the shift of the funding of social services from general taxation was slight. The immediate prospect of a reduction in direct taxes was therefore remote, and meanwhile there would be unpopularity from rising prices; not only would the poor be hit, but prices were, in the view of Maudling, what mattered most to women. There was therefore an even greater need for selective help for those who would suffer from rising prices and cuts in government expenditure. The rejection of universalism was all the more necessary, but there was a lack of serious thought and commitment to such a radical change in policy.[49] Despite the realization that selectivity was a prerequisite for tax reform, the policy group (where Keith Joseph and Margaret Thatcher were leading figures) when considering social services backed away from this hard choice.[50]

There was a natural tendency in considering tax revisions to draw up a balance sheet of gains and losses for particular sections of society. The package was, in Maudling's opinion, far too theoretical and did not pay sufficient attention to the effects on particular classes of taxpayers.[51] But such an approach was, in the opinion of Brendon Sewill, mistaken: the only result of ensuring that no one was much worse or better off would be to return to the present structure of taxation.[52] Rather, what was needed was a fundamental revision which would affect attitudes to work, and raise labour productivity. 'This reform of taxation was only worthwhile', remarked Arthur Cockfield, 'on the basis that the whole economy would change. If attitudes remained the same, then the reform would have failed.'[53] It was precisely the psychological impact of tax reforms which Edward Heath doubted. Why not, he wondered, achieve the same results by cutting public expenditure, introducing savings schemes and increasing wages?[54]

Already by 1970, policy was shifting from hard decisions about the future shape of taxation and the welfare state to easier options. The tax package offered a route to economic growth from which everyone would benefit in the long run, with immediate losers recompensed by selective benefits. The accumulation of capital by the moderately prosperous was linked to the creation of efficiency through changes in the financing of social services. What happened after 1970 was a redefinition of the connection between, on the one hand, efficiency and growth and, on the other, encouragement of property-ownership. Attention turned to the encouragement of home ownership with an extension of mortgage tax relief, and the development of pensions and savings schemes with tax breaks. By such means, small accumulations of property were encouraged but nothing was done to foster growth or to improve the buoyancy of the tax system. Denationalization could also be utilized. The party had a commitment to privatization, but had been hampered by the problem of finding buyers: the answer was to offer shares to a large number of small investors. By such means, argued Sewill, a policy of savings and ownership would provide the basis for a new electoral strategy.

In electoral terms, one of the Conservative Party's biggest handicaps is that we are considered to be a party of the rich while Labour always rates best as 'the party most likely to look after all classes'. The theme of saving and ownership helps to fulfill the suggestion . . . that we should turn this weakness to our advantage by showing that our escape mechanism – home ownership, occupational pensions, the security of savings – can be brought within the reach of all.[55]

Unlike the proposals of the tax package, the strategy was a blatant appeal to the self-interest of the middling groups with scant regard either for the creation of efficiency or for the well-being of the poor. Subsidies to owner occupation were complemented by increases in council rents which did nothing to target those most in need, who were suffering from the impact of VAT. The policy on selectivity was, as Rodney Lowe has argued, confused, and the aim of compensating the poor was a casualty.[56] The ambitions of the tax package were not achieved in the 1970s and the hopes of an inclusive policy, in which everyone would gain from higher growth and resources which would be available for a high standard of social services, were disappointed. The package also placed a great deal of stress upon improved utilization of labour and increased productivity. It was realized that a reform of trade union law would also be necessary, but the consequent tensions would be reduced by the proceeds of higher productivity which would permit higher wages. In the event, reform of trade union law was disassociated from the strategy of raising productivity by means of reallocating the finance of welfare to labour costs, and such reform was more easily portrayed as an attack on workers' rights. The demise of the tax package after 1970 meant that major issues were unresolved. By 1979, the economic and fiscal situation was worse, and the subsequent policy rested on a crude populist rhetoric of tax cutting which was innocent of the aspirations of the 1960s. Ironically, it was Mrs Thatcher as much as anyone who blocked the radical reform of the welfare system which might have created a more balanced package. The result of this earlier caution was that when she came to power she pursued a vision of an enterprise society which was less integrative, and showed less concern for casualties, than the opportunity state proposed in the 1960s.

*Notes*

1  The phrase is William Rees-Mogg's in Conservative Party Archive, Bodleian Library (hereafter CPA), CRD 3/7/6/5, William Rees-Mogg to James Douglas, 26 June 1965. I would like to thank Rodney Lowe for his comments on an earlier draft.

2  *The Campaign Guide 1959: The Unique Political Reference Book* (London, 1959), 19.

3  CPA, CRD 3/7/26/3, TPC/62/2a, Taxation Policy Committee 1963, 'Stable Savings', 30 September 1963.

4  For the concept of a 'fiscal constitution', see G. Brennan and J. M. Buchanan, *The Powers to Tax: Analytical Foundations of a Fiscal Constitution* (Cambridge, 1980).

5  These comments are based on the arguments of my forthcoming book, *The Ransom of Riches: Taxation and Politics in Britain since 1842*; aspects of the analysis are contained in 'Payment and Participation: Welfare and State Formation in Britain, 1900–1951', *Past and Present* 150 (1995), and 'How to Pay for the War: State, Society and Taxation in Britain, 1917–24', *English Historical Review* 111 (1996). The notion of the neutrality of the British state, and the attempt to exclude economics from politics, follows R. McKibbin, 'Why was there no Marxism in Great Britain?', *English Historical Review* 99 (1984), reprinted in *The Ideologies of Class: Social Relations in Britain, 1880–1950* (Oxford, 1990).

6  For a brief account of the review of 1964 to 1970, see J. Ramsden, *The Making of Conservative Party Policy: The Conservative Research Department since 1929* (London, 1980).

7  CPA, CRD 3/7/26/1, 'Taxation Policy, 1960 and After', 18 January 1960.

8  CPA, CRD 3/7/26/2, TPC (60)5, minutes of third meeting of Taxation Policy Committee, 30 June 1960; indeed, the starting point for payment of surtax had not been raised since 1920, when it was set at £2,000.

9  CPA, CRD 3/7/26/2, memorandum by James Douglas, 13 July 1960.

10  CPA, CRD 3/7/26/2, TPC (60)7, minutes of fourth meeting of Taxation Policy Committee, 15 July 1960.

11  Ibid.

12  CPA, CRD 3/7/26/26, Economist Intelligence Unit Report, 'Comparative Studies in Taxation: United Kingdom, France, West Germany, Sweden and USA: A Summary Report', April 1967. See also the comments on the lack of buoyancy of the tax system in CRD 3/7/6/1, EPG/66/44, Economic Policy Group, first draft of Swinton Discussion Weekend document, 2 June 1967 and CRD 3/7/26/38, EPG/66/114, Economic Policy Group, first draft of the final report on the reform of taxation, 16 January 1969.

[13] CPA, CRD 3/7/26/3, 'Expenditure and Taxation', 30 August 1960.

[14] There is a long list of discussion papers: see CPA, CRD 3/7/26/3, TPC(62)4, 'A Payroll Tax' [undated]; TPC(62)5, 'A Payroll Tax', 24 July 1961; 'Note on the French Payroll Tax', 27 July 1961; TPC(62)7, 'A Payroll Tax?', 27 September 1961; TPC(62)6, 'Indirect Taxes', 26 September 1961; J. Douglas to B. Sewill, 27 October 1961; TPC(62)12, 'Note on Payroll Tax: David Dear, 1 November 1961'; 'Payroll Tax: A Rejoinder by James Douglas' [undated]; TPC(62)13, 'Taxation Policy 1962', final draft, 1 November 1961 and TPC(62)14, redraft of section on payroll tax, 7 November 1961. For the Subcommittee on the Structure of Direct Taxation, see CRD 2/10/17, 'Note on how to Finance the Social Services for Discussion on 12 April 1961'; 'Note on a Payroll Tax', 7 June 1961; 'Note on a Sales Tax for Discussion on 28 June 1961'; 'The Need for a Corporation Tax and a Graduated Income Tax', R. Gresham Cooke, 23 November 1960; 'A Corporation Tax', 1 December 1960.

[15] CPA, CRD 3/7/6/1, A. Cockfield at eighth meeting, Economic Policy Group, 13 April 1967.

[16] The discussion of welfare is covered by R. Lowe, 'Social Policy', in S. Ball and A. Seldon (eds.), *The Heath Government: A Reappraisal* (London, 1996). The present chapter complements Lowe's discussion of social policy, and I am grateful to him for making it available and for his perceptive comments.

[17] CPA, CRD 3/7/26/26, Economist Intelligence Unit Report, 'Comparative Studies in Taxation'; S. Steinmo, 'Political Institutions and Tax Policy in the United States, Sweden and Britain', *World Politics* 41 (1988–9), 527–31.

[18] CPA, CRD 3/7/6/6, 'Swinton Policy Weekend 1967. Report', J. Douglas, 26 September 1967.

[19] CPA, CRD 3/7/6/9, PG/8/65/7, 'An Agenda', William Rees-Mogg [undated].

[20] CPA, CRD 3/7/6/10, PG/8/A/65/34, Policy Group on Future Economic Policy, Sub-Group A, Taxation, draft report, 23 September 1965; see also CRD 3/7/6/9, PG/8/65/28, third meeting of Policy Group on Future Economic Policy, 30 June 1965; CRD 3/7/6/1, EPG/66/44, Economic Policy Group, first draft, Swinton Discussion Weekend document, 2 June 1967.

[21] CPA, CRD 3/7/26/38, EPG/66/114, Economic Policy Group, first draft of the final report on the reform of taxation, 16 January 1969.

[22] CPA, CRD 3/7/6/10, PG/8/A/65/34, Policy Group on Future Economic Policy, Sub-Group A, Taxation, draft report, 23 September 1965.

[23] CPA, CRD 3/7/6/1, EPG/66/33, A. Cockfield to eighth meeting of Economic Policy Group, 13 April 1967.

24  CPA, CRD 3/7/26/3, TPC(62)4, 5, 7, 12 and J. Douglas to B. Sewill, 27 October 1961, 'Payroll Tax: A Rejoinder', J. Douglas [undated]. CRD 2/10/17, 'Note on how to Finance the Social Services for Discussion on 12 April 1961'; 'Note on a Payroll Tax', 7 June 1961. CRD 3/7/6/11, PG/8/B/65/2, Future Economic Policy Sub-Group B, 'Effects of Method of Financing Social Security Services', J. Douglas, 22 March 1965; PG/8/B/65/4, Notes on Second Meeting of Sub-Group B; PG/8/B/65/28, Policy Group on Future Economic Policy Sub-Group B, interim report from Sub-Group B to main group, 30 June 1965; PG/8/B/65/9, K. Joseph to E. Heath, 1 April 1965; CRD 3/7/6/1, EPG/66/43, tenth meetings of Economic Policy Group, 11 May 1967.

25  The dangers of the payroll tax are discussed in the material cited in the previous note; it might also be noted that there was concern in the USA that the payroll tax had been the most rapidly growing tax since 1945. There was little resistance to the tax, for it was assumed by the taxpayers that it offered benefits; and it was considered to be less onerous than the income tax. In fact, about half the employers' contribution fell on workers, and it was regressive for there were no exemptions. See J. A. Brittain, *The Payroll Tax for Social Security* (Brookings Institute, Washington DC, 1972).

26  CPA, CRD 3/7/6/11, PG/8/B/12, notes of the fourth meeting of Future Economic Policy Sub-Group B, 14 April 1965, and PG/8/B/17, notes of the sixth meeting of Future Economic Policy Sub-Group B, 12 May 1965; CRD 3/7/26/33, PG/13/65/41, fourth meeting of Policy Group on National Insurance Scheme, 6 May 1965; PG/13/65/56, seventh meeting of the Policy Group on National Insurance Scheme, 7 October 1965.

27  N. Kaldor, *Causes of the Slow Rate of Economic Growth of the United Kingdom* (Cambridge, 1966) provides the argument for a reduction in the service sector as a key to growth; he was adviser to the Chancellor of the Exchequer.

28  CPA, CRD 3/7/26/38, EPG/66/114, Economic Policy Group, first draft of the final report on the reform of taxation, 16 January 1969.

29  *The Campaign Guide 1964: The Unique Political Reference Book* (London, 1964), 35; CPA, CRD 2/10/17, Conservative Parliamentary Finance Committee, Subcommittee on the Structure of Taxation, 'Note on a Sales Tax for Discussion on 28 June 1961'; CRD 3/7/26/3, TPC(62)1, 'Indirect Taxation', 18 May 1961; TPC(62)2, 'Indirect Taxation', 19 June 1961; TPC(62)6, 'Indirect Taxes', 26 September 1961.

30  CPA, CRD 3/7/6/10, PG/8/A/65/1, notes on the first meeting of Sub-Group A; PG/8/A/65/28, 'Note by Nigel Lawson on Value Added Tax', 9 July 1965; PG/8/A/65/34, Policy Group on Future Economic Policy, Sub-Group A, Taxation, draft report, 23 September 1965; CRD

3/7/6/1, EPG/66/33, eighth meeting, Economic Policy Group, 13 April 1967; EPG/66/43, tenth meeting, Economic Policy Group, 11 May 1967; EPG/66/44, Economic Policy Group, first draft, Swinton Discussion Weekend document, 2 June 1967; CRD 3/7/6/3, EPG/66/87, Economic Policy Group, minutes of twenty-fifth meeting, 13 June 1968; EPG/66/103, Economic Policy Group, minutes of twenty-seventh meeting, 11 July 1968; EPG/66/85, Economic Policy Group, revised report on the reform of taxation, 30 May 1968; EPG/66/95, Economic Policy Group, 'Relative Merits of the Value Added Tax and the Retail Sales Tax: A Note by Professor A. R. Prest', 4 July 1968; CRD 3/7/26/36, minutes of the working conference on VAT, 16–18 June 1969. On the connection between VAT and profits taxation, see A. R. Prest, 'A Value Added Tax Coupled with a Reduction in Taxes on Business Profits', *British Tax Review* (September–December 1963), 336–47. Prest (who was a member of the subcommittee) was sceptical about VAT and preferred to extend the purchase tax and reform company taxation by confining it to undistributed profits or by imputing retained profits to shareholders and taxing them as income tax.

[31] There is an extensive nineteenth-century literature on the subject: most of the arguments were rehearsed in PP 1852 IX, *Select Committee on the Income and Property Tax* and PP 1861 VII, *Select Committee on Income and Property Tax*; for a discussion of the debate, see Daunton, *Ransom of Riches*.

[32] CPA, CRD 3/7/26/38, EPG/66/114, Economic Policy Group, first draft of the final report on the reform of taxation, 16 January 1969.

[33] CPA, CRD, 3/7/6/9, PG/8/65/34, Policy Group on Future Economic Policy, sixth meeting, 27 October 1965.

[34] National Economic Development Council, *Conditions Favourable to Faster Growth*; the case is assessed in R. C. Tress, 'A Wealth Tax is a Wealth Tax', *British Tax Review* (November–December 1963), and A. Peacock, 'Economics of a Net Wealth Tax for Britain', *British Tax Review* (November–December 1963).

[35] CPA, CRD 3/7/6/9, PG/8/65/28, second meeting of Policy Group on Future Economic Policy, 30 June 1965; CRD 3/7/6/10, PG/8/A/65/8, 'Note for Sub-Group A' [undated]; PG/8/A/65/10, third meeting of Sub-Group A, 14 April 1965; PG/8/A/65/12, 'The Taxation of Capital', F. A. Cockfield [undated]; PG/8/A/14, fourth meeting of Sub-Group A, 28 April 1965; PG/8/A/65/34, 'Policy Group on Future Economic Policy, Sub-Group A, Taxation, Draft Report', 23 September 1965.

[36] Peacock, 'Economics of a Net Wealth Tax', 396–7, 399; Tress, 'A Wealth Tax is a Wealth Tax', 406–7; J. R. S. Revell, 'Assets and Age', *Bulletin of the Oxford Institute of Statistics* 24 (1962); B. Millan, *Taxes for a Prosperous Society* (Fabian Research Series, 234).

37 CPA, CRD 3/7/6/9, PG/8/65/26, 'Comments by Mr William Rees-Mogg on Sub-Group A's Interim Report to the Main Group on Personal Taxation', 28 June 1965; PG/8/65/28, Policy Group on Future Economic Policy, third meeting, 30 June 1965; CRD 3/7/6/10, PG/8A/65/35, 'Comments by William Rees-Mogg on Sub-Group A's Draft Report', 27 September 1965. On the debate on the capital levy, see R. C. Whiting, 'The Labour Party, Capitalism and the National Debt, 1915–24', in P. J. Waller (ed.), *Politics and Social Change in Modern Britain* (London, 1987); and *idem*, 'Taxation and the Working Class, 1915–24', *Historical Journal* 33 (1990); Daunton, 'How to Pay for the War'.

38 CPA, CRD 3/7/10, PG/8/A/65/27, W. J. Biffen, 7 July 1965; CRD 3/7/6/3, EPG/66/87, minutes of twenty-fifth meeting, Economic Policy Group, 13 June 1968.

39 R. C. Whiting, 'Taxation', in H. Mercer et al. (eds.), *Labour Governments and Private Industry* (Edinburgh, 1992); I. M. D. Little, 'Higgledy-piggledy Growth', *Bulletin of the Oxford Institute of Statistics* 24 (1962).

40 CPA, CRD 3/7/6/3, EPG/66/85, 'Revised Report on the Reform of Taxation', 30 May 1968; EPG/66/87, Economic Policy Group, minutes of twenty-fifth meeting, 13 June 1968; EPG/66/88, 'The Reform of Corporation Tax and Capital Gains Tax', J. F. Chown, 17 June 1968; EPG/66/90, 'Revised Report on the Reform of Taxation. Note by Mr Cockfield. II The "Balance" of the Package: Investment Income – the Taxation of Companies', 18 June 1968; CRD 3/7/6/10, PG/8/A/65/3, 'Notes on Company Taxation', A. R. Prest, 23 March 1965; PG/8/A/65/7, 'The Taxation of Companies', A. Cockfield [undated]; PG/8/A/65/34, 'Policy Group on Future Economic Policy, Sub-Group A, Taxation', 23 September 1965; PG/8/A/65/17 and 18, minutes of sixth meeting of Sub-Group A, 12 May 1965; CRD 3/7/26/38, EPG/66/114, Economic Policy Group, first draft of the final report on the reform of taxation, 16 January 1969.

41 CPA, CRD 3/7/6/3, EPG/66/85, revised report on the reform of taxation, 30 May 1968; see also speech by Macleod to the Institute of Directors in 1969, CRD 3/7/26/38.

42 CPA, CRD 3/7/26/38, EPG/66/114, Economic Policy Group, first draft of the final report on the reform of taxation, 16 January 1969.

43 CPA, CRD 3/7/6/3, EPG/66/85, revised report on the reform of taxation, 30 May 1968.

44 CPA, CRD 3/7/26/38, EPG/66/114, Economic Policy Group, first draft of the final report on the reform of taxation, 16 January 1969.

45 Lowe, 'Social Policy', in Ball and Seldon (eds.), *The Heath Government: A Reappraisal*, 203, 213.

46 CPA, CRD 3/7/6/3, EPG/66/93, Economic Policy Group, minutes of

twenty-sixth meeting, 27 June 1968; see also EPG/66/97, 'Note by Mr Cockfield', 8 July 1968.

47  CPA, CRD 3/7/6/3, EPG/66/108, Economic Policy Group, twenty-eighth meeting, 26 July 1968.

48  CPA, CRD 3/7/26/41, Douglas to Heath, 20 May 1968, cited in Lowe, 'Social Policy', 196. For the computer estimates, see CRD 3/7/6/3, EPG/66/107 and 109; the results were discussed in EPG/66/108, Economic Policy Group, minutes of twenty-eighth meeting, 26 July 1968.

49  CPA, CRD 3/7/6/4, EPG/66/115, Economic Policy Group, minutes of thirty-first meeting, 3 December 1968; EPG/66/119, minutes of thirty-third meeting, 6 January 1969; EPG/66/121, thirty-fourth meeting, 30 January 1969; CRD 3/7/6/7, R. Maudling to J. Douglas, 3 July 1968; CRD 3/7/6/8, E. Heath to B. Reading, 7 February 1969; R. Maudling to I. Macleod, 13 March 1970; CRD 3/7/26/37, 'Tax Package. The Development of our Thoughts in Opposition', 27 July 1970; 'Tax Package. The Main Proposals and our Commitments', 29 July 1970.

50  CPA, CRD 3/7/6/11, PG/8/B/65/9, K. Joseph to E. Heath, 1 April 1965; PG/8/B/65/11, 'Note for Mrs Thatcher and Mr Geoffrey Howe: Sub-Group B's Discussion of the Economic Effects of the Present Method of Financing the Social Security Services', J. Douglas, 15 April 1965; PG/8/B/65/12, notes of the fourth meeting held 14 April 1965; PG/8/B/65/17, notes of the sixth meeting of Sub-Group B, 12 May 1965.

51  CPA, CRD 3/7/6/7, R. Maudling to J. Douglas, 3 July 1968.

52  CPA, CRD 3/7/6/7, B. Sewill to I. Macleod, 8 July 1968.

53  CPA, CRD 3/7/6/4, EPG/66/121, Economic Policy Group, minutes of thirty-fourth meeting, 30 January 1969.

54  Ibid. and CRD 3/7/6/8, E. Heath to B. Reading, 7 February 1969.

55  CPA, CRD 3/7/26/38, 'Saving and Ownership', B. Sewill, 3 January 1969.

56  Lowe, 'Social Policy', 199–205.

# Bibliography

Abrams, M., and R. Rose, *Must Labour Lose?* (Harmondsworth, 1960).

Addison, P., *The Road to 1945: British Politics and the Second World War* (London, 1975).

——, *Churchill on the Home Front 1900–1955* (London, 1992).

Adonis, A., *Making Aristocracy Work: The Peerage and the Political System in Britain, 1884–1914* (Oxford, 1993).

—— and T. Hames (eds.), *A Conservative Revolution? The Thatcher–Reagan Decade in Perspective* (Manchester, 1994).

Anderson, G. D., *Fascists, Communists and the National Government: Civil Liberties in Britain, 1931–1937* (Columbia, 1983).

Anderson, P., 'Problems of Socialist Strategy', in P. Anderson et al., *Towards Socialism* (London, 1965).

Atholl, Duchess of, *Women and Politics* (London, 1931).

Aughey, A., G. Jones, and W. Riches, *The Conservative Political Tradition in Britain and the United States* (London, 1992).

Ball, S., *Baldwin and the Conservative Party: The Crisis of 1929–1931* (New Haven and London, 1988).

—— (ed.), *Parliament and Politics in the Age of Baldwin and MacDonald* (London, 1992).

—— and A. Seldon (eds.), *The Heath Government: A Reappraisal* (London, 1996).

Banks, O., *Faces of Feminism* (Oxford, 1981).

Barnes, J., and D. Nicholson (eds.), *The Leo Amery Diaries*, I: *1896–1929* (London, 1980).

—— and A. Seldon, '1951–64: Thirteen Wasted Years?', *Contemporary Record* 1 (1987).

Bauman, Z., 'Sociology and Postmodernity', in P. Joyce (ed.), *Class* (Oxford Readers) (Oxford, 1995).

Beer, S., *Modern British Politics* (London, 1965).

Benney, M., and P. Geiss, 'Social Class and Politics in Greenwich', *British Journal of Sociology* 1 (1950).

Benney, M., et al., *How People Vote: A Study of Electoral Behaviour in Greenwich* (London, 1956).

Bentley, M., 'Liberal Toryism in the Twentieth Century', *Transactions of the Royal Historical Society* 6th ser, 4 (1994).

Bew, P., *Ideology and the Irish Question: Ulster Unionism and Irish Nationalism, 1912–1916* (Oxford, 1994).

Bhabba, H. (ed.), *Nation and Narration* (London, 1990).

Biagini, E. F., *Liberals, Retrenchment and Reform* (Cambridge, 1992).

—— and A. J. Reid (eds.), *Currents of Radicalism: Popular Radicalism, Organised Labour and Party Politics in Britain, 1850–1914* (Cambridge, 1991).

Birkenhead, Second Earl of, *The Life of F. E. Smith, First Earl of Birkenhead* (London, 1959).

Black, A., and S. Brooke, 'Labour and the Problem of Gender, 1951–1970' (forthcoming).

Blackaby, F. A. (ed.), *British Economic Policy 1960–74* (Cambridge, 1978).

Blackford, C., 'Wives and Citizens and Watchdogs of Equality: Post-War British Feminists', in J. Fyrth (ed.), *Labour's Promised Land? Culture and Society in Labour Britain, 1945–51* (London, 1995).

Blake, R., *Disraeli* (London, 1966).

——, *The Conservative Party from Peel to Churchill* (London, 1970).

——, *The Conservative Party from Peel to Thatcher* (London, 1985).

Booth, A., 'Britain in the 1930s: A Managed Economy?', *Economic History Review* 40 (1987).

Bowe, C. (ed.), *The Economics of Investment Subsidies* (London, 1976).

Boyce, D. G.,*The Irish Question and British Politics, 1868–1986* (London, 1988).

—— and J. Stubbs, 'F. S. Oliver, Lord Selborne and Federalism', *Journal of Imperial and Commonwealth History* 5 (1976).

Boyd, C. (ed.), *Speeches of the Right Honourable Joseph Chamberlain* (London 1913).

Brand, J., *The National Movement in Scotland* (London, 1979).

Brennan, G., and J. M. Buchanan, *The Powers to Tax: Analytical Foundations of a Fiscal Constitution* (Cambridge, 1980).

Brentford, Viscount, *Do We Need a Censor?* (London, 1929).

Briggs, A., *The Birth of Broadcasting* (London, 1961).

——, *The Golden Age of Wireless* (London, 1965).

Bristow, E., 'The Liberty and Property Defence League and Individualism', *Historical Journal* 18 (1975).

——, *Vice and Vigilance: Purity Movements in Britain since 1700* (Dublin, 1977).

Brittain, J. A., *The Payroll Tax for Social Security* (Brookings Institute, Washington DC, 1972).

Brittan, S., *Steering the Economy* (Harmondsworth, 1971) .

Brooke, S. J., 'Problems of "Socialist Planning": Evan Durbin and the Labour Government of 1945', *Historical Journal* 34 (1991).

——, *Labour's War: The Labour Party during the Second World War* (Oxford, 1992).

Brotherstone, T., 'Does Red Clydeside Matter Any More?', in R. Duncan and A. McIvor (eds.), *Militant Workers: Labour and Class Conflict on the Clyde 1900–1950* (Edinburgh, 1992).

Brown, S. J., 'Outside the Covenant: The Scottish Presbyterian Churches and Irish Immigration, 1922–38', *Innes Review* 62 (Spring 1991).

Buckland, P., *Irish Unionism*, I: *The Anglo-Irish and the New Ireland, 1885–1922* (Dublin, 1972).

Burk, K., *The First Privatisation: The Politicians, the City and the Denationalisation of Steel* (London, 1988).

Butler, D. E., *The British General Election of 1951* (London, 1952).

——, *The British General Election of 1955* (London, 1955).

——, *British General Elections since 1945* (Oxford, 1989).

—— and G. Butler, *British Political Facts 1900–94* (London, 1994).

—— and D. Kavanagh, *The British General Election of 1992* (Basingstoke, 1992).

—— and A. King, *The British General Election of 1964* (London, 1965).

—— and A. King, *The British General Election of 1966* (London, 1966).

—— and M. Pinto-Duschinsky, *The British General Election of 1970* (London, 1971).

—— and R. Rose, *The British General Election of 1959* (London, 1960).

—— and D. Stokes, *Political Change in Britain* (London, 1969).

Butler, Lord (ed.), *The Conservatives: A History from their Origins to 1965* (London, 1977).

Butler, R. A., *The Art of the Possible* (London, 1971).

Cairncross, A., *Years of Recovery: British Economic Policy, 1945–51* (London, 1985).

——, *The British Economy since 1945* (London, 1992).

Calder, A., *The Myth of the Blitz* (London, 1991).

Campbell, B., *The Iron Ladies: Why Do Women Vote Tory?* (London, 1987).

Campbell, J., *Nye Bevan and the Mirage of British Socialism* (London, 1987).

——, *Edward Heath: A Biography* (London, 1993).

Campbell, R. H., 'The Committee of Ex-Secretaries of State for Scotland and Industrial Policy, 1941–45', *Scottish Industrial History* 2 (1979).

Cannadine, D. N., *The Decline and Fall of the British Aristocracy* (New Haven, 1990).

Carr-Saunders, A. M., D. Caradog Jones and C. A. Moser, *A Survey of Social Conditions in England and Wales* (Oxford, 1958).

Carter, B., C. Harris and S. Joshi, *The 1951–55 Conservative Governments and the Racialisation of Black Immigration* (Warwick: Centre for Research in Ethnic Relations, Policy Papers in Ethnic Relations 11, October 1987).

Cecil, Lord Hugh, *Conservatism* (London, 1912).

Chalmers, M., *Paying for Defence* (London, 1985).

Charlot, M., 'Women and Elections in Britain', in H. R. Penniman (ed.), *Britain at the Polls, 1979* (Washington and London, 1981).

Chase, M., 'This is No Claptrap: This is Our Heritage', in C. Shaw and M. Chase (eds.), *The Imagined Past: History and Nostalgia* (Manchester, 1989).

Clarke, P., 'Margaret Thatcher's Leadership in Historical Perspective', *Parliamentary Affairs* 45 (1992).

Clarke, P. F., *Liberals and Social Democrats* (Cambridge, 1978).

Clarke, R., *Public Expenditure, Management and Control* (London, 1978).

Cockett, R., *Thinking the Unthinkable: Think-Tanks and the Economic Counter-Revolution, 1931–83* (London, 1994).

Coetzee, F., *For Party or Country? Nationalism and the Dilemmas of Popular Conservatism in Edwardian England* (Oxford, 1990).

Cohen, R., *Frontiers of Identity: The British and the Others* (London, 1994).

Colls, R., and P. Dodd (eds.), *Englishness: Politics and Culture, 1880–1920* (London, 1986).

Cooke, A. B., and J. Vincent, *The Governing Passion: Cabinet Government and Party Politics in Britain, 1885–6* (Brighton, 1974).

Coopey, R., and D. Clarke, *3i: Fifty Years Investment in Industry* (Oxford, 1995).

Cornford, J., 'The Transformation of Conservatism in the Late Nineteenth Century', *Victorian Studies* 7 (1963).

Cosgrove, R. A., 'The Relevance of Irish History: The Gladstone–Dicey Debate about Home Rule, 1886–7', *Eire-Ireland* 13 (1978).

Costello, J., *Love, Sex and War: Changing Values, 1939–1945* (London, 1986 edn.).

Cowling, M. (ed.), *Conservative Essays* (London, 1978).

Crafts, N., and N. Woodward (eds.), *The British Economy since 1945* (Oxford, 1991).

Craig, F. W. S., *British Parliamentary Election Results 1918–1949* (Glasgow, 1969).

——, *British Parliamentary Election Statistics, 1918–1970* (Chichester, 1971).

——, *British General Election Manifestos, 1900–1974* (Chichester, 1975).

——, *British Electoral Facts, 1832–1987* (Aldershot, 1989).

——, *British Parliamentary Election Results, 1885–1910* (Aldershot, 1989).

Crewe, I., 'Values: The Crusade that Failed', in D. Kavanagh and A. Seldon (eds.), *The Thatcher Effect: A Decade of Change* (Oxford, 1989).

——, and D. Searing, 'Ideological Change in the British Conservative Party', *American Political Science Review* 82 (1988).

—— et al., *The British Electorate, 1963–1987: A Compendium of Data from the British Election Studies* (Cambridge, 1991).

Cronin, J., *The Politics of State Expansion* (London, 1991).

Crosland, C. A. R., *The Conservative Enemy* (London, 1962).

Cunningham, H., 'The Conservative Party and Patriotism', in R. Colls and P. Dodd (eds.), *Englishness: Politics and Culture 1880–1920* (London, 1986).

Cunningham, W., *Politics and Economics* (London, 1885).

——, *Political Economy and Practical Life* (London, 1893).

Curran, J., and J. Seaton (eds.), *Power without Responsibility: The Press and Broadcasting in Britain* (London, 1991).

Curtice, J., 'Political Sociology 1945–92', in J. Obelkevich and P. Catterall (eds.), *Understanding Post-War British Society* (London, 1994).

Curtis, L. P., *Coercion and Conciliation in Ireland, 1880–1892: A Study of Conservative Unionism* (Princeton, 1963).

Daunton, M. J., 'Payment and Participation: Welfare and State Formation in Britain, 1900–1951', *Past and Present* 150 (1995).

——, 'How to Pay for the War: State, Society and Taxation in Britain, 1917–24', *English Historical Review* 111 (1996).

——, *The Ransom of Riches: Taxation and Politics in Britain since 1842* (forthcoming).

Davies, A. J., *We, The Nation: The Conservative Party and the Pursuit of Power* (London, 1995).

Davies, J., 'The End of the Great Estates and the Rise of Freehold Farming in Wales', *Welsh History Review* 7 (1974).

Davies, P., 'The Liberal Unionist Party and the Irish Policy of Lord Salisbury's Government, 1886–1892', *Historical Journal* 18 (1975).

Dean, D. W., 'Conservative Governments and the Restriction of Commonwealth Immigration in the 1950s: The Problems of Constraint', *Historical Journal* 35 (1992).

Dicey, A. V., *A Fool's Paradise: Being a Constitutionalist's Criticism on the Home Rule Bill of 1912* (London, 1913).

Dilks, D., *Neville Chamberlain, I: Pioneering and Reform, 1869–1929* (Cambridge, 1984).

Dixon, D., *From Prohibition to Regulation: Bookmaking, Anti-Gambling and the Law* (Oxford, 1991).

Douglas, D., *Land, People and Politics: A History of the Land Question in the United Kingdom, 1878–1952* (London, 1976).

Dow, J. C. R., *The Management of the British Economy 1945–60* (Cambridge, 1965).

Durant, H., 'Voting Behaviour in Britain, 1945–64', in R. Rose (ed.), *Studies in British Politics* (London, 1966).

Dutton, D., *'His Majesty's Loyal Opposition': The Unionist Party in Opposition, 1905–1915* (Liverpool, 1992).

Eccleshall, R., 'Conservatism', in R. Eccleshall et al. (eds.), *Political Ideologies* (London, 1984).

——, *English Conservatism since the Reformation: An Introduction and Anthology* (London, 1990).

Eden, A., *Freedom and Order: Selected Speeches, 1939–1946* (London, 1947).

Edgerton, D., *England and the Aeroplane* (London, 1991).

Elliot, W., *Toryism and the Twentieth Century* (London, 1927).

Emy, H. V., 'The Land Campaign: Lloyd George as a Social Reformer, 1909–14', in A. J. P. Taylor (ed.), *Lloyd George: Twelve Essays* (London, 1971).

Evans, J., 'Women and Politics: A Re-Appraisal', *Political Studies* 28 (1980).

Fair, J. D., and J. A. Hutcheson, 'British Conservatism in the Twentieth Century: An Emerging Ideological Tradition', *Albion* 19 (1987).

Fawcett, A., *Conservative Agent* (Driffield, 1967).

Feinstein, C. H., *National Income, Expenditure and Output of the UK, 1855–1965* (Cambridge, 1972).

Feldman, D., 'The Importance of Being English: Jewish Immigration and the Decay of Liberal England', in G. Stedman Jones and D. Feldman (eds.), *Metropolis: London* (London, 1989).

Ferris, P., *Sex and the British: A Twentieth Century History* (London, 1993).

Fforde, M., *Conservatism and Collectivism, 1886–1914* (Edinburgh, 1990).

Fielding, S., 'What did "the People" Want? The Meaning of the 1945 General Election', *Historical Journal* 35 (1992).

Finlay, R. J., 'Nationalism, Race, Religion and the "Irish Question" in Inter-War Scotland', *Innes Review* 62 (Spring 1991).

——, 'In Defence of Oligarchy: Scotland in the Twentieth Century', *Scottish Historical Review* 73 (1994).

——, *Independent and Free: Scottish Politics and the Origins of the Scottish National Party, 1918–1945* (Edinburgh, 1994).

——, 'National Identity in Crisis: Politicians, Intellectuals and the "End of Scotland", 1920–39', *History* 79 (1994).

——, 'Continuity and Change: Scottish Politics, 1900–45', in T. M. Devine and R. J. Finlay (eds.), *Scotland in the Twentieth Century* (Edinburgh, 1996).

——, *A Partnership for Good? Scottish Politics and the Union since 1880* (Edinburgh, 1996).

——, 'Imperial Scotland: Scottish National Identity and the British Empire, 1850–1914', in J. M. MacKenzie (ed.), *Scotland and the British Empire* (Manchester, forthcoming).

Floud, R., and D. McCloskey (eds.), *The Economic History of Britain since 1700*, III: *1939–92* (Cambridge, 1995).

Foster, R., 'To the Northern Counties Station: Lord Randolph Churchill and the Prelude to the Orange Card', in F. L. S. Lyons and R. A. Hawkins (eds.), *Ireland under the Union: Varieties of Tension* (Oxford, 1980).

——, *Lord Randolph Churchill: A Political Life* (Oxford, 1981).

Francis, M., 'Economics and Ethics: The Nature of Labour's Socialism, 1945–1951', *Twentieth Century British History* 6 (1995).

Freeden, M., *The New Liberalism* (Oxford, 1978).

——, *Liberalism Divided* (Oxford, 1986).

——, 'The Stranger at the Feast: Ideology and Public Policy in Twentieth-Century Britain', *Twentieth Century British History* 1 (1990).

Gailey, A., *Ireland and the Death of Kindness: The Experience of Constructive Unionism, 1890–1905* (Cork, 1987).

Gallup, G. H., *Gallup International Opinion Polls*, II: *Great Britain 1965–75* (New York, 1976).

Gallup Poll, 'Voting Behaviour in Britain', in R. Rose (ed.), *Studies in British Politics*, 3rd edn. (London, 1976).

Gamble, A., *The Conservative Nation* (London, 1974).

——, *The Free Economy and the Strong State: The Politics of Thatcherism* (Basingstoke, 1988).

——, *The Free Economy and the Strong State*, 2nd edn. (London, 1994).

Gardiner, A. G., *Certain People of Importance* (London, 1929 edn.).

Gilmour, I., *Dancing with Dogma* (London, 1992).

Girvin, B., *The Transformation of Contemporary Conservatism* (London, 1988).

Glennerster, H., *British Social Policy since 1945* (Oxford, 1995).

Glickman, H., 'The Toryness of English Conservatism', *Journal of British Studies* 1 (1961).

Goldthorpe, J. H., et al., *The Affluent Worker in the Class Structure* (Cambridge, 1969).

——, *The Affluent Worker: Political Attitudes and Behaviour* (Cambridge, 1971).

Grant, A., and K. Stringer (eds.), *Uniting the Kingdom? The Making of British History* (London, 1995).

Graves, P. M., *Labour Women: Women in British Working-Class Politics, 1918–1939* (Cambridge, 1994).

Green, E. H. H., 'The Strange Death of Tory England', *Twentieth Century British History* 2 (1991).

——, *The Crisis of Conservatism: The Politics, Economics and Ideology of the British Conservative Party, 1880–1914* (London, 1995).

Greenleaf, W., *The British Political Tradition: The Ideological Heritage* (London, 1983).

Greenwood, S., 'The Third Force in the late 1940s', in B. Brivati and H. Jones (eds.), *From Reconstruction to Integration: Britain and Europe since 1945* (Leicester, 1993).

Griffith-Boscawen, A., *Memories* (London, 1925).

Hall, P., *Governing the Economy: The Politics of State Intervention in Britain and France* (Oxford, 1986).

Hanley, D. (ed.), *Christian Democracy in Europe: A Comparative Perspective* (London, 1994).

Hannah, L., *The Rise of the Corporate Economy*, 2nd edn. (London, 1983).

——, *Inventing Retirement* (Cambridge, 1986).

Harris, N., *Competition and the Corporate Society: British Conservatives, the State and Industry, 1945–64* (London, 1972).

Harris, R., and A. Seldon, *Not from Benevolence* (London, 1977).

Harrison, B., 'Women's Suffrage at Westminster, 1866–1928', in M. Bentley and J. Stevenson (eds.), *High and Low Politics in Modern Britain: Ten Studies* (Oxford, 1983).

——, *Prudent Revolutionaries: Portraits of British Feminists between the Wars* (Oxford, 1987).

Hart, N., 'Gender and the Rise and Fall of Class Politics', *New Left Review* 175 (1989).

Harvie, C., *No Gods and Precious Few Heroes: Scotland 1914–1980* (London, 1981).

Haste, C., *Rules of Desire: Sex in Britain, World War One to the Present* (London, 1992).

Haworth, A., *Anti-Liberalism: Markets, Philosophy and Myth* (London, 1994).

Heath, A., et al., *Understanding Political Change: The British Voter 1964–1987* (Oxford, 1991).

Hennock, E. P., *British Social Reform and German Precedents* (Oxford, 1987).

Hills, J., 'Candidates, the Impact of Gender', *Parliamentary Affairs* 34 (1981).

Hinton, J., 'Women and the Labour Vote, 1945–50', *Labour History Review* 57 (1992).

——, 'Militant Housewives: The British Housewives' League and the Attlee Government', *History Workshop Journal* 38 (1994).

Hogg, Q., *The Case for Conservatism* (London, 1947).

Hollins, T., 'The Conservative Party and Film Propaganda between the Wars', *English Historical Review* 96 (1981).

Holmes, C., 'Immigration', in T. R. Gourvish and A. O'Day (eds.), *Britain since 1945* (London, 1991).

Howell, D. W., *Land and People in Nineteenth-Century Wales* (London, 1978).

Huntington, S., 'Conservatism as an Ideology', *American Review of Political Science* 6 (1957).

Hutchison, I. G. C., *A Political History of Scotland, 1832–1924: Parties, Elections and Issues* (Edinburgh, 1986).

Jalland, P., 'United Kingdom Devolution 1910–1914: Political Panacea or Tactical Diversion', *English Historical Review* 94 (1979).

James, A. J., and J. E. Thomas, *Wales at Westminster: A History of the Parliamentary Representation of Wales 1800–1979* (Llandysul, 1981).

Jarvis, D., 'Mrs Maggs and Betty: The Conservative Appeal to Women Voters in the 1920s', *Twentieth Century British History* 5 (1994).

——, 'The Shaping of Conservative Electoral Hegemony, 1918–39', in J. Lawrence and M. Taylor (eds.), *Party, State and Society: Electoral Behaviour in Modern Britain* (Aldershot, 1996).

Jay, R., *Joseph Chamberlain* (Oxford, 1981).

Jeffery, T., and K. McClelland, 'A World Fit to Live In: the *Daily Mail* and the Middle Classes 1918–39', in J. Curran, A. Smith and P. Wingate (eds.), *Impacts and Influences: Essays in Media Power in the Twentieth Century* (London, 1987).

Jefferys, K., *The Churchill Coalition and Wartime Politics, 1940–1945* (Manchester, 1991).

Jenkins, J. P., *A History of Modern Wales 1536–1990* (London, 1992).

Jenkins, R., *Mr Balfour's Poodle* (London, 1954).

Johnman, L., 'The Conservative Party in Opposition, 1964–70', in R. Coopey et al. (eds.), *The Wilson Governments, 1964–1970* (London, 1993).

Jones, B., *Parliamentary Elections in Wales 1900–1975* (Talybont, 1977).

Jones, G., 'The British Government and Foreign Multinationals before 1970', in M. Chick (ed.), *Governments, Industries and Markets* (Aldershot, 1990).

Jones, G. E., *Modern Wales: A Concise History c. 1485–1979* (Cambridge, 1984).

Jones, H., 'New Tricks for an Old Dog? The Churchill Government and Social Policy, 1951–5', in A. Gorst et al. (eds.), *British History, 1931–61: Politics and the Limits of Policy* (London, 1991).

——, 'The Conservative Party and Social Policy, 1942–1955' (unpublished Ph.D. thesis, University of London, 1992).

Jones, H., and M. Kandiah (eds.), *The Myth of Consensus: New Views on British History, 1945–64* (Basingstoke, 1996).

Jones, T., *Whitehall Diary*, II: *1926–1930*, ed. K. Middlemas (London, 1969).

Joyce, P. (ed.), *Class* (Oxford Readers) (Oxford, 1995).

——, 'The End of Social History?', *Social History* 20 (1995).

Kaldor, N., *Causes of the Slow Rate of Economic Growth of the United Kingdom* (Cambridge, 1966).

Kandiah, M., 'Lord Woolton's Chairmanship of the Conservative Party, 1945–1951', (unpublished Ph.D. thesis, University of Exeter, 1992).

Kavanagh, D., *Thatcherism and British Politics: The End of Consensus?* (Oxford, 1987).

—— and P. Morris, *Consensus Politics from Attlee to Thatcher* (Oxford, 1989).

Kellas, J., *The Scottish Political System* (Cambridge, 1984).

Kendle, J., 'The Round Table Movement and "Home Rule all Round"', *Historical Journal* 11 (1968).

——, *Ireland and the Federal Solution: The Debate over the United Kingdom Constitution, 1870–1921* (Montreal, 1989).

Kennedy, A. L., *Salisbury 1830–1903: Portrait of a Statesman* (London, 1953).

Kilmuir, Lord, *Political Adventure* (London, 1964).

King, M., 'The UK Profits Crisis: Myth or Reality?', *Economic Journal* 85 (1975).

Kingsley Kent, S., *Making Peace: The Reconstruction of Gender in Interwar Britain* (Princeton, 1993).

Kinnear, M., *The Fall of Lloyd George: The Political Crisis of 1922* (London, 1973).

——, *The British Voter: An Atlas and Survey since 1885* (London, 1981).

Koss, S., *The Rise and Fall of the Political Press in Britain* (London, 1990).

Kuhn, A., *Cinema, Censorship and Sexuality, 1909–1925* (London, 1988).

Lamb, R., *The Failure of the Eden Government* (London, 1987).

——, *The Macmillan Years, 1957–63: The Emerging Truth* (London, 1995).

Lawler-Wilson, W., *The Menace of Socialism* (London, 1909).

Lawrence, J., 'Class and Gender in the Making of Urban Toryism, 1880–1914', *English Historical Review* 108 (1993).

——, 'Party Politics and the Politics of Gender in Modern Britain' (unpublished paper, 1993).

—— and M. Taylor, 'The Poverty of Protest: Gareth Stedman Jones and the Politics of Language – A Reply', *Social History* 18 (1993).

—— (eds.), *Party, State and Society: Electoral Behaviour in Modern Britain* (Aldershot, 1996).

Lawson, N., *The View from No. 11: Memoirs of a Tory Radical* (London, 1992).

Layton-Henry, Z., *The Politics of Immigration* (Oxford, 1991).

Le May, G. H. L., *The Victorian Constitution: Conventions, Usages and Contingencies* (London, 1979).

Letwin, S. R., *The Anatomy of Thatcherism* (London, 1992).

Lewis, R., and A. Maude, *The English Middle Classes* (London, 1949).

Lindsay, T. F., and M. Harrington, *The Conservative Party, 1918–1979* (London, 1979).

Little, I. M. D., 'Higgledy-piggledy Growth', *Bulletin of the Oxford Institute of Statistics* 24 (1962).

Lovenduski, J., and P. Norris, *Gender and Party Politics* (London, 1993).

Lovenduski, J., P. Norris and C. Burness, 'The Party and Women', in A. Seldon and S. Ball (eds.), *Conservative Century: The Conservative Party since 1900* (Oxford, 1994).

Lowe, R., 'Resignation at the Treasury: The Social Services Committee and the Failure to Reform the Welfare State, 1955–57', *Journal of Social Policy* 18 (1989).

——, 'Social Policy', in S. Ball and A. Seldon (eds.), *The Heath Government: A Reappraisal* (London, 1996).

——, 'Milestone or Millstone? The 1959–61 Plowden Committee and its Impact on Welfare Policy', *Historical Journal* (1997, forthcoming).

Lubenow, W. C., *Parliamentary Politics and the Home Rule Crisis: The British House of Commons in 1886* (Oxford, 1988).

Lyons, F. S. L., 'The Irish Unionist Party and the Devolution Crisis of 1904–5', *Irish Historical Studies* 6 (1948).

MacDonald, C., 'The Radical Thread: Paisley Politics, 1880–1924' (unpublished Ph.D. thesis, University of Strathclyde, 1995).

Machin, G. I. T., *Politics and the Churches in Great Britain, 1869–1921* (Oxford, 1987).

Mackail, J., and G. Wyndham, *Life and Letters of George Wyndham* (London, 1925).

Macleod, I., *Neville Chamberlain* (London, 1961).

Macrae, G., *Sunshades in October* (London, 1963).

Mark-Lawson, J., et al., 'Gender and Local Politics: Struggles over Welfare Policies, 1918–1939', in L. Murgatroyd et al., *Localities, Class and Gender* (London, 1985).

Marsh, P., *The Discipline of Popular Government: Lord Salisbury's Domestic Statecraft, 1881–1902* (Hassocks, 1978).

Marwick, A., *British Society since 1945* (London, 1982).

Matthews, R. C. O., 'Why has Britain had Full Employment since the War?', *Economic Journal* 78 (1968).

Maybury, M., *The Truth About the Interwar Years* (London, 1949).

Mayfield, D., and S. Thorne, 'Social History and its Discontents: Gareth Stedman Jones and the Politics of Language', *Social History* 17 (1992).

McCallum, R. B., and A. Readman, *The British General Election of 1945* (London, 1947).

McClelland, K., 'Some Thoughts on Masculinity and the "Representative Artisan" in Britain, 1850–1880', *Gender and History* 1 (1989).

McCrone, D., *Understanding Scotland: The Sociology of a Stateless Nation* (1992).

McIntyre, I., *The Expense of Glory: A Life of John Reith* (London, 1993).

McKenzie, R., and A. Silver, *Angels in Marble: Working Class Conservatives in Urban England* (London, 1968).

McKibbin, R., 'Why was there no Marxism in Great Britain?', *English Historical Review* 99 (1984), reprinted in *The Ideologies of Class: Social Relations in Britain, 1880–1950* (Oxford, 1990).

McKibbin, R., 'Class and Conventional Wisdom: The Conservative Party and the "Public" in Inter-War Britain', in *The Ideologies of Class* (Oxford, 1990).

McLean, I., *The Legend of Red Clydeside* (Edinburgh, 1983).

McNeill, R., *Ulster's Stand for Union* (London, 1922).

Melling, J., *Rent Strike* (Edinburgh, 1983).

Melman, B., *Women and the Popular Imagination in the Twenties: Nymphs and Flappers* (London, 1988).

Mercer, H., *Constructing a Competitive Order: The Hidden History of British Antitrust Policies* (Cambridge, 1995).

Middlemas, K., and J. Barnes, *Baldwin* (London, 1969).

Minkin, L., *The Contentious Alliance: Trade Unions and the Labour Party* (Edinburgh, 1991).

Minogue, K., and M. Biddiss (eds.), *Thatcherism: Personality and Politics* (Basingstoke, 1987).

Mitchell, A., and P. O'Snodaigh (eds.), *Irish Political Documents, 1869–1916* (Dublin, 1989).

Mitchell, J., *Conservatives and the Union: A Study of Conservative Party Attitudes to Scotland* (Edinburgh, 1990).

Montgomery Hyde, H., *The Other Love: An Historical and Contemporary Survey of Homosexuality in Britain* (London, 1970).

Morgan, J. V., *The Philosophy of Welsh History* (London, 1914).

Morgan, K. O., *Wales in British Politics, 1868–1922* (Cardiff, 1980).

——, *Rebirth of a Nation: Wales 1880–1980* (Oxford, 1981).

——, *The People's Peace: British History, 1945–1989* (Oxford, 1990).

Morris, A. J. A., *The Scaremongers: The Advocacy of War and Rearmament, 1896–1914* (London, 1984).

Mortimer, J., 'The Changing Mood of the Working People', in J. Fyrth (ed.), *Labour's High Noon: The Government and the Economy 1945–51* (London, 1993).

Murphy, R., *Realism and Tinsel: Cinema and Society in Britain, 1939–49* (London, 1989).

Newburn, T., *Permission and Regulation: Law and Morals in Post-War Britain* (London, 1992).

Newby, H., *The Deferential Worker: A Study of Farm Workers in East Anglia* (London, 1977).

Nicholas, H. G., *The British General Election of 1950* (London, 1951).

Nicolson, H., *King George the Fifth: His Life and Reign* (London, 1952).

Nisbet, R., *Conservatism: Dream and Reality* (Milton Keynes, 1986).

Nordlinger, E., *The Working Class Tories* (London, 1967).

Norris, P., 'Conservative Attitudes in Recent British Elections: An Emerging Gender Gap?', *Political Studies* 34 (1986).

Norton, P., *Conservative Dissidents: Dissent within the Parliamentary Conservative Party, 1970–74* (London, 1978).

Offer, A., *Property and Politics, 1870–1914* (Cambridge, 1981).

O'Gorman, F., *British Conservatism from Burke to Thatcher* (London, 1986).

Oren, L., 'The Welfare of Women in Laboring Families: England, 1860–1950', *Feminist Studies* 1 (1973).

O'Sullivan, N., 'The Politics of Ideology', in N. O'Sullivan (ed.), *The Structure of Modern Ideology* (London, 1989).

Padgen, A. (ed.),*The Languages of Political Theory in Early-Modern Europe* (Cambridge, 1987).

Paul, K., '"British Subjects" and "British Stock": Labour's Postwar Imperialism', *Journal of British Studies* 34 (1995).

Pelling, H. M., *Social Geography of British Elections 1885–1910* (London, 1967).

Philip, A. B., *The Welsh Question: Nationalism in Welsh Politics 1945–1970* (Cardiff, 1975).

Phillips, G. D., *The Diehards: Aristocratic Society and Politics in Edwardian England* (Cambridge, Mass., 1979).

Porter, R. (ed.), *Myths of the English* (Oxford, 1992).

Potter, A., 'The Equal Pay Campaign Committee: A Case-Study of a Pressure Group', *Political Studies* 5 (1957).

Potts, A., '"Constable Country" between the Wars', in R. Samuel (ed.), *Patriotism*, III: *National Fictions* (London, 1989).

Pronay, N., 'British Newsreels in the 1930s: (2) Their Policy and Impact', *History* 57 (1972).

Pugh, M., *Women's Suffrage in Britain, 1867–1929* (London, 1980).

——, *The Making of Modern British Politics, 1867–1939* (Oxford, 1982).

——, *The Tories and the People, 1880–1935* (Oxford, 1985).

——, 'Popular Conservatism in Britain: Continuity and Change, 1880–1987', *Journal of British Studies* 27 (1988).

——, 'Women, Food and Politics, 1880–1930', *History Today* 41, 3 (1991).

——, *Women and the Women's Movement in Britain 1914–1959* (London, 1992).

Quinault, R. E., 'Lord Randolph Churchill and Home Rule', in *Reactions to Irish Nationalism, 1865–1914* (London, 1987).

Raison, T., *Tories and the Welfare State: A History of Conservative Social Policy since the Second World War* (Basingstoke, 1990).

Ramsden, J., 'From Churchill to Heath', in Lord Butler (ed.), *The Conservatives* (London, 1977).

——, *The Age of Balfour and Baldwin, 1902–1940* (London, 1978).

——, *The Making of Conservative Party Policy: The Conservative Research Department since 1929* (London, 1980).

——, 'Baldwin and Film', in N. Pronay and D. W. Spring (eds.), *Politics, Propaganda and Film 1918–1945* (London, 1982).

—— (ed.), *Real Old Tory Politics: The Political Diaries of Robert Sanders, Lord Bayford, 1910–35* (London, 1984).

——, '"A Party for Owners or a Party for Earners?": How Far did the

British Conservative Party Really Change after 1945?', *Transactions of the Royal Historical Society* 5th ser, 37 (1987).

Ramsden, J., *The Age of Churchill and Eden, 1940–57* (London, 1995).

——, *The Winds of Change: Macmillan to Heath, 1957–1975* (London, 1996).

Ranelagh, J., *Thatcher's People* (London, 1991).

Rasmussen, J., 'The Political Integration of British Women: The Response of a Traditional System to a Newly Emergent Group', *Social Science History* 7 (1983).

Revell, J. R. S., 'Assets and Age', *Bulletin of the Oxford Institute of Statistics* 24 (1962).

Rickard, R., 'The Anti-Sweating Movement in Britain and Victoria: The Politics of Empire and Social Reform', *Historical Studies* 18 (1978–9).

Riddell, P., *The Thatcher Era and its Legacy* (Oxford, 1991).

Ridley, J., 'The Unionist Social Reform Committee: Wets before the Deluge', *Historical Journal* 30 (1987).

——, 'The Unionist Opposition and the House of Lords', *Parliamentary History* 11 (1992).

Riley, D., *'Am I that Name?': Feminism and the Category of 'Women' in History* (Basingstoke, 1988).

Roberts, R., 'Regulatory Responses to the Market for Corporate Control in Britain in the 1950s', *Business History* 34 (1992).

Robertson, J. C., *The British Board of Film Censors: Film Censorship in Britain, 1896–1950* (London, 1985).

Rodner, W. S., 'Leaguers, Covenanters, Moderates: British Support for Ulster, 1913–1914', *Eire-Ireland* 17 (1982).

Rollings, N., ' "The Reichstag Method of Governing"? The Attlee Governments and Permanent Economic Controls', in H. Mercer et al. (eds.), *The Labour Governments and Private Industry: The Experience of 1945–51* (Edinburgh, 1992).

——, 'Poor Mr Butskell: A Short Life, Wrecked by Schizophrenia?', *Twentieth Century British History* 5 (1994).

Rose, S. O., *Limited Livelihoods: Gender and Class in Nineteenth Century England* (London, 1992).

——, 'Gender and Labour History', *International Review of Social History* 38, Supplement 1 (1993).

Said, E., *Culture and Imperialism* (London, 1994).

Salisbury, Lord, 'Disintegration', in P. Smith (ed.), *Lord Salisbury on Politics* (Cambridge, 1972).

Samuel, R. (ed.), *Patriotism* (London, 1989).

Sanderson, M., *The Universities and British Industry* (London, 1972).

Scannell, P., and D. Cardiff, *A Social History of British Broadcasting*, I: *Serving the Nation* (Oxford, 1991).

Schenk, C., *Britain and the Sterling Area: From Devaluation to Convertibility in the 1950s* (London, 1994).

Schwarz, B., 'The Language of Constitutionalism: Baldwinite Conservatism', in [Formations Editorial Collective] *Formations of Nation and People* (London, 1984).

Scott, Sir H., *Your Obedient Servant* (London, 1959).

Scott, J. W., *Gender and the Politics of History* (New York, 1988).

Scruton, R., *The Meaning of Conservatism* (London, 1980).

Searle, G. R., *Country before Party: Coalition and the Idea of National Government in Modern Britain, 1885–1987* (London, 1995).

Seldon, A., *Churchill's Indian Summer: The Conservative Government, 1951–55* (London, 1981).

——, 'The Churchill Administration, 1951–1955', in P. Hennessy and A. Seldon (eds.), *Ruling Performance: British Governments from Attlee to Thatcher* (Oxford, 1987).

Seldon, A., and S. Ball, *Conservative Century: The Conservative Party since 1900* (Oxford, 1994).

Seliger, M., *Ideology and Politics* (London, 1976).

Sellar, W. C., and R. J. Yeatman, *1066 and All That* (London, [1930] 1960).

Seymour-Ure, C., 'The Press and the Party System between the Wars', in G. Peele and C. Cook (eds.), *The Politics of Reappraisal* (London, 1975).

Shanks, M., *The Stagnant Society* (London, 1959).

Shannon, C., *Arthur J. Balfour and Ireland, 1874–1922* (Washington DC, 1988).

Shannon, R., *The Age of Salisbury, 1881–1902* (London, 1996).

Shepherd, R., *Iain Macleod* (London, 1994).

Shonfield, A., *British Economic Policy since the War* (London, 1958).

Siltanen, J., and M. Stanworth (eds.), *Women and the Public Sphere: A Critique of Sociology and Politics* (London, 1984).

Skidelsky, R. (ed.), *Thatcherism* (London, 1988).

Smith, A. M., *New Right Discourse on Race and Sexuality: Britain, 1968–1990* (Cambridge, 1994).

Smith, F. E., *Unionist Policy and Other Essays* (London, 1913).

Smith, H. L. (ed.), *British Feminism in the Twentieth Century* (Aldershot, 1990).

——, 'The Politics of Conservative Reform: The Equal Pay for Equal Work Issue, 1945–1955', *Historical Journal* 35 (1992).

Smith, J., 'Bluff, Bluster and Brinkmanship: Andrew Bonar Law and the Third Home Rule Bill', *Historical Journal* 36 (1993).

——, 'Paralysing the Arm: Unionists and the Army Annual Act, 1911–1914', *Parliamentary History* 15 (1996).

Smith, P. (ed.), *Lord Salisbury on Politics* (Cambridge, 1974).

Soldon, N., 'Laissez-Faire as Dogma: The Case of the Liberty and Property Defence League', in K. D. Brown (ed.), *Essays in Anti-Labour History* (London, 1974).

Solomos, J., *Race and Racism in Postwar Britain* (London, 1987).

Southgate, D. (ed.), *The Conservative Leadership, 1832–1932* (London, 1974).

Stannage, T., *Baldwin Thwarts the Opposition: The British General Election of 1935* (London, 1980).

Steinmo, S., 'Political Institutions and Tax Policy in the United States, Sweden and Britain', *World Politics* 41 (1988–9).

Stenton, M., and S. Lees (eds.), *Who's Who of British Members of Parliament*, III: *1919–1945* (Hassocks, 1979).

Stephensen, P. R., *Policeman of the Lord: A Political Satire* (London, 1929).

Stewart, A. T. Q., *The Ulster Crisis: Resistance to Home Rule, 1912–1914* (London, 1967).

Summerfield, P., 'The "Levelling of Class"', in H. L. Smith (ed.), *War and Social Change: British Society in the Second World War* (Manchester, 1986).

Sykes, A., *Tariff Reform in British Politics, 1903–13* (Oxford, 1979).

——, 'The Radical Right and the Crisis of Conservatism before the First World War', *Historical Journal* 26 (1983).

Tanner, D., 'Ideological Debate in Edwardian Labour Politics', in E. F. Biagini and A. J. Reid (eds.), *Currents of Radicalism* (Cambridge, 1991).

Taylor, A. J. P., *Beaverbrook* (London, 1972).

Taylor, H. A., *'Jix': Viscount Brentford* (London, 1933).

Taylor, M., 'Patriotism, History and the Left in Twentieth-Century Britain', *Historical Journal* 33 (1990).

Taylor, M. W., *Men Versus the State* (Oxford, 1992).

Tebbit, N., *Upwardly Mobile* (London, 1989).

Thane, P., 'Women of the British Labour Party and Feminism', in H. L. Smith (ed.), *British Feminism in the Twentieth Century* (Aldershot, 1990).

——, 'Towards Equal Opportunities? Women in Britain since 1945', in T. Gourvish and A. O'Day (eds.), *Britain since 1945* (London, 1991).

Thatcher, M., *The Downing Street Years* (London, 1993).

——, *The Path to Power* (London, 1995).

Thompson, F. M. L., *English Landed Society in the Nineteenth Century* (London, 1963).

Timmins, N., *The Five Giants: A Biography of the Welfare State* (London, 1995).

Tiratsoo, N., 'Popular Politics, Affluence and the Labour Party in the 1950s', in A. Gorst, L. Johnman and W. Scott Lucas (eds.), *Contemporary British History 1931–61: Politics and the Limits of Policy* (London, 1990).

Titmuss, R. M., *Essays on the 'Welfare State'* (London, 1958).

Tomlinson, J., 'Why was there never a Keynesian Revolution in Economic Policy?', *Economy and Society* 10 (1981).

——, 'Keynesianism and the Conservatives 1945–64: An Unfortunate Alliance', *History of Political Economy* (forthcoming).

Turner, J., 'Sex, Age and the Labour Vote in the 1920s', in P. Denley and D. Hopkin (eds.), *History and Computing* II (Cambridge, 1988).

——, *British Politics and the Great War* (New Haven and London, 1992).

——, 'Letting Go: The Conservative Party and the End of the Union with Ireland', in A. Grant and K. J. Stringer (eds.), *Uniting the Kingdom? The Making of British History* (London, 1995).

Turnor, C., *Land Problems and National Welfare* (London, 1911).

Vernon, J., 'Who's Afraid of the "Linguistic Turn"? The Politics of Social History and its Discontents', *Social History* 19 (1994).

Walker, L., 'Party Political Women: A Comparative Study of Liberal Women and the Primrose League, 1890–1914', in J. Rendall (ed.), *Equal or Different? Women's Politics 1880–1914* (Oxford, 1987).

Weeks, J., *Coming Out: Homosexual Politics in Britain from the Nineteenth Century to the Present* (London, 1977).

——, *Sex, Politics and Society: The Regulation of Sexuality since 1800*, 2nd edn. (London, 1989).

Weston, C. C., 'Salisbury and the Lords 1868–1895', *Historical Journal* 25 (1982).

White, R. J., *The Conservative Tradition* (London, 1950).

Whiting, A., 'An International Comparison of the Instability of Economic Growth', *Three Banks Review* 66 (1976).

Whiting, R. C., 'The Labour Party, Capitalism and the National Debt, 1915–24', in P. J. Waller (ed.), *Politics and Social Change in Modern Britain* (London, 1987).

——, 'Taxation and the Working Class, 1915–24', *Historical Journal* 33 (1990).

Wiener, M. J., *English Culture and the Decline of the Industrial Spirit 1850–1980* (Cambridge, 1981).

Willetts, D., *Modern Conservatism* (Harmondsworth, 1992).

Williamson, P., *National Crisis and National Government: British Politics, the Economy and Empire 1926–1932* (Cambridge, 1992).

——, 'The Doctrinal Politics of Stanley Baldwin', in M. Bentley (ed.), *Public and Private Doctrine* (Cambridge, 1993).

—— (ed.), *The Modernization of Conservative Politics: The Diaries and Letters of William Bridgeman, 1904–35* (London, 1988).

Wilson, T., 'Instability and the Rate of Growth', *Lloyds Bank Review* 83 (1966).

Wood, I. S., 'Hope Deferred: Labour in Scotland in the 1920s', in I. Donnachie, C. Harvie and I. S. Wood (eds.), *Forward! Labour Politics in Scotland 1888–1980* (Edinburgh, 1989).

Worsthorne, P., 'Too Much Freedom', in M. Cowling (ed.), *Conservative Essays* (London, 1978).

Worswick, G. D. N., and P. H. Ady, *The British Economy in the 1950s* (Oxford, 1962).

Young, H., *One of Us: A Biography of Margaret Thatcher* (London, 1989).

——, 'The Prime Minister', in D. Kavanagh and A. Seldon (eds.), *The Major Effect* (London, 1994).

Zweig, F., *Women's Life and Labour* (London, 1952).

Zweiniger-Bargielowska, I., 'Rationing, Austerity and the Conservative Party Recovery after 1945', *Historical Journal* 37 (1994).

——, 'Consensus and Consumption: Rationing, Austerity and Controls after the War', in H. Jones and M. Kandiah (eds.), *The Myth of Consensus: New Views on British History, 1945–64* (Basingstoke, 1996).

# Index